D0248909

A CONVENIENT SPY

WEN HO LEE and the POLITICS of NUCLEAR ESPIONAGE

DAN STOBER
and IAN HOFFMAN

SIMON & SCHUSTER
New York London Toronto Sydney Singapore

SIMON & SCHUSTER
Rockefeller Center
1230 Avenue of the Americas
New York, NY 10020

Copyright © 2001 by Dan Stober and Ian Hoffman
All rights reserved, including the right of reproduction
in whole or in part in any form.

SIMON & SCHUSTER and colophon are registered trademarks
of Simon & Schuster, Inc.

For information about special discounts for bulk purchases,
please contact Simon & Schuster Special Sales:
1-800-456-6798 or business@simonandschuster.com

DESIGNED BY LISA CHOVNICK

Manufactured in the United States of America

1   3   5   7   9   10   8   6   4   2

Library of Congress Cataloging-in-Publication Data
is available.

ISBN 0-7432-2378-0

ACKNOWLEDGMENTS

The intriguing confluence of intelligence, weapons science, and politics in the Wen Ho Lee affair drew us to this project and at the same time prevents us from giving proper credit to the many who gave so generously of their time and knowledge. They know who they are. Their trust, sense of justice, and patriotism are deeply appreciated.

We had an enormous, if harrowing time, the latter brought on by our ever-shrinking deadlines. For both, we would like to thank our editor, Robert Bender of Simon & Schuster. Bob's enthusiasm for national-security and nuclear topics led him to take a gamble on two unproven authors, and he managed to apply the lash with diplomacy and good humor. Our thanks also to Gypsy da Silva for her patience, skill, and joie de vivre, to the ever-vigilant Fred Wiemer, and to the other members of the Simon & Schuster team who kept us on track: Johanna Li, Liz McNamara, Linda Evans, Peter Vabulas, Bill Molesky, Thea Tullman, Gabriel Weiss, Martha Schwartz, and Sydney Wolfe Cohen. We also thank our agents, John Brockman and Katinka Matson.

We also would like to thank LANL archivist Roger Meade, James Mulvenon, and satirist Tom Tomorrow. Hundreds of people took the time to talk with us over the last couple of years, and some were kind enough to endure scores of phone calls. Among those were Bob Vrooman, Don and Jean Marshall, the Lee defense team, Bob and Kathy Clark, Bucky and Linda Kashiwa, Cecilia Chang, Notra Trulock, and Dobie McArthur, once described by his boss, Sen. Arlen Specter, as a one-man task force.

We are, however, most beholden to Joan and Maya, for their boundless patience and sacrifice. At the California end of this venture, Joan made writing a possibility with her cheerful decision to run house and family single-handedly for months, on top of her own career. A time zone away in New Mexico, Maya's gift for organization and deft literary skill—not to mention her selfless hours at the keyboard—made her a contributor to this book. Her unstinting help to Ian will never be forgotten nor can it be fully repaid.

We owe them both immeasurably.

To Jette, George, and Maya,
and in memory of Walter Goad, whose sense of justice
ultimately proved contagious. IMH

To Joan, whose encouragement and unflagging support
made it possible, and to Rachel, Kate, and Andrew,
for their loving patience. DRS

CONTENTS

PROLOGUE

"They Electrocuted Them, Wen Ho"

They furnished rooms like this starkly, to be devoid of distractions. Special Agent Carol Covert drew her chair closer. A red LED glowed on the video camera behind her left shoulder. Wen Ho Lee could see a shadowy reflection of himself and the drab sofa in its blank eye.

"Do you want to go down in history," she said, glaring at him, ". . . professing your innocence like the Rosenbergs to the day they take you to the electric chair? Do you want to go down in history with your kids knowing you got arrested for espionage? That's gonna happen, Wen Ho, if you're not careful."

The fifty-nine-year-old software writer sat primly, still wearing his windbreaker. He was five foot three and less than 130 pounds. Lee's hands worried around a Saturday edition of the *New York Times*. The front-page story, "China Stole Secrets for Bombs, Aides Say," told of a hunt for a Chinese-American spy at Los Alamos, the laboratory the world knew as the birthplace of the bomb.

Wen Ho Lee worked there. He was the Chinese American.

Lee looked into Covert's eyes. She reminded him a little of his daughter and her college friends: educated, intelligent, attractive. Covert had treated him respectfully, as an elder.

Lee never dreamed she could be like this, her face gone stony, her tone aggressive, threatening. How much did they know? Lee wondered. Did they know about his collection?

No, he decided. The questions were the same: What did he tell the Chinese?

For twenty years, he'd dutifully provided software so Los Alamos's bomb physicists could create more lethal weapons for America. The bombs never got used. But his snippets of code did. They were a kind of touchstone for verifying that the bombs worked before they were tested. In that sense his software won the Cold War as much as the weapons and their elitist inventors. They took him for a mediocre code jockey, if not a simpleton.

Software was his passion, a source of great fascination. Cooking up mathematical recipes—to compute the roil of rivers, stars, and nuclear weapons—was a wondrous thing. But Lee never quite won the admiration of his peers, and it pained him. In 1982, he had boasted to a stranger of designing nuclear warheads for a living.

The FBI's behavioral science experts suspected his braggadocio betrayed insecurity and a desire to be valued. He was, they believed, perfectly vulnerable to seduction by the Chinese. China's scientists were masterful at playing on egos, particularly of scientists eager to show off their knowledge.

Covert and her partner, John Hudenko, drew on Lee's pride and his desire to please. So they acted as his friends and confidants. The agents had said they needed Lee's expert help. A spy was feeding bomb secrets to China from inside Los Alamos National Laboratory, they told him. No one had ever caught such a spy red-handed. Only an insider like Lee could identify the mole.

It was this ruse—Wen Ho, expert advisor to the FBI—that drew him to this second-floor FBI office, above a post office in Santa Fe. He wasn't entirely taken in. In fact, on this Sunday in March 1999, it wasn't clear who was fooling whom. After his earlier encounters with the agents, Lee went home and wrote in a little blue notebook. He made character sketches and evaluated the personalities of the FBI agents.

————

But he'd been a fool to regard them as harmless. He was twice the fool now, sitting in this interrogation room. Without a lawyer.

The moment he walked in, Covert handed him a copy of the *Times*. In minutes, her voice rose and took on a menacing tone.

"I mean, look at this newspaper article! It all but says your name in here. The polygraph reports all saying you're failing!"

His daughter had read the story to him over the phone. She had told him not to come here, not to trust the FBI. Time to get a lawyer, Alberta had said, long-distance from North Carolina. Lee didn't like lawyers—too expensive—and what did they really do anyway? Lee still resented paying $200 for a lawyer to draft his will.

His reply was the same: "Why hire a lawyer? I haven't done anything."

It was all Alberta could do not to scream at him. Her father was as pig-headed as she was. Arguing wasn't going to change a thing. She'd hung up frightened and fuming.

Now in this bland interrogation room, as Covert hammered on Lee about his supposed failure of two polygraphs, everything was made nightmarishly clear: The FBI believed *he* was the mole.

Covert knew the vast majority of FBI counterintelligence officers never came close to getting a spy tried and convicted. All they needed from this odd little man was a confession. Otherwise, the case was a dud. Covert's supervisors in Albuquerque already had cabled Washington more than once: Lee appeared to be the wrong man, could they please look elsewhere?

But no. A congressional investigative panel was about to announce China's theft of information on nearly every U.S. nuclear-weapons design, due in part to the incompetence of the Clinton administration Justice Department. Then there was the *Times.* In one swoop, the paper had wrecked her investigation and made it impossible to close out.

Headquarters demanded an aggressive, no-holds-barred grilling. Covert was given a hasty crash course in hostile interrogation. She and Hudenko were to get as loud, as tough and abusive as necessary to wring a confession out of Lee. Not everyone thought this was a good idea, including Carol Covert. The timing was wrong, the ethics were questionable. Besides, Lee was a quiet man. He rarely got angry himself. His end of his conversations with the FBI had always been respectful, even deferential. She wondered whether this blitzkrieg interrogation might crush him, even drive him to suicide.

The evidence against Lee was thin. The Bureau's files were laden with suspicious tidbits, with the most damning hints of espionage coming from Lee himself. Now the FBI had no one but Lee to fill in the blanks.

What were two high-ranking Chinese weapons scientists doing in his Beijing hotel room in June 1988? One was the director of the Chinese equivalent of Los Alamos. There could be only one reason for such men to talk to a mid-level American programmer. They were hunting bomb secrets and somehow had fingered Lee as a valuable source.

Lee had told this story for the first time only three months ago, more than ten years after the event. Now he was offering a story of recurring memory loss, how his mind went blank after undergoing an appendectomy as a teenager, and then again after doctors cut away part of his cancerous colon in 1987.

Lee could recall waving off the Chinese scientists' advances. Nothing more. What else did they talk about? He didn't remember.

Covert raised her hand. "Don't!" Lee cried, cringing. She smacked the table hard. "I need an answer for Washington! As to why it took you ten years to remember something!"

The agents weren't buying this surgical amnesia story. Certainly nobody in Washington would.

"Wen Ho. This isn't important, Wen Ho! You know, I—I understand, but this isn't important. What's important is what's in that newspaper article," Covert said, pointing to the paper in his hand. Lee was on the front page of the *Times* but hadn't bothered to read it. He rarely read newspapers or watched the news anyway.

"What's important is what's going on in Washington," Covert explained. "And what's going on in Washington is they're saying back in Washington, 'Wen Ho Lee works at Los Alamos National Laboratories. Wen Ho Lee is failing his polygraph exams. Wen Ho Lee is not fessing up to everything he knows. Wen Ho Lee is approached by a nuclear scientist in his hotel room, and Wen Ho Lee has done something. And Wen Ho Lee is gonna be a nuclear scientist without a clearance and without a job.' And pretty soon, what's going to be in the papers is 'Wen Ho Lee is arrested for espionage.' "

"But I don't know about the—the law," Lee replied. "L-A-W. 'Cause I—I—I never studied law."

"You're going to learn real quick," Covert snapped.

Yet Covert knew she had few cards to play except what Lee himself had dealt her.

"Wen Ho, why?" Covert pressed. "Tell me this. When you were in that hotel room with Hu Side, why can't you remember anything else?"

Wasn't Lee flattered that the Chinese had treated him so grandly—dinners, museum visits for his wife, a trip to the Great Wall? After all that, Covert asked, didn't Lee feel grateful, obliged? Wouldn't it have been impolite, even dishonorable, to refuse them some small secret? Just a technical clue that he believed was unclassified? Wasn't he tempted to share his expertise?

"I want to know why you're failing the polygraphs," Covert told him. If he would just confess to a slip of the tongue, that would be understandable and, Covert hinted, the two agents could help him, could calm Washington down.

Lee wasn't giving in.

"I don't know, okay? I have no—I have no—I have no idea why, okay?" Lee said beseechingly. "And the second, in that hotel I don't remember anything except that question . . . I remember very well. I told them I don't know and I am not interested in discuss this problem.

"I do remember one thing," Lee told Covert. "I never say anything classified, I never say anything related to a nuclear weapon."

Lee was drained. He hadn't eaten since breakfast eight hours ago. He certainly didn't want to be here.

Covert tugged her chair closer and ratcheted up the pressure. Her eyes were only inches from his. "Do you know who the Rosenbergs are?"

"I heard them, yeah, I heard them mention," Lee replied.

"The Rosenbergs are the only people that never cooperated with the federal government in an espionage case. You know what happened to them? They electrocuted them, Wen Ho."

"Yeah, I heard," Lee said.

"They didn't care whether they professed their innocence all day long. They electrocuted them."

If the FBI came to handcuff him, Covert asked, what would he tell his son, his coworkers?

Lee was shaken. "I just tell them what you told me," he stammered out. "I say you people don't believe what I said and polygraph don't believe what I said. And whatever consequence I will take, okay. I'm—I'm—I'm—I'm sixty."

Covert pushed on: "Do you know what that means? It means you're going to be an unemployed nuclear scientist with no job, and if you get arrested, you'll have no money . . . You won't have a house."

"I will open a Chinese restaurant here," Lee began, "and you can give me . . ."

"You're not going to be opening any Chinese restaurant. You're going to be in jail, Wen Ho," Covert cut him off angrily. "And your kids are going to have to deal with the rest of their lives, people coming up to them and saying, 'Hey, isn't that your dad, that Wen Ho Lee guy that got arrested up at the laboratory?' . . . I see lots of problems for you. I see no job. I see no clearance. I see no way to keep your son in school. I see your family falling apart. All because of this."

Lee believed his job was safe, or so his boss had assured him. He didn't know more powerful forces were already at work. In a flurry of phone calls from Washington to Los Alamos, his fate was already being decided.

– 1 –

Nantou to Los Alamos

World War II had just begun in Europe when Wen Ho Lee was born—December 21, 1939. But by then, East Asia had been embroiled in conflict for years.

Japan's armies had swarmed into China in 1931 and again in 1937 to capture Shanghai and demolish China's capital in Nanking. Lee's birthplace on Taiwan, known as Formosa, or "Beautiful Island," had been under Japanese occupation for more than forty years, a prize for winning the Sino-Japanese war late in the nineteenth century. Japan's governors in Taiwan were so far from home that they were given extraordinary independence, power so complete they could act without orders from Tokyo. The Taiwanese derided these foreign leaders as the "Bumpkin Emperors."

On the mainland, Communists and Nationalists suspended their civil war in 1937 to fight the Japanese. But in Taiwan, Japan was consolidating its gain by embarking on a policy of "Japanization," stripping the Taiwanese of their native language and culture so they might become loyal imperial subjects. Taiwan's ethnic mix at the time was a blend of Polynesian natives and Han Chinese migrants, most coming in the last two centuries from Fujian Province across the Taiwan Strait. Wen Ho was less than two months old when the Japanese governor issued an order encouraging the Taiwanese to adopt Japanese names and learn Japanese. Lee learned to read the language.

Taiwan was to be a supply base for Japan's march into Southeast Asia. With a tropical climate that promised three rice harvests a year and a vast expansion in irrigated lands, the island became both the "Granary of Japan" and, via forced industrialization, a massive Japanese munitions factory. Associated industries—steel, chemicals, textiles, and machinery—mushroomed in Taiwan's cities. In fact, the year Lee was born marked the first time the industrial portion of the island economy outstripped agriculture.

Those wrenching changes were not as apparent in the island's rural interior. Lee's family lived close to the middle of the island, in Nantou, a landlocked county of mountains, foothills, and fertile valleys of farmland. Hsian Ko and Yi-wei Lee raised ten children, of whom Wen Ho was the fourth. All tended the family rice fields and banana trees; neither provided much money for the Lees. Like many farmers, they lived in a mud-and-thatch house that often had to be repaired after the summer monsoons. They were poor even by Taiwan standards. "At night, they would all sit around a table and read by candlelight," Lee's son, Chung, would say later, retelling the family stories.

Hsian Ko Lee had a passion for Chinese classical music, and his children shouldered extra jobs on the farm to buy him instruments. Yet Hsian Ko rarely found enough time to play them all, so the children ended up recipients of their own gifts. In this manner, Wen Ho and his siblings learned to play. Their mother, Yi-wei, though she could barely write, amazed her son by doing complex math in her head. Lee's stories of those times reveal a natural curiosity and a love of fishing and hunting wild boar with his brothers. He kept a monkey, a common pet in Taiwan.

The Lees' lives and language were distinctly rural, a simple family innocent of the larger world, exceedingly close. "My father was loved by everyone. He was the favorite sibling . . . everyone's favorite uncle," his daughter Alberta said.

Wartime brought harsh new realities. When Lee was four, the Japanese issued the "Taiwan Food Supply Control Order." To enforce the new rationing, soldiers came to the Lees' door and demanded to speak to the youngest child, apparently in the belief that the youngest would not lie. Wen Ho's parents ushered him to the door, where the Japanese soldiers pointed rifles at his head and asked, "How many bowls of rice have you had today?" The only correct answer was "One." And it was usually true: Lee would later talk of going hungry as a child.

Until 1943, the Japanese on Taiwan had boasted of their prowess at war, first against the Chinese and then the Americans at Pearl Harbor. The new food-rationing rules suggested that Japan's war effort was becoming strained. Confirmation came just over a year later as American bombs rained down on Taiwan's munitions factories and airfields. On September 2, 1945, the same day Japan signed the formal declaration of surrender on the deck of the USS *Missouri,* Allied Supreme Commander Douglas MacArthur ordered all Japanese forces on Taiwan to surrender to Generalissimo Chiang Kai-shek. Chiang led the army of China's Nationalist government, known as the Kuomintang or KMT, then encamped in Szechwan Province on the mainland.

Once again, Taiwan went to the victors of a war in which it had little part. The island was handed from one occupying army to another without a shot fired. The midwife in this transaction was the United States, despite its claim of being a champion of self-determination. The KMT had been fighting Communists, a higher national security interest for the United States than allowing a small island to determine its future. The Taiwanese lost their only chance at self-determination for the next forty-three years. Within six weeks, American ships guarded by U.S. warplanes carried 12,000 Kuomintang soldiers and officials into Taiwan's Keelung Harbor. The ragtag KMT Army marched straight to Taipei, where the new governor, Chen Yi, met them a week later, flying in on an American plane from Shanghai.

The Taiwanese quickly found the Kuomintang to be corrupt. It was aggressively diverting the island's industry and agriculture to supply Nationalist armies on the mainland. This triggered dire shortages of rice on Taiwan; prices shot up sixtyfold from September to November 1945. Sixteen months after the end of the war, Taiwanese rancor was at a peak. The pistol-whipping by KMT agents of a middle-aged widow selling contraband cigarettes on a Taipei street corner incited insurrection, which was brutally put down by the government. Troops fired indiscriminately into crowds and tortured or beheaded students and other intellectual leaders. Death estimates ran as high as 28,000. An entire generation of Taiwan's political and academic elite was wiped out or imprisoned. The "228 Incident," on February 28, 1947, left a deep imprint on the minds of the Taiwanese at home and abroad. It began forty years of martial law on the island.

In 1949, Chiang's main KMT forces were routed from the mainland by Mao Tse-tung's Communist Army. The KMT fled to Taiwan. Numbering about 2 million, they were a decided minority on the island. To lock in Nationalist power and to ensure power remained in the hands of his family, Chiang rewrote the Taiwanese constitution. He made effective use of a secret police to eliminate political opposition. Dissidents were imprisoned or executed; overseas Taiwanese who spoke against the regime were identified and blacklisted. The government exacted retribution on their relatives still on Taiwan.

It is unclear what effect KMT repression had on the Lee family or on Wen Ho personally. But the 228 Incident touched nearly every family on the island. Many Taiwanese became convinced the KMT was a worse evil than the Japanese.

The year 1949 also brought personal tragedy to the Lee family. Yi-wei Lee was diagnosed with tuberculosis. Medical care in rural Taiwan was poor, and Yi-wei knew the treatments would be enormously expensive. Not wanting to burden her family, she hanged herself by the rafters in the rice-drying room. A few years later, Hsian Ko was speared during a boar-hunting accident. Infection from the injury triggered a fatal stroke, according to Wen Ho's children.

"He was right there when it happened," Chung Lee recounted. "He grabbed him and basically held his father as he died."

Wen Ho's eldest brother, Wen Yih Lee, took charge of his siblings and assumed the role of father figure. Yet the double traumas—his mother's suicide and father's death—made a lasting impression on Wen Ho. Chinese culture places a premium on strong family ties, and Wen Ho was reared in the same tradition, among myriad aunts and uncles. But the loss of his parents made him crave the closeness of family even more.

Wen Yih Lee moved the family to northern Taiwan and launched a commercial fishing company. Wen Ho took refuge in his education. He studied English and would tutor himself by memorizing words while riding the school bus: "tree," "window."

"I study those—you know—go on the bus, you have nothing to do, so I just open my book and try to memorize," Lee would say later. "And when I go to school, I usually do very good on English, okay? Before my surgery."

At age sixteen, he suffered pains in his abdomen, and surgeons removed his appendix. A complication of the surgery was significant memory loss. As he would later explain: "I spent seven days in the hospital, and after that I go home for three weeks . . . recovery. And for the next whole year, the whole year, my memory goes way down . . . and I don't understand why, because I used to have a very good memory."

After the surgery, "I failed every day. I tried to remember, but as soon as I walked to the school, it was all gone. It's all gone! So my memory just suddenly go bad. And I did not recover my memory within, I would say, ten months or one year." Lee graduated Keelung High School in 1959, then went into Taiwan's Chinese Air Force for one year of mandatory military service. Once out, he earned a degree in mechanical engineering at Cheng Kung University in Tainan, on the southwest end of the island.

Wen Yih meanwhile had established a shipping business, cobbling together a small fleet of boats. But he yearned to take the whole family to the United

States for better jobs. Wen Ho was the first to go. He obtained a student visa in September 1964 and, financed by his brother, headed to California. He landed in San Francisco, a little bit of English and not much money to his name. To raise the cash for school, he got a job washing dishes at a Chinese restaurant in the city's Financial District. He decided to enroll at Texas A&M University, which had a reputation as one of the nation's better engineering schools— and one of the cheapest.

Lee hurled himself into his engineering classes with intensity. He shunned the ordinary trappings of college life. Rather than date or go to parties, he went to the library. For fun, he'd read a book and listen to classical music. Said office mate and fellow engineering student David Beers, "He was not a party guy. He kept pretty much to himself, but he was a very pleasant guy, a nice guy and a good student. He was a computer nut and liked mathematics. He was better at it than most of us."

When Beers got married, Lee borrowed a camera and took photos at the wedding. But in general, Lee kept a certain distance from everyone. A fellow student remembered him as a "nonentity." Although Beers dined with some of the other foreign engineering students, he never broke bread with Lee.

By 1966, Lee had his master's degree in mechanical engineering and, four years later, his Ph.D. He left little impression on his thesis advisor, A&M professor C. F. Kettleborough, who remembered him as "a pretty good, hard worker." Lee dedicated his dissertation to his parents. He bought himself a blue 1968 Ford Mustang. Within a year, he became a naturalized U.S. citizen and moved to California to begin both career and family.

Lee wasn't a Christian, but he was lonely and so joined a Taiwanese Christian singles group. His first outing was a trip to the Rose Bowl in Pasadena, and he helped car-pool in his Mustang. His daughter would later roll her eyes and laugh at the mental picture: "I just imagine all of these really clueless, charming, incredibly cute Chinese and Taiwanese sitting there trying to act really into football like they know what's going on, trying to drink beer, all wearing the same sweatshirt." Afterward, as he drove the new football fans to their homes, he made sure a pretty young woman named Sylvia was last. Then he took her to a soda shop.

Unlike Wen Ho, Sylvia had been born on the mainland, in Hunan Province, but was still young when her parents moved to Taiwan. She was a bright, poised "city girl" who grew up in Taipei, Taiwan's capital and a world away from Nantou. Years later, a visitor to the Lee home saw a photograph of her from the seventies and said she was rather attractive. Sylvia had a literature degree from National Taiwan University, a school originally founded by the Japanese and regarded as the island's most prestigious. She was almost exactly four years younger than Wen Ho. They were engaged five weeks after they met.

They moved around those first few years—eventually wending their way to Hackensack, New Jersey, where Sylvia gave birth to a son, Tse Chung, in August 1972. A year later, the Lees had a second and last child, a daughter to whom they gave the Western name Alberta.

The same year, Lee got a job at the National Reactor Testing Station in Idaho, a government-owned facility dedicated to nuclear power research. The site sprawled across the high desert, its remoteness perfect for the government's work on naval and civilian nuclear reactors, exploring new designs and safety issues.

Not long after Lee arrived, the lab took a new name, Idaho National Engineering Laboratory (INEL), and built a new computer center in Idaho Falls—a plain, one-story brick rectangle of utilitarian, two-person offices. It housed a total of about 150 workers, mostly scientists and engineers, plus computer operators. Lee worked in a small team of four engineers who studied nuclear-reactor safety.

The Lees made their family home in a simple, white ranch-style house, built a few years earlier on Oak Trail Drive, a street full of similar houses. It was one of Idaho Falls's nicer subdivisions, quiet and fairly free of traffic. The house had three bedrooms, a brick facade below the windows and a six-foot fence around the backyard. Most of the year, the ground was covered in snow.

The Lees were not socially active. In interviews, none of Lee's coworkers could recall anything about Sylvia Lee. She became a U.S. citizen in 1977 but still spoke English haltingly and appeared to keep to herself. Almost no one came to the house for dinner even though Wen Ho richly enjoyed cooking—and fishing. He soon found a stream, Willow Creek, a trickle of rainbow-trout water northeast of Idaho Falls. His way of socializing outside of work was to invite people fishing. Fellow engineer Steve James received an invitation after he fixed Lee's blue Mustang. Afterward, Lee shared his favorite recipe for steamed fish. "He called it the Chinese way of fixing trout, and I wrote down the recipe and tried it a few times and I liked it," James said much later. "I remembered him being humorous about it. The biggest fish you could catch in Willow Creek was about an eleven-inch rainbow trout. So his recipe was phrased in terms of 'Cut one eleven-inch rainbow trout in four pieces.' He wasn't the most anglicized. He seemed to have a lot of trouble with written and spoken English."

Lee's coworkers found him likable and hardworking, perhaps a little naïve. But Lee didn't share many of his thoughts beyond that recipe and a few fishing invitations. "He was a very secretive person. It was rare to hear him say anything about his personal life in any way. For instance, I don't remember him saying anything about his wife or kids," James said. "He seemed particularly isolated, particularly a loner, compared to anyone else."

Chuck Nalezny worked more closely with Lee than anyone else in the team. "I never knew anything about his personal life. I don't ever remember him mentioning his family or where he'd gone to school or even where he came from," Nalezny said. "He worked hard, seemed pleasant."

James Lime, another Chinese American on the team, got a glimpse of Lee's personal thoughts from a smattering of talk on a few fishing trips to Willow Creek. "I do know his loyalty was to Taiwan, toward independence," Lime said. "Just from our small talk, I know he was a very strong Taiwanese person. He wanted independence for the republic of Taiwan."

Lee's job at INEL focused on a piece of computer software, or code, called BEACON, for Best Estimate Advanced Containment. Its purpose was to predict the pressure and temperature inside a reactor-containment vessel during an accident. BEACON was a fairly simple two-dimensional code for answering questions. If cooling water stopped flowing around the nuclear-reactor core, when would steam from the overheated core create enough pressure to rupture the containment vessel? Or if the containment vessel had a crack, how much steam might escape and what would happen inside the vessel?

Lee's specialty was hydrodynamics, the study of fluids—including gases— and the ways they behave in all kinds of environments. Before World War II, hydrodynamicists used paper-and-pencil calculations for the design of ships and airplanes. But during the war, new classes of problems arose that had no exact solution. Instead, they required estimates or approximations, so scientists taught computers to crunch large calculus problems to reach the needed approximations.

The U.S. Nuclear Regulatory Commission was the "customer" for INEL's work, in fact was paying for research in reactor-safety software at several government labs at the time. The NRC's regulatory staff was desperate for ways to check the integrity of reactor designs proposed by General Electric, Westinghouse, and others. BEACON was troublesome, however; the software crashed a lot. The small team looked in part to Lee to fix the code. And he possessed a wealth of ideas. But in the end, BEACON was a bust. It wasn't reliable enough to be useful.

Team supervisor Larry L. Wheat, a nuclear engineer, concluded that Lee knew his field well, was intimate with the scientific literature on two-phase hydrodynamics as well as a host of related sciences. But Wheat discovered Lee was less skilled at translating that knowledge into the equations that BEACON and the Idaho team needed.

"He was fine from a personal standpoint. He seemed very nice and very friendly and fit in well with the work group," Wheat recalled. "You could ask him questions about the subject we were working on, and he seemed to have good knowledge of the literature. He'd read a lot of material about it. We had some trouble getting him to apply that knowledge to the project. He was perhaps not able to translate that knowledge into the work. And ultimately he was dismissed from our project because of that."

In other words, he was fired or at least asked to resign. He never told his coworkers the reason for his departure. Nalezny had been on vacation. "He just sort of disappeared. I was really surprised," he said. "I came back from annual leave and he was gone." Wen Ho Lee already had left for a new job, moving expenses paid, at another government lab, Argonne National Laboratory.

Argonne's history was built on the legend of the University of Chicago's Metallurgical Laboratory, where Italian physicist Enrico Fermi and his team of fifty hand-built the world's first nuclear reactor in a university squash court. Los Alamos might be the birthplace of the bomb, but the Met Lab was the birthplace of the Atomic Age and the United States' first national laboratory. After the war, at a forested site twenty-five miles southwest of Chicago's Loop, scientists and engineers labored to make nuclear power safe and cheap.

The Lees and their two young children set up house in Downers Grove, about ten miles from the lab. Lee shared an office with computer scientist Bob Schmitt in a flat-roofed, cement-block building. "He was a very likable person and a very gentle man," Schmitt said. Lee opened up more with his Argonne coworkers than he had at INEL and chatted up a storm on technical issues. He was excited about his field and his work, and it showed.

"As was the case with many scientists, he was anxious to share what he knew with other scientists and to share their understanding," Schmitt said. "He was a typical exuberant scientist."

"He seemed like a decent sort of guy in that he was helpful and talkative. If anything, he kind of rambled on a bit . . ." on scientific issues, said Hank Domanus, a fellow code developer on the team. "Overall, I think he was a competent guy. He was a good resource to have online. He was kind of like a pack rat, a resource kind of guy. You'd have a question and he'd go into his files and pull something out or a name of someone he'd come across."

Lee assembled an impressive and well-organized personal library of his work and published articles about other code approaches, plus manuals on how to use them. But, as at INEL, some of his coworkers felt his value to the team was less than Lee himself perceived. "What I heard was that he was technically capable but he was not particularly anybody that was a superstar of any sort. He knew the subject and was someone who could contribute. [But] it was not like this was someone we have to go out and recruit, nor someone who was irreplaceable when he left," said Rich Valentin, who headed the applied-mechanics section of which Lee's team was a part. Nonetheless, Lee "had a pretty strong opinion of his own work." Argonne hydrodynamicist Robert Lyczkowski came to know Lee later and figured he was entitled to that opinion: "He was about the only person I ever worked with who really understood what all this multiphase flow was really about."

But several of those who worked with Lee at the time agreed with Valentin's assessment. Lee was not "one of the superstars we have come through here," Domanus said. "He talked a good talk, and I'm not sure if he could walk the walk."

The team of twenty or so scientists and engineers was headed by William T. Sha and did hydrodynamic modeling much as Lee had done in Idaho. Coworkers said Sha recruited Lee as a two-phase–flow expert and that he came with good recommendations from INEL. Sha was born on the Chinese mainland and had a prodigious memory for faces, names, and personal details that never ceased to amaze his staff. The word on Sha was beware: He had a volcanic temper and a conviction that he knew good work from bad. Anyone who ran afoul of this conviction would be driven out of the team.

Sha had his team working on software for advanced reactors cooled by liquid metal. If they were ever to be fielded, the NRC would need software tools to make sure they were safe. The reactors never caught on, however, and the money dwindled. Sha was under pressure to cut staff. "Bottom line was, we needed to get rid of some people," Schmitt said. "Not very many people know how to get rid of employees, and Bill happened to do it very poorly, in almost everyone's opinion."

Sha's problems with Wen Ho Lee grew not only out of tight funding. The two men disagreed vehemently on fundamental issues of science and software. Sha questioned the numbers emerging from Lee's equations. And he ordered Lee to try a different approach; Lee was sure it would fail and said so. Sha was loud and bitter, his shouting echoing down the hall. The arguments left Lee wringing his hands and anxious about his job. "He was beaten down," Schmitt said. "It was loud and angry, a very ugly situation."

"Everybody had difficulties with Sha. The guy was a slavemaster," Lyczkowski said. "He just didn't like anybody who disagreed with him, so you did whatever he said and didn't disagree with him."

"It seemed that occasionally he would get into a disagreement over technical issues, and he would argue and harangue the employee until they left or went on to some other place of employment. It just got too much to bear," Schmitt said. In Lee's case, Sha berated him almost daily, peppering his technical criticisms with personal attacks.

"Wen Ho Lee was definitely technically more capable than Bill Sha," said Domanus. "Bill Sha just kept pounding on you until you put in your six to nine months and then you moved on." Lee followed the pattern. Argonne had insisted he stay more than a year to be fully reimbursed for his moving expenses from Idaho. He left November 30, 1978, a year and a month after he arrived.

His first two career steps had been unsuccessful. But the future looked brighter. Lee was headed for northern New Mexico's high desert, to Los Alamos Scientific Laboratory. It was nirvana of sorts for a hydro-code developer. In the field of nonanalytic hydrodynamics—the fluid-behavior problems that could be studied only by computer simulation—Los Alamos was where it all began.

– 2 –

The Hill

When Wen Ho Lee brought his family to Los Alamos in December 1978, he drove across the opaque Rio Grande, a green river clouded by the silt of canyons and irrigated farms in southern Colorado and northern New Mexico. The highway beyond, snaking up stunning cliffs of volcanic ash and basalt, was rutted dirt when the first wave of European émigrés and American scientists arrived for the 1940s Manhattan Project. Los Alamos back then was a secret military installation; birth certificates bore a Santa Fe address, "P.O. Box 1337."

Isolated by design, Los Alamos sat on a volcanic plateau referred to simply as "the Hill." The U.S. Army erected tall fences, placed sentries and tanks at the gates. Even before the scientists arrived, they imposed their own security, voluntarily withholding publication of the atom's promise of bombs of unbelievably destructive power. At Los Alamos, lab director J. Robert Oppenheimer resisted compartmentalization. He wanted researchers on different pieces of the project to collaborate. The atmosphere of collegial give-and-take infused a secret wartime project and became ingrained in lab culture.

By 1978, the gates, tanks, and guards on the edge of town were gone, yet Los Alamos was still very much a company town steeped in the mystique of the Project and its icons.

A semblance of a normal town—shops, hotels, and offices—had grown over the old barracks-style wartime structures of Site Y, the Los Alamos code name during the Project. Fuller Lodge, the timber home to countless colloquia during the war, was still standing, as was "Bathtub Row," a line of cozy timber-and-stone houses that, having bathtubs, had been reserved for some of the Project's leading lights—Fermi, neutron discoverer Sir James Chadwick, Hans

27

Bethe, Norris Bradbury, Stanislaw Ulam. Beyond these remnants of history, Los Alamos was an architectural hodgepodge: seventies kitsch stood side by side with adobe and California ranch homes and the kind of inexpensive wood houses that the old Atomic Energy Commission built by template at every nuclear facility under its command.

Across Omega Bridge from the town, the lab itself was much the same story—there was no architectural harmony in the sixties and seventies offices, and a warren of trailers. There was no identifiable aesthetic except a sense of the utilitarian, the workmanlike pragmatism of engineers, which Los Alamos had in spades. The Cold War was on; no time for frills.

———————

Lee came to a lab that had only recently begun to hire Chinese Americans in any number. For many years, the government had refused to grant security clearances to anyone with relatives behind the Iron Curtain or in China, but by 1978 there were more than a dozen Chinese-American families on the Hill, most from Taiwan, some from Hong Kong, Singapore, and Malaysia.

Living on the Hill meant either Los Alamos or White Rock, a cluster of subdivisions built close by on finger mesas stretching to the southeast. The government had sold land for a dirt-cheap $200 an acre to specially selected developers capable of building a hundred or more houses a year. By the time the Lees arrived, White Rock was almost built out.

Lee met with a salesman for the Home Planning Development Company and picked a plain, ranch-style house—three bedrooms, one and three-quarters baths, one of thirty-two standard floor plans. It was brown, one of five standard paint jobs. Nearly everyone else in town kept the builders busy customizing the cookie-cutter homes—an extra fireplace, real shutters, or an added foot of wall—but not Lee. His house, like him, was frugal and simple.

The street name, Barcelona, was plucked from the air by salesmen for its romantic appeal to young families. Near Christmas, the moment the framing was done, before his new house had walls or roof, Lee thumbtacked a photograph of his family to the fireplace mantel.

Next door, another new house was going up. One day, Lee spotted his new neighbors checking the construction and scrambled over the mounds of dirt and debris to greet them. He grinned at Don and Jean Marshall. "My name's Wen Ho—as in Ho, Ho, like Santa Claus," Lee said. The Marshalls thought he was charming, if a tad quirky. The Lees moved into their new house in April 1979, the Marshalls a month later.

Both the Marshalls, like Lee, were code writers at the lab. To their mutual delight, their children were roughly the same age. The Lees had just enrolled Chung in the third grade and Alberta in the second. Don Marshall dug a sandbox in his backyard and erected an A-frame to ward off the unrelenting high-desert sun. The four kids imagined they had a beach in the shade, a garden hose for their ocean, and wet sand for castles.

Jean taught piano on the side, and in a few months, Chung and Alberta Lee were pupils in the Jean Marshall School of Music. Her living room was designed to double as a concert hall. The two families gardened. Lee brought over fresh vegetables and fruit. Jean Marshall shared her flowers and every year wheelbarrows of soil recycled from her roses. Don Marshall lent Lee his concrete mixer for making borders; Lee without fail always repaid the favor with a Chinese roasted chicken, finely chopped and, according to a number of recipients, delectable.

The Marshalls became warm friends with Wen Ho and Sylvia, who didn't seem to have many close friends.

If Lee was quirky, the town he'd chosen was a haven for the eccentric as well as the brilliant, often as not in equal doses. Los Alamos was the most affluent spot in an impoverished state and boasted more Ph.D.'s per capita than any other town in the world. Everything from the minutiae of town government to family squabbles was dissected and analyzed to a fare-thee-well. "Too many Ph.D.'s" was a popular local lament.

It was nonetheless gauche to address anyone as "Doctor." In the late 1970s, Los Alamos had the relaxed air of a college campus, branching into unclassified science under the direction of lab director Harold Agnew.

Yet almost everybody had some connection to nuclear science, usually to hydrogen bombs and missile warheads. Genetics research began as a desire to understand the effects of radiation on the residents of Hiroshima and the workers in the American bomb plants. Likewise, Los Alamos astronomers knew their research would be used to help warheads steer more precisely to their targets. The lab's geophysicists and seismologists conducted basic research but were hired primarily to study underground nuclear blasts, including the tests of other countries.

The town's curling streets were quiet, full of woodsy houses and well-kept gardens. Above the town was the ski area, Los Alamos's second. Weaponeers had cleared earlier slopes by wrapping necklaces of high explosive around the trees. Far to the east, across the desert, the sun rose over the snow-capped San-gre de Cristo—Blood of Christ—Mountains, named for their salmony hues at sunset or, according to legend, the blood of Spanish missionaries slaughtered by rebelling Indians.

The townspeople were comfortable with the lab's work. Its inventions killed more than 200,000 Japanese at Hiroshima and Nagasaki, but perhaps saved countless more Americans and Japanese who might otherwise have died in the invasion of Japan. The Bomb was an instrument of peace, the theory went, by making war too horrific to contemplate. Inside the lab's weapons divisions, many scientists wrestled with the ethical implications of their jobs. But often, they compartmentalized or rationalized their role: Didn't they have a moral obligation to provide the best for the arsenal of democracy? Actual use of nuclear weapons was a political decision, not theirs. Surely no president would be mad enough to order a nuclear strike unless the survival of the nation and democracy were at stake.

By and large, the children of Los Alamos grew up in a Norman Rockwell–like normalcy, albeit often with no clear idea of what their fathers did for a living. "We had forts in the woods and BB-gun wars and hide-and-seek until ten o'clock at night and kick-the-can," said native James Rickman, the son of two Los Alamos schoolteachers. "The only thing that was different was that there were very few ethnic people. I think we had one black kid."

In the Lees' neighborhood, kids holed up in a fort just behind the Lee house, a planked affair with a roof, stocked with comic books, food, bottled water, and a first-aid kit. A rival "gang" had a fort several blocks away.

Los Alamos teenagers attended the best high school in the state, its budget fattened by federal subsidy. A large percentage of Los Alamos High School grads made it to the Ivy League. Kids were often hard-driven to succeed. A grade of C was "a life-changing event," Rickman said. Wen Ho and Sylvia Lee expected as much of their children as any parents in town. "Growing up in Los Alamos, you learn intelligence is the primary value," Alberta Lee said. "That was definitely true in my family."

The town was not immune to drug and alcohol problems. Acid Canyon, right in the middle of town, got its moniker by soaking up twenty years of radioactive chemicals from plutonium processing. The effluent stopped in 1964 but the name stuck, a reference to teenagers and LSD.

Lee nudged Chung and Alberta into an overachiever's schedule early in life—piano lessons, youth soccer league, mandatory household chores and study periods, Chinese lessons on the weekends. It was Wen Ho, more often than Sylvia, who oversaw and participated in their children's activities. He made their lunches and wrote their names on the brown bags in Chinese characters. He was the volunteer assistant to the soccer coach, he helped with homework, he lobbied the piano teacher to tutor his kids in the classics—no wasting time on the blues, swing, or ragtime. By age ten, Alberta was lugging a cello at least as big as she was to soccer practice.

The Chinese Americans in Los Alamos kept an eye out for new arrivals and welcomed them to social gatherings. Wen Ho and Sylvia hosted bridge games, but Wen Ho's preferred instrument of hospitality was the fishing trip. "Many people would tell you that was their first exposure to Wen Ho and to fishing," said particle physicist Jen-Chieh Peng, who arrived in Los Alamos a few months before the Lees. "Of course, I went fishing with him once on the [Rio] Chama. He caught on the order of ten and I caught zero. He was going to teach me. I think he considered himself an expert."

By 1981, the Chinese community numbered at least twenty families, and a majority decided to form the Los Alamos Chinese Cultural Association. The idea was to celebrate traditional Chinese food, language, music, and art—and share it all with non-Chinese. "I and others said we need an organization so we can get together and celebrate the holidays and really let the local people know about Chinese culture," remembered Hsiao-Hua Hsu, a friend of the Lees and cofounder of the cultural association. "My thought at the time was that ordinary Americans would join and we could share our culture. It never happened."

Peng called Los Angeles and San Francisco with orders for Chinese textbooks, movies, and produce. These were shipped to Los Alamos or hauled by friends driving eastward. Association leaders rented classrooms or the library reading room to show Chinese movies and Fuller Lodge or the nearby community building for celebrations of the Chinese New Year. Parents took turns instructing all of the children in Mandarin, usually on Sundays.

Lee's first position in the lab was in Q Division, largely recycled out of the defunct N Division, where research into nuclear-powered rockets had lost public support and funding. Q Division—the Q being a physics symbol for energy—was to make nuclear power safe by anticipating accident scenarios and advising governments on reactor designs to thwart them.

Lee's first office was in Technical Area 52, in the top of a new three-story cinder-block building, insulated in Styrofoam and coated in light tan stucco. A pair of woodpeckers had carved a nest in the foam, so the walls emitted an odd ticking sound. Lee worked alongside other staff members of Q-9, the reactor-safety-code-development group. The centerpiece of their work was a large chunk of software called TRAC, for Transient Reactor Analysis Code, a cousin of the codes Lee had worked on in Idaho. TRAC had beaten an Idaho code for the endorsement of the Nuclear Regulatory Commission. The winnings came in the form of research money; the new office building was part of the prize.

TRAC was designed to predict the outcome of reactor accidents starting with a leak of cooling water. The question TRAC was to answer was this: When would the uncooled reactor core become hot enough for the metal cladding on the nuclear fuel rods to crack open and release highly radioactive metals, perhaps molten fuel, into the bottom of the reactor vessel?

As experts in the study of moving fluids, Lee and colleagues worked on honing TRAC to simulate sudden and huge breaks in the 30-inch pipes that supply cooling water to a nuclear reactor. It was a worst-case scenario that began and ended within seconds. Their task changed dramatically on March 28, 1979, when a valve malfunctioned at the Three-Mile Island reactor in Pennsylvania and operators who misread the danger signs further reduced the flow of cooling water. No one knew exactly what was happening in the reactor core, nor could anyone venture into such a highly radioactive environment to find out.

The Nuclear Regulatory Commission staff called Los Alamos, and a core of Q-9 scientists began re-creating the accident using TRAC. They had to overhaul the code massively—with new equations—because the Three-Mile Island incident was a slow accident, taking a full day, much longer than the accidents TRAC was designed to model. In the end, the code predicted correctly that at least some of the fuel rods had cracked open and leaked molten fuel into the bottom of the reactor vessel.

Lee and coworkers spent the first half of 1979 refining the code, plugging in new math, and retuning the code with experimental data from Idaho, Japan, and Germany. From there, Lee's work ranged from basic hydrodynamics theory to simulating huge, liquid-natural-gas spills and the concentrations of pollution downwind of coal-fired power plants.

Colleagues thought he was an ordinary, hardworking code developer. "He was sort of a quiet fellow and did his job," said James Sicilian, Lee's immediate supervisor.

Unbeknown to coworkers, Wen Ho Lee had begun sending unclassified research papers back to his homeland. It remains unclear, based on what is known of his conversations with the FBI, whether Lee began sending U.S. scientific material to Taiwan officials in Washington while he was at Argonne or Los Alamos. His bosses said he never asked permission, nor was there a requirement to do so for openly published scientific literature.

A portion of the scientific data Lee handled at Argonne was restricted. Known as "Applied Technology," it was not to be shared with foreign scientists or referenced in any scientific publications. Yet the data was not classified—it had nothing to do with nuclear weapons—and the only reason for restricting its publication was so U.S. government laboratories could trade it to France, Germany, and Japan in exchange for their data, at cost savings to all concerned. Applied Technology was merely a bargaining chip.

"It was a way we can leverage the money we put into it and trade it back and forth," said Argonne's Valentin.

The data held unique value for the refinement of reactor-safety codes and, although the U.S. government might prefer that it be kept confidential, none of Lee's supervisors could see any national-security harm from his sharing it.

"It was in everybody's interest to make sure reactors everywhere were safe," Sicilian said. Lee should have abided by the restrictions on information given him and "he shouldn't on his own recognizance have decided to share it. But that's an employment issue, not a security issue at all."

Nonetheless, Lee's willingness to send restricted information overseas suggested a disregard for the rules.

By 1980, Lee would later tell the FBI, Taiwan was requesting that he send specific Los Alamos documents. In intelligence parlance, Lee was receiving a "tasking list." Although Lee was dealing in unclassified documents, spy catchers view a tasking list as evidence of a relationship that could lead to espionage.

The FBI was familiar with Lee's contact at Taiwan's unofficial embassy, the Taipei Economic and Cultural Representative Office in Washington, D.C. He was an intelligence officer for Taiwan.

Lee had crossed a line, and no one in the U.S. government yet knew about it.

In July 1979, Lee was given access to more sensitive information. He was hired into the TD, or Theoretical Design, Division at Los Alamos. Housed in the lab's Administration Building, TD Division was the inner sanctum of U.S. weapons science, a place where scientists designed the lion's share of the most sophisticated nuclear arsenal in the world.

Lee began studying shock dynamics, namely the effects of shock waves on metals and other materials. His job was to perform experiments inside computers. But those experiments would take on a complexity he'd never attempted before.

Earlier the software with which Lee worked could simulate water and steam—two-phase flow—in a byzantine maze of pipes and obstructions such as a nuclear-reactor core. But the flows were relatively slow and the structures more or less fixed. In his new job, everything moved at supersonic speeds. Nothing stood still.

He would be dealing with phenomena found virtually nowhere on Earth outside of nuclear weapons. Metals would be crushed under incredible pressures, turn to molten liquid, then energized gas. Shock waves would race at supersonic speeds and turn inside out.

The pioneer of this realm of fluid dynamics was a brilliant mathematician, John von Neumann, whom J. Robert Oppenheimer lured to Los Alamos from Princeton in 1943. Von Neumann realized no math existed that could deliver precise solutions for the extreme turbulence created inside an imploding atomic bomb. So he invented it. He worked out methods for approximating the effects of shock waves at a given point in a sphere—the imploding ball of plutonium that was the heart of the first atom bomb. Von Neumann was a magnificent engineer as well: He designed the first computing machine that could store instructions, and so he is one of the fathers of the modern digital age.

In later years, scientists at Los Alamos and elsewhere carried von Neumann's work ahead to found the field of computational fluid dynamics, Wen Ho Lee's chosen field. By the time Lee reached the Theoretical Design Division, Los Alamos was designing sophisticated H-bombs using software that was generations beyond von Neumann's original one-dimensional approach.

Von Neumann's algorithm—the step-by-step instructions for computers to perform the math without "thinking"—was kept shrouded in classification by the Atomic Energy Commission into the 1950s, which struck Los Alamos physicists as odd. Von Neumann's work was novel, even ingenious for the day. But it was mathematics, not nuclear bomb secrets. So began a long clash between weapons scientists and the government for which they invented enormously destructive bombs.

The scientists at Los Alamos took secrecy to heart. Their consciousness was seared by the blinding flash of H-bombs and the angry boil of fireballs reaching miles into the heavens. A nuclear test was a horrifying and awesome experience. Blast waves buffeted them miles away and were powerful enough to kill fish offshore, triggering shark frenzies around the Pacific atolls. The weaponeers locked their work in safes every night and had their office mates check the locks. They rarely spoke of their work outside of the lab's walls. And they surrendered claim to the coin of scientific legitimacy, the publication of their work. But they also harbored a growing disdain for government authorities and lawmakers who seemed to think everything about a bomb was a state secret.

– 3 –

A Neat and Delicate Package

*W*hen *Lee was transferred* into the lab's Theoretical Design Division, his days of building computer models of nuclear reactors were over. He would now create and maintain the codes used by the bomb designers. He was thirty-nine years old.

The codes were complex mathematical constructions that attempted to replicate the action inside an exploding weapon. Code writers built them line by line, typing in instructions and equations. "Five lines a day is really all you can do if it's completely debugged," noted Lee's fellow code writer Bob Clark. The longer codes contained hundreds of thousands of lines.

If properly built, a code could predict, to some extent, how a new, untested design might behave. For that reason, the mathematical models were the basic tool of weapons design. The successful detonation of a bomb in the desert at the Nevada Test Site was the ultimate confirmation of both a new weapon design and the codes used to conceive it.

The codes, however, were far from perfect. "A code is an approximation of what you think is nature," one Los Alamos code writer said. In the desert, a bomb might blow up with 20 percent less energy than the code had predicted. If the code writers or weapons designers understood the reason for the mistake, they would change the basic physics of the code. If not, they simply added a "fudge factor" to the code, to make the computer prediction match the "ground truth" of the actual nuclear explosion. The code jocks adjusted these "knobs" in the software until the answers came out right, even if the underlying physics were not understood completely.

Lee and others in X Division, as the Theoretical Design Division was soon renamed, created codes inside their computers by breaking down the object under study—an imploding bomb, for example—into a grid of small, more manageable areas, known as "cells." The grid itself was called a "mesh." Each cell was represented by dense mathematical equations that calculated the pressure, temperature, density, and movement of the material within the cell. The answers formed a snapshot of the bomb at one instant in time. Then the code would take a "time step" of a small fraction of a second and begin calculating the next snapshot. A full run of a weapons code on a Cray supercomputer could last overnight or even days.

There were two basic types of codes, Eulerian and Lagrangian. In Eulerian codes, the imaginary mesh was stationary. As the bomb exploded, the material in the bomb—plutonium, high explosives, neutrons—moved from one cell to the next. Lagrangian codes were different. The cells moved as the material moved, so that a single cell would track the same bit of material throughout the explosion.

Writing code is a cerebral, not a physical, activity. Lee sat at his desk and typed at the keyboard of his computer terminal. As a hydrodynamicist, he used high-level math to describe how metals as heavy as plutonium—one of the heaviest materials on Earth—flow like gases when subjected to the extreme heat and pressure of a nuclear weapon. He also modeled the shock waves in weapons that, as one scientist said, "bang around in these things all over the place." He was often alone in his office, quietly employing numbers to describe the most violent mechanisms that humans have ever invented.

A line of code could be a train of math symbols incomprehensible to the layperson, or something as simple as "read the eos data from the file seseos." This told the computer to go to something called the Sesame Tables and gather some data about the physical properties (eos, or "equation of state") of a particular material, such as plutonium. The data were then fed into the churning code.

One of Lee's first assignments in X Division was to help create part of a code named Big Mac, which would become a workhorse at the lab, used in the design of a nuclear warhead known as the W88. When Los Alamos won the assignment for the warhead from the Pentagon in 1982, the scientists knew it would be America's most prominent nuclear weapon. In the triad of U.S. deterrence—bombers, land-based missiles, and submarine missiles—the submarines were king, and the W88 was destined for them.

The W88 would be the warhead for the Navy's new missile, the Trident II D-5, with a range and accuracy beyond existing missiles. Its target would be the missiles of the Soviet Union. The Navy insisted that the lab deliver a warhead just as small and light as past warheads but far more powerful in order to "dig Soviet missile silos out of the ground."

From the beginning of the nuclear age, the weapons designers at Los Alamos sought to make their bombs smaller, lighter, and more powerful. They spoke of yield-to-weight ratios and yield-to-size ratios. In 1952, they took a great step forward with the invention of the hydrogen bomb.

The H-bomb was in essence a heavy metal box known as a "radiation case." Inside the box, at one end, was a plutonium atomic bomb. At the other end was the fusion fuel capsule. When the plutonium exploded, it created a dense river of fast-moving X-rays, which flowed through the box, reflected off the walls, and converged on the fusion fuel capsule with great force. The fuel, compressed and heated to extremes, fused and exploded.

The two parts of the bomb were given names. The atomic bomb (in which the plutonium atoms "fissioned" or split in half) was called the "primary." The hydrogen fusion explosive was called the "secondary."

The first experimental H-bomb was as big as a house. The drive to make H-bombs smaller began immediately. The W88 warhead could trace its lineage to those early days of Los Alamos. But some of its roots lay elsewhere, eight hundred miles away in California. In some ways, the W88 was the result of a deep sibling rivalry.

In 1952, a month before Los Alamos scientists tested the H-bomb, America opened its second nuclear-weapons lab in the dusty ranch town of Livermore, an hour southeast of Berkeley and San Francisco. Edward Teller, the Hungarian-born physicist who had helped conceive the H-bomb, campaigned for a second lab on the grounds that Los Alamos was not pursuing his dream of thermonuclear explosives with sufficient enthusiasm.

Having already lost the H-bomb race, Livermore opted instead to become the "new ideas" lab. The orders from its young lab director, Herb York, were clear: "Whatever you do, don't do it like Los Alamos." For the researchers in the lab's Small Weapons program, that meant make "a fission bomb that was anything but spherical." At the time, the Los Alamos standard primary was a ball of plutonium inside a larger sphere of high explosives that crushed the plutonium into a critical mass.

Physicist Jim Wilson suggested imploding a stick of plutonium with just two detonation points, one on each end. A spherical weapon, by comparison, had as many as thirty-two detonators. Wilson's coworkers were dubious. The implosion could never be precise enough to drive the stick to a critical mass, they said; molten metal would splatter in all directions.

Undaunted, Wilson arranged a demonstration. In the sunlight outside his office, he rigged up two garden hoses so that they were aimed directly at each other. When the spigots were turned on, the jets of water met in the middle, canceling out each other without splattering. "The angle you aim them at is what's critical," Wilson told his audience. "You have to do it head-on—very head-on."

When Wilson's "pipe bomb," code-named Cleo I, exploded in a live nuclear test in the Nevada desert in 1955, Livermore scientists were jubilant. But Norris Bradbury, the Los Alamos director, was less impressed. He would later joke that Cleo I was so loaded up with plutonium that it "would go off if you threw it in the corner." Nevertheless, the bomb's shape had potential for artillery shells and missile warheads.

In 1956, the Navy was investigating the prospect of launching missiles from submarines. At a planning meeting with Navy officials, Teller "outbid" Los Alamos for the job of designing the small nuclear warhead for the missile by predicting that Livermore scientists could achieve more yield with less weight than Los Alamos.

The challenge of the small warhead involved not just weight, but also size and shape, for the warhead had to be shoehorned into its reentry vehicle, the bullet-shaped metal shell that carried the warhead to its target. Spherical primaries were fat and didn't fit well in the narrow confines of the reentry vehicle. The difficult fit was a problem in search of Livermore's solution, the nonspherical primary.

By the summer of 1957, the nuclear pipe bomb had morphed into an oblong shape of hollow plutonium, surrounded by a similarly shaped shell of high explosives. It looked like a cross between a sphere and a cylinder, as if someone had squeezed a basketball until it became a watermelon and then slapped a detonator at each end. The designers called it the Robin, sometimes the Robin's Egg, because it looked a little like an egg.

The narrow primary was one wheel of the bicycle; the Livermore inventors now needed the other wheel, a high-yield fusion secondary. The physicists opted to abandon the cylinder shape that was then in common use in favor of a uranium sphere. They stuffed the sphere with fusion fuel and more uranium. The added uranium would supply the extra yield the designers needed.

Thus the bomb drew its destructive power from several nuclear explosions: a plutonium fission blast from the primary, a uranium fission detonation in the secondary, and the fusion explosion in the secondary. To maximize the yield, even the radiation case (the "box" that held the primary and secondary) was fashioned from a fissionable metal.

When this new secondary was successfully tested on a Pacific atoll in 1958,

Teller was ecstatic, exclaiming, "Wonderful, wonderful," and musing, "Boy, we really did it, didn't we?" This combination of oval primary and spherical secondary, invented in 1958, provided the prototype of missile warheads to come, including the W88.

The innovative design was inspired by rivalry between Livermore and Los Alamos, as well as the more obvious motivation provided by the Cold War. The rivalry was intense, sometimes bitter. At Livermore there was an expression that said it all: "Always remember, the Soviets are the competition, but Los Alamos is the enemy."

Livermore's reshaped warhead, the W47, went to sea on the Polaris, the first submarine missile, in the 1960s. Its invisibility beneath the ocean provided an invulnerable ability to launch a retaliatory strike that would slaughter millions of Russians if the Soviet Union attacked the United States.

The Polaris program played another role in the evolution of the W88. It was the first missile to carry more than one nuclear warhead. When the third version of the Polaris missile was put on submarines in 1964, every missile carried three warheads, each with a yield equivalent to 200,000 tons of TNT. The Navy had wanted a megaton warhead, but settled on the idea that three smaller explosions could do just as much damage and kill just as many people as one big one. The Navy called the arrangement CLAW, for Clustered Atomic Warheads. The three warheads would be aimed together, coming down around a city in a triangle. Multiple warheads would also have a better chance of defeating an antimissile defense system around Moscow.

Even before the CLAWs were on station, the planners were deeply engrossed in their next idea, MIRV, for Multiple Independently Targeted Reentry Vehicles. If one missile could deliver three warheads, why not aim them at three different targets instead of one? The reentry vehicles (RVs) would ride in a "bus" atop the missile. As the bus traveled its intercontinental arc above the Earth, it could drop off an RV here, another there, like the mailman. One missile could do the work of three, or six, or a dozen.

The world's first MIRVs were deployed in 1970, on top of the Minuteman III missile in underground silos in the American West. The warhead, the W62, was a Livermore design. There were twelve per missile, each with a yield of 170 kilotons. A year later, the Poseidon submarine-launched missile, the successor to the Polaris, was also loaded with MIRVed warheads from Livermore.

Finally, in 1973, Los Alamos broke the iron grip that Livermore had held on strategic missiles for sixteen years. The Navy was building a new, bigger sub, the Trident, and this time the contract for the MIRVed warhead went to Los Alamos. The lab produced the W76, with a yield of 100 kilotons. Each Trident missile could carry eight to fourteen of them, independently targeted.

Los Alamos was now the Navy's lab of choice, so it was no surprise that when the time came for the Navy to seek an even bigger sub and bigger missile, the Trident II D-5, it went to Los Alamos for the bigger warhead. The Navy wanted a high yield, around half a megaton, to guarantee destruction of buried targets. At the same time, the Navy insisted on warheads small and light enough for eight of them to fit atop a single missile and fly 4,000 nautical miles.

To make the design job even more difficult, the cone-shaped reentry vehicle for the W88, as this new weapon was designated, would be longer and thinner than most. The narrower the cone, the faster it would fly down toward its target, reducing the chances that it would be blown off target by winds. Accuracy was everything for the W88. The Navy did not want to miss the Soviet missile silos.

Added together, these requirements demanded a warhead with a higher yield-to-volume ratio than any previous warhead, by far. Every trick would have to be employed to wring out the last kiloton of yield. The W88 would have to "take advantage of all the technologies known in the weapons business."

X Division's design plan was to make the primary as small as possible, with just enough power to ignite the secondary, and then to load up the secondary with as much highly enriched uranium as would fit. Similar devices had been tested by the lab's engineers and physicists in live nuclear explosions beneath the Nevada desert during the mid-1970s, years before Los Alamos won the contract for the W88 in 1982.

The scientists provided names for their creations. The secondary was called Cursa, after a bright star. The primary was christened Komodo, after the Indonesian lizard, the Komodo dragon, that rips apart its prey with tooth and claw.

The W88 design called for Cursa and Komodo to be placed inside a peanut-shaped radiation case, with the primary nestled inside one end and the secondary at the other. The "peanut" was made of "depleted" uranium, a variety of the radioactive metal that will not sustain a chain reaction on its own but will fission within the environment of an exploding warhead. "At that point you could fission your grandmother's underwear," quipped one Los Alamos scientist. The peanut was about a yard long, approximately 9 inches in diameter at the primary and 14 inches at the secondary. The explosive yield was equivalent to 475,000 tons of TNT, thirty-two times that of the bomb that shattered Hiroshima in 1945.

The primary of the W88 was squeezed into the nose of the reentry cone, a configuration known as "primary forward." The larger secondary sat at the base of the cone.

One of the "secrets" of the W88 and most other H-bombs is that they are more a fission weapon than a fusion weapon, despite the fearsome reputation of the hydrogen bomb as something that uses uranium or plutonium only as a "trigger" for the fusion reaction. The W88 gets most of its deadly power from the ordinary fissioning of uranium and plutonium.

The W88 went into production in 1988, the most "optimized" weapon in the world, the evolutionary conclusion of decades of bomb-making. Chinese scientists ranked the W88 as the warhead they admired most. Four hundred W88s were manufactured and sent to sea. Everything in the warhead was stretched to the limit, making it difficult and expensive to produce.

The impetus for such an extreme weapon came in no small measure from the competition between Los Alamos and Livermore. The Soviets built warheads that were less sophisticated and heavier than U.S. models. To compensate, they simply built larger missiles. But this lack of refinement had no discernible effect on the ability of the Soviet weapons to deter the United States from military action against the Soviet Union.

Some scientists believe the W88 is the wrong weapon for the post-Cold War era. If the W88 develops problems as it ages, as have other warheads—difficulties such as corrosion, cracks, or microbubbles in the plutonium—its complexity could make fixing it difficult without nuclear testing, which the United States abandoned in 1992.

But whatever the reservations, the Los Alamos weaponeers clearly had earned the right to brag that they had built, in the words of former lab director Harold Agnew, a "neat and delicate package."

The complexity inherent in simulating nonspherical primaries fueled the development of more sophisticated computer codes such as those used to design the W88. Wen Ho Lee worked on some of those codes and had access to others.

The W88 Nuclear Warhead

Designed at Los Alamos National Laboratory, the W88 nuclear warhead is United States' most "highly optimized" nuclear weapon. For its size, it creates a more powerful explosion than any other weapon. The W88 is carried on Trident II submarine-launched missiles, which can deliver the warheads thousands of miles with great accuracy. The W88 explodes with the force of 475,000 tons of TNT, roughly 32 times the energy of the bomb that destroyed Hiroshima in 1945. The warhead was built to attack missile silos in the Soviet Union.

The W88 gets its power from a mix of exploding plutonium, uranium and fusion fuel.

1. The "Primary" is a plutonium fission bomb. Codenamed "Komodo," its watermelon or football shape (some fission bombs are spherical) allows it to squeeze into the narrow end of the re-entry vehicle.

2. The "Secondary" is compressed by a flood of X-rays from the exploding primary, a process called radiation implosion. The X-rays superheat the outer surface of the secondary (the tamper), driving it symmetrically inward, a reaction known as ablation. Inside the secondary, the fusion and fission reactions feed on each other. The secondary is codenamed "Cursa."

3. The "Radiation case" is also known as the "peanut" because of its shape. It channels the X-rays from the primary to the secondary. The chambers around the primary and secondary are ellipses, to better focus the X-rays.

4. Plastic foam fills the radiation case. X-rays from the primary superheat the plastic into a hot, energetic gas known as a plasma. The plasma "tunes" the X-rays to make for a more uniform implosion of the secondary.

5. The tritium reservoir. Radioactive tritium produces helium as it decays, reducing the boosting power of the gas. This is a problem for the W88, because of the difficulty of frequently changing the gas in the tight confines of the submarine. One of the key features of the W88 is a system, known as Terrazzo, that filters out the helium from the tritium reservoir.

Re-entry vehicle
Protects warhead from heat of re-entering atmosphere after flight through space.

High explosives
The plutonium "pit" is uniformly imploded to a critical mass by two types of explosives, one burning faster than the other.

Plutonium pit
Plutonium 239 is the fission fuel.

Tritium and deuterium
A mixture of the gases is injected into the "pit" under high pressure just before detonation to "boost" the explosion.

Lithium-6 deuteride
The fusion fuel. Neutrons from the exploding primary convert lithium deuteride to tritium and deuterium, isotopes of hydrogen. The gases then undergo a fusion reaction and explode; hence the name, "hydrogen bomb."

Uranium 235
At the center of the secondary is a hollow sphere of uranium 235 known as the "sparkplug." The sparkplug is stuffed with Lithium-6 deuteride. Together they provide a fission and fusion explosion.

More uranium 235
The heavy uranium tamper around the secondary helps to compress the fusion fuel, then undergoes a fission explosion.

Uranium 238
The radiation case is made of U-238. Less likely to fission than its cousin, U-235, it will nonetheless explode in the flood of neutrons produced inside the warhead.

REID BROWN

All were kept on the classified section of the Los Alamos lab's main network. In April 1988, Lee began to do a very curious thing. He secretly moved copies of several of the classified codes to the unclassified side of the laboratory network, where they were vulnerable to access by thousands of lab employees without security clearances and to theft through the internet.

This was a flagrant violation of security rules. By February 1992, he had copied twenty-six files containing weapons-design data into the unclassified side. He began with five versions of a code used to design primaries, then shifted to files related to two other codes. Among the files were a set of slides depicting a nuclear warhead. He left all the files on the unclassified network for as long as eleven years.

−4−

The China Connection

Long before the W88s went to sea and were targeted on Soviet silos, the Cold War was thawing on several fronts. Outside formal diplomatic channels, weaponeers of the United States and the Soviet Union were edging toward a wary détente on their own. Scientists on both sides were talking, first at international conferences and eventually inside one another's labs.

They pried for details of each other's weapons programs, and almost subconsciously they discovered that their counterparts raised families, thought, and invented much as they did. Decades of enmity fell away. It was for many like walking through the looking glass. They confirmed what each knew all along—that their competitor was extremely capable of inventing massively destructive weapons. Yet Russians and Americans alike found that neither side was inclined to use those weapons. This realization became the premise of an uneasy trust.

As the Americans and the Soviets learned about each other, China kept its weapons program tightly sealed. No one in the Soviet Union or the United States knew much of China's nuclear doctrine, its scientists or capabilities. Even so, neither the Russians nor the Americans viewed China as much of a competitor in numbers of arms or sophistication.

They were in many respects dead wrong.

A friendship between two University of Chicago alumni—one American, one Chinese—led to the gradual unveiling of China's program.

Harold Agnew and Chen Ning "Frank" Yang had become acquainted as classmates and protégés of Nobel laureate Enrico Fermi. The Italian physicist had created new and unusual radioactive elements by bombarding uranium with neutrons, then had gone on to build the world's first nuclear reactor. He was in this sense the father of the Atomic Age.

Agnew was a wry, outspoken Coloradan, with twinkling hazel eyes and a bearing that blended cowboy and gentleman scholar. History and Agnew's adventurism had given him a front-row seat in this new nuclear era. He was on the famous Fermi team that laid graphite bricks for the first nuclear reactor under the University of Chicago stadium. Fermi sent him ahead to Los Alamos in early spring 1943, and at the end of the Manhattan Project, Agnew flew aboard the instrument plane alongside the *Enola Gay* as it bombed Hiroshima. The well-known aerial photographs of the mushroom cloud rising over the wrecked city are his.

By 1970, when he was drafted as director of the then Los Alamos Scientific Laboratory, Agnew had formed extensive ties linking the worlds of politics and science. He was strict, blunt, and notoriously tight with money, but employees regarded him as eminently fair and came to see him as one of the lab's strongest directors. Lab weapons scientists were impressed that, as director, he personally launched the half-megaton warhead project that became the W88, a kind of hands-on role not assumed by succeeding directors. Agnew also pushed the laboratory's boundaries into unclassified, basic research. Under his leadership, Los Alamos became truly multidisciplinary and multicultural.

Yang came to Chicago after the war, at age twenty-four. The son of a mathematics professor, Yang was a quiet, affable workhorse of a scientist, well connected in China's physics community and prolific in his publications. He studied under Fermi; Edward Teller was his Ph.D. thesis advisor. Yang taught particle physics at Chicago for a few years and went on to become a force at Princeton's prestigious Institute for Advanced Studies, where director J. Robert Oppenheimer tried to draft Yang as his successor.

He was clearly brilliant: Yang and longtime coauthor Tsung-Dao Lee shared the 1957 Nobel Prize in physics. Altogether, Fermi's 1949 doctoral class produced four Nobel laureates.

Yang later became one of the first high-profile overseas Chinese to visit the People's Republic and began working for stronger Sino-U.S. relations.

"I knew both China and the United States and loved both countries," he later wrote. ". . . I knew I had the responsibility to help build a bridge of friendship and understanding between the two countries."

Yang became the first president of the National Association of Chinese Americans and lobbied heavily for the normalization of Sino-U.S. diplomatic relations. As one high-ranking American scientist put it, "He had one foot in China, one foot in the United States." Not long after Yang's visit to China, President Richard Nixon and his National Security Advisor, Henry Kissinger, launched secret overtures that opened the door to U.S.-China relations.

In January 1979, with his retirement a few months away, Agnew got an invitation to a head-of-state reception at Washington's Ritz-Carlton Hotel. The United States and China had just established normal diplomatic relations, and Vice Premier Deng Xiaoping was paying the first U.S. visit by a high-level official of the People's Republic.

Agnew sensed Yang was behind the invitation. He made his way down the reception line, greeting the Chinese entourage. A few minutes later, noted Chinese nuclear physicist K. C. Wang approached Agnew. Yang appeared, introduced the men, and urged Agnew to dine with Wang in a back room. Wang was then deputy director of the Second Ministry of Machine Building, a name and bureaucracy that the Chinese adopted from the Soviet weapons program.

"He was Mr. Nuclear Physics in China at the time," Agnew said.

Wang made casual inquiries about Agnew's scientific interests. "Defense science," Los Alamos's director said. Wang nodded. "That's nice." And the conversation wound down to small talk.

Two weeks later, Agnew received a formal invitation to come to China. His host would be one of the PRC's premier physics professors, Yang Fujia. Agnew was scheduled to attend a laser-fusion meeting in Japan that summer and agreed to go from there to Shanghai, where Yang was chairman of the Nuclear Physics Department at renowned Fudan University. Yang met the newly retired Agnew and his wife, Beverly, in the Shanghai airport. Yang was nattily attired in Western clothing and had a long, studious face framed in plastic glasses and a thick shock of black hair. He greeted Agnew warmly. Suddenly six men approached them. Yang seemed perplexed and not a little frightened.

"He was as befuddled as I was," Agnew recalled. "They kind of moved him aside and told me to come with them. All he said was, 'I don't know these people. You don't have to go with them.' "

The men did not say much, but they seemed friendly and eventually mentioned that K. C. Wang sent his greetings and would join them later. They asked Agnew, his wife, and Yang to come with them. Agnew sensed that the gang of six were weapons scientists. Yang was still leery, but Agnew's curiosity was piqued: Few if any Americans knew China's weapons scientists, much less talked to them. Here was a unique chance.

The Chinese set up the Agnews at a hotel and planned a whirlwind tour for their guests. The first stop was Beijing, where they hoped Agnew would give a talk in the Great Hall of the People, the home of the National People's Congress. Its granite and glass façade towers over the east side of Tiananmen Square.

Agnew agreed and found himself at a podium in front of thirty or more Chinese weaponeers. He spoke about Los Alamos, stressing its unclassified research and ties with academia. By Yang's reaction to the weaponeers at the airport, it was clear that China's weapons physicists and academic physicists were separate communities, unknown to each other. The weapons scientists were obviously well-educated and understood English. Their leader, Chen Neng Kuan, and several others in fact had trained in the West. Chen left his science career in the United States in 1959 to answer Premier Zhou Enlai's call for overseas scientists to build the Bomb for China. Agnew didn't know it, but Chen ranked among China's top weapons managers. His team had conducted over a thousand experiments exploring the principles for detonating atom bombs and supervised the crafting of the vital explosive assembly for China's first bomb.

Over the next weeks, the weaponeers served as the Agnews' tour guides. They showed off Beijing's Forbidden City, its ornate botanical gardens, and the Great Wall. Underneath Beijing, the Agnews walked inside one of the world's largest nuclear-bomb shelters, mile upon mile of walkways, hospitals, shops, even a power plant so Beijing's elite could survive a holocaust. While in the city of Guilin, they dropped into a music store where the proprietor was playing a bamboo flute. Agnew was captivated by its sound and bought it. Later at a hotel, he had trouble positioning on top of the flute the fine tissue-like paper that served as its reed. Aggravated, he knocked at Chen's door and asked if Chen could get the flute to work.

"He picked it up and immediately started playing," Agnew said. Chen looked at Agnew over the flute, eyebrows raised, and in a moment the tune changed. Agnew recognized the new melody. "He was playing 'Onward Christian Soldiers.'"

Intrigued, Agnew asked where Chen had learned the hymn. Chen said he'd attended a Yale-sponsored missionary school as a boy in Beijing. The best and brightest were sent to the United States to study; Chen went to Yale. His experiences with Americans had largely been positive, though he bitterly recounted an incident in which a barber refused to cut his hair because he was Chinese.

Agnew's inaugural trip was almost wholly academic in tenor and substance. The Chinese were exceedingly genteel. "We had a nice visit," he said. "They didn't really ask any questions, not much anyway."

The Chinese nonetheless were aware of the research going on at Los Alamos and understood it. "It was clear their intellectual level was very high," Agnew said. "I sensed that anything public, they had copies of it."

Back in New Mexico, Agnew filed a report that set U.S. intelligence officials on their ear: He had gotten a peek at the scientists inside one of the world's most secretive weapons programs. China's program was a black hole, its plans and its personalities virtually unknown. Agnew pulled out photographs and a tiny spiral notebook in which the Chinese had helpfully written their names in both Mandarin and English. The lab's intelligence chief, Danny B. Stillman, had Agnew's report typed up, classified it, and sent it to the CIA. The CIA's nuclear-weapons analysts were intrigued by what Agnew had seen and heard. Here was a rare glimpse, and they wanted more.

U.S. scientists already knew much, or at least had made educated guesses, about China's deployed nuclear arms. Their chief sources were technical and primarily generated information on nuclear tests. Surveillance satellites in the late seventies featured resolution down to a few centimeters—if one knew where to look. Seismic sensors and hydroacoustic arrays could capture the vibrations of nuclear detonations by land and sea. (But some intelligence tricks that worked against the Soviet Union were useless against China. To literally piece together models of Russian warheads, the United States sent boats to the splash-down zone of Soviet missile tests. Pieces of the missiles' mock warheads were pulled from the ocean and reassembled. One U.S. physicist recalled the eerie feeling of standing next to a perfect replica of a Russian warhead. But the Chinese typically tested their missiles over dry land.) But best of all was radiochemistry, the analysis of the radioactive debris of nuclear tests.

H-bombs are factories for enormous quantities of radiation and a zoo of radioactive elements, some found nowhere else on Earth. The job of the radiochemist is to capture, study, and—using a computer—reassemble these bits of fallout back into the design of the original bomb. For this, scientists ran the same software used to design American nuclear weapons but in reverse. The cloud devolved, inside the computer, from fragments and energy back into the bomb itself. Los Alamos scientists dissected hundreds of nuclear tests in this way and came to believe they could discern just about any bomb design from a mere whiff of its radioactive fallout, captured by Air Force planes.

For decades, radiochemistry provided the United States with the firmest intelligence on the yield and at least approximate designs of arsenals in Russia, France, and of course China. China's nuclear tests were deep in the Gobi Desert, isolated from prying eyes. But China's radioactive clouds wafted high into the atmosphere, then eastward over the Sea of Japan, where the Air Force and the radiochemists were waiting.

These bits of technical intelligence were a gold mine. But they disclosed little about larger questions of Chinese nuclear-force structure, doctrine, and plans for the future. The answers lay in China's weapons-design experiments and in the minds of its scientists and military leaders. Agnew's report whetted the appetites of the analysts at the CIA and the Defense Intelligence Agency.

Seeking to exploit the opening, Los Alamos intelligence chief Stillman cast about for the right kind of scientist-spy. He tapped a brash young executive at Los Alamos, George A. "Jay" Keyworth II, then head of the lab's Physics Division. Agnew, too, urged him to go.

Then in his thirties, Keyworth offered a piercing, impatient gaze that belied his youthful exuberance. His Bostonian family had seen to it that Keyworth was well educated, from his early days at a northeastern prep school through Yale and Duke universities. He was a vivacious physicist, a protégé of Edward Teller who shared his mentor's enthusiasm for science and technological solutions to defense problems. Keyworth was quick to grasp the implications of scientific discoveries and perhaps just as quick to dismiss those who disagreed. He counted Silicon Valley pioneer David Packard as a close friend and was renowned at Los Alamos for his love of fine food, cars, and accommodations. Agnew warmed to his energy and forceful persona. But the elder scientist was a dyed-in-the-wool skinflint and chided Keyworth frequently about his champagne tastes.

Keyworth had been to the Soviet Union and disliked it immensely, being especially disdainful of the lack of stalls, seats, or sanitation in restrooms. "It was just awful," he said. (CIA operatives awarded Keyworth a cobalt-blue toilet seat as a jibe at his fastidiousness.) While hardly enthusiastic about visiting China, Keyworth's admiration for Agnew overrode his reluctance. The results would have a subtle influence on Sino-U.S. relations through the 1980s.

A new CIA liaison to Los Alamos schooled Keyworth in playing a critical role in this new intelligence game abroad.

The product of a long, blue-collar Dutch lineage, Robert S. Vrooman was a compact man with thinning sandy-blond hair and mirthful brown eyes behind wire-rim glasses. He grew up in Syracuse, his mother a homemaker who raised five sons, and his father an engineer on the New York Central Railroad. They divorced in 1949, and Vrooman's grandparents took over his rearing just outside Pittsburgh, in "a dirty little steel town." After high school, he mulled becoming a minister and spent two years at a Methodist seminary in Rochester, New York.

He never finished his graduate work at the University of Rochester because "the draft was breathing down my neck."

He joined the Air Force as an air controller, assigned briefly to Kirtland Air Force Base on the south side of Albuquerque. "They grabbed me and shipped me off to Vietnam," Vrooman said, where in 1964 he began a standard two-year tour coordinating air rescues and air strikes from a mobile radar unit.

After the war, Vrooman went back to graduate school at the University of New Mexico, working toward a master's degree in international relations. One day, he noticed a commotion on campus, a gaggle of students shouting at a hapless figure in a window. It was a CIA recruiter. Vrooman decided on a lark to go talk to him. Jack Hansen was a Mormon; in fact, he caught hell from fellow agents for recruiting only other Mormons. He and Vrooman became friendly; Vrooman broke Hansen's Mormon streak.

He was accepted into operations training in 1969 and was assigned as a domestic case officer. He debriefed U.S. travelers who went abroad and tried to recruit foreign nationals in the United States to be spies. Vrooman had some successes, as well as some headaches, dealing with defectors from China and Warsaw Pact countries. His postings took him from Washington, D.C., to St. Louis to Denver and, finally, Los Alamos.

In 1979, Vrooman and his wife set up their house in White Rock, equipped with a safe and a secure telephone, and he began work as CIA liaison to the lab. Vrooman was an avid reader of natural history, astronomy, physics, a variety of sciences. Talking to the scientists made it all come alive for him. He realized he was sitting on an incredible reservoir of foreign intelligence, and he didn't really have to do much but write it up on the agency's pink forms and send it in.

The lab was, he found, an embarrassment of riches. Dozens of scientists were traveling to the Soviet Union and elsewhere. Better still, unlike businessmen, the scientists were technically adept enough to understand what they saw and heard. The CIA debriefings were not mandatory. Lab scientists were told, "You certainly don't have to do this, but we'd like you to sit down with these intelligence people." The scientists often were captivated by this cloak-and-dagger aspect of their jobs and usually agreed.

Among the lab's globe-trotting scientists, Keyworth was a special case. He would be hunting in China for detailed information about the weapons program and the men and women inside it. He would be tasked, in intelligence argot. The agency sent a team of field operatives down from Denver to Keyworth's house in Pojoaque, a small town on an Indian reservation twenty minutes east of Los Alamos.

"They gave me tips, taught me methods—'Here are some ways you can do things.' It was just like the spy books, writing things that can't be seen," Keyworth said. "They left it for me to decide what to use. I learned what a spy is."

Vrooman and the agents warned him not to play James Bond. He would bring back plenty if he comported himself just as he was, a fellow scientist. "What they were trying to tell me and what Bob was trying to teach me is the best way to get information out of there is to go over as a scientist and be a colleague," Keyworth said.

The CIA's analysts in Langley, Virginia, had hundreds of questions they wanted Keyworth to answer. It took weeks to weed out the arcane and trivial. High on the agency's wish list: What amount of Soviet weapons technology was on the ground in China? Where were the Chinese research sites, and who in the weapons program seemed to be a rising star, an up-and-comer likely to be in charge one day? The CIA, in other words, was hunting potential spies for the United States—and using a U.S. scientist as their spotter.

The agency's questions hammered home to Keyworth the fact that he was walking into virtually unknown territory. Agnew had barely scratched the surface of China's weapons program.

"I was stunned to learn how little we knew about it," Keyworth said.

For decades, U.S. intelligence had been preoccupied with the Soviet Union. Washington was chockablock in Sovietologists who scrutinized every syllable coming out of the Kremlin. But inside the Beltway, there were few recognized authorities on Chinese politics, personalities, intelligence, or arms. Washington cared about China chiefly as an outgrowth of policy on the Soviet Union. Sinologists as a result were a rarity outside academia.

The Carter administration was keen to develop Nixon's opening of China to a new level of strategic partnership. It sought to cultivate China as an ally, an Eastern counterweight to Soviet power.

Hundreds of American military officers journeyed to China to share their knowledge of tactics, logistics, and joint operations. A second army of American scientists offered access to U.S. science and technology. It was a time of opportunity, as well, for the United States to learn more of China's capabilities and intentions. No one else would get as close a look at the Chinese nuclear program as Keyworth. Beyond acting as a scientist-spy, he had been given a unique diplomatic aim: He was to convince China to stop testing its nuclear weapons in the atmosphere and move its blasts underground, as the United States and the Soviet Union had.

In 1980, Keyworth flew into Shanghai and, as Agnew had before him, met Yang Fujia. But the identity of his real host floored him.

General Zhang Aiping was a veteran of the Long March, chief of the commission overseeing China's first bomb test and first commander of the Lop Nur test base headquarters. By the late 1970s, he was the PRC's senior administrative statesman for defense science. For years, he had run the powerful Commission of Science, Technology, and Industry for National Defense, or COSTIND, as its deputy director. The panel was the central authority for dividing up China's sparse technical resources between the competing interests of nuclear and conventional arms. Then approaching his mid-seventies, Zhang was on the verge of greater power, soon to be named minister of defense.

Keyworth was awed.

"The Chinese choose to match their top one-hundredth of one percent with our little team," he said of Zhang. "He was twenty-five levels above me, I was just a scientist from Los Alamos. He was running their defense complex."

It was a pattern that would be repeated in the hosting of military officers and diplomats as well. A classified report for the CIA concluded it was no accident: The Chinese deployed high-level officials as a power play, a means to gain leverage in one-on-one exchanges and to engender a sense of obligation among foreign visitors. Keyworth offered a more pragmatic explanation: "It's the nature of a hierarchical government that they don't trust those farther down the ladder. So they had to send their top guys."

Zhang and Keyworth talked of China's military strategy for defending against the Soviets. It had not evolved substantially from Mao's concept of People's War. In the event of a Soviet invasion, the army would retreat southward, using cities as defensive bulwarks and relying on sheer manpower to win the war of attrition.

"It's simple," Zhang told him. "We lose 500 million people, and then we prevail."

The neutron bomb was part and parcel of this strategy. At the time, however, the United States had no idea China was interested in developing the weapon. The United States had concluded that the neutron bomb was not useful. It was designed to explode high over a battlefield, bathing enemy soldiers in a lethal wave of radiation while the shock wave from the explosion remained small enough—in theory at least—to inflict only minimal damage to buildings. The United States built the bomb in the 1970s to halt columns of Soviet tanks invading densely populated West Germany, but it was never deployed. The Germans had little faith that any nuclear weapon could be exploded without widespread destruction.

China did not have the same worries about its border with the Soviet Union.

"For you," Zhang agreed, "the neutron bomb has no use. But for us, well . . . You have this game in the United States—bowling? You bowl. We need to bowl neutron bombs over the Soviet border."

Keyworth was installed in a presidential guest house in Beijing ringed by machine-gun–toting guards. There were cooks and cleaners—all operatives for the Ministry of State Security, as later visitors would discover. During the Agnew trips, he believed, the Chinese were tentative. "They were still feeling us out," Keyworth said. "When I went, I was prepared. I had questions. And they were prepared, too."

He was virtually certain the house was bugged. So he would turn the shower on full-blast and stand in the steam dutifully recording each day's events on microcassettes—the one CIA technical device that he had brought with him. He recorded what he learned, what he was asked, what the Chinese seemed to know and not know. For security, he stowed the tapes inside his pillowcase as he slept and carried them on his person every minute of the day.

Often, Keyworth would get a phone call, and a group of scientists would show up in midafternoon, loaded with questions.

"The Chinese were getting pretty aggressive about asking things pointblank. But it was easy to deflect them," Keyworth said. "You know what's classified and what's unclassified. And you know what you're supposed to come back with. And you know where the line is. It's all a matter of judgment," he said.

He declined to answer many questions, ignored others as though he hadn't heard. And sometimes he resorted to subterfuge. Once, he was riding in a caravan of vehicles after a banquet, and one of his fellow passengers, Chen Neng Kuan, turned in the front seat and demanded an answer.

"Now you're going to tell me: What's in the black box?" he asked, referring to the so-called nuclear football, a suitcase that contains U.S. launch authorization codes and accompanies the president wherever he goes.

"I feigned horror," Keyworth said. "I said I wanted to get out of this car right away. Stop the convoy!" The scientist quickly withdrew the question.

Once, however, Keyworth was assailed by questions in a more academic setting, and subterfuge was no use. He was giving a talk about inertial-confinement fusion, or ICF, a process in which scientists in a laboratory use lasers to simulate the thermonuclear burn in H-bombs. In later years, ICF research would become largely unclassified, but in the early 1980s it was still heavily shrouded in secrecy. Keyworth delivered a seminar on ICF, took a seat and then opened the floor to questions.

The Chinese appeared to know about secret U.S. experiments to measure the exact conditions necessary for fusion ignition. The question the U.S. scientists—and now the Chinese—sought to answer was: What were the lowest pressures and temperatures needed for ignition?

The Chinese scientists began by asking Keyworth what the Americans used as fuel for laser fusion. Obviously, tritium and deuterium, Keyworth said. Even a college physics student knew the mixture of the two gases was the easiest kind of hydrogen fuel to ignite. "You just make a ball of it," Keyworth said.

One Chinese scientist pressed for the precise threshold conditions for igniting that fuel. The answer lay in secret U.S. experiments and was classified, but Keyworth decided to couch his answer in a simple, playful analogy that wouldn't give away any secret: "If you drop the ball on the floor, it will go off. It's that easy."

When Keyworth returned to Los Alamos, he reported the incident as the kind of problem likely to confront U.S. scientists in China and his way of finessing the situation. Yet some Los Alamos scientists feared Keyworth's analogy amounted to an indiscretion. Years later, these fears were taken up as facts by China's critics in Congress. Keyworth's analogy was branded a slip-up, evidence that U.S. scientists couldn't be trusted to keep secrets from the Chinese.

"I bust a gut laughing," Keyworth said. "This is completely unclassified, right out of a freshman physics textbook."

Keyworth's intended message back at Los Alamos in 1980 was that the Chinese used ostensibly academic gatherings to probe for weapons secrets.

"No question, one had to be on one's toes," Keyworth said. "You had to be tricky."

Keyworth went back to China several times in 1980 and 1981, staying weeks at a time and bringing home more microcassettes. His secretary transcribed these, and Stillman and Vrooman scrutinized the results to eliminate any bit of information that might tend to identify Keyworth as the source. Then the transcripts went to the CIA.

The agency blended and correlated them with other intelligence. The final reports went to the National Security Council in the White House, Keyworth believes.

"Everything we brought back went into the policy-making apparatus,"

Keyworth said. Besides technical insight into China's nuclear-weapons program, he delivered intelligence on China's plans and intentions. "In 1979, we knew virtually nothing," Keyworth said. "By 1981, we knew a large fraction of the strategic intelligence, the big questions."

His reports were an eye-opener. China's weapons program was as massive as the Manhattan Project and could boast at least as many top-flight physicists. The difference was that the brains behind America's first atomic bomb fled Los Alamos and its fences for academia after the war. China's weapons intellects stuck around for decades and mentored a new generation of weaponeers. They were deep in talent and knowledgeable in the black arts of designing and building nuclear weapons. Most had been educated in the West or in Russia when the Soviet Union was providing weapons assistance to the Chinese.

U.S. nuclear-weapons experts had known of the Sino-Soviet nuclear cooperation but had suspected the actual transfer of technology would be slight. Instead, Keyworth found, the Soviets had started reactors and factories in China for producing nuclear-weapons components. The Russians withdrew in 1959, before finishing their work, and left the projects in shambles. But they also left behind bits of information and advanced technologies that made China more than just a newcomer to the nuclear club.

"We believed they would stop short of sharing actual technology," Keyworth said. "We were absolutely and totally wrong."

China prided itself on breaking the developed world's monopoly on nuclear weapons. "When we first started," Keyworth said, "we had no idea the Chinese would get an ICBM that could strike the continental U.S. We thought of them as a third tier. And they're not."

The U.S. Department of Energy, the federal bureaucracy overseeing the weapons labs, was to know nothing of Keyworth's true purpose in going to China. Nor was the University of California, the contractor that had operated Los Alamos since the Manhattan Project. Vrooman sat down with Keyworth after each trip to fashion his mandatory trip report in a way that preserved DOE's ignorance. Unlike the CIA and other intelligence agencies, the Energy Department lacked the proper categories of classification and compartmentalization to protect human sources—Keyworth and the scientists in China. Just as important, the DOE was a growing and intrusive bureaucracy in the eyes of the weapons labs, and Vrooman and Keyworth didn't see any reason to invite meddling or second-guessing by some paper pusher in Washington.

To an outsider, Keyworth believed, his stint of gathering intelligence was indistinguishable from a straight scientific visit. "I would not have even known this was an organized intelligence operation if I hadn't gone to the other side and seen what it looks like."

———————

In May 1981, Keyworth was about to leave for China again, this time to tour its desert test site at Lop Nur, when he received word from the White House. President Ronald Reagan was about to nominate Keyworth as his science advisor and director of the Office of Science and Technology Policy. Keyworth knew it was "childish," but he still wanted to go. But Reagan wanted him on the job as soon as possible.

American curiosity about Lop Nur went unsated for almost a year. But in 1982, Agnew said he would accept a Chinese invitation—if the trip featured a tour of the test site. He had two other conditions: The CIA must provide him a map of China and airfare for his wife. The CIA was quick to agree. Getting similar information out of other countries had cost millions; airfare was chicken feed.

Agnew was flown to western China and driven over rutted highways for hours to reach Malan, the hometown for China's Lop Nur test site. Lop Nur bears a resemblance to the Nevada Test Site; both are expanses of desert sandstone and dust, ringed by barren mountains, torturously hot in summer. But there the similarities end.

The Lop Nur Nuclear Weapons Test Base lies along the ancient Silk Road, a link for goods and ideas between China and the Mediterranean. It was an exceedingly dry expanse where less than an inch of rain fell a year. Soldiers and scientists could watch water drawn for washing or cooking vanish within minutes. The skyline to the northwest is dominated by the reddish crest of the Kuruktag mountain range. Elsewhere, the desert of Lop Nur extends out to a vanishing point that shimmers on the horizon. The base itself is four times larger than the biggest Russian test site, seven times larger than the Nevada Test Site.

In the evenings, Agnew dined in the home of Gen. Zhang Zhishang, commander of the test site. A large gray safe squatted incongruously in the middle of the living room. The food was good, the conversation cordial. They swapped tales of life at nuclear test sites, comparing Nevada and Lop Nur.

To Agnew's relief, there were few questions about weapons science at Los Alamos.

"No rubber-hosing whatsoever," Agnew said. "The only thing they wanted to know from me was detonation sets," the arrangement of detonators on the surface of the primary's high-explosive shell. "They would say, 'Have you ever thought of doing this or that?' And I would only say, 'Well, that is an interesting idea.' "

The Chinese did probe for details of U.S. underground testing, performed in vertical shafts. China typically detonated its bombs in horizontal tunnels, which made it easier to acquire data from the bomb and accompanying instruments for verifying its efficiency. But in 1982, perhaps due to Keyworth's influence, the Chinese already were digging vertical shafts and making ready for true underground tests.

Agnew's escorts showed him a movie and color photographs of Chinese atmospheric tests that no American had witnessed, then took him out on the stark, dusty expanses of Lop Nur and showed him the tunnels they dug for testing. No American had ever visited China's test site, much less seen preparation for a nuclear test.

As the Chinese talked of their nuclear facilities, Agnew remembered his map and pulled it out to identify the locations. The Chinese scientists and military officials gathered around and laughed, pointing at the bottom of Agnew's map. It read: CENTRAL INTELLIGENCE AGENCY.

Agnew was embarrassed. "They just thought it was pretty funny."

It was obvious to Agnew the Chinese had been collecting their own intelligence. They knew much about the American weapons program that was not widely published. And they possessed low-level classified information on at least one American nuclear-weapons system that was brand-new.

The Chinese were curious about the Mk 12A, the reentry vehicle for Los Alamos's W78 warhead. At that moment, General Electric was manufacturing Mk 12As and, since December 1979, the Air Force had been retrofitting the new reentry vehicles onto Minuteman III missiles, stationed in silos in various midwestern states. The Chinese explained that they had read details of the reentry vehicle and warhead yield in a *Washington Post* article. They were interested in discovering how the Americans could fit a warhead in the reentry vehicle's tight confines.

"They just said, 'How do you do that?' " Agnew said. "It was never very insistent, just more like admiration. Like you have a new car, and people say, 'That's really neat.' "

Agnew reported the exchange but didn't personally view Chinese possession of the information as much of a concern. Nuclear yields were technically classified, but every nuclear power used its tests in part to telegraph its capability to a potential adversary.

As another example, the Chinese complained about the failure of parachutes they used when dropping a bomb for a test. Early parachutes developed tears and later versions sometimes failed to open. Later, when Agnew got back to Los Alamos, he located a somewhat dated Air Force manual on parachutes and mailed it to Chen Neng Kuan.

"I got a note back saying, 'Thank you very much. You sent us last year's. We have this year's.' "

———

Looking back, Agnew said, "I wasn't really very clever in I guess what you'd call being a spy. I never wrote anything down." But his trips to China did more than provide a glimpse inside a closed weapons program. They opened the door for other U.S. scientists to learn more and perhaps influence China's weapons policy.

On his return, Agnew decided he'd had enough. The travel was grueling for a man in his sixties. It was again time for young blood, and the choice was Keyworth's protégé and successor in his former job as Physics Division director.

John C. Browne was a particle physicist who, as a graduate student at Duke, had helped Keyworth with his thesis research. Browne had none of Keyworth's advantages growing up. Coming from a family of modest means, Browne was prodded by his father to excel both in baseball and in his studies. After earning an undergraduate physics degree at Drexel University, he went to Durham, North Carolina, and teamed up with Keyworth for experiments on Duke's accelerator.

The two became close friends, and Keyworth says he advised Teller to hire Browne at Lawrence Livermore, where Browne cut his teeth on weapons physics. Browne came to Los Alamos in 1979 as a group leader in Keyworth's Physics Division, which was then building an accelerator that would produce the most intense proton beam in the nation. In 1981, then-laboratory director Donald Kerr agreed to Keyworth's request, and Browne inherited not only the division but his friend's duties in China.

Browne was warned that the Chinese would press for classified information. He still wasn't quite prepared for what he found when he and his wife, Marti, went to China in 1985.

Browne was scheduled to give a number of talks and after every one came a barrage of questions about American secrets. "I would just basically say, U.S. law is pretty clear and I can't answer the question," he said. "And they said that was okay."

His audience would ask unclassified questions, then come back for an-other try. "It's clear that they were in a mode—and I knew that going over there—that they were going to probe for anything they could get," Browne said.

The Chinese treated the Brownes with the same hospitality as they did the Agnews and Keyworth. But their persistence in seeking weapons secrets wore on him. He felt wary at every talk. "There was this feeling or undercurrent of al-ways pushing for information," Browne said.

That wasn't all. At the time, anti-American sentiment in China was run-ning high. And on several occasions, the Brownes and their hosts emerged from restaurants into hostile crowds that were yelling something angrily in Chinese. Browne realized the chants were meant for them, but the Chinese scientists were reluctant to give a translation. He at last refused to go any farther until he knew.

"Finally, they told me," Browne said. "They were shouting, 'Foreigners, go home. Foreigners, go home.' " They did. And Browne never went back.

He filed a thick report back at Los Alamos and was debriefed by the FBI and the CIA. Then he went to see Keyworth at the White House. Browne told his friend that he felt unsafe in China and worried about other scientists going.

"My recommendation was I wouldn't send anybody over there who didn't know what they were getting into. And if they go, they should go in pairs," Browne said.

Keyworth agreed. "I think with John they decided to see how far they could go," he said later. "I felt if it was going to go any further, we needed professional people along"—meaning CIA handlers on site, in China. Keyworth sought the advice of a high-ranking CIA officer detailed to work for him.

The officer nodded as Keyworth recounted Browne's complaint, then shifted chairs in front of Keyworth's desk. "As the CIA, I must tell you these vis-its are valuable for national security and should be continued," he said. He got up and sat in the other chair. "But as the science advisor, I must recommend you end them immediately."

The message was clear for Keyworth. If the CIA wanted to keep sending Los Alamos scientists to China as spies, the argument was the agency's to make. Keyworth picked up the phone and asked for an immediate meeting with Na-tional Security Advisor William Clark.

Soon after, he was in Clark's office and recounting Browne's story.

"We need to end this," Keyworth told him.

The recommendation was "sensible," Clark agreed. "I'll do it."

The CIA was furious. It appeared that Reagan's science advisor was shutting down its most productive source of intelligence on the Chinese nuclear program. He had gone and now was closing the door behind him.

Keyworth assumed his recommendation was taken and the scientist-spy episode in China was over.

In truth, it was just beginning.

– 5 –

Tiger Trap

At the end of the workday on Friday, December 2, 1982, Wen Ho Lee sat down at his office desk and made a brief phone call to California that would change his life in ways he could never imagine. His call was prompted by news that another Taiwanese-American nuclear scientist, this one at Lawrence Livermore, was in some kind of trouble and had lost his job. The situation could have implications for Lee as well, because, as he understood it, the other scientist was caught doing something Lee himself had been busy at, providing unclassified documents to the government of Taiwan.

Lee placed the call, and Gwo-Bao Min came on the line from his suburban Bay Area house a few minutes from the lab. Lee introduced himself in Mandarin as a weapons designer at Los Alamos, the holder of a Q clearance. The "weapons designer" description was an exaggeration, of course.

Still speaking in Mandarin, Lee mentioned a mutual friend, another Livermore scientist who had spoken to Lee about Min. Then Lee got down to business. He had contacts with Taiwan, he bragged, and offered to help Min find out who had "squealed" or "made little reports" on him. Maybe they should get together and talk.

Min attempted to tone Lee down, saying, maybe we shouldn't talk about this now. Min didn't seem interested, and he got off the phone fast. Lee's strange call must have been confusing to Min, as it was to the FBI agents secretly taping all of Min's phone calls. For Min and the agents knew what Lee did not—that Min, though Taiwanese by birth, had not been helping Taiwan. Instead, the agents believed, Min was a spy for the People's Republic of China, a man who had given away highly classified secrets about the design of the neutron bomb and other nuclear weapons. The FBI code-named their investigation of Min "Tiger Trap."

Gwo-Bao Min was born in Taiwan in 1939, a few months before Wen Ho Lee. In 1962, after graduating from National Taiwan University in Taipei with an engineering degree, he came to the United States. He earned a master's degree in engineering from West Virginia University, then, in 1970, a doctorate in aerospace engineering from the University of Michigan. He became a U.S. citizen and went to work for Lawrence Livermore in 1975. He and his wife settled into a modest but comfortable ranch-style home in nearby Danville to raise their children.

His coworkers found him friendly and capable; to his friends, he was a kind man and a good father. Occasionally, he talked of going into business with his family. He worked in the lab's D-Division, where researchers did systems studies, looking at nuclear issues from a larger perspective than the design of one weapon. It was not unusual for D-Division scientists to go to the lab's technical library and check out papers on a wide range of issues. At one point, Min worked on missile defense, the precursor of the Reagan-era Star Wars program.

In 1979, Min talked with Chinese scientists. Later, a spy inside China provided U.S. intelligence with clues that pointed to Min as a security risk. FBI agents from the San Francisco Field Office tore into every part of his background, followed him around, and obtained a special warrant from the secretive Foreign Intelligence Surveillance Court in Washington to monitor his telephone and perhaps bug his house.

The agents discovered that in his trips to the lab library, Min had accumulated a mass of data about a variety of weapons, well outside of his job responsibilities. A team of experts, including scientists from Los Alamos, "did a job on his office," compiling lists of every document he checked out. The volume of material would climb just before his trips to China. "You could almost tell when he was leaving," according to one team member.

When Min was stopped in an airport in 1981 en route to China, he was carrying papers with detailed answers to five questions, including one about the two-point detonation system for primaries that made miniaturization of missile warheads possible.

The investigators were convinced that Min had given away the design of the W70, the warhead for the Lance missile, popularly known as the neutron bomb.

If so, China would gain twice over. First, with the neutron bomb itself, and second, by learning how to reduce the size of the plutonium primaries in its own warheads. The W70 contained a primary that was exceptionally small, despite its spherical shape. U.S. officials worried that China could use the primary in a "road mobile" missile launched from the back of a truck.

China tested its own neutron bomb on September 25, 1988.

Investigators thought they knew the identity of Min's contact with Chinese intelligence. But when the FBI agents finally made their move in 1981, rounding up and questioning both Min and the supposed contact, they were unable to get confessions from either. Bill Cleveland, the agent who headed the investigation, thought he had pushed Min "right to the brink" of confessing. "I really thought I had him," Cleveland told his coworkers.

FBI officials went to federal prosecutors and recommended prosecution, but the Justice Department felt the evidence was too weak. The case lacked a confession or any proof of "transfer," such as a photograph of Min handing over documents to the Chinese. Additionally, a long court proceeding ran the risk of unmasking the U.S. asset—the spy—in China.

Min was told he could resign from the lab or be fired. He quit in February 1981, and went into the trading business, traveling often to China, trips missed completely by the FBI. When Cleveland, on assignment in Beijing, ran into Min, it was startling for both of them. Min seemed to think that Cleveland had followed him all the way across the Pacific Ocean.

Even after Min was interrogated and forced from the lab, the FBI kept up its surveillance, convincing a judge to renew the wiretap. From the agents' experience, some suspects grew complacent when they had beaten the rap. Others might panic at the attention and call for help.

The wiretap led to nothing, however, except Wen Ho Lee. When Cleveland's agents first listened to Lee's voice, a year after Min's dismissal, they had a hard time understanding his name. Certainly, none of them had ever heard of him. But the conversation, confusing as it was, alarmed them. Here was a nuclear-weapons scientist making an unsolicited phone call to a spy suspect, offering help. Even the most favorable interpretation of Lee's scrambled understanding of the facts led to the conclusion that he was eager to form an alliance with someone he thought had been fired for passing U.S. documents to a foreign country in violation of security rules. The FBI quickly launched an investigation, under the guise of a scheduled review of Lee's security clearance. But the agents did not question Lee for another year, not wanting to spoil the secrecy of the wiretap on Min's phone by moving sooner.

Finally, on November 9, 1983, agents went to talk to Lee. As always, the diminutive scientist was smiling, polite. They asked general questions, to test him, to see if he would lie. Did he know Gwo-Bao Min? Had he called him? Offered aid? Lee denied all, claiming he had no idea of how to get in contact with

Min. His denials, an agent would say later, were unequivocal. The agents thanked Lee and went away. Six weeks later they came back, armed with evidence from the wiretap, which they showed to Lee. Now his story changed. Yes, he admitted, he had called Min.

As the agents listened, Lee explained about his aid to the Taiwanese government, how he had begun sending unclassified reactor-safety documents, beginning in 1977 or 1978, and had performed consulting work. "Lee indicated that starting about 1980, he would receive requests for papers and reports from the Taiwanese embassy, which he would then copy and mail to the embassy," as Attorney General Janet Reno would later testify. Lee said he thought Min was doing the same thing, and he was concerned. Lee was edging closer to the truth, but was still holding back. It was the beginning of a recurring pattern, in which Lee would retreat under pressure, not telling the full story until it was unavoidable.

By then the FBI had obtained toll records for Lee's office phone and knew that he had phoned the Coordination Council for North American Affairs, the equivalent of Taiwan's embassy in Washington, during the same period that he had called Min. But Lee denied making the calls.

The agents were interested in something else that day. Min was still very much on their minds, and they had a plan to snare him. They asked Lee to cooperate, to participate in a "false flag" operation against the same scientist he had offered to help a year before. Lee agreed. With the FBI tape recorder rolling once again, Lee telephoned Min, pretending to be an agent of China, seeking Min's partnership in espionage. When the phone call fizzled, the FBI paid for Lee to travel to Min's Danville home. Wired with a hidden microphone, he knocked on the door. There was a brief conversation, but Min did not respond to Lee's enticements and the false flag was over. In the end, Lee had become a player in the intelligence game, as both suspect and servant of the government.

Another month went by. Lee agreed to the Bureau's request for a polygraph. On January 24, 1984, Lee went in for the test, and now had a slightly different story about Taiwan. Some of those unclassified documents he had mailed to Washington, he said, carried a special marking, NOFORN, for "no foreign dissemination." It wasn't a crime, but Lee had played fast and loose with the security rules. According to a secret report compiled by the government, "Wen Ho Lee stated that his motive for sending the publications was brought on out of a desire to help in scientific exchange." Lee had also said "he helps other scientists routinely and had no desire to receive any monetary or other type of reward from Taiwan."

He now also admitted making the calls to Taiwan's unofficial embassy.

With that off his chest, Lee passed the lie detector test. He was no spy, the examiner ruled. Still, he was a walking security risk, a holder of a high-level clearance who had winked at the rules and then lied about it. People had lost their security clearance for less.

Tiger Trap was an important case to the FBI. It increased the Bureau's worry level about scientists giving away secrets. "I'm more afraid of a visiting physicist than I am an intelligence agent," fumed Ed Appel, an agent in the San Francisco office. "I worry about the scientist who shares his formula with the other guy because they have a wink, a smile, and a handshake, or they're going to save the world together."

Tiger Trap remained an open case, but a secret one. Lee's role was so far from center stage that almost no one at Los Alamos knew about it. His clearance was not revoked; no disciplinary action was taken. An opportunity to head off the trouble ahead was missed.

– 6 –

The Narrow Neck of the Hourglass

The era of Los Alamos scientists spying on China as agents of the CIA ended with Agnew, Keyworth, and Browne. But a less organized form of intelligence gathering by scores of Los Alamos scientists traveling to China for conferences and lab visits continued unabated. Some of the trips were still "sponsored," i.e., paid for, by the CIA. The distinction was that these scientists were not "controlled" by the intelligence agency. They went to their physics conferences in Beijing primarily for science, but when they returned to New Mexico, they were debriefed for whatever tidbits they had picked up from the Chinese weapons researchers.

The visits did not occur in a vacuum. During the Carter and Reagan years, the White House, the State Department, the Defense Department—everyone in Washington—was promoting ties to China. The United States was cultivating an ally by sharing intelligence, military technology, and science. The People's Republic, meanwhile, sent its own ears and eyes to the U.S. nuclear-weapons labs.

In 1979, Wang Ganchang, a German-trained physicist who had been deeply involved in creating China's first bomb, led one of the first delegations to Los Alamos. The Chinese were seasoned specialists in nuclear physics and plasma physics, the study of hot energized gases that are created among other places in nuclear weapons. Several of the Chinese, like Ganchang, were weapons veterans.

Staffers from Los Alamos's Physics Division and the Controlled Thermonuclear Reactions Division, where researchers were trying to build a fusion nuclear reactor, joined as hosts to the Chinese. Their guests were clearly envious of the Americans' expensive equipment. The Chinese were technically competent—intelligent, creative, and steeped in the literature of their fields—but they couldn't compare to the Americans in the realm of big-ticket science.

One evening, the Chinese and the Americans came together for a dinner party at the home of CTR Division Director Harry Dreicer, a physicist who had formed friendships with Chinese students while getting his doctorate at MIT. He invited many of Los Alamos's Chinese Americans to meet the visiting scientists.

"I knew they'd be interested," Dreicer said. "And there was the issue of making the visiting delegation feel at home, having people who spoke the same language."

Los Alamos's Chinese community was largely Taiwanese. Some of them had grown up in Taiwan knowing little of the People's Republic except through the propaganda of the anti-Communist Kuomintang Party that ruled the island. They were curious about these mainlanders. "They were a mystery to us," said one of them, Jen-Chieh Peng. "We were born in Taiwan and we only read about China. Most of us had never been there."

They found the Chinese to be well educated, although rusty in their social skills, a result of isolation in their laboratories. "There was a lot of ice to be broken," Peng said.

Wen Ho and possibly Sylvia Lee were at the party. They broke the ice and made connections with high-level Chinese scientists. In years to come, Sylvia Lee would become a key figure in the growing relationships between the American and Chinese weapons scientists. Her role, as translator, host, and tour guide, would be the best thing about her career at the lab. The joys of that position would provide a welcome diversion from troubles at home and the difficulties she encountered in her regular job as a secretary at the lab.

To the outside world, the Lees' domestic life was tranquil, even enviable. Chung and Alberta Lee were well liked and high performers in school, music, and athletics. At home, life was centered in the kitchen, where Wen Ho, with maternal care, cooked and helped the children with their homework. Food was affection. He fed everyone, including all of Alberta and Chung's friends. He gave fruit from his trees to the neighbors ("Won't you share in our good fortune?") and drove his children to friends' doors at Christmas to deliver Chinese-style roasted chickens.

Family friend Cecilia Chang was struck by his tenderness when, on a camping trip, he waited for the children as they crawled from their tents in the morning and wiped their faces with a warm towel. The loving motion of his hand stuck in Chang's memory.

Lee provided his children with everything his own troubled childhood lacked. He was breadwinner and caregiver, an all-in-one parent.

Privately, however, the Lees' marriage was beset by resentments and dysfunction. Wen Ho took over the traditionally female tasks of cooking, cleaning, and rearing of the children. Sylvia was not up to his obsessive standards for homemaking.

In November 1980, Sylvia Lee had found work as a secretary at the lab and not long after made a leap to data analysis, as a computer technician. She was a TEC-2, a job defined as requiring minimal experience and involving fairly simple tasks under direct supervision. She entered data into computer codes, ran the codes for scientists, and eventually did some code writing. But she quickly ran into difficulties.

At first, her supervisors chalked up Sylvia's problems to a language barrier. Her English was muddled by a thick accent, and she hardly could practice at home; Wen Ho favored Mandarin as the family's language. "My communication with her was labored at best," said Allen S. Neuls, who supervised Sylvia Lee on and off during her fourteen years at the lab. "Most of the time, I couldn't understand her, and I really tried hard at it."

When given assignments, Sylvia nodded and even repeated out loud the elements of the task, but coworkers came to realize those responses did not signal that she understood. "The language issue certainly entered into it. But how much of it was language, how much was technical, how much was a lack of desire to understand, I don't know," Neuls said. "She certainly was one of the hardest people to communicate with that I ever worked with."

The group's TEC supervisor, Janet Wing, and others found Sylvia difficult to get to know and grasped for a cultural explanation. But none of the other Chinese Americans in the group presented the same problems. It was clear Sylvia Lee was socially isolated. Over time, problems with her work mounted.

"Somehow the projects she was assigned never quite worked out. Whether this was her fault or the person she was working for wasn't clear," Wing said.

In the winter of 1980–81, a delegation of Chinese laser physicists came to Los Alamos, led by one of the highest-ranking female scientists in China, Madame Su Wie, chairwoman of the Chinese Academy of Sciences. The academy shared coordination of science and nuclear-weapons work with the government.

Before the event, coordinator Jean Andrews Stark received a phone call from Sylvia Lee, who had started working at the lab only a few months before. She told Stark that she had heard a Chinese delegation was coming to town. Could she help out by translating? Her offer was accepted and turned out to be propitious. When Madame Su was struck with diarrhea, it was comforting for her to have another woman around who spoke Chinese.

From this beginning, Lee's role grew with the number of arriving Chinese guests. When there was translating to be done, she was there, whether it was a conversation or a document. When Chinese scientists came to town, she played tour guide and host, inviting them to dinner at the Lees' home on Barcelona Drive, where Wen Ho served tea and cooked Chinese vegetables from his garden. She translated letters from Chinese to English, English to Chinese, for scientists of Los Alamos and the Institute of Applied Physics and Computational Mathematics (IAPCM) in Beijing. She made overseas phone calls. She coordinated meetings.

As time went by, she developed her own relationships with the Chinese. They would correspond directly with her, asking her to mail them papers or unclassified documents. She became the narrow neck of the hourglass, with everything passing through her hands. Sometimes her husband helped out as well. "Both sides would pass messages back and forth through the Lees," explained Bob Vrooman, who was the CIA liaison to the lab when Madame Su came calling. "The Lees would write in Chinese and say, 'Would you ask so-and-so to bring this information when he comes next week?' "

Typical was a note that came in on letterhead stationery from IAPCM, the Chinese equivalent of Los Alamos. It listed three Los Alamos reports by their laboratory publication number. Sylvia Lee routed it to a clerical worker with her handwritten comment, saying, "[t]he Deputy Director of this Institute asked these paper. His name is Dr. Zheng Shaotang. Please check if they are unclassified and send to them. Thanks a lot. Sylvia Lee."

In a telex to Lee about an upcoming visit, a Chinese scientist wrote, ". . . I will be very happy if we can learn something in computational hydrodynamics and get some papers."

Sometime around 1984, FBI Agent Dave Bibb recruited Sylvia Lee as an FBI informant. Bibb, a big man who reminded some people of a country sheriff, was the Bureau's agent at the lab. He frequently made the forty-five-minute drive up the mesa from his desk in the Santa Fe resident agency. He wanted Sylvia Lee to identify people for him, both the names of Chinese scientists coming to Los Alamos and the U.S. scientists traveling to China. He wanted copies of the correspondence and documents that went back and forth. Lee was eager to oblige.

Bibb had a nickname for Sylvia. He had jokingly referred to Madame Su Wie as "Madame Sue-eee," as if he were a farmer calling a pig to dinner. After that, Sylvia somehow became "Miss Piggy." It wasn't meant as an insult. It was Bibb's sense of humor.

Sylvia Lee apparently was not privy to Bibb's jokes. Dealing with the FBI was a pleasure; Bibb was always so nice to her. It was ironic, of course, that she was helping one FBI agent while others had investigated and polygraphed her husband for his telephone call to the spy suspect in Livermore.

———————

By 1984, Bob Vrooman had spent five years as the CIA liaison to Los Alamos. He had dashed off countless reports to agency headquarters outside Washington with secret details of Chinese nuclear weapons, insights gleaned by Los Alamos scientists. He now decided to make Los Alamos his permanent home. He retired from the agency to take a job with the lab. He moved in with people he knew well, the staff of the lab's intelligence division. It was run by Danny Stillman, a bright, quirky physicist who had grown up in Seattle and loved the world of spy-versus-spy. Stillman liked to make his own decisions and take matters into his own hands; Vrooman felt right at home.

His job was to handle administrative details for the fifty-person staff, but of course he kept an interest in the intel business, sometimes sitting in as Los Alamos scientists just back from China told what they had learned. The office's formal name was International Technology, reflecting its mission to divine the secrets of other nations' nuclear weapons. In the days before the lab established a separate, formal counterintelligence program, Stillman oversaw that area as well, making him in charge of both spying and spy catching.

One of Stillman's tools was to read other people's mail. "I asked the mailroom to send me all the mail postmarked to go out of the country," Stillman recounted. He found "all kinds of stuff" by reading the mail. Lab scientists were being thanked "for all the material you gave us in your last visit." Wen Ho and Sylvia Lee sent a "lot of letters." In one, Wen Ho Lee wrote to someone in Pakistan, sending publications on code problems. Pakistan was on the U.S. government's list of "sensitive countries." It had a nuclear-weapons program but had not yet detonated a bomb. There was no evidence, however, that the information Lee supplied with his letter had any relevance to nuclear weapons.

Around 1985 another player entered the game, a CIA agent from the Denver station named Dan Wofford. CIA agents like Wofford would come and go at the lab, often undercover. To protect their identities, the lab issued them the same blue badges worn by regular lab employees.

Wofford was with the CIA's Foreign Resources Division, the officers who recruit foreigners to be spies for the United States. Across the country, the agency loved to recruit foreign students, send them back to their homelands and wait patiently for years while they rose to positions of importance. Los Alamos, with its share of young Chinese students doing postdoc studies, was an obvious hunting ground, although the brightest tended to stay in America instead of going home. Wofford might also prowl among the ranking Chinese nuclear-weapons scientists coming through the lab on a regular basis. In the vernacular, Wofford was spotting and assessing.

When Wofford and Bibb met with Vrooman to discuss the China target, Sylvia Lee's name and her role as the go-between came up quickly. Soon Sylvia was providing names and intelligence to the CIA as well as the FBI. She was a CIA "support asset." A dozen or so times, Lee, Wofford, and Bibb met clandestinely in hotel rooms, with the CIA picking up the bill. But Lee apparently never knew she was dealing with the CIA. She was led to believe that Wofford was just another FBI agent.

The period of the eighties was a fertile time for developing intelligence on the Chinese weapons program. Vrooman described the process this way: "The most difficult thing for an intelligence officer interested in collecting information from scientists is getting continuing access. Intelligence officers do not normally mix well in scientific gatherings or social events. They stick out. (You can spot an intelligence officer among a group of scientists very easily. His socks match.) Thus, intelligence officers have to resort to using friendly scientists to get information for them. This can range from simple interviews after contact with a foreign scientist to elaborate training and preparation. I have done both . . . When Americans do it, it is good. When others do it, it is bad."

Throughout the 1980s, a continuous parade of Los Alamos scientists, perhaps sixty in all, flew to China to give talks, attend conferences, or visit nuclear-weapons facilities. Most of these trips were paid for by Los Alamos. Others were sponsored by the CIA, the Defense Intelligence Agency, or the Chinese government.

Some of the Los Alamos scientists were from the lab's weapons programs, visiting their counterparts, while others worked in unclassified physics or areas such as the human genome project. Most of them would return to a debriefing from the FBI, the CIA, or Stillman's in-house intelligence operation in International Technology. Sometimes the returning visitors would tell their stories at Stillman's weekly staff meetings. The debriefers would write up reports and send them off to Washington, where a body of knowledge about the Chinese program was growing.

Unlike Agnew, Keyworth, and Browne, these travelers left the lab for China without being formally tasked to collect specific data. That legal distinction meant they were not agents of the U.S. government. But it made little practical difference. The "defensive" briefings they received before departing, ostensibly to coach them in repelling unwanted questions from the Chinese, provided them with some targeting hints as well. At Los Alamos in the mid-1980s, the intelligence and counterintelligence staffs were the same people.

———————

Wen Ho Lee, meanwhile, was diligently pursuing his career. During the eighties, he collected a salary that grew from $37,000 to $62,000 a year. He wrote code in X Division, the lab's center for weapons design. His immediate group was X-7, Computational Physics. His office was at the heart of the Los Alamos lab, which sprawled out over 43 square miles of winding roads, canyons, and forests. He labored in a plain government space where he had a desk and computer workstations—one connected to the X Division open network and the other tied to a closed and secure network that also hosted powerful supercomputers.

Lee was friendly with his coworkers but didn't gossip. He brought his own lunch and ate it at his desk. He was frequently on the phone with his wife or his children, offering them advice. At evaluation time, his bosses usually wrote that he met or exceeded his job requirements; but he was not a technical star. He was considered middle-of-the-pack at best. He lacked connections to the lab's power structure, both inside the fence and in his outside social life. He was, said Judith Binstock, one of his office mates, "too unimportant for anyone to gossip about."

He filed things away like a pack rat. He kept detailed notes of things other people wouldn't even write down. He filled his shelves with three-ring notebooks, "row after row of notebooks labeled in Chinese," Binstock remembered. "I assumed it was notes on whatever he had done in his whole career. He kept everything."

He collected manuals for codes as if it were a compulsion. "You wanted to know something about somebody's code, you'd go to Wen Ho and he'd pull out the manual," said his friend and neighbor, Don Marshall. Lee even helped write a user's manual.

Lee worked in a weapons lab but showed little interest in nuclear weapons. He was absorbed in algorithms and codes—not the devices themselves. He put significant effort into writing papers for publication or presentation at conferences, sometimes using classified codes to run the calculations. Binstock thought fear drove him to frantically crank out papers. "At one point, he told me how many times he had been RIF'ed [given notice of a "Reduction in Force," a layoff], and it was quite a few. He held up a number of his fingers."

In all his years at the lab, Lee wrote about forty papers, many of them with coauthors. Frequently, Lee organized the work and ran the codes, while his coauthor contributed the important ideas, as in his paper with Bryan A. "Bucky" Kashiwa, "On Cell-Centered Lagrangian Hydrodynamics." Relatively few of Lee's papers appeared in peer-reviewed journals.

Lee also liked to travel. He attended conferences in Sydney, Venice, Stuttgart, San Francisco, and Budapest, among other cities. He went back to Taiwan every couple of years. In March 1985, he flew to a beach resort at Hilton Head, South Carolina, for a scientific conference. Sitting in the back row were two Chinese scientists wearing Mao jackets who could not have been more obvious, according to Lee's friend and fellow code writer Bob Clark. They were there to meet U.S. scientists, and they befriended Clark and Lee. "You know what they're doing," Clark said. "Everybody does. That's why they're there."

One of the scientists, Li De Yuan, was from the IAPCM in Beijing, China's equivalent of Los Alamos. Li and Lee, who shared an interest in Lagrangian codes, struck up a conversation. That budding relationship led to an invitation for Lee and Clark to participate in a conference in Beijing in 1986. They accepted, with the blessing of Los Alamos officials. Surprisingly, in light of her low-level position, Sylvia Lee was invited to present a paper at the same conference. Years later, this invitation would raise concerns when Sylvia Lee came under suspicion.

For Wen Ho Lee, born and raised in Taiwan, this 1986 journey was apparently his first trip to the land of his ancestors. The Lees decided to take Alberta and Chung with them.

Before they left, Sylvia met once again with Bibb and Wofford, the FBI and the CIA, in a hotel room, to talk about what kind of information might be gathered. This time, her husband went with her. Wofford spoke with the Lees in Mandarin, which Bibb did not understand. Supposedly, Wofford was translating their conversation for Bibb—a seemingly unnecessary complication since, of course, both Lees spoke English. It seemed to Bibb that Wofford would chat with the Lees for several minutes, then summarize the conversation in one sentence. Later, it occurred to Bibb that Wofford was tasking the Lees, right in front of him, without his knowledge.

The Lees arrived at Beijing's Friendship Hotel in June for the 10th International Conference on Numerical Methods in Fluid Dynamics. Wen Ho had prepared two papers, unintelligible to the layman, "High Explosives Modeling in 2-D Euler Code for Shaped Charge Problems" and "PIC Method for Elastic-Plastic Flow." Lee and Clark gave "poster presentations" of their papers, pinning them to a wall at the conference hall for anyone interested.

Lee was busy in Beijing making friends with the Chinese scientists. "It's obvious they would chat him up with the idea that maybe one day they would get information from him," said Clark. "You might say he was friendlier than he should have been with these guys."

When a nuclear-weapons scientist named Li Wei Shen came to see Lee, asking for help with a code problem, Lee offered his advice. The scientist said he was having problems with "tangled mesh," a common predicament with Lagrangian codes. Sometimes, the mesh on the computer screen would get itself tangled into shapes like bow ties or boomerangs, and the calculation would crash.

This was Lee's forte, as Li well knew. Lee provided him with a formula used in U.S. nuclear-weapons codes to deal with the tangled mesh problem. The formula, however, was unclassified and had a wide range of uses outside of weapons work.

One afternoon during the trip, Lee and Clark traveled across town to the IAPCM. While Clark gave a talk to the Chinese scientists, Lee translated for him, writing on a blackboard. At night, there were banquets and dinners at scientists' homes. Presumably, the Lees were gathering names for their FBI and CIA handlers.

Sylvia Lee seemed pleased to be in Beijing. She was eager to show "all things beautiful" in the city to her children and her friends the Clarks—Kathy Clark had come with her husband. Wen Ho was kind as always, photocopying pages from travel books to give to Kathy and Bob. There were bus tours and trips to the Great Wall. Both families took vacation time for additional travel around China.

When they got home, Wen Ho and Sylvia went to meet with Bibb and Wofford for their debriefings. The Lees apparently brought them some documents. What they told the FBI and the CIA about Li Wei Shen is unknown, but later, when Wen Ho went through the more mundane task of filling out a travel report for Vrooman's internal-security section, he wrote nothing about Li's request for help with the tangled mesh. Vrooman did not debrief Lee about the trip until two years later.

As time went by, the Lees and Clarks, like numerous other Los Alamos scientists before and after them, began to receive letters and holiday cards from the Chinese scientists they had met.

Nineteen eighty-seven was life-changing for Lee in a very personal way. In the spring, he was diagnosed with colon cancer and faced the possibility he might die. He flew to a Houston hospital, where "they took off twelve inches from my colon," he said later. Sylvia was so worried she got sick herself. He was off work for five weeks but, in typical style, didn't mention his brush with mortality to his close friend Cecilia Chang. Only when she noticed that he had stopped eating red meat and sugar did he tell her. He wants to share everything he has, Chang thought, but not his misery. When he did talk about his cancer, he simply said, "I'm just happy to be alive."

He didn't smoke or drink alcohol; now he didn't eat red meat or sugar. He turned to his backyard garden and New Mexico's rivers, harvesting a bounty of fresh fish and vegetables for his own fusion of Chinese and Southwestern cuisine.

By now, the Tiger Trap case was being briefed to senior management at the weapons laboratories. The FBI had never arrested Gwo-Bao Min, but the briefers left little doubt that the FBI believed that a calamitous loss had occurred. The neutron bomb was almost certainly compromised, the agents said. If all the documents Min kept in his office safe had been given to China, the loss would have included information about several warheads and the secret to small football-shaped primaries such as those used in the W88. Tiger Trap prompted officials to look at the "insider" threat in addition to the traditional reliance on the physical security of barbed wire, armed guards, and document-handling rules. But Wen Ho Lee's name did not come up in the presentations.

Stillman knew of Lee's involvement, of course. He had his counterintelligence responsibilities, and he had flown to Livermore to look through Min's office as part of the damage assessment. He had informed Sig Hecker, the Los Alamos lab director. Hecker had approved Stillman's plan for keeping a quiet eye on Lee.

In February 1987, DOE officials briefed Hecker and the directors of Lawrence Livermore and Sandia, the Albuquerque lab that engineers the non-nuclear portions of nuclear weapons. That spring, Vrooman learned about Tiger Trap for the first time, but not yet about Lee's role. In June, Bill Cleveland, the FBI agent who had unsuccessfully pushed Min for a confession, briefed senior management at Los Alamos.

Now there was pressure for the labs to create their own formal counterintelligence organizations. Hecker chose Bob Vrooman to create it at Los Alamos. The man who had spent twenty years in the spy business, who had played a key role in sending Los Alamos scientists to China, and whose career had benefited from the visits, was now in charge of monitoring those visits.

Vrooman was exactly what the lab wanted. He thought the scientific trips were worthwhile, that the risks could be handled. "I did not hide my biases," he said later. "My biases were that lab scientists should talk to foreign scientists and vice versa. I have a bias towards collection; I think it's stupid to sit behind a wall and not know what the other side is doing." Hecker agreed: "He made it clear he's not an FBI guy." Hecker didn't want a cop or former FBI agent but someone whose loyalty would lie with the lab.

Meanwhile, the FBI was becoming increasingly agitated about the free-thinking scientists in New Mexico and California who kept traipsing off to China. The notion of a Los Alamos bomb designer with a head full of secrets crossing the border into China, out of sight and out of control, was unfathomable. The mental image of Chinese nuclear-weapons physicists being welcomed into Los Alamos with open arms was equally painful.

The Chinese knew how to take advantage of American visitors, according to the FBI. Surprise them with a hotel room visit or a banquet at the end of a long, tiring day. Put them off balance, flatter them, surround them, press them for information. For some scientists, there was an added emotional pitch: We're a poor country, struggling to modernize, to catch up. Help us; it won't hurt America.

In 1988, Wen Ho and Sylvia Lee were invited back to China for a June computational physics conference, chaired by his friend from the Hilton Head conference, Li De Yuan. His paper this time was "Material Void Opening Computation Using Particle Method." Vrooman was worried about Sylvia Lee's lack of sophistication. He discussed the situation with Bibb, the Lees' FBI agent, but didn't block the visit.

After dinner one evening in Beijing, the phone rang in the Lee's hotel room. The only account of what happened next is Lee's own, delivered more than ten years later. The caller was Zheng Shaotang, an administrator at IAPCM who had corresponded with both of the Lees. Zheng asked if he could drop by. Lee said yes. Sylvia was not there. A few minutes later, Zheng showed up at the door with Hu Side, a well-known Chinese nuclear-weapons figure who would later head China's entire program. The two ranked several steps in importance above Lee.

First, there was small talk.

"How's it going? Did you enjoy the tour I arranged for you?"

Then Zheng got to the point.

"Does the United States use a two-point detonation system on the W88?"

Lee responded that he couldn't talk about it and wasn't interested. Zheng dropped the subject. After a few minutes of chitchat about families, Zheng and Hu left. It was a classic Chinese espionage approach for scientific information. The FBI looked upon such encounters—a late-night visit by high-ranking officials—as an indication that secrets may have been passed.

When Lee got back to the lab, he filled out his trip report. He wrote in the names of ten Chinese scientists he talked with but left off Hu, the most prominent. The report made no mention of the hotel-room meeting.

Bob Vrooman went to Lee's office to debrief him. According to what Vrooman later wrote in his journal, Lee gave a talk at IAPCM on shaped-charge explosives, the type that might be used in an antitank weapon. It wasn't his paper; he had borrowed it. "He was not probed for info on codes," Vrooman wrote. "Lots of good questions but no inappropriate questions."

The journal entry ended with "Went with guys on sightseeing tour. No relatives in China, family in Taiwan."

-7-

Alarm Bells

Even without knowing of Wen Ho Lee's hotel room encounter, Vrooman had reason to be suspicious of the Lees' dealings with the Chinese—or at the least concerned about their vulnerability.

In two trips now, 1986 and 1988, Lee had reported that no one had asked him any questions about classified matters. Vrooman was left with an uncomfortable feeling about Lee. "They were hitting on everybody else, what the hell are they missing him for?"

The Chinese seemed to know not only which visiting scientists from Los Alamos worked on weapons but exactly what they had worked on. They sometimes casually mentioned the subjects of papers those scientists had written decades before. And ever since Agnew's 1979 visit, the Chinese had dropped their reticence about asking classified questions. They were polite, but direct and persistent.

"You'd be sitting around after dinner and talking physics and all of a sudden the Chinese would whip out a napkin, draw a primary, and say, 'OK, where are the detonation points?' " Vrooman said. "It was not subtle, the Chinese were not inscrutable at all."

Wen Ho wasn't the counterintelligence chief's sole worry. By May 1988, Sylvia's problems at work had reached a crescendo. Coworkers began to believe that her difficulties in communicating were a ruse for getting out of assignments that she felt were beneath her. And she often was away from her regular duties for days, even weeks, working with the Chinese or for the FBI and the CIA.

Her group leader, Harold Sullivan, was fed up. Sylvia would tell her supervisors that she was the official China liaison for the lab director's office. That had been going on for seven years, ever since Madame Su Wie's visit.

"She would come in and say, I am going to wherever. And off she went, and we didn't do anything," Sullivan said.

Once, he and Deputy Group Leader Bill Gregory tried to quantify her work with the Chinese—the amount of her time it absorbed—because her entire salary was coming out of their budget. The group's bread-and-butter work was nuclear-reactor safety, and new reactors weren't being built, so Sullivan was struggling to make ends meet for the group. Moreover, Sylvia Lee was making office phone calls to China, sometimes racking up thousands of dollars of long-distance charges on the group phone bill.

"We never could get an answer," Sullivan said. "I went to everyone I knew."

It also became clear that Wen Ho was helping her with her work, at least by coaching her over the phone. Whatever their domestic problems, Sylvia respected her husband's computer skills and took his advice.

"She was very worshipful of her husband," said Wing, the TEC supervisor. "She felt if he did something, it was better than anyone else could do. That caused some problems for the people she was working with. They would want her to do something one way, and it wasn't the way Wen Ho told her. She always felt she was improving on things by following his advice, which really complicated things for the person who wanted the work done their way."

Soon the situation got worse. Sylvia Lee was running a code for modeling the operation of antiarmor munitions for a scientist named Rich Davidson. The code simulated what happened inside a particular type of antitank shell that used high explosives to liquefy metal inside the shell and squirt it forward as a molten spear for penetrating the tank armor.

One day in the spring of 1988, Davidson gave Lee an assignment that she apparently found too menial. She refused, and when Davidson persisted, she turned obstinate. She hid the depth of her anger, but it quickly became apparent.

Davidson soon learned Lee had erased the project files. The work was at a lower classified level—the interior design of the shell was proprietary, a shared secret of a private company and the U.S. government. Sylvia had destroyed those files as well as unclassified ones.

In a panic, Davidson reported the incident to Bill Gregory, his immediate supervisor, and then phoned Sullivan, who was in Washington, D.C.

"I dropped everything I was doing and came back, flew in that very night,"

Sullivan said. The next morning, Sullivan and Gregory called Lee in for a meeting, and she quickly became upset. According to her supervisors, she said Davidson didn't value her work, so she had taken it away.

Sylvia told them that she had copied some or all of the files from the lab's secure or Red network—used for classified computing—to the open or Green network, where unclassified files resided. She had locked up those files with a password and refused to give them up. Sylvia then had destroyed the originals on the Red network.

Sullivan was aghast. Now on top of a worsening personnel problem, he and Gregory faced a security violation. "I told her that what she did was something we couldn't stand, and she would have to go back and reconstruct all that stuff," Sullivan said. "Then she played that game of 'I don't understand,' and I was ready to fire her on the spot.

"I had never had a case that people would tell me they absolutely would not do something, and there's no way of getting them to do it," he said. "This was a case when she just said no." Sullivan ordered her to retrieve the project files. He gave her a deadline of a few days and told her to work on nothing else. Her job depended on her success. If she failed, Sullivan warned, she was gone.

Lee recovered some of the files but not all. A few of the lost files were classified. The lab's computer staff had to "sanitize" her directory, erasing all files to eliminate any classified information from the network. Sullivan began preparing to terminate her.

Lee was one step ahead. She complained to the lab's Human Resources Division, and a decision was made to put her on paid leave during an investigation. After three months, a Human Resources staffer asked that she be reinstated. She had language problems, and her life at home was very difficult, the staffer explained. Her husband verbally humiliated her, treated her as though she were stupid. He not only had assumed all of her responsibilities at home, but apparently was doing much of her job for her, also sometimes at home, the staffer told supervisors.

The bottom line: Sullivan couldn't fire her. All he and Gregory could do was place a written reprimand in her personnel file. Sullivan blamed political correctness and Sylvia's apparent ties to lab management.

"She was a woman, she was a TEC, she was ethnic, and she had some connection with the laboratory director," he said.

Sylvia Lee never forgave Sullivan and Gregory. She was overheard saying she would "get even," a statement that sounded threatening. For years afterward, she treated them coolly, would not look them in the eye, and communicated with them as little as possible. They were stuck with an employee who wasn't working out and, it seemed, wasn't working much at all—at least for them.

The CIA and the FBI caught wind of Sylvia's work problems and intervened as well. Bibb visited Sullivan to ask about them, and two CIA agents came by. They didn't come straight out and tell Sullivan not to interfere, he said, but they strongly implied they wanted Sylvia to continue in her job.

"By then I was beginning to think the less I knew about this the more I liked it," Sullivan said. "It was obvious that she had a job that she was supposed to do and a lot of times she wouldn't or couldn't do it, and the reason she gave was she was doing something for the laboratory . . . Finally, we just gave up."

Sullivan's complaints didn't go unheard, however. They added to Vrooman's growing concerns about the Lees.

In June 1988, while Wen Ho and Sylvia were in Beijing, Vrooman and his counterpart at Sandia National Laboratories began voicing mutual counterintelligence concerns about the increasing back-and-forth exchanges between the Chinese and U.S. weapons labs.

"There's something you should know," Jerry Brown, Sandia's counterintelligence director, said.

He filled Vrooman in on Wen Ho Lee's role in Tiger Trap. It was a detail Vrooman should have been told years ago. Brown told him about the phone call, captured on wiretap, in which Lee offered his help to a spy suspect. It was then that Vrooman learned Lee had admitted to passing export-controlled documents to Taiwan.

Brown and Vrooman decided to check in with the China Unit at FBI headquarters.

Three weeks later, three FBI foreign counterintelligence experts listened as Vrooman laid out his conundrum: The Lees had committed security violations, had close ties in China, and were visiting the IAPCM, the Chinese Los Alamos. Both Lees appeared naïve and might be vulnerable to Chinese manipulation. Sylvia's work problems could result in disgruntlement, even resentment. On the other hand, the Lees were currently working with the FBI and had cooperated with the CIA.

The Bureau's experts were unequivocal: Deny further travel to the PRC and find someone else to deal with the Chinese. Better safe than sorry.

While in Washington, Vrooman met with three other FBI counterintelligence agents. Two of these, Craig Schmidt and Jim Shaw, later would become intimately familiar with the contradictory nature of the Lees' dealings with the Chinese—Schmidt as a manager in the Bureau's National Security Division and Shaw as counterintelligence chief in the FBI's Albuquerque Field Office.

Vrooman flew back to Los Alamos and the next day took the elevator to the fourth floor of the Administration Building, where he laid the facts and the FBI's advice before the lab director. Siegfried S. Hecker, known to all as Sig, had led the lab for less than two years. An immigrant himself, Hecker had grown up in Poland and Austria, seen his father pressed into service in the Nazi Army, then lost him on the Russian front. Hecker came to Los Alamos rail thin and stayed that way, being fanatical in his exercise habits. He ran at lunch, skied in winter, and biked the rest of the year. His energy and his memory were legendary.

He was a metallurgist by training and spent his early years at the lab studying plutonium.

Hecker's blind spot was human interaction. In public, he showed a talent for oratory but often came off as cool, even haughty. Later in his career, he would be heavily criticized for ordering one of the largest layoffs in lab history in anticipation of budget cuts that failed to materialize. Privately, however, he was warmer, more engaging; most of his immediate staff judged him a good and shrewd boss. Vrooman was one of them. He told Hecker that Sylvia was billing herself as the official liaison to China for the lab director's office.

"That's ridiculous," Hecker said. "She's not working for the director's office."

He told Vrooman to draft a letter for his signature, telling Sylvia to stop acting on the lab's behalf with the Chinese. He also wanted to bar her access to secrets.

But Sullivan had already made sure Sylvia Lee received no further classified assignments after the debacle with Davidson and the destroyed files.

Vrooman went to see Jean Andrews Stark and told her to stop using Lee as a translator. Stark replied that she'd heard Sylvia had just received a phone call from IAPCM director and weapons scientist Zheng Shaotang. Zheng, the equivalent of a U.S. weapons-lab director, apparently had commented on the good time that he had with Sylvia during their last meeting.

A few days later, an executive of the lab's laser-fusion program gave Vrooman more worrisome news: Zheng Shaotang's son, Zheng Pujei, recently had boarded at the Lees' home while visiting Los Alamos en route to college.

Vrooman was increasingly concerned about the Lees as security risks, but evidently did not feel the need for urgency in cutting Sylvia Lee's ties with the Chinese. He knew the FBI and a number of lab scientists still needed her.

"It's not, 'Oh my god, we've got a spy.' This is simply somebody I think is vulnerable," he said years later.

As a consequence, Hecker's instructions were not fully carried out for more than a year. Vrooman neglected to draft the letter informing Sylvia of the change for six months.

Vrooman was submerged in another crisis: The General Accounting Office, the investigative arm of Congress, was preparing a damning report on lab visits by foreign scientists. Hundreds of foreign scientists—the greatest numbers from the Soviet Union and China—were coming to the weapons labs. And lab security personnel such as Vrooman were not running what the GAO termed "background checks" on them.

Vrooman got the job of drafting Los Alamos's response. The GAO's "background checks" were more accurately called indices checks and amounted to running a visiting scientist's name through CIA and FBI databases of foreign intelligence operatives. Vrooman thought they were a waste of time and often produced false hits. Many foreign scientists had common names and would be incorrectly flagged out of confusion with real spies. Security staff would have to cancel the visit or not renew the jobs of valued foreign scientists.

What irritated Vrooman more was his conviction that the "background checks" were wrongheaded in the first place. Intelligence agencies knew professional spies were easy to spot in a visiting scientific delegation and didn't have the technical background to understand the value of what they saw and heard. Most nations, Vrooman figured, stole scientific secrets the way he had—by sending their own scientists. And those were typically "clean," untainted by a history of spying or any other nefarious activities that might trigger suspicions in a foreign laboratory.

For six months, Vrooman knuckled down to do battle with the GAO, while Sylvia Lee—the potential security risk—continued as the lab's go-between with China. Vrooman explained his failure to end her contact with the Chinese in two ways: The FBI's Bibb was still getting useful information out of her, and a sizeable number of lab scientists depended on her translation services. Cutting both parties off was going to be a hassle, Vrooman knew. Finally, in mid-February 1989, he carried a draft to Hecker, who rejected it as too harsh. Hecker signed a softer, kinder version two days later.

"I want to let you know that I appreciate your efforts on behalf of our relations with our Chinese colleagues," the memo said over Hecker's signature. "Again, thanks for your help over the past years."

Vrooman delivered it personally and told Sylvia to stop acting as liaison. She took the news silently, nodding.

A month later, the FBI's Bibb reported that Sylvia planned to attend a fluid mechanics conference the next year in China. She had been invited to give another paper and evidently was willing to pay her own way if the lab refused.

Then word trickled in from around the lab: Sylvia was still phoning China, still translating for scientists, still receiving letters from Zheng Shaotang. And Wen Ho Lee wanted to accept an invitation to the same conference as his wife.

Finally, in October 1989, Vrooman persuaded John Birely, the head of the lab's weapons program, to deny any travel to China by the Lees. Two months later, Vrooman, Bibb, and Sullivan met Sylvia and ordered her to stop contacting the Chinese for anyone at the lab. She agreed, and contact appeared to stop—almost a year and a half after the FBI had advised it.

The Lees' heady days in the middle of two nations' nuclear-weapons programs were over, for good. Or so it seemed.

– 8 –

ASKINT Meets *Guanxi*

Even as Los Alamos was ending Sylvia Lee's China connection, a new venue was opening. It began with a picnic.

In 1988, two Los Alamos scientists who worked in intelligence in the International Technology Division (ITD), Danny Stillman and nuclear chemist Nerses H. "Krik" Krikorian, met five Chinese weapons scientists at a conference in Albuquerque. Their lunch together in a city park began more than a decade of intelligence gathering in China by scientifically trained intelligence officers.

Over sandwiches, Stillman suggested that the Chinese tour the National Atomic Museum, an impressive array of U.S. nuclear warheads, bombs, and missiles on the edge of Kirtland Air Force Base there in Albuquerque. The museum is open to the public. Stillman phoned the museum and asked about bringing Chinese citizens. The museum staff was only too pleased to host them.

"They said sure, and they really rolled out the red carpet," Stillman said.

The Americans watched as the Chinese crowded around cone-shaped reentry vehicles and talked excitedly. They were clearly guessing the size of the components inside.

The Chinese were deeply appreciative. Chinese society relies on interwoven personal relationships called *guanxi* (pronounced *gwan-shee*). Friendships as deep as kinship are sustained by a continuum of reciprocal favors and expectations. Stillman had performed such a favor, and the Chinese scientists were indebted. So they invited him to see their nuclear-weapons facilities.

Stillman and Krikorian began plotting what information to seek. Stillman spread out a map of China on a picnic table on Krikorian's patio in Los Alamos. They knew the Chinese had built a home for the Ninth Academy, the collection of institutes doing nuclear-weapons work. The question was where.

In the 1950s, the Chinese built their first nuclear-weapons research facilities close by the Soviet border to facilitate technical assistance from Russian weapons scientists. The PRC's Northwest Academy was near Mongolia, in isolated, high-desert plateau country, very much like Los Alamos's mesa tops. Yet the laboratories themselves were designed and laid out exactly like Arzamas-16, the primary nuclear-weapons lab of the Soviet Union. Russian advisors swarmed into China and joined in building copies of Soviet uranium plants, plutonium production reactors, and other factories. But the Russians pointedly withheld vital pieces of machinery, factory blueprints, and, most of all, a detailed bomb design that would include a prototype.

China's engineers probed for the shape of the primary and received only insulting, vague replies: "It is similar to a watermelon rind."

"How do you wrap the product?" they asked.

"Just as you would wrap an apple."

But by early 1959, the Russians were ready to hand over the final, most valuable bits of the bomb puzzle, according to stories that Russian scientists later related to the Americans. Workers at Arzamas-16 loaded crates of weapons-design documents and the prototype bomb into a railroad boxcar. But, the story goes, they lacked a signature on the shipping manifest, some final authorization from Moscow. Unable to reach the head of the Soviet weapons program, Arzamas-16 officials called the Central Committee for the Communist Party, laid out their dilemma and were put on hold. In a few minutes, a voice came on the line and instructed them to replace the bomb in secure storage and set fire to the railcar.

The Soviet withdrawal fired the resolve of Chinese at home and abroad. Peasants by the thousands fanned out to dig uranium ore by hand. And hundreds of thousands more began building factories, processing bomb components and more, an extraordinary campaign that engaged 900 factories, institutes, and schools. Decades later, veteran workers in the Chinese weapons program still wore shoulder patches bearing the logo "596"—the year 1959 and the month of June, when the Soviets formally reneged on their promise to help the Chinese build a bomb; "596" also was the code name for CHIC-1, China's first nuclear test device.

The Chinese never could stomach total dependency on the Soviets and had begun looking for a new research location. It was to be safe from surveillance and attack by the Soviets.

"I figured their new site had to be somewhere in the Sichuan Province," Stillman said.

A Chinese delegation was in Los Alamos at the time. Stillman talked to them about his scientific field—the prompt-burst reactors that Los Alamos used to make whopping amounts of neutrons and gamma radiation in an attempt to simulate comparable radiation levels from the detonation of a nuclear weapon. Stillman asked whether the Chinese had such a thing. They did indeed, in Sichuan Province. At a place never seen by surveillance satellites. Stillman wanted to go.

———————

Securing funding and approvals for the trip took months, and by the time Stillman was ready, civil unrest had sprung up nationwide in China. In mid-April 1989, the death of popular reformist Hu Yaobang triggered mourning and then protests in every major Chinese city. In late April, students from forty universities across China traveled to Beijing and joined workers and students there in a protest encampment in Tiananmen Square. They erected a tent city, chanted slogans, and called for reforms aimed at making Communist leaders more accountable to the public will.

By May 20, party leaders feared the workers and students were gaining allies in the military and in their paranoia declared martial law. On the night of June 3, officials of the White House listened in shock to intercepted radio transmissions in which People's Liberation Army (PLA) elements from distant provinces were ordered to clear Tiananmen Square at all costs.

The most violent episode of the Tiananmen Square tragedy actually unfurled several miles outside the square, on streets approaching from the west. There, PLA troops encountered a blockade of angry demonstrators, more workers and common people than students, and mowed them down with gunfire. Hundreds were killed, more than 10,000 wounded. The army swept the square without much resistance, but the final death toll was variously estimated between 700 and 2,700. Chinese leaders then embarked on weeks of arrests, quick trials and jailings, even executions, that left Western leaders reeling.

The State Department decided the immediate policy response would be a cessation of all Sino-U.S. military contacts and arms sales to China. Soon after, Secretary of State James A. Baker answered administration critics in Congress by announcing a suspension of international loans to China and by saying he had advised President Bush to freeze all high-level contacts with the Chinese.

The ban on high-level contacts slowed but didn't stop Stillman. In April 1990, he made the first of ten trips. As a partner, he took his new deputy, Houston T. "Terry" Hawkins, a former intelligence analyst at the Defense Intelligence Agency and the Defense Nuclear Agency. He was a bulldog of a man whose eyes narrowed when he grinned, which was often. Hawkins taught Sunday school back in Los Alamos and was in fact an ordained Baptist minister.

Before coming to Los Alamos, he had worked in the Air Force program that monitored foreign nuclear tests by seismic and radiochemical data. There and at DIA, Hawkins had studied China's weapons program, read the classified reports, and heard the briefings. He jumped at the chance to see the program.

The two men didn't hide their trade; they sent résumés to the Chinese beforehand. China's scientists knew they were coming to gather intelligence.

They flew into Hong Kong, then Shanghai, where they were met by a staff member of Fudan University's Center for American Studies. Once again, Fudan's Yang Fujia was their host. After two days' delay in obtaining a flight, they flew to Chengdu, where they found themselves in a sea of Mao jackets and a more conservative society than Shanghai. Chengdu was the capital of Sichuan, China's most populous province and a haven for nuclear science and technology, but insulated by distances that slowed liberalizing influences.

Chinese scientists drove the Americans to Mianyang, where workers were finishing the centerpiece of the Chinese nuclear program, a city devoted to scientists and engineers.

Science City featured a sprawl of laboratories, homes, and stores, even a miniature version of Disneyland, complete with a water flume, for entertaining the children of scientists and engineers. Stillman and Hawkins had been forewarned: The scientists of Mianyang were among China's best and brightest but could seem like peasants—backward, uncultured—the result of decades of isolation.

China's scientific leaders in the late 1980s worried about this isolation. "They felt like their technical staff was being taken out of the mainstream," Hawkins said. Science City was part of the solution. "This," explained one senior Chinese weapons designer and executive, "is what I have to do to attract staff. We keep losing people to the West."

Mianyang—which translated as "dim sun"—lay under almost perpetual cloud cover, shielding it from satellites, and was deep in the Chinese interior, inaccessible to surveillance aircraft. The laboratories and institutes themselves were scattered in several valleys, often hundreds of kilometers from one another. The Chinese designed the site to be an unwieldy target, capable of partially surviving Soviet attack. But this defensive design came at the price of scientific interaction: Scientists of one institute might have to drive hours to work with colleagues in another institute.

Hawkins and Stillman were told they were the first Westerners to see the area since Marco Polo. Science City hadn't been occupied yet, and there were few accommodations for foreign travelers—just a small hotel downtown and a new café nearby.

For days they toured Mianyang's laboratories. The Chinese had built many of the same weapons-research facilities as were found at Los Alamos and Lawrence Livermore. Most were featured in a thick color brochure issued by the Chinese Academy of Engineering Physics, which as China's DOE ran Mianyang. Hawkins felt lucky to get a copy. "When I was in DIA doing real intelligence work, I would've given ten million dollars for this book," he said.

For testing and refining nuclear primaries, the Chinese had a radiographic hydrotest facility that could take X-ray pictures of a mass of metal being imploded by high explosives. The machine helped scientists explore new high-explosive systems without nuclear testing. The Chinese had several particle accelerators, one that Hawkins described as "bolt for bolt, a copy of one at Livermore."

Stillman and Hawkins asked questions, Stillman writing down copious details in small notebooks. It was the inauguration of a practice Stillman came to call ASKINT—"ask intelligence"—as opposed to HUMINT, the intelligence gathered by human spies, and TECHINT, the intelligence derived from technical means such as satellites. In China, the nuclear-weapons program had been a black box, sealed from the light of scrutiny. Now Stillman discovered that he could walk around and map the dimensions of machines and buildings by counting his paces. What he didn't know, he found he had only to ask. The Chinese proved very open and even corrected the scribbling in his notebook.

"They'd take it away from me and say, 'No, you don't understand. Here,' " he said. "Then they'd write in my book to correct me."

Later the Chinese sent photos to Stillman to commemorate his trips. In every one, Stillman is pictured off to the side, scribbling away.

The Chinese stressed that they wanted information about their weapons program to reach decision-makers in Washington.

"They always said, 'Take this to the highest levels of your government,' " Stillman said.

————

Six months later, Stillman was back in China with his deputy, Hawkins, their boss, John Hopkins, the head of Los Alamos's nuclear-weapons program, and Hopkins's wife, Adele. The prize of the trip was a tour of the Chinese Nuclear Weapons Test Site at Lop Nur, the first by an American since Harold Agnew had visited eight years before.

The Chinese of course knew Stillman led the intelligence division at Los Alamos. And they had dug into the backgrounds of John and Adele Hopkins as well. At the time, she was working as an analytical chemist in Los Alamos's plutonium-handling facility, checking the purity of various batches of the metal. But years before, Adele Hopkins had written a paper on robotics. The Chinese had a copy and made a point of asking her about it.

"They really checked us out carefully," her husband said.

In fact, the Chinese seemed to have copies of every unclassified Los Alamos paper. The Southwest Institute of Fluid Physics at Mianyang, the Institute of Applied Physics and Computational Mathematics in Beijing, and several other Chinese research labs housed huge archives of research papers by U.S. scientists.

Stillman and the Hopkinses were met in Shanghai by Yang Fujia and Robert S. Daniel, a former CIA operative and chief of intelligence for the U.S. Department of Energy. Daniel was a rugged, straight-talking Virginian, formerly one of the state's Republican congressmen. Energy Secretary James Watkins, a former admiral, had wanted an intel chief with strong experience, and Daniel's operations background filled the bill.

Yang Fujia and weapons scientists escorted them to the Shanghai Institute of Nuclear Research. Five days later, the Americans flew to Chengdu for a more in-depth look at Mianyang.

They asked questions, took notes, and hopped a plane to Urumqi, the capital of Xinjiang Province and the most inland city in the world. Its Mongolian name translates as "beautiful pastureland." Urumqi had been a trade and cultural center on the northern route of the Silk Road two thousand years before. Lop Nur is only 165 miles from Urumqi as the crow flies, but it took most of a day to get there by Chinese military Jeeps.

China's weaponeers took their detonations underground in 1982 and had since tested nine devices in tunnels and shafts. The Chinese took the Americans to several test holes. The Americans asked to see the area of atmospheric testing but the Chinese declined—the radiation in spots remained too high and the roads were impassable.

The Chinese obviously wanted the Americans to know they had learned most of the tricks of setting up and instrumenting underground tests. Data on a nuclear detonation is crucial for getting higher efficiencies and refining weapons-design software. But American diagnostic techniques for nuclear tests are mostly unclassified, and what was published the Chinese clearly had.

The Americans were nonetheless awed, which was precisely what the Chinese desired. They knew the Americans would report their observations. Presumably, Washington could be made to understand that China was not a third-rate nuclear power. But more importantly, they knew their weapons research had breadth and depth unappreciated by foreigners and by their own countrymen. They craved peer recognition, and this group of Americans provided it.

"There's a tendency on the part of most Americans to think we have a monopoly. I think the Chinese felt we didn't give them the respect they deserve," Hopkins said. "We've got a lot of equipment, sophisticated lathes, experimental machines, computers. But the Chinese have a tremendous number of well-trained scientists who sit at their desks all day long thinking about nuclear weapons. I think they wanted to brag just a bit. And I think we were impressed."

The Chinese didn't share the intricacies of their weapons designs. But the Americans carried home photographs and notebooks full of details and names—a portrait of Chinese nuclear-weapons research and its leading minds.

"My impression was they didn't withhold anything," Daniel said. "They didn't show us a bomb design or anything like that. But as far as where we went, they didn't say we couldn't go there."

The gleanings of the trip were fed to analysts at Los Alamos and DOE headquarters. They sifted and collated the pieces, then drew estimates—based in part on comparisons with earlier American weapons research—of where the Chinese were headed. The final product was classified and sent to the CIA and the DIA, where it was blended with other intelligence for briefings to the National Security Council and elsewhere.

"It wasn't an intelligence scoop," Daniel said, "but they got a very good idea of how the Chinese were going about things."

American scientists harvested details of other nations' nuclear programs as they traveled and went to scientific conferences. But in the 1980s and '90s, no other non-ally offered the Americans greater access to its weapons facilities than China. Daniel saw intelligence on other nations' nuclear programs but "nothing compared to what we were seeing in China."

Under the unspoken rules of *guanxi,* it was China's turn. Its scientists now had a right to expect favors of the Americans and began nudging for reciprocation.

"It was not terribly overt," Hopkins said. "I think they wanted to build into us a feeling of obligation. There were just certain things we couldn't do."

As the Americans left Lop Nur, the Chinese made their expectations known to Stillman: "We have shown you all of our nuclear facilities. We have shown you our test site. Now we want to come see yours."

"I'm sure I can get that done," Stillman assured them.

It took two and a half frenetic years. Stillman was lobbying the Bush and Clinton administrations on behalf of the Chinese, returning for more visits to China and taking similar trips to Russia and Kazakhstan. Russia's weaponeers opened their doors to Stillman as well.

While awaiting word from Washington, the Chinese asked for other favors. They wanted a sophisticated machine known as a computer tomography system, which they called an ICT. They said it was to be used to examine welds on large-diameter oil pipelines. The Americans regarded the ICT as a dual-use technology: Tomography was used in the U.S. weapons program to check welds or otherwise image nuclear-weapons components, as well as to assemble 3D images of imploding mock-ups of primaries, a boon for designing more efficient implosion systems.

Stillman did some homework. He researched U.S. suppliers of tomography systems. Then the Americans heard that the Chinese did, in fact, intend to divert the ICT to nuclear-weapons research in Mianyang. Hawkins notified the Commerce Department that the application was fraudulent and it was denied.

During the October 1990 visit, Hawkins had asked Yang whether he could arrange a private meeting with Chinese engineers most knowledgeable about PRC command-and-control technology for Chinese nuclear weapons. Yang agreed. That same night, the Americans met two engineers of China's Fifth Institute, the equivalent of Sandia National Laboratories.

According to Stillman, Hawkins opened the discussion with them by saying that he had been authorized by the U.S. government to gauge Chinese interest in obtaining a Permissive Action Link (PAL) system, the closely guarded locks on U.S. nuclear weapons that prevent their unauthorized use. Surely the Tiananmen Square incident had taught China's leaders that they might lose control of the gray PLO in a popular uprising. Some PLA leaders had sided with the students. Had those sympathies grown, China's party leaders might have lost their grip on their last resort to power. Fear of losing that control had, in fact, been a leading motivation behind the massacre.

The two Chinese engineers were receptive. They asked for a CAT F PAL, the most sophisticated U.S. bomb lock. China had no such locks on its weapons, relying instead on storing warheads separately from the missiles.

PAL systems had been pioneered at Sandia in 1960, after the government realized its weapons were at risk. Early PALs were combination locks. Later versions used digital keys, remote controls, and encryption. A CAT F PAL used a twelve-digit key and reportedly allowed remote disabling of the bomb.

Stillman carried China's pitch forward, lobbying officials in both the Defense and Energy departments. He argued, why not give the Chinese one of our earlier, less sophisticated PALs? U.S. defense officials were divided. On one hand, giving away PALs might preclude accidental or unauthorized launches that in turn could escalate to a nuclear exchange—the silver-screen scenario laid out in *Fail-Safe*. On the other hand, sharing PAL technology could aid a foreign power in defeating U.S. weapons locks.

But no one was willing to stick his neck out. Giving anything that smacked of nuclear-weapons technology to the Communist Chinese, especially after Tiananmen Square, was clearly out of bounds.

The Chinese were irritated but polite to Stillman. They thanked him for his effort. All was fine; they had gotten a PAL from the Russians.

But within a year, the Chinese were back. The Russian PAL was "no good." Stillman renewed his lobbying but with the same negative result. The Clinton administration was no more eager than the Bush administration to look like it was giving away nuclear-weapons technology to the Chinese.

The fact that Stillman couldn't deliver favors to the Chinese brought protests. Weapons designer Hu Side chided him for not getting the tomography system "after all we did for you."

But Stillman knew the rules of the *guanxi* game. Merely trying was enough. Stillman was permitted continued access to Chinese nuclear facilities. And he and his traveling companions meanwhile kept bringing back intelligence. Much of their take simply filled in the holes left by Agnew, Keyworth, Browne, and innumerable others, or it was used to validate or invalidate the intelligence community's theories and information from other sources.

Stillman's access to Chinese nuclear facilities went on for years. After all, the Chinese had a story to tell Los Alamos and Washington, and Stillman was their emissary.

"The only relationship you can have is one where both sides do something for one another," said Paul D. Moore, a former veteran counterintelligence analyst for the FBI. "If you want to know what you can get from the Chinese, you look at what they're asking from you. But you don't really have to deliver in a Chinese relationship, all you have to do is try. They don't always know what you can get your hands on."

Ultimately, Stillman felt his way into a delicate equilibrium with the Chinese, and it served him well through the 1990s and beyond.

The Americans did in fact deliver on the most crucial Chinese favor, or at least part of it. They arranged for the highest-level Chinese delegation ever to visit the U.S. weapons labs.

Bringing the upper echelon of the Chinese nuclear-weapons program to the United States took a direct appeal by Stillman to George Tenet at the National Security Council. Tenet made a phone call, and the Chinese delegation was approved.

It would be a rare opportunity to persuade the Chinese to stop testing and to adhere to the international norms of the nuclear club.

–9–

The Collector

One day in April 1988, when he was forty-eight years old, Wen Ho Lee pulled up his office chair to the Sun workstation in his X Division office and began a secret, unauthorized project that was most unusual and would change his life. He set out that day on the arduous, obsessive task of collecting—or stealing, depending on your point of view—his own personal tape library of the secret computer codes used to design America's nuclear weapons. He didn't tell anyone what he was doing or why.

A passerby peering into his office from the hallway would have noticed nothing unusual. Alone in his office, staring at the screen, Lee was perpetually typing at the keyboard, surrounded by the clutter on his desk, looking as he always did when he was writing code.

His project continued off and on through the next nine years. His office computer was the tool he used to travel out into the lab's computer networks, where he hunted his digital prizes. He traveled around electronically in one of the most powerful computing centers on Earth. From his keyboard, he typed Unix commands to Cray supercomputers and IBM data-storage machines, copying, moving, saving, renaming files. His efforts were methodical, if sometimes clumsy. He took classified files as he would books from the shelves, often from the directories of other code writers.

He then assembled them into groups and placed each group into a larger holding file known as a TAR file. Days or weeks later, he downloaded the TAR files to a machine equipped with a tape drive and sitting in an unsecured trailer outside the security fence. Then he used the tape drive to make copies of the weapons-design codes on cassette tapes the size of a small paperback book. In the history of Los Alamos, no one had done anything quite like it. Lee's collection was like none in the world.

Lee's scheme would have been far simpler if his office workstation had been equipped with a tape drive, but tape drives were banned from X Division for security reasons. He would have to transfer his weapons files into an open computing network, where tape drives were allowed.

One of Lee's interests was an important code named Big Mac. It *was* big—223,000 lines long—a workhorse two-dimensional code used to design secondaries and some primaries. When a weapons designer asked Big Mac to test the latest brainstorm for a new secondary, the code would run nonstop on a Cray supercomputer for hours, perhaps days, solving complex equations written by code writers like Lee.

Big Mac had been created in X Division around 1979. Lee had played a small role in its creation, and later updated one of its hydrodynamic packages. His input was in the section of the code used to design primaries, his specialty. "Wen added a package to our code that, altogether, was probably less than a thousand lines of work," John Romero, the team leader for Big Mac, would later say. In other words, Lee's contribution was less than one-half of 1 percent.

Lee began his capture of Big Mac at his keyboard, first logging into X Division's local network using his personal employee number, 08885 (known at the lab as a Z Number), to gain access. He then made his way down this local network to the workstation of Steve White, the code writer who kept the Big Mac files.

Lee copied an entire directory of Big Mac files from White's computer. He put his haul—main directory, subdirectories, files—into one TAR file of 20 megabytes. Once he had Big Mac in a TAR file, he saved it in his secure directory, "lee333," on the lab's Common File System, a massive digital storage facility built by IBM. In choosing names for his TAR files, Lee typically made no attempt to disguise their content, using names that accurately described the files. He may well have named this file "lee333/tar.BigMac."

The next afternoon at two-thirty, the collector was back at work. To move Big Mac onto the open side, he first had to trick the computer into believing that the weapons code was unclassified. He typed "CL=U." The abbreviation stood for "classification level equals unclassified." It was a lie. But the computer system couldn't tell. The lab's cyber security ran on the honor system. If the owner of a file declared it was unclassified, the system believed it.

For security, the Los Alamos computer system was divided into halves, each half called a partition. The Green, or open, partition was for unclassified computing. The Red partition was for secure, classified computing, such as bomb calculations. The rule was that all classified files had to stay on the red partition, where security was tightest.

Lee now logged into another computer, one that existed for a narrow purpose. Its proper name was Machine C, but it was more often called the Washing Machine. It was used to "down-partition" files from the Red to the Green. Lee then called up his Big Mac TAR file on the Washing Machine and typed a "modify p" command to move the file from the Red to the Green. The Washing Machine would have rejected the request if Lee had not already changed the marking on the file to "U," for unclassified.

It took yet more steps for Lee to move the file into his own directory, "kf1," on the Green partition.

Now all he needed was a tape drive. He had found one in an office in a trailer outside the fence of X Division. The trailer, known as T-15, belonged to scientists from the theoretical division and was decidedly low-security, often unlocked. In the trailer was a Sun workstation equipped with a tape drive. It was used by Kuok-Mee Ling, a researcher who knew Lee casually. Lee asked to use the hard drive to download "some files" from the unclassified network. Ling obliged, going so far as to write down his user name and password on a slip of paper and giving his colleague a tutorial on operating the equipment.

Always one to keep notes, Lee filled a sheet of paper, in a mix of English and Chinese, with a detailed sixteen-step process for making tapes. He titled it, "How to Use the T-15 Machine." The tape itself, he noted, was a 3M 6150. It was a generic size commonly used for backup tapes and was readily available. Lee had special-ordered a pack.

The gist of Lee's handwritten instructions was that he would use the password, "trasopme," to download his file from the main computer system to the hard drive of the Sun in the trailer. Then, finally, he could slip the tape into the computer and capture Big Mac for his collection.

Leaving nothing to chance, he drew a diagram of the tape drive, with arrows and labels. At the bottom of the page, he wrote, in Chinese characters, "To extract the tape, move the door at the top to the left."

Armed with Ling's password, Lee returned to T-15 many times in 1993 and 1994 to make tapes for his collection. He vacuumed up not just the codes themselves, but many of the auxiliary files that went with them. He grabbed data files that included physics data on how materials—plutonium, for instance—behaved at the extreme pressures and temperatures found in nuclear weapons.

Many of these were known as equation-of-state data. Some were available in the open literature. But other data were gathered from measurements made during live nuclear tests and were closely guarded.

He moved 1,600 files in all. Perhaps more surprising, he took files that described the shapes and sizes of the interior components of nuclear weapons, what the code writers called "the contours." The files, called input decks, represented a bomb that a scientist wanted to test in cyberspace. The researcher plugged the input deck into the code, and the code ran a simulated explosion, offering a prediction of how well the bomb would perform.

To get the input decks used with Big Mac, he went straight to the source, Steve White, the keeper of the code. Whatever Lee said to White was persuasive. White gave Lee a directory of input decks, all TARed up into a file. Lee downloaded them onto tape. Lee had less luck with another code writer, Jay Mosso. Mosso sent Lee away empty-handed because Lee didn't have a need to know.

Half the files Lee picked up were preexisting collections put together by code teams or weapons scientists, such as secondary specialists Mike Clover and Tom Hill. Hill was a coworker and friend of Lee beginning almost as soon as Lee arrived at the lab in 1979. Hill had been to Lee's house, and their kids had gone to Piñon Elementary School together in White Rock. Years later, when Hill found out what Lee had done, he was so angry that he never spoke to him again, even when they saw each other in the grocery store or the gas station.

Each time Lee downloaded a classified file to the trailer, he went astray of the rules by taking classified material outside a secured area. Worse yet, after he made the tapes, about seventeen in all, he left copies of the code in the Green partition, where they were vulnerable to attack by hackers coming in from the Internet, or available to anyone who had Lee's password. For years the files sat there unnoticed, even though Lee had given them revealing names.

In the 1993–94 period when Lee was making many of his tapes, someone using his user name, "whl," and his password logged in to RHO, an unclassified Cray supercomputer, from the University of California at Los Angeles. The log-ins came from machines named "zuma.pic.ucla.edu" and "venice.pic.ucla.edu," computers that were used by a large number of people. On a half-dozen occasions, the log-ins came on days when Lee was moving around files or making tapes. Alberta Lee was a student at UCLA at the time, and later said she was logging in to play Dungeons and Dragons on the Internet.

Always persistent, Lee labored on his codes-to-tape project on seventy different days, taking more codes, moving more files around, making more tapes. He moved codes around most often in the afternoon, but he usually went over to T-15 to make the tapes around lunchtime or after hours, when fewer people were around. He was flagrantly violating security rules at every turn, marking classified files "U" and down-partitioning classified codes.

In keeping with his penchant for making notes, Lee wrote down the details of his tape collection. He recorded the names of the files, their size, and how they were grouped together onto tapes, which he labeled Tape B through Tape N.

Tape N was the last tape, recorded in 1997, three years after he finished the others. By then, the rules in X Division had changed and Lee had his own tape drive. This time, he downloaded the files directly from the Red side to his own office. His library was complete.

––––––––––––

The weightiest delegation of Chinese nuclear-weapons managers ever to visit the United States arrived in February 1994, led by Hu Side, the new chief of China's Academy of Engineering Physics. There were six of them, four scientists and two engineers. Among them, they ran the Chinese program.

The American contingent was headed by Lab Director Sig Hecker; Danny Stillman, the one-man intelligence operation, now largely retired; and Terry Hawkins. All three had been to China, and in fact, the get-together was a reciprocal invitation in return for the intelligence-rich tours of China's facilities by Stillman, Hawkins, and others.

The Americans had spent years laying the groundwork for the trip. Even in an administration eager to engage China, bringing the brain trust of China's weapon establishment into the lab prompted sweaty palms. Classified faxes flew back and forth to Washington, laying out agendas and drawing boundaries around certain topics.

The U.S. scientists were the vanguard of the Clinton administration's effort to pull China into the international arms-control community. U.S. intelligence reported that China was selling missiles in the Middle East and supplying nuclear technology to Pakistan and North Korea. The Americans at Los Alamos were trying to persuade China's scientists to stop this sharing of dangerous and destabilizing weapons technologies. (Over lunch the Chinese denied assisting North Korea. "Why would we help North Korea," one of them remarked. "Do you help Mexico?")

Unlike diplomats, the scientists could toss around ideas without the burden of being official representatives of U.S. foreign policy. The State Department, however, was deeply involved in the planning of the visit.

Before arriving at Los Alamos, the Chinese delegation had hopscotched from San Francisco to Berkeley, Livermore, and Stanford University. Only the Nevada Test Site was off-limits to the visiting Chinese.

On February 23, the two sides gathered in a conference room on the second floor of the Los Alamos library, named after J. Robert Oppenheimer, to talk arms control. Hawkins was standing in the front of the room, giving a talk with the viewgraphs that are a part of every talk at the lab. Stillman, the doorkeeper for this low-profile, unannounced event, was sitting in a chair against the back wall. A table with cookies and tea was nearby.

The door opened and Wen Ho Lee walked in uninvited, wearing a coat and tie instead of his habitual jeans and casual shirt. ("I'm not sure I've ever seen him in a coat and tie," his friend Bob Clark would say later. "There is some story about Wen Ho not being able to get into a casino in Monte Carlo because he didn't have a jacket.")

Stillman, who didn't recognize Lee by sight, stood up and approached him. "Can I help you?"

"They're my friends," Lee said, motioning toward the Chinese.

It was hard for Stillman to imagine that these senior scientists were friends of someone he didn't even know. There was Yang Fujia, the president of Fudan University and the director of the Shanghai Institute of Nuclear Research; Peng Hangsheng, the associate chief engineer of the China Academy of Engineering Physics (CAEP); and Hu Renyu, the director of CAEP.

Then there was Major General Qian Shaojun, the military's leading voice on arms-control issues, and Brigadier General Ye Lirun, the chief engineer of the Chinese nuclear test site.

Finally, there was Hu Side, the very nuclear-weapons designer who had asked Lee about two-point primaries in the Beijing hotel room six years earlier—and had gone on to design China's first miniaturized nuclear weapon.

"Who?" Stillman asked Lee. "Who's your friend?"

Lee pointed to a Chinese scientist who had been sitting next to Stillman.

Stillman asked the Chinese scientist if he knew Lee. The scientist lifted his glasses and peered at Lee. "I don't know him," he said.

Stillman was puzzled but allowed Lee to stay in the room to listen to the remainder of Hawkins's talk. Afterward, there was a break for stretching and snacking. Lee, having now correctly identified Hu, approached him in the back of the room. As the other Americans watched, the small-time code writer from Los Alamos was warmly embraced by the leader of the Chinese nuclear-weapons program. There were smiles, "a lot of bowing and exchanging cards" as they chatted in Mandarin. It was too much for Stillman to bear. He didn't speak Mandarin, so he asked someone who did to walk over and "find out what's going on over there."

Stillman's emissary returned to say that Lee had been introduced to him as someone who had come to China and advised the Chinese weapons scientists on codes. "They're thanking him for help with codes," the man said.

Stillman was alarmed. He could think of no way for Lee and Hu to be close friends or even know each other. Moreover, Stillman was one of the few people at the lab who knew about Lee's Tiger Trap phone call in 1982, which only added to his suspicion.

After his conversation with Hu, Lee walked out of the conference room. But, according to one participant, he returned late in the afternoon to invite the Chinese delegation to dinner, as he had with previous Chinese visitors. As far as is known, the Chinese declined.

Three of the Americans in the conference room that February morning— Stillman, Hawkins, and Rod Thurston, a weapons scientist working in Hawkins's intelligence office—reported the incident. Was the relationship between the two men based on espionage? From Lee's perspective, of course, the incident might have looked completely different. Perhaps he had heard that his acquaintance from his 1988 trip to Beijing was at the lab. Maybe he just went to say hello. After all, Lee and his wife had been taking care of visiting Chinese for more than a decade. Perhaps he thought it would improve his status to be seen in such lofty company as Hu Side. "He probably forgot that he had failed to list Hu on his trip report," a friend of his mused.

Stillman sent off a written report about "the Hug" to FBI Agent Dave Lieberman, the Bureau's counterintelligence agent in Santa Fe.

Lieberman asked Washington headquarters to do some checking on Lee but didn't do much else. He began working, ever so slowly, toward an interview with Lee. He never did talk to him.

– 10 –

Kindred Spirits

The Department of Energy's chief counterintelligence investigator in 1995 was a former Air Force inspector by the name of Dan Bruno. He was DOE's legman for chasing down hints of espionage. One day in May, he was called to his boss's office in a secure, underground suite in the bowels of the Forrestal Building. DOE's hulking, gray headquarters was a jarring contrast with the whimsy of the Smithsonian Castle and its lively gardens across Independence Avenue. Bruno's boss was Notra Trulock, the director of both intelligence and counterintelligence for the department's nuclear labs and factories. With a budget of $35 million, Trulock indirectly controlled hundreds of federal and contractor employees scattered around the country.

Beneath the floor ran the wires for the computer, the secure phones, and the encrypted fax machine. There were no windows in his office or anywhere else in NN-30, as Trulock's shop was known. The basement of the Forrestal Building was one giant, sealed vault—a secure compartmented information facility or SCIF, in government speak—with copper-lined walls to prevent electronic eavesdropping from the outside. From around the world, secret cables flowed in, distillations of reports from the far-flung U.S. intelligence community. The data was often gleaned from newspapers, technical journals, radio broadcasts, or the Internet, but it was just as often the product of satellites, covert listening stations, and spies.

Anything having to do with energy or nuclear weapons was shipped to the NN-30 analysts. Did a new pipeline in Azerbaijan mean the West was losing its grip on the region's oil? Did a shipment of niobium to South Korea mean the Koreans were working on a new reactor, something capable of producing plutonium? Did the earth-moving equipment visible in a spy satellite photo of Lop Nur mean the Chinese were preparing a nuclear test? Forty scientists and engineers, drafted from government agencies and private industry, all with security clearances, did the analysis. They consumed intelligence and they produced it; the reports came in and the analyses went back out, often to the White House.

NN-30 boasted experts in missiles, oil and gas production, and the high-precision, seven-axis lathes that could be used to machine plutonium for critical bomb parts.

Bruno was a career counterintelligence investigator, but Trulock had come up on the other side of the business, as an intelligence analyst, a specialist on the military of the Soviet Union. He was the son of an Indianapolis fireman, one of a long line of English immigrants and gunsmiths stretching back to the 1700s.

Trulock at age forty-seven cut a fireplug of a figure. He favored blue shirts, lively ties, and suspenders to offset his office attire of standard charcoal.

He had become DOE intelligence chief a year earlier but had been handed responsibility for the counterintelligence operation almost as an afterthought in a department reshuffling. Coworkers thought him highly ambitious. They whispered that Trulock dreamed of being CIA director. He liked to talk and formed his opinions quickly, sometimes too quickly. An assistant swore that Trulock told him, "We need one good espionage case to make this program grow. There's one spy out there and we're going to find him." Trulock later denied saying this.

Sitting behind his desk, Trulock told Bruno, "We've got a problem here. The Chinese have stolen the design of the W88." He paused to let the enormity of the statement linger in the air for a moment. The Chinese had copied it and tested their own version underground in the remote desert at Lop Nur. Trulock did not seem to have any doubts. A couple of his "bomb wizards" had pored over classified intelligence data and come to that conclusion.

Bruno was stunned. He could think of nothing more profound to say than "Yikes!" Neither man was a scientist, but they both knew what this meant. The W88s were, that day and every day, on ultrasilent *Ohio*-class submarines beneath the Atlantic Ocean, ready to fly away on Trident missiles at a moment's notice. Each warhead was stuffed inside a narrow nose cone as tall as a ten-year-old child and capable of raining down at 15,600 miles an hour—faster than Mach 20. No other weapon on Earth could deliver as much deadly force so rapidly and accurately.

Bruno thought immediately of Ethel and Julius Rosenberg, executed in 1953 for their role in passing the first atom bomb designs from Los Alamos to Russia during World War II. To Bruno, the Rosenbergs were the icons of nuclear treason.

Nothing since then could equal what he had just heard.

Bruno didn't know much about nuclear weapons. He did know the Chinese didn't have anything like the W88. It was the premier U.S. warhead, the pinnacle of weapons evolution, with a design so compact that eight could be packed atop the Trident II D-5 missile. Both missile and warhead were engineered to sit for a dozen years inside a submarine, always on hair-trigger alert. Minutes after a D-5 was launched, the warheads would make a fiery descent, one by one unerringly striking separate targets. To think of Chinese missiles with multiple warheads aimed at the United States was terrifying to Bruno.

He suggested to Trulock that they turn the whole thing over to the FBI, immediately. By law, the FBI had exclusive jurisdiction over criminal espionage investigations, and this sounded like espionage to Bruno. Trulock agreed. Bruno went back to his office, telephoned the National Security Division at FBI headquarters, and then went over to brief them. The agents didn't see enough evidence for an investigation. "We're not going to open. Call us if you get more."

Stuck with the case, Trulock and Bruno charted a path. They would pull together a blue-ribbon panel of nuclear and intelligence experts, a scientific working group to review the evidence. With a solid, scientific report, maybe the FBI would reconsider.

––––––––

Trulock was an Indiana conservative who had voted for both Reagan and Clinton. He had graduated with a political-science degree from Indiana University and then joined the Army, which sent him to the Defense Language Institute in Monterey, California, in 1971 to learn Russian. The Army Security Agency shipped him to West Germany during the Cold War, where he spent his time with earphones on, listening to the radio traffic of Soviet soldiers across the border. After a soldier in his unit went AWOL in Czechoslovakia, apparently into enemy hands, the Soviets suddenly changed their radio frequencies. It was an early lesson in the game of spy-versus-spy.

Trulock then worked several years in Maryland for the supersecret National Security Agency, the world's largest electronic-eavesdropping organization. He still donned the earphones, but he also advanced into analysis of the intercepted communications, specializing in the command-and-control systems of the Russian military, including its nuclear forces. He loved every minute of it. In the 1980s, he shifted to consulting at the National Defense University, doing studies for the Pentagon on Russian military affairs.

He reluctantly left the Beltway in 1990 and headed for the high desert of New Mexico with his wife and two children, hoping the climate would improve their son's health. He accepted a job at Los Alamos's Center for National Security Studies and was immediately miserable. He was a political analyst among scientists, an inside-the-Beltway mover stuck in the outback. The scientists themselves seemed supremely arrogant. When the Center went defunct, Hopkins, as head of the weapons program, and Stillman, as intelligence chief, tried persuading several group leaders to hire Trulock but found no takers.

Trulock believed he was promised a job as Stillman's deputy but found that the job had been given to Terry Hawkins instead. Trulock once clashed mightily with Hawkins. "We need scientists, not social scientists," Hawkins shouted at Trulock. Trulock denied any heated exchange. "Hawkins and I never had a cross word," he said.

Trulock quickly managed to get involved in a large, Washington-based study of the Soviets' nuclear capability and began commuting to the only place that felt like home, a town he called "the most powerful city in the world." For his work on the project, he received the Intelligence Community Seal Medallion from CIA Director James Woolsey. Trulock put in for a change-of-station, citing personal reasons that included better care for his ailing wife. He left New Mexico for good in 1993 to accept an intelligence job at Energy Department headquarters.

Trulock carried more than bad memories from Los Alamos. He had listened to the tales of scientists traveling to China and Russia by the hundreds and saw an unguarded gleam in their eyes when they returned.

"They came back looking like they just had a lap dance in a strip club," he would say later.

A number of scientists at Los Alamos were leery of the developing coziness with the Russians, and Trulock was said to share their skepticism. He reportedly commented at one point that only a fool would assume the Cold War was really over.

But Trulock knew the U.S.-Russia exchanges were a kind of sacred scientific glasnost blessed by everyone from Congress to the State Department to the White House. They were saving the world by securing Russian nuclear bombs and plutonium. The whole relationship was politically off-limits to Trulock's counterintelligence operation.

But the Sino-U.S. exchanges weren't. They had no heavyweight political cover. And Trulock already was suspicious of the chuminess of Stillman and Hawkins with Chinese weaponeers. He would hunt for spies in the Chinese exchanges, rather than the Russian visits, he said, "because we could."

Trulock hardly was alone in his suspicions. They were shared by Bobby Henson, a former hydrogen-bomb designer working in Los Alamos's intel group. The two men had strong personalities. Together, Trulock and Henson reinforced each other's beliefs in a way that steered events that summer in 1995.

Beijing's bombs were something of an obsession for Henson. The round-faced physicist was a pit bull—short, compact, tenacious, unpredictable. He grew up in Teague, a town of 3,146 on the Texas plains. He hardly knew his mother, who had died when he was a boy. His father was an auto mechanic, moving from garage to garage and finally setting up his own shop. Henson watched his dad, eager to learn the inner workings of engines. He graduated from the local high school in 1956 with no clear idea of what to do with himself. Engineering, either petroleum or electrical, was said to be the best thing to study, so off he went to Texas A&M. A quiet Taiwanese student named Wen Ho Lee was in the Aggie engineering program at the same time, but the two did not meet until years later, working in the same division at Los Alamos.

A professor liked Henson's spirit and his toughness, and steered him toward a physics Ph.D. Henson eagerly went off to California one summer to work on nuclear-reactor design for General Atomics in San Diego. The company was heavily staffed by Los Alamos scientists, some of them former weaponeers who saw promise in the fair-haired Texan. They prodded him to apply at the lab and hinted that his application would find a warm reception. It did, and Henson went straight behind the fence into designing thermonuclear secondaries.

By 1995, Henson was balding but as intense as ever. He had a temper that could flash at a moment's notice. He said exactly what he thought and didn't worry about hurt feelings.

Henson's fascination with the Chinese program had begun in 1967, when a mentor at Los Alamos asked him to study China's first bomb, detonated with much fanfare three years earlier. It was a large ball of uranium, a starter bomb that made China a nuclear power. Henson analyzed the radioactive fallout from the test, gathered by Air Force planes secretly flying the borders of China. Full-scale models of foreign bombs had been mocked up from little more than fall-out data and intuition.

Henson went on to scrutinize each of China's forty-five known nuclear tests. Beijing had never built small warheads, the kind the Americans had mastered in principle by 1958. China's military leaders were famous for boasting that when it came to nuclear deterrence, crude bombs were just as effective as sophisticated ones. The Chinese warheads remained large and heavy.

The subterranean shockwaves created by China's tests in 1992 and later, recorded as wiggling lines on seismographs around the world, showed some of the explosions were getting quite small, producing a lower "yield," as the bomb designers called it. To Henson, this meant that China was learning how to build smaller primaries. And that was not good news. When it came to primaries, smaller was better. A more compact warhead meant more warheads per missile. A lighter warhead lent itself to a lighter, longer-range missile with solid fuel, allowing greater mobility. A launch submarine could patrol farther from the enemy's coast, safe in deep waters. A truck-mounted launcher might travel every night to a new hiding place deep in China's interior. Both would be harder for U.S. surveillance satellites to track, thus harder for U.S. missiles to target and destroy. Smaller and lighter therefore meant China's nuclear missiles would be far likelier to survive an attack, get off the ground, and strike back at multiple targets. The majority of China's long-range missile targets were thought to be U.S. cities.

For the September 25, 1992, test, Henson noticed, Chinese scientists used a horizontal tunnel for the first time since 1980 and ran an unusually large set of fiber-optic cables out of its entrance. That implied the bomb or test device was surrounded by an extraordinary number of sensors; it was heavily "instrumented," in weapons lingo. Something unusual was going on. The yield ended up at just a few kilotons. All the available evidence, in Henson's eyes, suggested that the Chinese had made a jump to smaller H-bombs. "They quit driving a Model T and started driving a Corvette," he said later. The question was, how did China make the leap? Could it build such a hotrod? Anyone could design a clumsy leviathan that required an oversized bomber or missile for delivery, but creating something small and elegant ("technically sweet," as Robert Oppenheimer had said), that took skill. American weaponeers were the best in the world, and it had taken them many years to perfect miniaturized primaries. Stillman and Hawkins might have been convinced the Chinese were great weaponeers, but in Henson's eyes, there was no way the Chinese were good enough to develop small primaries so suddenly. They had to have stolen American design secrets.

If secrets were slipping away, Henson thought, you didn't have to look far to see how it could happen. He had never been a fan of the back-and-forth visits between the U.S. and Chinese weapons scientists. He thought everyone was freelancing angles, working contacts. Los Alamos scientists, it was said, could best be described as "3,000 entrepreneurs linked by a common janitorial service." Chinese visits to the three U.S. nuclear labs had swelled in the early 1990s to 500 a year.

The cross-Pacific visits provided too much opportunity for mischief, for inadvertent disclosures, Henson feared. He already had complained about the Chinese visits, but to no avail. He concluded that no one at Los Alamos wanted to hear about spies, especially not lab directors.

"It's all out of control," Henson grumbled.

In the summer of 1994, he walked over to the lab's Physics Auditorium one afternoon to hear a talk by Chinese theoretical physicist Sun Cheng Wei. Sun was an explosives expert; he worked on nuclear primaries. Henson listened intently as Sun reviewed his country's nuclear-weapons program. He was gesturing with his hands, forming a large round shape in the air. For decades, Sun said, China's scientists had created ball-shaped primaries. Then Sun shifted his hands much closer, fashioning a different geometry. "But these last few years," he said, "we've just been working at these watermelons."

In his chair in the small auditorium, Henson sat bolt upright. Sun had not only spilled the secrets of the Chinese program, but he had blurted out one of the secrets of U.S. thermonuclear warheads as well. His head swimming, Henson wondered if there was some way to have Sun's speech retroactively classified. But he knew his colleagues would never risk disturbing their lab-to-lab visits by reporting up the chain of command that a Chinese scientist in a very public speech—the room was full of uncleared people, even wives with baby strollers—had announced the very secret of miniaturizing nuclear warheads.

The "secret" was fairly obvious to many people outside government who studied nuclear weapons. But it was classified Restricted Data nonetheless. Sun's speech suggested Henson's suspicions were on track, that the Chinese tests starting in 1992 were aimed at perfecting an aspherical primary. In a few months, the last piece of Henson's puzzle would fall into place.

In January 1995, Henson was helping out Trulock's intelligence analysts in NN-30 when he got word that a classified cable was waiting for him in the office's highly secure walk-in vault. The guard chatted amiably as Henson signed in. Henson walked inside alone to a document bin. Like several documents in the vault, the top cable was edged in blue, denoting "Sensitive Compartmented Information" that came from human spies. Everyone in NN-30 had a high-level security clearance, but only a few specialists were allowed to read blue-border reports.

Henson began reading. The cable did not identify the source of the information—no gender, not even a code name—all to protect a valuable spy.

The spy was a Chinese nuclear expert who had been recruited years earlier by U.S. intelligence agents. The bomb tested in September 1992, the spy confirmed, was indeed miniaturized and used a hollow plutonium core in the shape of a watermelon. The primary—the oblong plutonium shell wrapped in high explosives—was about as wide as a soccer ball. A follow-up test used a similar core surrounded by insensitive high explosives. Both tests detonated as predicted.

Henson could hardly believe it. It had taken American scientists more than a dozen tests to make really small primaries work. But to succeed with the more difficult insensitive high explosives as well on the first try? No way. Not without help from the United States. He had them dead to rights. Henson put the folder back together and signed out, not saying a word to the guard. He walked quickly into the office of Larry Booth, a Los Alamos intelligence analyst also on loan to DOE. Booth shared his office when Henson was in town. Booth's side was neat as a pin; Henson's a ziggurat of papers.

"We got to talk serious," Henson said. He told Booth what he'd read. Booth wanted to see for himself. They went back to the vault and Henson showed him. "This stinks like doo-doo," Henson said. "So. Do we tell anybody?"

News of the Chinese stealing American bomb secrets was sure to be unwelcome at Los Alamos. The two men believed it was espionage, but they couldn't be certain. If they reported it, there might be recriminations. Booth settled the issue. "I think we have to report it. I don't think we have a choice."

Henson agreed. The Texan always enjoyed a good fight. Perhaps now the DOE and Los Alamos would see the error of unfettered contact with the Chinese.

The two scientists wrote up their report and printed it out on paper edged in red and black stripes, denoting the classification Special Intelligence. In April, they went to see Trulock. "Hell, yes, I want to hear this," he said.

The implications were too serious for Trulock to rely on Henson's shoot-from-the-hip assessment. Trulock wanted another expert opinion. He assigned Henson and Booth a third partner, John Richter, a big, blustery Los Alamos physicist—another Texan. He was known at the lab as the king of primaries, the "guru of gurus" on the subject of plutonium explosives, as Trulock said.

————————

Richter had been in the business for thirty-seven years. As a young man, his student deferment had kept him out of the fighting in Korea. No sooner was the ink dry on his University of Texas doctorate than Richter had signed on with Los Alamos as penance for missing the war. The late summer of 1958 was a frenzied time. In just two months, the United States and the Soviet Union would enter into a moratorium on nuclear testing that, so far as anyone knew, could last forever. It might be the very last chance to tinker with the bombs and warheads, or to create some new ones before the designs were frozen forever. Los Alamos's designers had no time to tutor Richter, so he plunged into learning the lab's weapons codes.

By 1961, the moratorium was over, and within a year Richter tested his first nuclear weapon, a modified version of the W33, a warhead packed into a 155mm artillery shell. He went on to play a role in designing more than forty experimental nuclear explosives. Trulock was fond of saying that if Richter were a country, he would come in fourth in terms of testing experience. Richter had a penchant for advanced designs that employed unusual shapes and materials to push weapons in new directions. Many other designers worked on incremental improvements, but Richter "was the lord on high of everything else, the oddball designs," as he himself described it. "I did all these crazy things, and they even paid me."

Other weaponeers came and went. But Richter loved living in Los Alamos, a half-hour drive from his cherished Santa Fe Opera. By the late 1970s, he was leading the Los Alamos scientists who invented primaries. He was the group's institutional memory, the graybeard who knew all the tricks, what had succeeded or failed and, most importantly, why.

Called to Washington in May 1995, Richter went straightaway to the vault holding the blue-bordered cable that had inspired Henson to cry espionage. "It was very sensitive HUMINT [human intelligence]," Richter said later. "If it got back to the originating country, they could trace it back to the source and he'd be gone." Typical of intel, the spy's report was vague, like "looking through a keyhole with a piece of handkerchief covering the opening."

Richter saw immediately that China's September 25, 1992, test had a low yield that suggested its scientists were testing only the primary. The "soccer ball" statement got his attention. It was a pretty close description for the width of the Komodo. Richter had supervised the Komodo's designer, Ralph Douglas Johnson, and knew the years of tweaking that went into its design. He also knew Johnson had inherited thirty years of weapons refinements, a whole generation of nuclear tests. The odds of the Chinese nailing such a weapon in one shot were slender. Still, Richter wasn't certain the Chinese success signified espionage. But who was ever sure in this game?

On May 25, Richter, Henson, and Booth signed a new analysis memo to

Trulock. In their judgment, it was probably espionage, and likely involved the W88. "When they said it's the primary for the most modern weapon in our arsenal, I said, 'Oh shit,'" Trulock recalled.

The three scientists were used to the world of intelligence, where reports were bandied about by fellow analysts before gathering dust in a safe. None of the three expected what would happen next.

Trulock pounced on the report. Within days, he was telling Bruno and others its conclusion of probable spying as though it were fact. The man who had supposedly wished for one good spy case had found one. Now all he had to do was find the spy. Soon, he and subordinates in NN-30 were sitting in an office, batting around the names of potential suspects. Someone jotted down the names. Years later, a U.S. Department of Justice review team headed by federal prosecutor Randy Bellows would find the handwritten list, dated June 6. No one would own up to it, no one could seem to recognize the handwriting. But Sylvia and Wen Ho Lee were there, listed as "Li/Lee/Le + wife," as was Peter Lee, a former Los Alamos scientist who was quietly being investigated for suspicion of espionage.

Trulock and Bruno would deny that they had been in the room when any suspect list was made. Henson was there, though he said he didn't participate in naming suspects. He was certain Bruno was present, as well as Trulock, Larry Booth, NN-30 staffers Carl Henry of Los Alamos, and Fred Wettering on loan from the CIA. Justice Department investigators could not discern what caused the Lees to be listed at that early date. Regardless of the rationale, the Lees' names were on a suspect list weeks before the scientific working group began debating whether espionage had ever taken place. The start of an investigation was still months away. The handwritten list also included non-Chinese names. Among these, Henson said, were Los Alamos's Danny Stillman and Terry Hawkins.

With the Henson-Booth-Richter analysis in hand, Trulock was propelled on a mission. He began warning people in the DOE and FBI of "potential espionage involving nuclear weapons data." Among the first he warned was John Lewis, the FBI deputy assistant director in charge of the National Security Division. A few days later, Trulock was on a flight to New Mexico for a preliminary briefing with Los Alamos director Sig Hecker.

"It was pretty clear that he was convinced there was Chinese espionage," Hecker said of his meeting with Trulock. "And the rest of the case was to try to demonstrate we're infiltrated by Chinese spies."

Trulock asked for experts to help in the analysis and was steered to Michael Henderson, a veteran primary designer at Los Alamos who enjoyed a reputation as an even-handed leader, the kind of scientist who was skilled at drawing consensus from a pack of fellow scientists.

The same day, June 28, Bruno issued a handwritten proposal for an "administrative inquiry"—an AI, for short—which is a non-FBI survey of evidence that espionage indeed has occurred.

Bruno's memo called for the creation of the scientific working group to "assist in the development of a logical investigative effort." The scientists would chart the evolution of the W88 design "allegedly copied by the PRC." They would identify documents containing the compromised warhead data and list lab staff who worked on the weapon or had access to the data. Lastly, they would brief the FBI and get clearance to launch the administrative inquiry. In the end, the scientists weren't allowed to perform most of these tasks.

Bruno also wrote: "An initial consideration will be to identify those US citizens, of Chinese heritage, who worked directly or peripherally with the design development. (NOTE: This is a logical starting point based upon the Intelligence Community's evaluation that the PRC targets and utilizes ethnic Chinese for espionage rather than persons of non-Chinese origin.)"

His statement suggested that Chinese Americans would be a focus right from the beginning.

The Bellows team later concluded that Bruno's memo "does not support an allegation of racial bias" partly because the "proposal was never implemented" and because Bruno "was simply acknowledging the fact that the PRC specifically targets ethnic Chinese for espionage purposes. . . . consistent with the view of veteran FCI [foreign counterintelligence investigators.]"

But experts in Chinese intelligence methodology say the Chinese target not only ethnic Chinese but anyone with access to science and technology information. Secondly, according to former FBI China counterintelligence analyst Paul D. Moore, PRC targeting of ethnic Chinese does not translate into a judgment that ethnic Chinese are more likely to spy for China and so does not justify targeting of Chinese Americans as potential suspects solely because of their ethnicity.

On July 5, Lee's name came up again. In a secure-telephone conversation with NN-30, a Livermore counterintelligence official identified four people who were "relevant to compromises to the PRC," according to the Bellows report. Lee apparently was included because of his cameo appearance in the Tiger Trap investigation.

Bruno maintains that he never heard Lee's name until six months later.

On July 10, the working group got started. Analysts from NN-30 and the CIA were present. But it was not, however, the broad scientific panel of weaponeers described in Bruno's plan. Henderson and many of the invited designers and engineers from Los Alamos, Livermore, and Sandia had yet to arrive.

Trulock asked the partial panel to "evaluate the available intelligence to determine whether they could eliminate espionage as a probable source for the advancement in the Chinese nuclear weapons program," according to the Bellows review. The analysts who dominated the panel's first meeting soon realized they needed more experts in nuclear-weapons design and development. They had a lot of work to do before ruling espionage in or out.

Trulock nonetheless began spreading the word in intelligence circles: His boys had figured out that the Chinese had stolen the W88. Trulock wanted people to know he was onto something big. Several NN-30 staffers thought it was premature to sound the alarm outside of DOE. Trulock had little grasp of the technical details. He was the kind of man who could mistake a possibility for a certainty.

"One of the biggest fears in the office was, 'Oh my God, did Trulock go down to the White House and report that? He doesn't know what he's talking about!' " Richter said later.

Even before the scientific panel began its debate in earnest, "Trulock grabs the ball and says, 'I'm going for a touchdown, screw you guys,' " Henson recalled.

Trulock's first briefings that summer were to Charles Curtis, the undersecretary of energy, and to Energy Secretary Hazel O'Leary. Curtis recognized the seriousness of the matter immediately. If the Chinese had pilfered secrets out of the weapons labs, that was a problem of astounding proportion.

O'Leary passed word to White House Chief of Staff Leon Panetta, and Curtis phoned CIA Director John Deutch.

Back in NN-30, Henderson took charge of a fuller, blue-ribbon panel. The Los Alamos contingent—Henson, Booth, Richter, and Henry—now were joined by Reid Worlton, a veteran bomb physicist from the lab. Sandia sent George Kiminiak. Longtime primary designer Bill Quirk led a group from Lawrence Livermore. More experts from the CIA and the Pentagon's Defense Intelligence Agency rounded out the panel.

Henson was confident that his analysis would be compelling to anyone.

He'd sold Booth and Richter; the rest would be as easily persuaded. But as the full working group assembled under Henderson, he began to learn he was wrong.

Starting in late July, the weapons designers from the laboratories began to catch up with the NN-30 analysts in their understanding of the intelligence reports. As a result, the analysts lost the information advantage that had given them influence over the panel's early deliberations. A number of weapons designers and the CIA's analysts began making noises about indigenous development—perhaps the Chinese could make the jump to smaller, more refined primaries on their own or with help from the Russians. Soon, a majority of the panel was leaning toward rejecting the conclusion of espionage, and some of this majority came from Henson's own lab.

Suddenly, the arguments of Henson and his fellow NN-30 analysts got a boost from an unexpected quarter—the Chinese themselves.

Henry caught wind of intriguing new data over at the CIA. He and the other DOE analysts were not allowed to tell the panel of its existence, however, unless they cleared it with the CIA first. Trulock took the matter up with Curtis, who called Deutch. It was a huge trove of documents, and the story behind it was so strange that no one at the agency knew what to make of it.

Earlier in 1995, a middle-aged Chinese man who claimed to be a missile expert carried an armload of documents into the offices of Taiwan's internal-security service. In spy parlance, the man was known as a "walk-in" defector—an unknown who presented himself without invitation. Tucked in his stack was a twenty-page gem apparently prepared for the PRC's First Ministry of Machine Building, home to the designers and builders of China's missile forces. Dated 1988, the memo laid out in text, diagrams, and graphs the characteristics of both Chinese and U.S. weapons. It was a five-year strategic plan for China's future missile developments and suggested that U.S. weapons—especially the W88—were the standard against which China's new missiles and warheads should be measured. There were text descriptions and crude hand sketches of the cone-shaped reentry vehicles for a long list of U.S. strategic weapons: the W88, the W87, the W78, the W76, the W62, and the W56—the warheads of the Trident, MX, and Minuteman ICBMs—as well as the W80 cruise-missile warhead.

Taiwanese leaders passed the defector and the documents to the CIA, stationed in the American Institute in Taiwan, the organization that served as the informal U.S. embassy in Taipei.

The defector repeatedly went back to China for more documents, bringing more than seven hundred in all, totaling thirteen thousand pages. The CIA flew a team to Taiwan to begin translating. Their first effort was glancing—titles primarily, plus the most intriguing documents on U.S. nuclear weapons.

The walk-in defector failed a CIA polygraph, specifically on the question of whether he was operating for a foreign intelligence agency. And the agency noted that the quality of his material seemed to decline on subsequent trips from China. Intelligence agents flew him to America, where the FBI and the CIA were never quite sure what to make of him and his stash of documents, whether he was a true defector or a controlled agent sent to spread disinformation. Worse yet, he was difficult to handle, at one point running off to New Orleans in pursuit of a woman.

The agency suspected the walk-in could be a dangle, a pawn used by Chinese intelligence to manipulate the Americans. Everyone had a theory to explain why, if he were a dangle, Beijing might have sent the documents—to intimidate Taiwan, to dissuade the United States from entering a future conflict on Taiwan's side, to feed misinformation to the CIA, or to divert attention from a more valuable mole still in place. Perhaps it was just somebody's mistake. Richter drafted a white paper suggesting that China wanted to know whether its intelligence was correct. China supplied its best information on nuclear design, then sat back to watch for a reaction that would confirm its accuracy. It was "reverse intel."

No one knew. Regardless, the walk-in documents were clearly full of classified U.S. information. China's motives seemed irrelevant.

Several of the working group scientists went to Langley and examined a number of long boxes of the Chinese papers. "It was a whole pisspot full of documents," Henson said, a handful of reports on nuclear weapons buried in reams of missile documents.

The analysts seized on the walk-in documents as reinforcement of their belief that espionage had occurred. They feared the documents might represent just a fraction of what the Chinese had learned about the W88.

But in coming weeks, as the larger panel reviewed the translations, several panelists were far from certain that Henson's intelligence and the walk-in material bore any relationship to one another. Details on the range and accuracy of U.S. missiles, for example, while technically classified, were widely available and could even be downloaded from the Web site of the Federation of American Scientists in Washington. The Federation researchers had sifted through congressional records to glean their information, and there was no reason the Chinese could not do the same.

Nor were the panelists especially bothered by the sketches of U.S. reentry vehicles. Photographs of several of the reentry vehicles were widely published.

Others had been depicted in drawings of missiles—the Trident, for example—released by defense contractors.

Still, the description of the W88 was intriguing. The text correctly said the primary was "two-point aspherical" and the secondary was spherical. A diagram accurately depicted the primary forward and the secondary aft—an arrangement found in the W88 and a few other U.S. weapons. The diameter of the radiation case around the primary was correct at 230 millimeters, or about nine inches. The rad case diameter around the secondary was accurately listed as 344 mm, or about 14 inches. The Chinese had the warhead's weight nailed, as well as its "stay-out zones," areas within the reentry vehicle that the manufacturer was to keep free of obstruction.

With the walk-in document in hand, Trulock's panel of "wise men"came together in mid-August and early September to hammer out a formal assessment in the secure conference room. China's scientists clearly had designed miniaturized primaries. But how?

"Everyone agreed there had been some hanky-panky," said Henderson, the panel chairman.

Exactly what role espionage played in China's advances was hidden in the ambiguities of the intelligence. The scientists and Trulock's intel analysts rushed in to fill the void. "You get three pieces of a thousand-piece puzzle and try to figure out what it is," one panelist said. "People read in their own prejudices."

———————

The Henson school of thought argued for a master spy, a Cold War mole sharing blueprints with the Chinese.

On the opposite end of the spectrum, Livermore's Bill Quirk became spokesman for the idea that China's new warhead was largely indigenous. Spying was of some help. But the Chinese could draw on a talent pool of more than one billion. Their scientists were skilled. And the secret to miniaturized warheads was obvious—change the shape of the primary. If American scientists could invent miniaturized warheads in the 1950s, why couldn't the Chinese do it in the 1990s?

Besides, the Chinese didn't abruptly come up with the watermelon idea just in time for their breakthrough test in 1992. All during the semiofficial lab-to-lab visits of the 1980s, Chinese designers had peppered the Americans with questions about two-point detonation systems.

A third camp wondered how the Americans had answered those questions. These scientists suggested China had garnered nuclear secrets from multiple sources over multiple years and used them to guide its weapons-design effort. Tiger Trap's Min alone could very well have given up the idea of two-point detonation. Tips from other Americans—as well as the Russians and open-source literature—could have steered the Chinese down the most fruitful paths, saving time and nuclear tests.

Henderson tallied their comments in a list of bullets. China appeared to be pursuing a "W88-like aspheric primary." And espionage had been of "material assistance." But China could have arrived at new warhead designs largely on its own. And there was no evidence that its scientists had made an exact copy of the W88.

Henson grew angry. His view was represented by just one bullet, and only weakly.

The rest of the panel realized that China had acquired at least some classified numbers—the weight, shapes, and outside diameters of W88 components. But that was all. No detailed diagrams of the innards, the real nuts and bolts of the bomb.

Henson couldn't believe what he was hearing. Everyone in the room—even his Los Alamos colleagues—seemed to be lining up against him, even if they couched it diplomatically. He stood up and cursed every member of the panel. "Every one of you knows they stole this," Henson seethed. "To say otherwise is stupid and ignorant. And, in my opinion, it is unpatriotic."

An uncomfortable hush fell over the room. Scientists fidgeted and peered at their legal pads. Henson launched into a harangue. He accused the panel of engaging in sophistic naïveté that had no place in intel analysis. Henson's tone was contemptuous. He didn't give a damn. Sure, it was theoretically possible for the Chinese to make a huge leap to compact H-bombs, Henson said. But what mattered was probabilities—was such a leap likelier than not? "If you're going to play analyst, you have to talk probabilities," he said. Saying the Chinese had done this on their own, Henson argued, was as ludicrous as saying the space shuttle was going to crash that moment into the conference room.

Henderson, the chairman, rose to calm the waters and defend the panel's deliberations. Henson was having none of it. He jabbed a finger at Henderson. "You come out with your report," he said. "I'll write a dissent and tell the truth."

The Los Alamos contingent felt compelled to appease Henson. Richter, Booth, and Worlton had all worked alongside him. One by one, they announced they wanted more time before voting on a panel-wide consensus. Henderson was disappointed. "We almost had an agreement here," he said. "All right. Let's take a breather and come back at it."

The panel took a break. Henson's face was crimson. He hustled Booth off to Trulock's office. Once inside, Henson began yelling again.

"Okay. Don't worry," Trulock said. "I'll check into this." The intel chief went off in search of Henderson and pulled him aside. He proposed a cooling-off period, delaying the vote for another meeting. Henderson agreed. They would pick up where they left off later.

Back in his office, Trulock was wearing a Cheshire cat grin when Henson and Booth showed up again in the doorway. "I'll take care of it," he told them. Booth offered to sway Richter and Worlton toward a conclusion of espionage. Trulock waved him off. Don't bother, he said. "Henderson can bring his bullet list in here. The next time I go to the bathroom, I'll be sure to take it along and use it on my ass." Trulock later denied making this statement.

The weaponeers on the expert panel had introduced ambiguity and nuance that undermined Henson's original claim that China had stolen the W88 design. But Trulock never called the panel back together for a formal meeting to take a vote. The scientists went home to their laboratories. Trulock's analysts remained in Washington and began crafting a message closer to the original conclusion of espionage, according to Bellows's later investigation. All they had to do was sell the FBI on Bruno's administrative inquiry.

Trulock and his analysts had now shifted the pertinent question again. Earlier, it had gone from "Was espionage involved?" to "Was the W88 lost?" Now the answer was being contorted and a new question would be pursued: "Who gave it away?"

– 11 –

A Shallow Pool

*N*otra Trulock took the list of nine bullets produced by his working meeting and locked it in a safe. It didn't line up with his own belief that out-of-control visits between Los Alamos scientists and their Chinese counterparts had led to spilled secrets. To the contrary, the panel's assessment (with Henson dissenting) was that China may have made the breakthrough to small primaries on its own, with some help from espionage and open-source information.

Trulock then began a series of briefings that the Bellows team later described as misleading. According to Bellows, Trulock substituted his personal opinion—that China had stolen the design of the W88—for the panel's conclusions. Trulock played a key role in promoting the espionage theory, and not for the last time.

Soon after the final meeting of the experts, Trulock sent a letter to the FBI, confirming that Bruno would launch his administrative inquiry, known in the business as an AI. Bruno's unwritten personal goal was to produce a finding that would force the FBI to take over. His feeling was, "If they won't open a case on it, then I'll drag them into it." Bruno said he never saw the bullets. His understanding of the case came directly from Trulock, who said the panel had concluded that China had stolen "the concepts, the essential information of the W88 design." It was a false predicate for an investigation, Bellows would report, and it would send investigators off searching for a spy and a "crime which was never established to have occurred."

On October 31, 1995, Trulock, Bruno, and Larry Booth, one of Trulock's analysts from the working group briefed the FBI on their belief in the apparent theft of the W88. Among the agents who gathered in the basement offices of NN-30 was T. Van Magers, a China specialist out of Tampa who would help Bruno with his inquiry. David Lieberman, the counterintelligence agent in Santa Fe investigating Wen Ho Lee and the "Hug" incident, was also flown in for the briefing. Trulock led the briefing. Booth put a poster up on the wall, with parallel time lines tracking similar development of Chinese and U.S. nuclear weapons. The point was that China had gotten to the small primary in fewer tests than the United States. The implication was espionage. "The timeline looked good," Bruno remembered. "The presentation Booth gave made complete logic. There weren't any holes in it."

Trulock did not mention the working group's list of bullets and its conclusion that the Chinese advances may have occurred indigenously, and that there was no evidence that China had built a copy of the W88. Instead, he left the impression that the group had come to the unanimous assessment that China's advances were the direct result of espionage. The DOE briefers were "misrepresenting their own assessment as the working group's conclusion," the Bellows team later wrote. It would be years before the FBI realized it had been misled—a situation that could have been avoided had the bureau accepted an invitation to send a representative to the working group's earlier deliberations.

The FBI made another critical mistake by not immediately taking jurisdiction of the investigation after the October 31 briefing. The head of intelligence for the Energy Department had just reported a case of nuclear espionage, which should have set off a legal trip wire in the bureau, as Bellows later concluded. Catching spies was by federal law the exclusive responsibility of the FBI. Had the FBI taken the case immediately, the debacle that followed might have been avoided.

During the briefing, Bruno showed the FBI his own viewgraphs and explained how he would conduct his "paper check" investigation. The plan was loaded with problematic assumptions, beginning with the notion that a spy had given away the secrets of W88. Perhaps the most striking was the assumption that the loss probably occurred as a result of the interactions between U.S. and Chinese nuclear-weapons scientists. There was nothing in the walk-in document to suggest that, but the hypothesis dovetailed neatly with the views of Trulock and Henson, who distrusted the back-and-forth visits.

Bruno said he would compile lists of employees of U.S. nuclear-weapons facilities who had access to W88 information and had either traveled to China or mingled with Chinese delegations visiting the United States. Bruno had been taught in counterintelligence classes that China went after U.S. secrets through human interaction, rather than stealing documents in the middle of the night. It was the Chinese modus operandi. Instead of bribery or blackmail, the Chinese would invite an American scientist to dinner in Beijing, "get him in a room, and say, 'Oh, we've got a professor here who wants to ask you something,' and then there's a battery of people asking questions.

"If you're from the homeland, these guys will say, we found your grandmother lives on the third floor of the apartment building. We can get her on the first floor," producing a profound sense of obligation in the visiting scientist. It was Bruno who picked the name "Kindred Spirit" for the investigation. He thought the Chinese would reach out to U.S. scientists with sympathy for China, people who felt "a kindred spirit with a particular regime." He would later deny he was thinking specifically of Chinese Americans.

Bruno focused on the lab-to-lab visits for another reason—he didn't know what else to do. "I'm looking at a cold case"—any loss of secrets was at least eight years old—"So I figure the only shot I got is the personal interactions."

What he *didn't* do was examine the original intelligence evidence, establish exactly what had been compromised, and search out documents containing that information. So Bruno was off to find a suspect without having investigated the crime.

To prevent leaks, Bruno would not conduct any interviews. By his account, he told the FBI that he would not be searching for clues at the Pentagon or in the plants of defense contractors involved in manufacturing the W88 reentry vehicles. "That's outside my sandbox," he said. As he remembered it, there were no objections. For Bruno and the FBI, it was a critical error.

As it turned out, after limiting the inquiry to DOE sites, Bruno avoided DOE headquarters out of fear, he said, that any hint of an investigation would spread quickly there. He also skipped two important production facilities, the Rocky Flats plant in Colorado, where plutonium was shaped for weapons primaries, and the Pantex plant in Texas, where weapons were assembled. Although W88 design information was available at both sites, there had been no contact with the Chinese, so Bruno wrote them off. That left the three nuclear-weapons design labs, Lawrence Livermore, Los Alamos, and Sandia. Sandia was eliminated when Bruno was told Sandia had received a DOE exemption from keeping records of foreign travel, even though a Sandia official told the investigator that the lab had all the design information for the W88 and was even a repository for design documents. This narrow focus was "a major failure," the Bellows team later concluded.

Kindred Spirit would be the biggest case of Bruno's twenty-seven years in counterintelligence. Most of his career had been spent with the Air Force in Europe. He saw himself as a "simple man," the first in his family to go to college, a gregarious guy with street smarts. In his off hours he played guitar in a band with his brother and some buddies. He defined counterintelligence as "finding out who's trying to get into our knickers."

In February, Bruno flew to New Mexico with his new partner, Magers. "He's a lawyer, a typical Southern gentleman, and he knows the Chinese target like the back of his hand," Bruno said. They drove to Los Alamos, where, in response to their request for travel records, Vrooman's deputy, Terry Craig, had stacked boxes of paperwork along one wall of an office, practically to the ceiling. Most of the documents were expense account forms, filed by employees seeking reimbursement for travel. It wasn't just China; there were trips to France, Israel, and elsewhere. Bruno and Magers sorted through the pile. So it came to be that of all people in America with some connection to nuclear weapons, the suspects in the W88 case would come only from those whose travel records were stacked in an office in New Mexico one week in February 1996.

The working assumption was that the espionage had occurred between 1984, when the W88 entered the engineering design stage at Los Alamos, and early 1988, when the walk-in documents were dated. Looking for travel to China during those years, Bruno came up with a list of employees from Lawrence Livermore and Los Alamos. The Los Alamos list had 70 names. He later mentioned all of them in his secret report, under the heading, "Identification of Los Alamos National Laboratories Employee Travel to the PRC, 1984–88."

A third of those identified had traveled to China on vacation, including three employees who went as chaperones for the Santa Fe High School band. About forty of the seventy had no access to classified information. Two of them didn't even have security clearances.

Bruno and Magers had also planned to compile a list of lab employees who had spent time with Chinese delegations at the lab. But, unable to find a paper trail, they eliminated that potential group of suspects.

The documents weren't producing too much evidence, but, while standing around talking, Bruno said, he picked up an interesting tip from Vrooman. There was an employee named Sylvia Lee who had acted as a translator and liaison with the Chinese. She put more time and effort into that task than into her regular job and pushed it until she got in trouble with her boss. Maybe Bruno should check her out—and her husband, too. By Bruno's account, this was the first time he had ever heard of the Lees, even though their names were on the informal suspect lists from the previous summer.

Vrooman didn't mention that Sylvia Lee had performed her liaison role with permission of lab management, or that she had been a source for the FBI and the CIA. Bruno knew nothing about this. His partner, Magers, knew about Sylvia Lee's relationship with the FBI, but he didn't say anything about it either.

Vrooman arranged for them to meet with Jean Andrews Stark, the administrative assistant who had helped organize one of the first Chinese visits and who knew Sylvia Lee. Bruno and Magers drove down the hill to Santa Fe and met Stark for coffee at the La Fonda Hotel. For a cover story, they told her that they were doing an analytical study of relationships between the Chinese and U.S. labs. Stark talked for a while, and then said, "But you know, Sylvia Lee interacted with them more than I did."

"She was the hostess with the mostest," Bruno concluded. "She was Miss Volunteer."

Later on, Bruno found a brief FBI memo in Wen Ho Lee's security file, offering a sketchy description of Lee's big security incident, his 1982 phone call to the Tiger Trap suspect in California. It left an impression on Bruno. "I'm Italian, but I don't call John Gotti and say, 'Come on John, I hear the FBI's after you, can I help you?' "

Bruno said he was kept in the dark about the FBI's inquiry into the Hug, Lee's embrace of Chinese weapons administrator Hu Side in 1994.

Vrooman was concerned that his visitors were misunderstanding the widespread distribution of classified warhead documents, so he introduced Bruno and Magers to weapons scientist Bill Anderson, who explained that documentation was scattered across the country at facilities that made various parts of the weapons. The Pentagon and its contractors had copies as well. But the tutorial did nothing to change the scope of the AI, which remained focused on Los Alamos and Lawrence Livermore.

Bruno might have benefited from conversations with more scientists, but he was reluctant to conduct interviews for fear that news of the investigation would spread across the labs. There was, of course, one group of scientists that would have been ideal to interview—the members of the working group, who doubted the W88 had been stolen. Bruno was just a short walk from the offices of the Los Alamos members, but he never interviewed them.

As Bruno and Vrooman talked together at the lab about possible candidates for a "short list" of suspects who would be recommended to the FBI for further investigation Vrooman questioned some of the names, such as an employee who lacked a security clearance or access to the W88. According to Vrooman, Bruno replied that it didn't matter; the Lees were the real suspects and the other names would just fill out the list. Bruno later denied saying that.

Bruno was wary of Vrooman, who had lectured him that the Cold War was over and urged Bruno to look upon the lab-to-lab visits with a more sophisticated worldview. To listen to Vrooman talk, Los Alamos was "Happy Valley," a land where there were never any security problems. Vrooman and Terry Craig's opinion of Bruno was no more charitable. Craig described him as an "over-promoted cop." Vrooman said Bruno was "lost" at Los Alamos, that his work was not "intellectually rigorous."

Bruno went to Lawrence Livermore by himself. Magers pulled out of the case in order to travel to China on FBI business. "It just shows how much importance they [the FBI] placed on this case," Bruno said. Bruno ran into more difficulty in Livermore. An employee who had been asked to search for W88 documents looked in only one vault, ignoring the others scattered across the lab. His arbitrarily limited search mirrored Bruno's own investigation. Then another miscue. Because Bruno incorrectly believed the entire design of the W88 was compromised, he reasoned that the spy had to have access to the blueprints of the warhead. When Bruno discovered that the blueprints had not arrived at Livermore until 1990, at least two years after the compromise, he effectively eliminated Livermore from further investigation. He did not know that only partial details of the W88 were obtained by China, details that could have circulated in Livermore well before the blueprints arrived. As a result of Bruno's misunderstanding, "an entire national laboratory and all its employees were excluded," the Bellows team would later conclude.

Bruno wrote the administrative inquiry report back in Washington. He had written his first draft, naming the Lees as suspects, *before* he searched the travel records at Livermore. His final report was eighty-nine pages long, including four lengthy lists: Employees of Los Alamos and Lawrence Livermore who traveled to China (including the Los Alamos parents who went as band chaperones), and Chinese citizens who visited either of the U.S. labs. In addition there was the short list of suspects, Bruno said, with a few paragraphs about each.

Then Bruno got to the point: The FBI should open an investigation and pay special attention to Wen Ho and Sylvia Lee. He laid out the evidence as he saw it. Both had been to China. Lee had access to W88 data and had gotten involved in the Tiger Trap case. Sylvia Lee had "aggressively" inserted herself into dealings with the Chinese.

Then there was this: In the early 1960s, Sylvia had attended National Taiwan University at the same time as Peter Lee, a former Los Alamos scientist who was, as Bruno was writing his report in 1996, under investigation for espionage. Bruno found this coincidence "profound," especially in light of the fact that Peter Lee and his wife had once lived a few houses away from Wen Ho and Sylvia Lee in White Rock.

Bruno wrote: "It is the opinion of the writer that Wen Ho Lee is the only individual identified during this inquiry who had opportunity, motivation and LEGITIMATE access" to information about the W88.

The report's language was inconsistent, from speculation that the W88 "may have been compromised" to the conclusion that the Chinese had built "almost a total duplicate of the W88 warhead."

The Bellows team review of the AI a few years later was merciless: a "slapdash affair . . . a deeply flawed product . . . a woefully inadequate and cursory investigation . . . poorly written." "The selection and focus on just one suspect (and his wife) was wrong. It is not that Wen Ho Lee should not have been a suspect. It was that Wen Ho Lee should not have been the *only* suspect.

"The AI should have been a *sieve* resulting in the identification of a number of suspects. Instead, it ended up as a *funnel* from which only Wen Ho and Sylvia Lee emerged."

Trulock removed the scientists' bullet list from his safe at least once over the next three years. In May, just before Trulock sent the edited final Administrative Inquiry to the FBI, Deputy Energy Secretary Curtis insisted on a personal briefing by the experts, whom Trulock had dubbed the Kindred Spirit Advisory Group, or KSAG.

The weapons scientists returned to Washington and the NN-30 conference room, where they verified that their bullets were still accurate and prepared slides based on them for the briefing with Curtis.

Curtis received an accurate briefing on the KSAG findings and asked that the FBI be notified. "This accurate briefing, however, never left DOE," the Bellows review team concluded. Instead, the FBI received the AI and its flawed statement that the Chinese apparently had copied the premier warhead of the U.S. nuclear arsenal.

After Bruno delivered his AI to Trulock on May 28, 1996, someone made dramatic editing changes before Trulock forwarded the report to the FBI. "The final report transmitted to the FBI was the product of an editing process that ultimately converted the AI from a broad identification of potential suspects to a virtual indictment of the Lees," the Bellows team concluded. Bruno's AI included a plan for further investigation that Magers had written and sent from Florida. Magers had realized that the W88 information was widespread, so he suggested the FBI widen the scope of the investigation. But before Bruno's report was forwarded to the FBI from Trulock's office, Magers's suggestions for more work were removed, making the AI seem "a more thorough and comprehensive document than it actually was," as the Justice Department later noted.

Other sections disappeared as well. Where Bruno had written, "The investigative team must conduct records reviews etc., at several other locations before this inquiry is concluded," the text was deleted and replaced with "However, based upon a review of all information gathered during this inquiry, Wen Ho Lee and his wife, Sylvia, appear the most logical suspects."

The name of a third Los Alamos employee identified as a logical suspect also disappeared from the report before it was sent to the FBI. The Justice Department later concluded that the name was wrongly removed "to make the case against the Lees look stronger."

Bruno said his short list of suspects had nine names on it, including about three Asian Americans. By the time the Administrative Inquiry reached the FBI, the list had grown to twelve names, half of which were Asian.

According to Notra Trulock, when he turned over the Administrative Inquiry report to the FBI in the summer of 1996, Craig Schmidt, the agent who would oversee the FBI investigation from Washington, said, "It's Wen Ho Lee and we're gonna get him."

Bruno would later say that he was surprised that the FBI would take his "cursory investigation" and launch a criminal investigation of the Lees, ignoring all other suspects or theories. "It was just a stupid Administrative Inquiry," he said.

-12-

Mass-Market Espionage

It was a steady paycheck, not cloak-and-dagger allure, that brought Paul D. Moore into the counterintelligence game. The FBI recruited him right out of a classroom at Georgetown University, where the Jesuit-trained linguist was eking out a living teaching Chinese translation.

The Bureau was scrambling to find Chinese translators. President Nixon and Secretary of State Henry Kissinger had launched the era of Ping-Pong diplomacy, and China was sending missions to the United States and the United Nations. Moore was a ready-made solution to the Bureau's problem. Smart, well educated, he didn't have the kind of liabilities that could delay his security clearance—extensive travel or relatives in China whose treatment might give the PRC too much leverage over an FBI employee.

After a few years as a translator, Moore was drafted in 1975 into what was then called the Intelligence Division as the Bureau's chief China counterintelligence analyst, a position he held for twenty-three years. The very first document he read in his new job depicted Chinese intelligence as almost exclusively using ethnic Chinese as gatherers of information.

The FBI's first China cases, decades before, were called "ship-jumper cases." Chinese nationals appeared to slip into the United States and obtain jobs cooking and washing dishes. The Bureau suspected they were spies. "The question was, are they running an intelligence operation?" Moore said. "Well, no. They just wanted a better job."

In time, however, the FBI discovered genuine Chinese espionage cases. And the spies were almost uniformly ethnic Chinese. Moore and colleagues set out to answer the question of why. It strained reason to believe that Chinese Americans were somehow more inclined than any other group in a polygot society to betray the United States. So what really was going on? The Chinese, for their part, saw to it that he had plenty of data.

When the Carter Administration established normal diplomatic relations with China in 1979, the United States sweetened the deal for China by offering a broad array of exchanges in intelligence, military technology, and science. Instances of Chinese spying on U.S. science and technology skyrocketed into the dozens.

"China doesn't do a lot of intelligence activity in the United States until 1979," Moore said. "And then—boom—they're all over everybody."

The Bureau compared notes with counterintelligence agencies in other countries. "Everybody's having the same problem with China," Moore discovered.

Even decades before 1979, China already had a well-placed mole deep inside the CIA.

Larry Wu-Tai Chin was born in Beijing and educated at a top university. American soldiers allied with the Chinese in World War II selected Chin as a translator and interpreter for the U.S. Army Liaison Office. His facility in English and three Chinese dialects made Chin valuable to the Americans. He saw the job as his ticket to the United States and a chance to become rich. "Larry loved money," said one former FBI official.

His roommate, a physician named Wang Li, was a devout Communist. When in 1948 Chin began translating for the U.S. consulate in Shanghai, Wang introduced him to a Communist official who asked Chin to "help China." As Mao's armies swept China, the consulate moved to Hong Kong and, before long, Chin was being regularly debriefed about his new American friends by Chinese intelligence officers.

In 1951, he was drafted by the U.S. State Department to interrogate Chinese POWs in Korea. On his return to Hong Kong a year later, Chin reportedly fingered for the Chinese exactly which prisoners had cooperated with the Americans. Later he took a job on Okinawa with the Foreign Broadcast Information Service (FBIS), a CIA division that translated foreign broadcasts.

Every other year, the CIA gave him paid leave to return to Hong Kong. According to published reports, Chin used the trips home to detail U.S. intelligence needs to Chinese handlers four times between 1952 and 1961. A professional Chinese intelligence officer named Ou Qiming became his lead contact. When Chin was promoted to an FBIS job in California, the Chinese set him up with a courier in Toronto. Chin was naturalized as a U.S. citizen in 1965.

Within five years, the CIA wanted to promote Chin to FBIS headquarters in Arlington, Virginia. To get the necessary security clearance, he first had to pass a polygraph examination. He admitted a number of vulnerabilities—he gambled and was a bit of a ladies' man—but nonetheless passed the polygraph and won a top-secret clearance and access to CIA headquarters.

His new job made Chin privy to classified reports about China from the CIA, the Defense Department, and the State Department. He could monitor the flurry of diplomatic and military cables coming out of China and discuss them with U.S. intelligence analysts. Chin was especially useful to the agency's covert arm. The Directorate of Operations asked Chin to translate into English reports from spies in China, as well as their instructions from U.S. case officers into Chinese. Chin had access to National Intelligence Estimates on China and the rest of Asia. These analyzed spy reports, signals intercepts, and satellite surveillance, and revealed much about American intelligence gathering.

Chin was delighted to come upon a classified memo in which President Nixon notified Congress in the early 1970s of secret plans to reestablish relations with China. Chin later wrote that when he saw the memo he was "overjoyed" and wanted to be sure the Cultural Revolution didn't lead China to dismiss the overture as an "imperialist trick." Chin secreted the document in his shirt, took it home, photographed it, and the next morning slipped the document back into place. Two days later, he handed the film to his courier at a Toronto shopping mall. During the 1970s, Chin kept his handlers apprised of the Nixon-Kissinger team's negotiating positions. For all this, the Chinese paid Chin handsomely.

Chin retired from the CIA in January 1981 and was awarded one of the agency's highest medals for distinguished service. The Chinese, likewise, honored him that summer at a secret banquet, during which top intelligence officials gave him $50,000 and the honorary rank of deputy bureau chief in intelligence.

The same year, a clever CIA operation aimed at penetrating China's Ministry of State Security (MSS) paid off. A senior Chinese intelligence officer, Yu Qiangsheng, identified Chin as a Chinese mole to a spy catcher at the CIA. Yu carried the MSS file on Chin out of China in his 1985 defection to the United States.

On November 2, 1985, three FBI agents conducted an interrogation of Chin. It was the counterintelligence version of a high-stakes poker game, the FBI laying out card after card to call Chin's bluff.

They showed him photographs of senior Chinese intelligence officials. He denied knowing any of them.

Then, Special Agent Mark Johnson read a statement to him: "On February 4, 1982, you took off from JFK airport. You arrived in Beijing on February 6 and stayed at the Qianmen Hotel, Room 533. There was a dinner in your honor, and a presentation making you a Deputy Bureau Chief in the Ministry of Public Security."

"Are you serious?" Chin asked.

"Very serious," Johnson said. "Do you know a Ou Qiming?"

"No," Chin replied.

"On May 31, 1983, you took a flight from Dulles, arriving in Hong Kong on June 1. You met with Ou Qiming on June 3, 5 and 14, and later on September 17. You told him you had a fight with your wife, and that she had sworn out an assault complaint against you."

The poker game was over. "Only Ou would know that," Chin said.

He offered to become a double agent against China. The agents asked for details of his past spying as a measure of his future value. Chin talked of what he had done for more than an hour. The FBI rejected using him as a double and arrested him.

During his trial in early 1985, Chin admitted to giving secrets to China but said he did it with pure motives, to bring China and the United States closer together. He was convicted of espionage, conspiracy, and tax evasion. On February 20, he asked a jail guard for a plastic bag to tidy up his cell. Later, alone, he pulled the bag over his head, tied it around his neck with a shoelace, and asphyxiated himself.

He left behind a last will and testament. "I love China," he wrote. "I have done nothing to hurt the United States."

———

The Chin case was unusual, not just for his level of access to U.S. intelligence, but for the way the Chinese ran him. He was recruited, assigned handlers, given a courier, paid by some estimates as much as $1 million. He was run as a classic recruited agent in the same tradition as the spies of the Soviet Union, the United States, and virtually every other nation.

Most of the world's intelligence agencies rely primarily on money to recruit spies. After greed, case officers play upon the desire for revenge, followed distantly by personal problems. An intelligence officer will offer sympathy and support, whatever the target finds lacking in his or her own life.

But China's intelligence-gathering methodology is typically very different. China's spies are motivated by a sense of cultural and social obligation. They spy for friends or for the *idea* of China—not the People's Republic, but the 5,000-year-old Middle Kingdom, the heartland of Chinese culture.

PRC intelligence gathering seems almost tailored to beat spy catchers at their own game. China's spies are rarely paid or equipped with handlers and couriers. No James Bond gadgets, no elaborate subterfuge. This makes life harder for counterintelligence officers the world over, who are trained to look for vulnerabilities, for fat bank accounts or extravagant spending habits. They watch for suspicious behavior, for clandestine meetings, surreptitious signals, and the hiding of cash and documents, the classic dead drop under a footbridge.

PRC spies tend to deliver science and technology intelligence in China through a conversation with a scientist in the same field. Even if counterintelligence agents could mount effective surveillance inside China, spying looks like a social gathering. "In Chinese intelligence, you see two people sitting on a couch. So your forensic accounting is useless. The social aspect of it puts up a gigantic smoke screen," Moore says.

"We're into a very different kind of intelligence operation. We're used to naughty," he says. "This is not about naughty, it's about nice. China is interested in people who are good . . . They want you to help China. They want you to do it because it's a good thing to do. China doesn't want you to steal, they want you to give things to them."

The recruitment pitch often is as simple as "We consider you a friend of China. Do you see yourself as a friend of China?" The obvious problem for China is, most people don't fall for the pitch. As a result, China's spying method is enormously inefficient, slow, and piecemeal. So China works the numbers. The approaches are massive in scale, but the primary targets are the people who appear most likely to hear China's plea for help. And those people, Moore says, are primarily ethnic Chinese.

"The principles are the same that govern junk mail and telephone solicitations," he says. "You can sell this product most easily to people of Chinese ancestry. So the Chinese are dialing into the Chinese-American area code . . . And 98 percent of the time, the people who end up responding positively to the pitch are of ethnic Chinese ancestry."

The sales job is wasted on the vast majority of people, whether ethnic Chinese or not. Moore estimates that fewer than 5 percent of ethnic Chinese respond.

"We knew that Chinese Americans were approached rather frequently to help China covertly, but they only *occasionally* agreed to do so," Moore said. "Ethnicity could not be made to work as a predictor of espionage or other clandestine intelligence activity."

Recruited spies in fact produce the smallest amount of intelligence for China, Moore believes. The People's Republic relied more on a massive yet incremental approach to intelligence gathering that was known in counterintelligence circles as the "grains of sand" method. The expression came from a playful analogy: Imagine a vast ocean beach, in which the sand is an intelligence target coveted by every spy agency. One night, the Russians surface in a submarine, and commandos paddle ashore in a rubber raft. They fill a bucket with sand and carry it back to Moscow for analysis. Meanwhile, the Americans task a satellite to orbit unseen overhead and take hundreds of high-tech images, complete with spectrographs in every frequency range. Experts analyze them exhaustively and file thick reports. The next morning, the Chinese send 10,000 sunbathers. As the sun goes down, they return home, shake out their towels and produce a mound of sand—more secrets than anyone else.

China began vacuuming up untold masses of information, bit by bit, in the late 1970s, and, as far as is known, continues to do so today. The greatest volume by far comes from open publications—newspapers, magazines, TV news, and scientific literature. The Chinese specialize in archiving, then disseminating these to its scientists. A Chinese spying manual reads like a librarian's dissertation.

China's second most prolific source of intelligence is an army of students, the tens of thousands of Chinese youth who come to the West every year. According to Moore, the Ministry of State Security and the Defense Science and Technology Commission watch their progress from afar, wait until a select few gain valuable positions in industry and government, then ask them, "Do you think of yourself as a friend of China?" An extremely small percentage agrees to supply information, often just bits and pieces.

China gets the third largest amount of intelligence from PRC visitors—scholars, businessmen, military officers, and scientists. With both visitors and recruited agents, high-ranking Chinese scientists perform double duty as hosts and intelligence officers.

This practice carries risks. China's scientists are amateurs, unschooled in espionage tradecraft. What they do know is precisely the kind of information they need and how to manipulate the collegial, give-and-take dynamic of scientific intercourse to get it.

Their job is to bring foreign scientists onto their own turf in China, build social bonds with them, flatter them, then maneuver them into feelings of friendship and obligation. It reminds Moore of Rock Hudson's bachelor pad of 1950s cinema: He lures female seduction targets home, presses a button and—presto!—a leopard-print sleeper sofa drops out of the wall, a full bar rolls out, the lights dim, and strains of Mantovani emerge from the stereo.

China designates its own Rock Hudsons in the realm of science.

"China's able to bring out the heavy hitters," Moore said. "One of your roles as a Chinese leader is to meet and greet people and be part of the collection effort. The Chinese call it reception work."

The opening play is often genteel hospitality. The Chinese are highly solicitous of a visitor's desires for food, comfort, sightseeing. In one approach, for example, an American scientist might be taken on a daylong trip to the Great Wall and worn down physically or lavished with kindnesses that wear him down psychologically. Later the same day, a visitor might be invited to a banquet in his honor. He might arrive to find himself the only American in the room. Getting a scientist alone is an integral part of the play. As a rule, Moore says, the Chinese never try to get information from more than one person at a time. They add liberal doses of excellent food, alcohol, and charm. Then they outnumber the visitor with scientists probing for classified information.

"You're tired. You're not in a fit state to operate heavy machinery. They know how to flatter you. 'You're so smart, you know a lot,'" Moore said. "Then you're surrounded by people who are every bit as smart as you are. They say, 'China is a poor country.' You get that almost screamed at you. 'China is not a threat to anybody, especially not the United States. If you could help out in just a little way, you could perhaps help millions of people.'"

Many corporate and government visitors to China, including scientists, are usually told to avoid discussing certain topics. They know what they can say and are to decline questions about anything forbidden. Chinese scientists are skilled at turning aside that "no" and finding information behind it. They might say, according to Moore, "You are so knowledgeable and accomplished that I bet you know at least a hundred things that would help me immensely and not hurt U.S. interests one little bit." Invariably, some people will search their memories to see if there isn't something that they can give up.

These are standard PRC techniques for eliciting information from visitors of any ethnicity. The idea is to exploit them, to make them feel embarrassed or obligated to give up some iota of forbidden information.

Unlike recruited spies, who willingly give away information to China, the people who mistakenly give up information are likely to be of non-Chinese background, Moore says. They are targeted and exploited not on the basis of obligation but on what they know. Because far more non-Chinese Westerners than Chinese hold knowledgeable positions in targeted companies or institutes, they are targeted more for exploitation and thus also end up providing more information. They are not recruited spies but the information is still "stolen" in a sense and so amounts to espionage.

It was therefore inaccurate for the DOE's Dan Bruno to contend that the PRC "utilizes ethnic Chinese for espionage rather than persons of non-Chinese origin." Likewise, his proposal to begin looking among Chinese-American scientists for suspects in the purported theft of the W88 was misguided.

By the mid-1990s, the notion that China targeted ethnic Chinese for spy recruitment was gospel among U.S. spy catchers. Its authority was reaffirmed by another FBI espionage case, codenamed "Royal Tourist." The suspect was a Chinese-American scientist working in a U.S. weapons lab. And the details provided a template into which Wen Ho Lee fit perfectly.

Few people who knew Peter Hoong-Yee Lee could imagine his betrayal of the United States. He was a quiet but personable scientist who was regarded highly for his expertise in nuclear diagnostics; Lee was a laser specialist who excelled at mining scientific data from laser-fusion experiments.

Lee had every reason to despise the People's Republic of China. His father had been a general in the Chinese Nationalist Army that Mao's forces drove from the mainland to the island of Taiwan. His uncle stayed behind and was executed by the Communists. Lee was born on Taiwan and, like Sylvia Lee, attended the prestigious National Taiwan University. There is no evidence that Peter Lee and Sylvia knew each other, though the Energy Department's Bruno would later note the coincidence and suspect they were partners in a spy ring.

After graduation, Lee began working for the global conglomerate TRW Inc. in California, performing research under contract with Lawrence Livermore National Laboratory. Three years later, he joined Livermore scientists exploring the application of inertial confinement fusions, or ICF, to the understanding of nuclear weapons. Soon he became head of a Livermore laser-research team that focused on diagnostics.

During that time, Lee was deeply involved in the secret fusion experiments that the Chinese had asked Keyworth about in 1980. Lee's marriage to a Jewish woman created conflict with his father; his brother had adhered to the family tradition of marrying Chinese women. Desperate to win back his father's respect, he sent research papers home for his father's perusal.

In 1980, Lee made his first trip to the mainland, primarily as a translator for a team of Livermore laser physicists. One evening, a Chinese scientist paid a visit to his hotel room, much as Zheng and Hu came to Wen Ho Lee's room. Over breakfast in the morning, Peter Lee told a colleague of the visit. The colleague reported the conversation to Livermore security when they returned, but Lee made no mention of the visit in his trip report, just as Wen Ho Lee failed to report his hotel-room encounters.

The Chinese invited him to return, and he and his wife spent five weeks in December 1981 and January 1982 at the Shanghai Institute of Optics and Lasers. He later said he found China's premier laser facility in abysmal condition and set about improving it. He asked the Chinese for certain high-tech instruments and, finding them unavailable, decided to fashion them out of whatever he could find. Colleagues said he showed the same ingenuity and resourcefulness in his work in the United States.

While in Shanghai, China's cultural capital, Lee became intrigued by what he saw and heard. "He fell in love with the history and the art, the mystique," said Thomas J. Cook, a Los Alamos scientist who worked on the case. "China is an ancient country with old roots, and I think he was pretty taken with it."

During one of his early trips to China, Lee apparently became acquainted with Chen Neng Kuan, a manager of high-explosives research on China's first bomb who ascended the ranks of the CAEP and became a perennial host to Americans. It was Chen who played the flute for Harold Agnew and peppered Jay Keyworth with sensitive questions. He would play a crucial role in the seduction of Peter Lee.

Soon after making Chen's acquaintance, Lee started a correspondence with Chinese scientists that amounted to more than six hundred letters, phone calls, and e-mails over the next sixteen years. The Chinese asked him to send copies of many unclassified research papers. Lee dutifully went to the Livermore lab library, copied them, and sent them to China, as Wen Ho Lee apparently did for both Taiwan and China.

In 1984, Lee left Livermore for a job at Los Alamos, where he performed mainly unclassified work on the physics of hot, energized gases such as the plasmas found in ICF experiments.

He returned alone to China in 1985, this time to its nuclear-weapons research center in Mianyang. One night, he accepted an invitation to come to Chen's hotel room. Chen began asking questions that could only be answered with classified information. Lee initially resisted.

"China is a very poor country," Chen said. "We have only one nail to drive and we can't miss it. If I ask you questions, would you just nod yes or no?"

Lee nodded.

Chen pulled out a pencil and paper and began to sketch a hohlraum, the thimble-sized hollow cylinder containing a glass globe of hydrogen fuel, the target in laser-fusion experiments. He began asking questions that Lee knew were classified, but Lee nonetheless answered first by nods, then in words.

The next day, Chen picked up Lee at his hotel and took him to another hotel room, this one packed with some of the leading weapons scientists of the

Chinese Academy of Engineering Physics. Among them was Yu Min, a brilliant weapons designer regarded as China's Edward Teller. Yu and several of the scientists praised Lee's work for its intellectual rigor and creativity. It was a heady moment. The Chinese began asking questions, and for the next several hours, Lee answered them.

China's scientists had deftly shifted Lee from a helpful colleague to a spy recruit, said the FBI's Moore. "Now he's behaving like someone who's a willing, cooperating party in a Chinese intelligence operation."

Many of the answers Lee gave came out of a paper he had written in 1982 that was classified Secret Restricted Data. It described measurements that could be used, in slightly modified form, to gauge the efficiency and operation of thermonuclear weapons in underground tests. For a weapons scientist, getting high-precision data from nuclear tests was essential to refining nuclear weapons from large, bulky devices to leaner, lighter, and more efficient warheads. That's exactly what China was pursuing in the 1980s—a new generation of warheads to fit atop road-mobile and sub-launched missiles.

Twelve years later, Lee was asked by FBI agents, "Is there any question they could've asked you that you would not have answered?"

"No," Lee replied.

———————

No published account of the Peter Lee case indicates the reason the FBI came to investigate him for espionage. But according to sources, U.S. intelligence reports indicated Lee was cooperating with China's weaponeers. Agents acquired enough incriminating evidence for a special, secret federal court in 1985 to approve an electronic surveillance warrant. The FBI tapped his home and office telephones, one of which was connected to a fax machine. They monitored his e-mail at work, and they installed at least one microphone in a ceiling vent in Lee's home. Then they waited.

Nothing happened for years.

In May 1991, Lee was rehired by TRW for a space and electronics team in Redondo Beach, California, that was working on antisubmarine warfare. They were researching a new way of "seeing" submarines, not with sonar but with microwave radar. In theory, the technology would allow surveillance aircraft to track submarines through subtle wakes on the ocean surface.

In April and May 1997, Lee and his wife went to China for what he described on a TRW form as a pleasure trip. In fact, he was a guest of the Institute of Applied Physics and Computational Mathematics, the Beijing home of

China's elite nuclear-weapons designers. At IAPCM, Lee delivered a seminar on microwave radar to roughly thirty high-ranking Chinese scientists. To demonstrate its application to antisubmarine warfare, Lee displayed a photograph that he had brought with him of a surface ship's wake. He drew a graph and showed the Chinese scientists ways to filter out natural and man-made interference so they could detect wakes, such as that of a submerged submarine.

Lee went home and filled out a TRW post-travel questionnaire denying "any requests from Foreign Nationals for technical information" or attempts to persuade him to reveal classified information.

He was unaware that the FBI had followed him to China. But he soon got a big clue that something was amiss. In July, his wife was dusting the ceiling vent and the FBI's microphone fell out.

The agents knew their microphone had been discovered and the case would be lost if they didn't act fast. In August, agents interviewed Lee in a Santa Barbara, California, hotel. Congressional investigators later speculated that the location of the interview in a hotel rather than an FBI office suggested the agents wanted to "turn" Lee as a double agent. Lee admitted that he lied on his TRW travel reports, but he insisted he had paid for the May trip with his own money.

Soon after, Lee sent an e-mail to a Chinese scientist asking him to create receipts showing his payment for lodging, airfare, and other trip expenses. It was a fatal mistake. The FBI still was monitoring his e-mail and spotted the request even before the Chinese did. When Lee presented the falsified receipts to the FBI, agents confronted him with his own e-mail and phone calls arranging for them. An FBI polygrapher tested him and found Lee deceptive when answering such questions as "Have you ever deliberately been involved in espionage against the United States?" and "Have you ever provided classified information to persons unauthorized to receive it?"

Lee broke down and admitted to giving his May talk to the Chinese about the microwave radar technology, as well as divulging classified laser-fusion information twice in 1985. The agents pressed him for the details of other talks he'd given to the Chinese in previous years. Lee began explaining laser fusion to the FBI, evidently enjoying his role as teacher. He didn't know they already had been well coached by technical experts from Los Alamos and Livermore. When Lee claimed that he had performed no classified research, they confronted him with classified papers that he had written or edited.

The interview was videotaped, and some who have seen the tape were struck by the way Lee appeared to crumple. His smile disappeared, his voice softened, and he began to admit sharing information with the Chinese for more than a decade. In the end, he wanted to bring China's scientific capabilities closer to those of the United States. His tenure as a recruited agent of China grew out of ego and insecurity—his unfulfilled desire to please his father—and his "scientific enthusiasm," as Lee's attorney put it.

Lee pleaded guilty on December 8, 1997, to charges of attempting "to communicate national defense information to a person not entitled to receive it" and lying to a government agency. He faced a maximum sentence of fifteen years in prison and a fine of up to $250,000. He was sentenced March 26, 1998, to a year in a halfway house and ordered to perform 3,000 hours of community service and pay a $20,000 fine.

It took the FBI twelve years to get enough evidence to close Royal Tourist. The job of preventing and interdicting Chinese spying wasn't getting any easier. A Chinese espionage case still looked for all the world like a friendship. How could a spy catcher possibly tell them apart? The answer clearly didn't lie with ethnicity, although some counterintelligence officers mistakenly thought so.

"Friendship covers a lot of ground, and you're not going to take a hard line against it," Moore says. "So you ask, 'How does China regard the difference between people who say they're your friend and the people who will cross a line for you?'"

The crucial distinction for the Chinese is confidentiality. The rules of *guanxi* demand it. Sensitive favors require discretion. So counterintelligence agents began looking for evidence of friendships that American scientists wouldn't report or acknowledge.

"It's the kind of relationship where he doesn't feel comfortable telling you about it. And what occurs to the counterintelligence officer is that he knows it's improper in some way," Moore said.

The FBI used other indicators of improper relationships to spot evidence of Chinese spying—lying, travel to China, security violations, implication in a previous intelligence case.

"That's a big one," Moore says. "Most of the names you see are not new. They were just on the periphery of another case."

When DOE fingered Sylvia and Wen Ho Lee in its administrative inquiry, the FBI jumped in with both feet. Wen Ho Lee was loaded with indicators for Chinese espionage. He had called a spy suspect whom he didn't know and offered help. He had admitted violating export controls by passing documents to Taiwan. A top Chinese weapons designer had embraced him and thanked him for "help with codes." He had been to China twice and repeatedly entertained Chinese weapons scientists in his home.

To the FBI, Wen Ho Lee could hardly have looked more like a spy.

– 13 –

The Out-of-Towner

Since the FBI had broken up the Rosenberg-Fuchs nuclear spy ring, the Albuquerque Field Office, headquarters for New Mexico, had slipped a few notches. To be sure, the office produced hefty case numbers—lots of arrests and convictions per capita, the statistics that mollify headquarters. But these were at least as attributable to demographics and location as to investigative prowess.

New Mexico is a thinly populated desert state with a Mexican border, well situated as a hideaway for fugitives and a transshipment point for narcotics. For serious crimes, the FBI also serves as the police for the twenty-three Indian tribes that occupy 4.7 million acres of land.

The Albuquerque office is a quality-of-life, backwater posting: It offers an easier-going pace, more than three hundred days of sun a year, mind-boggling expanses of blue sky. For some agents, it's an ideal spot for closing out a career or decompressing after high-pressure jobs at headquarters and in major metro areas.

Such was the attraction for Special Agent David Lieberman and his wife. Once, the couple had enjoyed a romantic vacation in Santa Fe. In 1990, the opportunity came to return. They wanted to escape Washington, D.C., where Lieberman had worked on a legal review team in the Freedom of Information Act Unit. Working FOIA, Lieberman felt he was a valued player. But his wife had just gotten a degree at American University and was ready for change.

Lieberman was a lawyer; he'd gotten his degree as an in-stater at the University of Nebraska. He was slightly built, a pale man about 5 feet 3 inches with dark brown hair. Early in his FBI career, Lieberman worked in Chicago and Alexandria, Virginia, doing foreign counterintelligence and criminal cases.

Foreign counterintelligence, or FCI, was held in high esteem in the Bureau before the end of the Cold War. It was cerebral, methodical, long-view kind of work.

Lieberman regarded FCI as a pleasure, a challenge, and an honor. What better place to hunt spies than a tourist paradise? His assignment in 1991 to the Santa Fe Resident Agency as the FBI liaison to Los Alamos would be an eye-opener.

Supervisors of the Santa Fe RA didn't have much time or patience for skull-duggery up at the weapons lab. Lieberman tried to visit the laboratory several times a week, meet the intelligence and counterintelligence officers, talk to the scientists, and figure out what this strange lab on the Hill really did.

But Lieberman didn't get far. He was besieged by other assignments and soon felt snowed under. The worst were background checks. Headquarters requested investigations of major federal nominees, judgeships, or executive posts. Field agents were expected to drop everything and develop reports on the nominees.

Lieberman complained but meekly—his protests in any event produced meager effect on his workload. Whether he bore a disproportionate load or couldn't juggle competing demands on his time, Lieberman was overwhelmed.

"Counterintelligence was not a priority—at all—for this division. None," he said. "They were interested in drugs, bank robberies, and Indian crime."

A poor performance in counterintelligence had given the Albuquerque Field Office one of the worst black eyes in the FBI. In 1985, a massive FBI surveillance team in Santa Fe let slip a fired CIA agent who was suspected of giving secrets to the Soviet Union, including all of the innermost details of agency spies and the operation of the CIA's Moscow station.

Edward Lee Howard had been trained by the FBI itself in the art of eluding surveillance. On Saturday, September 21, 1985, he slapped together a crude "jib"—a jack-in-the-box contraption—that he had learned to use in the CIA. It was a sawed-off broomstick with a coat hanger for shoulders, his wife Mary's Styrofoam wig holder for a head, and a leftover CIA disguise wig. Late in the afternoon, Ed and Mary Howard left their Eldorado home, ostensibly for dinner on Santa Fe's Canyon Road, presuming they were being watched by a large surveillance team the Bureau had brought in from around the country. The FBI in fact had a video camera trained on the Howard home from a construction trailer nearby, but a lone, young agent missed their departure, reportedly because of sunset glare on the video monitor.

At the restaurant, the Howards even called a babysitter at home, where Ed knew the FBI had a wiretap on his phone, and announced where they were eating. An agent appeared, and the Howards left. They drove off with him in tow. As they rounded a curve, Ed Howard bade his wife of ten years goodbye, flipped the dummy into place in the passenger seat and jumped out of the car, rolling into the bushes.

The next day, he hopped a flight to New York, charging the ticket on his TWA Getaway Card to needle the FBI. Back in Albuquerque, a sharp young assistant U.S. attorney named Robert Gorence began drawing up a warrant for Howard's arrest, unaware that his first spy suspect already was far from New Mexico. A few days later, Howard rang the doorbell at the Soviet embassy in Helsinki.

The Howard incident crippled careers and blackened the FBI's reputation. In the late 1980s, FCI agents in New Mexico continued to make an unimpressive showing. Russian and East German intelligence operatives showed up in Santa Fe for reasons unknown. The FBI decided to tail them.

The operations were pure Keystone Kops. The FBI men were conspicuous in Santa Fe's tourist-laden plaza. One observer saw two men sitting on a cast-iron park bench and figured they were lovers—Santa Fe being a southwestern gay and lesbian mecca. On a closer look, the men were obviously law enforcement of some stripe, with wires trailing out of their ears. Teenagers on bikes and skateboards had them pegged right away and yelled to one another: "Car 54, where are you?"

The East Germans and Russians appeared to enjoy the game. They handily dodged the tails by ducking into a shop, hotel, or restaurant and walking out the back. It was child's play.

This was the atmosphere when Lieberman arrived in 1991, not knowing that he—and the Albuquerque Field Office—would soon be at the center of the nation's most closely watched spy case since Aldrich Ames.

———

After DOE's first mid-1995 briefing to the FBI on Kindred Spirit, the Bureau figured the Chinese must have penetrated Los Alamos very deeply to make off with an actual warhead design. The question was, how widespread was the penetration? Was it a case of loose-lipped scientists, a single dedicated mole, or an entire Chinese spy ring? To avoid tipping off the quarry, the Bureau decided to put a hold on the 1994 Hug investigation of Wen Ho Lee and his code aid to the Chinese. Lieberman was told not to conduct any interviews. Kindred Spirit was to remain a closely held secret, at DOE, at Los Alamos, and in the FBI.

As a result, nothing would happen on the 1994 lead for almost a year.

Lieberman was only too relieved. His workload, as he saw it, was crushing enough.

In the spring of 1996, knowing Kindred Spirit was imminent, Lieberman decided to lobby for help at FBI headquarters. He dropped in on the head of the FBI's China Unit, explained he was strapped for time and could use some more manpower. Lieberman was told to take up the matter with Staffing.

It was, in Lieberman's eyes, a bureaucratic blow-off. He gave up and went home to New Mexico.

That April, Hawkins caught wind of Kindred Spirit and was angry that he had been left out. He now was director of the Nonproliferation and International Security Division but still had responsibility for the lab's intel analysts. He discovered Trulock had used these analysts without his knowledge for Kindred Spirit, claiming that Hawkins couldn't be told because he was too close to the Chinese and could be considered a suspect. Later, Hawkins laughed at the idea. "I'm sure I was [a suspect]," he said. Vrooman suggested that Trulock kept Hawkins in the dark to avoid criticism of his investigation.

On May 28, Trulock shipped the heavily edited administrative inquiry to the Bureau. The FBI added a document officially opening the case. It was captioned "Lee, Wen Ho and Lee, Sylvia."

The package arrived in early June in Santa Fe. Lieberman was taken aback. The AI was a daunting tome, thick with all the attachments. He skimmed through it and got to the meat, Bruno's investigative note. Bruno had "exhausted all logical 'leads' regarding this inquiry" that he was legally permitted to explore. Bruno suggested that Lee's motive to pass W88 information to China was to "enhance" his stature in the "eyes of high ranking PRC personnel." Sylvia and Wen Ho Lee were the obvious suspects.

The message to the FBI, the Bellows team later found, "was that the FBI need look no further within DOE for a suspect. Wen Ho Lee was its man . . . [T]he FBI should never have accepted this message."

Lieberman inherited all of the ills that Trulock's intelligence office built into Kindred Spirit—the misrepresented "theft" of the W88, the slipshod administrative inquiry, and a report edited to portray the AI as a complete investigation.

Lieberman's superiors in Washington bore the burden of blame for allowing the DOE to establish the "crime" and name two suspects to the exclusion of hundreds, if not thousands. It was understandable for the FBI to leave the assessment of whether nuclear espionage had occurred to the Energy Department. But the same deference to DOE on its administrative inquiry was, in the words of the Bellows review team, "inexplicable." "On matters related to the identification of a suspect in a counterintelligence investigation, the FBI *was* the expert."

FBI Headquarters then compounded its error by dumping all of this on a single, overworked agent, quite probably in the wrong field office. The Albuquerque Field Office was the wrong place to send a high-profile spy case, and Lieberman was the wrong agent to assign to it.

"It's not the way to handle anything that's a big investigation," a former official knowledgeable about the case said. "You don't send it out to the backwater of America and assign it to someone part time."

Lieberman was no China spy catcher. He didn't know Mandarin. And his supervisors already regarded him as lacking in capability. One of them told the Bellows review team that working with Lieberman was "like pushing a cart with a dead donkey," raising the question of why he was assigned.

Yet Lieberman himself deserved a sizeable share of blame for the manner in which he first took up the case. Based on conversations with Vrooman, he had good reason to believe that DOE had misstated the crime and delivered a deeply flawed AI. Lieberman in fact had telexed Washington with those observations starting in 1995. In 1996, he could have pulled back, questioned the AI to superiors, and perhaps stopped Kindred Spirit before it went further awry. He didn't.

He didn't, for example, examine the Energy Department's rationale for excluding suspects other than Wen Ho and Sylvia Lee. Nor did he take the rudimentary step of traveling to Washington so that he could familiarize himself with the purported "crime" by studying the intelligence or talking to the scientists who did. Instead, two agents in Washington conducted those interviews. They were told that the compromised weapons information was scattered at DOE and Defense Department locations across the country, an observation that might have led the FBI to question the singular focus on Los Alamos. The agents also were told that the intelligence did not show any compromise of certain secret and unique design features of the W88, undermining assertions in the AI and Trulock's briefings that the entire design of the warhead had been stolen. But the two agents were insufficiently versed in the case to pick up these clues that something was wrong. Lieberman might have gotten the message if he had done the interviews.

In lieu of going to Washington, Lieberman could have interviewed the Los Alamos and Sandia scientists who had been part of the Kindred Spirit Advisory Group. At least five of them were within an hour's drive of his office in Santa Fe.

In short, Lieberman didn't question the logic or conduct of the AI, though he had reason to. Headquarters had opened an espionage case on the Lees, and Lieberman merely took it as his lot to investigate them.

As the Bellows review team later concluded: "The FBI's own lack of investigative interest in looking beyond Wen Ho Lee and Sylvia Lee magnified each of the AI's defects. Mistakes made during the AI were not corrected during the subsequent FBI investigation. Locations ignored during the DOE AI were also ignored by the FBI. Individuals missed by the AI were also missed by the FBI. . . . Leads identified, however fleetingly in the AI report, were not pursued by the FBI."

In fact, Lieberman believed he wasn't to do much of anything for another month. He believed, based on a conversation with the China Unit's Craig Schmidt, that he was to sit tight until an entourage from headquarters could come to New Mexico and brief a select group at Los Alamos on the launching of the case.

In the meantime, a piece of information came in that Lieberman couldn't ignore. Wen Ho Lee's next-door neighbors believed he was a spy for China.

It was not uncommon for coworkers, jilted spouses, and neighbors to suspect lab employees of spying. The lab counterintelligence office investigated about thirty such reports a year. Almost none of them came to anything.

Lee's neighbor Norman Pruvost had reported his suspicions to Danny Stillman, Los Alamos's former intelligence chief and a Lieberman contact at the lab. Pruvost and his wife, Lynn, knew Lee not only as a neighbor but as a coworker. Norm worked in X Division, and Lynn had worked as a secretary in the same group as Wen Ho Lee.

The apparent basis for their suspicions was twofold: As a secretary, Lynn Pruvost had noted that Lee used the copying machine frequently. When others approached the machine, Lee appeared to gather his materials quickly and leave, as though he did not want anyone else to see what he had been copying.

The other half of the Pruvosts' suspicions had to do with their telephone. Periodically, strong interference could be heard on the handset. FBI agents would come to refer to this phenomenon as "the burping telephone." The Pruvosts apparently believed their phone difficulties were directly related to a satellite dish that the Lees had installed in their yard. It was perhaps three feet in diameter and mounted on a platform.

As an intelligence chief, Stillman knew the interference could be consistent with the use of a burst transmitter, a form of SRAC, or Short-Range Agent Communications that sends quick bursts of compressed and generally encrypted information. A host of European spy agencies used them. He and Pruvost speculated that Lee could be copying weapons codes at work, breaking them into transmittable chunks at home, and sending them via satellite to the People's Republic of China.

Lieberman called the Pruvosts, and they agreed to come by the Santa Fe Resident Agency for an interview while en route to errands in Albuquerque, but then the Pruvosts never showed up. Lieberman left phone messages at their home; none were returned. Lieberman finally called Stillman, who called back later to say that the Pruvosts "didn't want to get involved."

It looked like a dead end. Back in Washington, Schmidt was dismissive. "The Chinese don't use SRAC," he scoffed.

On July 2, Schmidt and Jerry Doyle of the FBI's China Unit touched down in Albuquerque, and the next morning, after gathering New Mexico agents, drove to Los Alamos. They met Hecker in the director's conference room. Hawkins, Vrooman, and Craig arrayed themselves around the table, along with Larry Runge, who was in charge of all lab security, including Vrooman's counterintelligence shop.

The FBI talked of a rigorous investigation—the loss of nuclear-weapons designs was a dire threat to national security. Interdicting a spy is tough, however, and the evidence against Lee so far was slim. It would be necessary to catch Lee in the act of giving secrets to the Chinese. It was crucial not to tip him off— or anyone who might be working with him.

"Well," Hecker said, "should I get his clearance pulled?"

"God, don't do that!" Schmidt said. "He'll sue you!"

Lee was to remain in his regular job, his clearance intact, while the FBI performed every possible covert investigation. Terry Craig was to be the Bureau's chief point of contact at the Los Alamos lab. Knowledge of Kindred Spirit was to be limited to those in the room. No one else was to be briefed unless they absolutely had a need to know.

A few days later, Lieberman came to Los Alamos and met with Vrooman and Craig. As usual, the agent was anxious about his pressing workload. He said he wasn't sure about the amount of time that he could devote to the case. Vrooman and Craig told Lieberman that there were limits to what they could do as employees of the University of California, which ran the lab. But they could at least help him get started. They could give Lieberman printouts of Wen Ho Lee's badge-reader access—the FBI would know every time Lee entered a secure area of the laboratory and perhaps spot unusual activity. To help decipher the badge-reader lists, Vrooman handed over a list of the lab's most sensitive areas for weapons research. Craig called the technicians in charge of the lab's phone network and arranged to get monthly readouts of Lee's phone calls.

Lieberman received all of these in short order. Los Alamos never heard another word from him about them.

In November, Craig offered an idea to nudge Lieberman along. Los Alamos had seen at least one case of a scientist sending classified information by e-mail, either by mistake or because he felt too rushed to have the e-mail independently reviewed for classified content. As a result, the lab's computer security staff had installed a system for monitoring incoming and outgoing e-mail. Craig mentioned it to Lieberman.

Lieberman consulted the FBI's National Security Law Unit (NSLU). Its lawyers were interested. Did this mean the FBI could access Lee's e-mail without a warrant? Lieberman asked Craig for more information. Los Alamos's computer-security group supplied documents that justified lab searches of computers, including e-mail, for waste, fraud, and abuse. Craig also supplied information about the lab's new online computer-security training. Employees who finished the course signed a one-page statement that included a reminder that the lab could audit the contents and use of their computers.

Craig confirmed that Lee hadn't completed the training. As a consequence, the NSLU team was uncertain about a computer search without a warrant. Perhaps Los Alamos could search its employees' computers, but what about an FBI search in the context of building a criminal espionage case? Weeks later, Lieberman said the NSLU was uncomfortable with searching or monitoring activities on Lee's computer unless it displayed a warning banner of the type then in use at other government and contractor facilities. When Lee logged on to use his e-mail, did his computer screen display a message warning of government access to his computer in order to check for waste, fraud, and abuse?

To answer this question, Craig simply showed Lieberman what happened on his own computer—no banner when booting up the machine or logging on for e-mail.

Craig had gotten Lieberman's approval to ask such questions of lab computer-security personnel, without revealing anything about the case. Craig did look in Lee's personnel file, and it contained no indication that Lee had been notified of the lab's ability to search his computer.

X Division, where Lee worked, had its own computer staff and designated computer-security officer. Had Craig asked, the X Division staff would have told him that division computers did, in fact, display a warning banner to users. A check of Lee's computer-user file in X Division also would have revealed that in 1995, Wen Ho Lee had signed a statement acknowledging the lab's right to search his computer.

But Craig felt he could not ask questions anywhere else in the laboratory unless specifically requested by the FBI. It was only the Bureau, as Craig saw it, that had federal authority for conducting criminal espionage investigations.

Instead of pursuing the matter further, Lieberman never forwarded the documentation that Craig gave him to the NSLU, so the question of computer searches and monitoring lay idle. If the FBI or the lab had looked at Lee's computer files, they would have discovered that he had placed a storehouse of nuclear-weapons codes on the unclassified network, in harm's way.

The FBI did take other investigative steps, however. Agents won approval from Attorney General Janet Reno for a "mail cover," the photocopying of the outside of Lee's mail, and a "trash cover" to study the Lees' home refuse.

Right before Thanksgiving, Deputy Energy Secretary Charles Curtis called an urgent meeting of several national lab directors and their security staffs. Curtis said the foreign-visitors program was out of control. Scientists were stretching the limits of permitted topics for foreign interaction, they were making their own rules or dodging the rules by meeting off site, and virtually no one was keeping track of their foreign contacts. Foreign scientists and intel operatives were targeting many of the DOE labs, not just the weapons-design labs, for a host of technologies with military and commercial applications. As soon as possible, Curtis wanted the labs to restart background checks and report on their potential vulnerability to foreign intelligence gathering. DOE's list of "sensitive subjects" that were prohibited from conversation with nationals of countries seeking weapons of mass destruction would be broadened; scientists would be more restrained in what they could talk and write about.

Several lab directors agreed, but Los Alamos balked. The indices checks were still useless. Hecker and Vrooman suggested that DOE study the risks and benefits of foreign exchanges. Curtis agreed and assigned the task to Trulock.

Just before the meeting, Vrooman and Trulock had a conversation on the side. It was clear that the Chinese used their senior scientists to try to pry classified information out of U.S. weapons scientists. According to Vrooman, Trulock suggested that the real risks were ethnic Chinese. Vrooman said Trulock argued that DOE should not allow ethnic Chinese to work on classified science. Trulock has since denied this conversation ever took place.

"The notion that Asian Americans should not be assigned to classified projects—that's just preposterous," he would say later.

On December 6, Vrooman relayed Trulock's alleged comments about ethnic Chinese as security risks to Hecker and Hawkins. Both were incredulous. In the previous months, Vrooman had talked to a number of scientists who had worked on the intelligence analysis that launched Kindred Spirit. He now argued to Hecker and Hawkins that the whole investigation was a mess: It wasn't clear that the Chinese had copied the W88. It was becoming increasingly evident that the same information was available not just at DOE's labs but at DOE headquarters, the Pentagon, and a number of Defense Department contractors. And there was no evidence that weapons information was lost from Los Alamos.

That wasn't all. Vrooman argued that Bruno's AI was either sloppy research or a pretext to finger Wen Ho Lee. The AI was riddled with holes, he said. Several people who had access to the W88 did not appear in the AI at all. On the other end of the equation, four of the twelve leading suspects had no access to the W88, one had no Q clearance at all. Several were, however, ethnic Chinese. Lastly, Vrooman said Bruno had identified Lee as a likely suspect before coming to Los Alamos to investigate. Vrooman recalled hearing Bruno say, "I know it's the Lees. I just have to fill in some other names to make it look good."

Hecker was annoyed. The FBI had talked of an aggressive investigation but had not delivered. It was wrong, he said, for allegations against a lab employee—especially an allegation of stealing a weapons design—to languish without being resolved. Get the FBI moving on this, he told Vrooman. The bureau needed to dig up some hard evidence or eliminate Lee as a suspect.

Within a few days, Vrooman passed Hecker's request to the FBI's Albuquerque office. He also talked to Lieberman, who again complained that he was overworked and had little time for Kindred Spirit.

Lieberman's relief would come soon enough. In January 1997, he was overjoyed to learn he would be getting a transfer out of New Mexico, back to headquarters. Within a few weeks, Vrooman's complaints of the lack of FBI action reached Craig Schmidt, the agent supervising the case from Washington.

Schmidt was incensed. He had sent two agents to Albuquerque to help out with Kindred Spirit. What was going on? He dialed up Lieberman. "What happened to the two guys I sent you?"

Lieberman was flustered. "What two guys?"

His confusion was understandable. Two rookie FBI agents had arrived in the Albuquerque Field Office, but Lieberman's superiors had diverted them into standard criminal investigations without telling him.

Lieberman told Schmidt that he would be coming to Washington soon. Perhaps they could grab a beer or a bite to eat?

Schmidt was irate. "The only reason I'd go to dinner with you is to watch you choke on a chicken bone."

-14-

The FISA

In February 1997, Special Agent Jim Levy took over the case, and within a few weeks it was jolted back to life by Wen Ho Lee himself. Word got to the FBI that the scientist wanted to hire a Chinese graduate student—a citizen of the PRC—as a summer intern. Genong Li, twenty-six, held engineering degrees from Xi'an Jiaotong University (in the city best known to Americans for its famous army of ancient terra cotta figures) and was working on his doctorate in mechanical engineering at the University of Pittsburgh. He was the nephew of a Chinese scientist who had spoken to Lee about the internship. As always, Lee was happy to help out. Li's assignment at the lab was to "work on unclassified 2-D Lagrangian code to help our current research work on code development."

Although Chinese grad students were welcomed at the lab, Lee was an espionage suspect, and his every action was viewed through that prism. To the FBI, Lee's desire to hire a PRC citizen was a warning flag. The agents believed that Lee had invited Genong Li to Los Alamos National Laboratory "for the purpose of giving him access to classified information." As the FBI saw it, Li would be the conduit through which Lee's treasonous disclosures would be channeled to China. Lee's request, which would have once been seen as routine, now pushed the FBI to seek approval for electronic surveillance of his home and office. Levy began by obtaining a photograph of Genong Li and his resume from Vrooman.

With no real evidence against Lee, the FBI turned to a wiretap for help. Nobody knew exactly what the crime was, where it happened, or when. Levy had been given a suspect to investigate, rather than a crime to solve. With a wiretap, he could listen to the phone conversations and hope for luck. Maybe he would catch the Lees saying something incriminating, then confront them with the proof and get a confession. This was standard fare in spy cases. The FBI had recorded the phone calls of Peter Lee and Gwo-Bao Min, the weapons-lab scientists suspected of spying for China.

Getting an ordinary criminal court judge to sign off on a wiretap authorization for the Lees was out of the question, since there was no evidence they had committed a crime. The FBI would have to take its request to the U.S. Foreign Intelligence Surveillance Court in Washington. That special court was created to operate in secrecy, dealing only with national-security issues. It could approve a request for a phone tap, a clandestine search of an office or home, and secret monitoring of e-mail and computer files. Under the Foreign Intelligence Surveillance Act, or FISA, the seven-member court could even authorize FBI agents to sneak into homes and hide microphones in air-conditioning vents, as in the case of Peter Lee.

"The FBI loves FISAs," said a congressional aide who has followed the Bureau. And the FISC loves to give them, approving an average of roughly 800 a year—or more than two a day including weekends—in the 1990s.

Levy would have to put together an application to send to prosecutors in the Justice Department, who would present it to the court. Quietly, so as not to alert Lee, he began assembling evidence of what seemed suspicious behavior by Wen Ho and Sylvia Lee. In May, he picked up a new piece. A review of Lee's Visa credit card records showed that five years earlier, on December 10, 1992, he had charged $108.21 to a Hong Kong travel agency, TC Tours Travel. A week later, there was another charge at the same travel agency for $764.60.

Lee, who loved to travel, was then in Hong Kong on a lab-sponsored trip to present a paper ("Strong Shock Tube Problem Calculated by Different Numerical Schemes") at the International Conference on Computational Engineering Science.

The FBI saw the situation this way: "Based on Hong Kong's proximity to China and records indicating purchases for the Lees from a travel agency in Hong Kong, the FBI believes that these records may indicate that while in Hong Kong, Lee Wen Ho purchased transportation from Hong Kong to Beijing and returns. Such travel, if it occurred, was not reported to DOE, and may have provided Lee with a covert opportunity to meet with Chinese officials."

On June 30, 1997, the FBI sent its application to the Justice Department's Office of Intelligence Policy and Review (OIPR). By mid-August, the paperwork had landed on the desk of Allan Kornblum, the OIPR's deputy counsel for intelligence operations. He thought the case "important and urgent." Like others unfamiliar with the weapons labs, Kornblum was "shocked by the facts, the idea that this guy is making official trips to the PRC to meet with his counterparts in nuclear-weapons design. I couldn't believe that."

Kornblum assigned the case to an attorney who worked through the Fourth of July holiday weekend drafting a surveillance application for the court. But when Kornblum read it, he found it wanting.

The application's sixteen-page FBI affidavit was a hodgepodge of fact, observation, and opinion summing up everything the FBI knew about the Lees. At first glance, it seemed a convincing stew of suspicion. But on closer examination, the scattered pieces did not fit together well. There were mistakes and omissions that offered a distorted view of the Lees' activities.

The affidavit began with this questionable assumption, taken from the Department of Energy inquiry: "DOE counterintelligence and weapons experts had concluded that there was a great probability that the W88 information had been compromised between 1984 and 1988 at the nuclear-weapons division of the Los Alamos laboratory." The memo made no mention of the weapons experts at the DOE, the CIA, Los Alamos, and Lawrence Livermore who almost unanimously disagreed with that assumption. Nor did it point out that the FBI had not confirmed the assumption on its own. Echoes of Notra Trulock's briefings reverberated in the wiretap application.

The affidavit took for granted that the Lees were the most likely suspects. The theory was that "he had access to the relevant weapons data, while she had access both to him and to visiting Chinese delegations."

Sylvia Lee was "extremely close" to Chinese scientists, perhaps closer than anyone at the lab. The FBI cited a note written by her asking a lab employee to send a copy of an unclassified paper to a Chinese nuclear-weapons official. "Moreover," it said, Wen Ho Lee had "aggressively" sought to interpret for one delegation, even though he wasn't very good at it. The omission of the Lees' long service as informants—especially Sylvia Lee's—with CIA officer Dan Wofford and FBI agent Dave Bibb was breathtaking. "It is at least inconsistent to ask folks to cooperate with the government and at the same time contend that what they're doing is nefarious," one of Lee's lawyers would later say.

The memo described Sylvia Lee's vengeful destruction of computer files and threats she made against coworkers. It noted that the Lees had gone to China in 1986 and 1988 for conferences and had traveled on vacation while they were there. There was no indication that the trips, including the vacation travel, were similar to visits by numerous other Los Alamos scientists. As Attorney General Janet Reno later put it, "It wasn't as if they snuck off to the PRC."

The FBI affidavit cited the Visa card charge at the Hong Kong travel agency, the Hug incident and Hu Side's comments that Lee had been helpful with codes, and Lee's summer intern, Genong Li.

The suspicious aspect of Li's hiring, according to the FBI, was that Lee wanted him to work on Lagrangian hydro codes. Lab officials supposedly told the FBI that there was no such thing as an *unclassified* Lagrangian code. The FISA application was plainly wrong on that point, however. Unclassified Lagrangian codes are widely used in industry and academia, by astrophysicists modeling the cosmos and engineers designing sprinkler systems for commercial buildings. In fact, anyone with a computer modem can download a free copy of a two-dimensional Lagrangian hydro code from Los Alamos.

Also in the FISA memo, of course, was Lee's strange 1982 phone call to the Tiger Trap suspect at Lawrence Livermore and Lee's denials that he had made the call. But how did that make Lee a spy for China? As Reno later pointed out, Lee thought the conversation was about Taiwan. In its discussion of Tiger Trap, the letterhead memo contained a striking error. It reported that Lee had agreed to assist the FBI in its investigation of Gwo-Bao Min, the Tiger Trap suspect, but that his offer had not been accepted when, in fact, Lee had visited Min at his California house wearing a microphone, at the request of the FBI.

On another issue—the Visa card charges at the travel agency in Hong Kong—the circumstances carried less weight with the Justice Department lawyers than with the FBI agents. As Reno would later explain, "because somebody goes to Hong Kong and incurs a $102 travel bill, that does not show that they go to Beijing [any more than Taipei], but even if they go to Beijing, you had hundreds of scientists coming to, and students coming to, Los Alamos, and a large number of scientists going to Beijing."

Even the 1994 Hug incident, which the FBI put great stock in, was brushed aside. To the Bureau, the warm embrace and Hu Side's acknowledgment that Lee had helped China with codes was evidence of a clandestine relationship, given that Lee had never reported any previous contact with the high-ranking official. But the Hug lent itself to another, more benign interpretation, countered the Justice Department. Lee had entered a room full of Los Alamos scientists, openly sought out Hu, and begun a conversation that attracted everyone's attention. As Reno later said, there was "nothing clandestine about it."

Certainly it was evidence that Lee had helped the Chinese with codes and calculations that might be useful to their weapons program, but the codes could very well be unclassified.

The memo also implied that the Chinese might be interested in Lee because he worked on the lab's "legacy codes," older codes that had been bench-marked by actual nuclear tests, before testing ended in 1992. The same could be said about many other code writers at Los Alamos.

———————

In several areas, the FISA application had chronology problems. On the one hand, the investigation was about the supposed loss of the W88, which had to have happened by early 1988, because the walk-in document was dated then. Thus, any suspicious activity after 1988 was irrelevant to the loss of W88 data. Even the Lees' 1988 trip to Beijing was not a factor, since they went in June and the walk-in document was dated earlier in the year.

On the other hand, to get FISA approval, the FBI had to show that there was a strong probability that the Lees were *currently* engaged in espionage. The Jus-tice Department lawyers felt that "all of the most interesting things [Tiger Trap and the Hug] that would qualify him for coverage were too distant in time." The evidence had a "staleness issue."

The more fundamental problem was a lack of evidence that the Lees had had anything to do with the purported loss of the W88. The FBI had not "suffi-ciently demonstrated a connection" between the suspects and the crime, the OIPR lawyers complained. The failings of Bruno's administrative inquiry were now coming back to haunt the FBI. There was no probable cause to believe that the Lees were "agents of a foreign power" or were engaged in "clandestine intel-ligence gathering activities," as the law required. The FBI agents disagreed, ar-guing that the separate pieces they had collected formed a mosaic of probable cause, that the "totality of the circumstances" merited electronic surveillance.

But there was yet another basic problem. The FBI had been given a list of a dozen suspects by the Department of Energy, but the Bureau had investigated only Wen Ho and Sylvia Lee, ignoring the others. Then, repeating Bruno's AI, agent Levy claimed that the Lees stood out from the others on the list. But how, Kornblum asked, could you know the Lees stood out if you didn't investigate the others?

The Justice Department review of the FISA application was in essence a cri-tique of the FBI investigation, with the judgment that it was inadequate. OIPR would not present the application to the judges. Two more draft applications were prepared, both rejected by OIPR in August of 1997 and sent back to the FBI for more investigation. John Lewis, the chief of the FBI's National Security Division, was troubled enough to take the unusual step of going directly to At-torney General Reno with a plea to have the FISA request reviewed again. It was, and was again turned down. Nothing happened after that; Justice officials thought the FBI was gathering more facts, while FBI agents believed the matter was dead.

———————

Neither side seemed to grasp the larger issue, that the DOE's administrative inquiry upon which the FBI based its investigation was hopelessly flawed. Trying to find out how the W88 data was lost by focusing on the dozen names Dan Bruno had developed while browsing travel and expense reports at Los Alamos had little relation to reality.

There was something else questionable about the FISA application that went unchallenged. The document clearly argued that one legitimate reason for investigating Sylvia and Wen Ho Lee as potential spies, one cause for wiretapping their telephones, was that they were Chinese Americans.

The FISA application listed eighteen pieces of evidence to justify a wiretap. As congressional investigators later paraphrased the application, "it was standard PRC intelligence tradecraft to focus particularly upon targeting and recruitment of ethnic Chinese living in foreign countries (e.g., Chinese-Americans)." This piece of "evidence" was not something the Lees had said or done. It was simply that they were Chinese Americans.

Another item on the FISA list: "It was standard PRC intelligence tradecraft, when targeting ethnic Chinese living overseas, to encourage travel to the 'homeland'—particularly where visits to ancestral villages and/or old family members could be arranged—as a way of trying to dilute loyalty to other countries and encouraging solidarity with the authorities in Beijing." The apparent implication was that the judges on the FISA court should view a trip to a conference in Beijing by a Chinese-American scientist in a different light than the same trip by a European-American scientist. The ancestry of Chinese-American scientists could be used as evidence against them.

"Every time Lee's motive was discussed, it came down to his ethnicity," said Bob Vrooman.

With Lee under investigation, there were questions about his job duties and access to classified information. In April 1997, after Vrooman held meetings with DOE security officials and FBI agents, a decision was made to keep Lee away from new weapons codes but allow him to continue working on the older "legacy" codes. One consideration was that a move to unclassified work might alert Lee that he was under investigation. By August, however, the FBI had dropped any objections to moving Lee to non-weapons work. FBI director

Louis Freeh mentioned the decision to Notra Trulock and another DOE official, but word never reached Los Alamos, and Lee stayed in place.

That summer, on orders from National Security Advisor Sandy Berger, CIA
analysts studied the original Kindred Spirit intelligence. They obtained the
Kindred Spirit Advisory Group bullets and found their own analysis agreed in
many ways. In September, the agency faxed its report to the FBI. It was clear the
CIA thought Trulock's claims were off the mark. Freeh jotted notes to the effect
that there was "a fundamental contradiction between what DOE had told the
FBI and what the CIA was telling the FBI." Apparently no one passed word to
the case agent, Levy.

According to the Bellows review team, the FBI was "handed and fumbled
an extraordinary opportunity to discover the fact that the Administrative Inquiry fundamentally mischaracterized the predicate for the investigation." As a
consequence, "[f]rom May 30, 1996, until early 1999, the FBI investigated the
wrong crime."

Freeh repeated his advice in October, saying DOE could pull Lee's clearance
without concern for harming the case. This time Jim Levy told Vrooman, but
Lee still was not moved. Vrooman later said he didn't want to jeopardize the
FBI's investigation. It was the same year that Lee used the tape drive on his X
Division computer to make the last tape in his collection of weapons codes.

The Bellows review team would later fault the OIPR lawyers for failing to
obtain a wiretap warrant. But Bellows's report also slapped the FBI for misstat-
ing facts in its application.

During this period of time, an order went out from Trulock's office to the
nuclear-weapons labs, directing them to conduct a security study that involved
cataloging the names of Chinese Americans, according to two officials who
have seldom agreed on anything, Trulock and Vrooman. Both men said the
study was blatant racial profiling.

Vrooman recalled that Los Alamos, Lawrence Livermore, and Sandia were
ordered to compile the list, including not just naturalized citizens like the Lees,
but also second-generation Asian Americans. The list was to include their
names, the programs they worked for, and a system to monitor their travels.
Vrooman said managers at the labs refused to do the study, which they thought
was improper if not illegal.

Trulock said the study was commissioned not by his intelligence shop, but
by security officials in another part of DOE headquarters. Before the project
was halted, he said, he was shown charts containing names. Someone else in
DOE, Trulock said, wanted to know "how many Wen Ho Lees were working on
defense programs, how many Asian Americans."

-15-

Flying the False Flag

In the spring of 1998, a new counterintelligence agent arrived at the Santa Fe FBI office for assignment full-time to the Los Alamos lab. Carol Covert was a skier, and from the FBI office above the post office she could get to the Santa Fe Ski Area in a thirty-minute drive up a winding mountain road, banked by rock cliffs and aspen groves. The opposite direction, west toward Los Alamos, offered nearly as beautiful a drive—and another ski area, less frequented by tourists.

Covert was in her mid-forties, an attractive woman with reddish-brown hair. Her last two posts with the Bureau had also been in counterintelligence, in California and at headquarters. She was specially trained in the gathering of crime-scene evidence and computer investigations. Computers were an interest she had in common with her husband, a retired IBM employee and also an avid skier. From him she acquired the surname that was the source of much ribbing in the Bureau.

Vrooman found Covert to be the best of the FBI counterintelligence agents who had been assigned to Los Alamos. The intelligence and counterintelligence officials at the laboratory loved her; she was smart, motivated, and dedicated to working counterintelligence. She came to Los Alamos frequently and talked to scientists about their research and their travels abroad. Lab officials took her into their confidence.

Stillman shared with her the Pruvosts' suspicions about their neighbor, Wen Ho Lee. The FBI hadn't shown much interest in the Pruvosts' theories, and Covert was leery of poaching on Levy's case. But she decided to look into it with Stillman.

They timed the interference on the Pruvosts' phone and found it occurred at precise intervals of 93.2 minutes. They also discovered that other people in the neighborhood seemed to be having interference on their phones. They wanted to set up an electronic surveillance station inside the Pruvosts' home, aimed at the Lees'. But that would require a surveillance warrant, and they weren't sure they had enough evidence. They then decided to check with other federal authorities on the existence of a Chinese satellite on an orbital path over Los Alamos.

Eventually, their inquiries ended up at U.S. Space Command, the arm of the military that tracks satellites and space debris. Space Command reported three satellites over Los Alamos with orbital periods roughly matching the interference in the neighborhood. Two of the satellites were American; one was Russian. None was Chinese.

The episode of the burping telephones of White Rock was over without resolution. It added nothing to the Lee case. But the Pruvosts, according to acquaintances, remained convinced they were living next door to a spy.

That spring, Lee was cultivating a second career as a consultant, and had talked to lab acquaintances about it. He began working as a paid consultant in the late 1980s for a Taiwanese friend.

In March 1998, Lee secured lab approval for a multiweek trip to Taiwan to see two elderly sisters and to deliver two papers on shaped explosives at Chung Shan Institute of Science and Technology. Chung Shan was the site of Taiwan's secret nuclear-weapons program before it was abandoned in the 1980s under pressure from the United States. Just before he left, Lee called the lab's computer help desk and asked a technician whether he could remotely access the classified lab network from abroad. He could not, the technician told him.

Lee flew alone to Taiwan, his airfare paid by Chung Shan. He met the president of AsiaTek Inc., a defense firm with ties to Chung Shan and an interest in Lee's code skills. In May, he used a Chung Shan computer to log on to the *unclassified* Los Alamos network. He plucked two unclassified code files from the mass of weapons codes he had stored there, and copied them across the Internet to Taiwan. Chung Shan's computers—and every computer along the Internet path between Chung Shan and Los Alamos—could have captured Lee's passwords and commands.

Every keystroke he made was a potential free pass to the collection of Los Alamos's nuclear-weapons design codes that he had left on the unclassified network since the late 1980s. The FBI later found no evidence that anyone at Chung Shan or anywhere else accessed those codes, but Lee's actions that May posed a tremendous security risk. The FBI and the Energy Department later would regret not tracking Lee's actions during his trip abroad.

By the summer of 1998, the Lee case was two years old, and the FBI had made effectively zero progress. Case agents Lieberman and Levy had acquired virtually no evidence for a prosecution.

Levy, in the words of one supervisor, was a "reject." But his Albuquerque supervisors weren't making his job any easier. He maintained a criminal case there while working the Lee case in Los Alamos, a four-hour round trip away. Levy was a bundle of nerves. It seemed nothing could persuade the Office of Intelligence Policy Review to forward a FISA warrant application to the Foreign Intelligence Surveillance Court.

The Bureau couldn't listen on the Lees' phone and had erroneously concluded that Wen Ho's e-mails and computer were out of bounds. The FBI had no traction on him whatsoever.

That summer, agents decided to try one of the riskiest tactics in the counterintelligence game. They would mount a false-flag operation: An agent pretending to be a Chinese intelligence operative would contact Lee and try to entice him into doing or saying something incriminating.

Typically, a false flag is the counterintelligence equivalent of a Hail Mary pass in football, a last resort. A false flag in a China case was challenging because the FBI had few agents who were fluent in Mandarin. Running one against Wen Ho Lee was especially dicey: It was exceedingly rare to target an American citizen who had already been used to run a false flag on another suspect, as Lee had on Gwo-Bao Min in 1983.

It was a gamble. What if Lee recognized the operation and panicked? As one veteran FBI counterintelligence agent put it: "You gotta have your bag packed correctly to do a false flag, or it won't work. They are hard to do. You have to know it all. You don't want to contradict what the target knows about the service you supposedly work for. . . . You have to know the code words, the technique to show you are from the service. You have to establish your bona fides."

The FBI took weeks to prepare. It lined up an agent who was fluent in Mandarin and briefed him on the evidence. But just before the scheduled date for contact with Lee, the agent learned he was being sent to a post in Beijing. The FBI didn't want to muddy the waters by having him testify at a spy trial.

Instead, the Bureau quickly drafted another Chinese-speaking agent. But the new agent had grown up in Hong Kong and spoke the Cantonese dialect, with a Hong Kong accent. Chinese intelligence personnel—both of the Ministry of State Security and COSTIND—primarily spoke Mandarin, just like

Lee. Running a false flag in the wrong language of the intelligence service *and* the target was a matter of questionable judgment.

On an August morning, the agent phoned Lee's office in X Division and got no answer. It was an annoying delay for the encampment of FBI agents in two adjoining rooms of a Santa Fe hotel. Covert called Craig at the lab: "We can't reach him. Could you go see if he's in?" Craig walked by Lee's office, and there he was. Try again, he told Covert.

This time the agent connected and introduced himself as a Chinese government representative just passing through New Mexico. Immediately his language seemed to be a liability. Lee seemed puzzled on the other end of the line, perhaps even suspicious. He asked the agent to repeat his name and spell it in Chinese characters.

Having gotten past the name ordeal, the agent asked the question that had been agreed upon beforehand: "Has the Peter Lee case caused any trouble for the Chinese at the laboratory?"

According to Bureau and lab sources, Lee didn't seem interested in answering, but he was curious about exactly which branch of the Chinese government his caller represented. By his comments, Lee seemed to show a familiarity with Chinese organizations involved in intelligence gathering. The agent asked whether Lee would have lunch with him, and Lee cautiously agreed. First, Lee said, he would have to check with his superiors. He got a callback number for the agent.

A few minutes later, Lee phoned the agent and said he would not be able to meet with him. The agent again tried talking Lee into a meeting, but it was no use. He told Lee that he would still be in town the next day and would call again. Lee politely said goodbye and hung up. The agents exchanged looks of disappointment. He hadn't taken the bait. The false flag, so far, was a failure.

In retrospect, the agents suspected Lee had called his wife after the first conversation and she had cautioned him against a meeting.

Covert asked the lab counterintelligence staff to locate Lee's car. They found his Oldsmobile Cutlass Supreme in a parking lot. The FBI set up surveillance and saw Lee put a file box in the trunk, then drive home for lunch.

Whatever conversation Wen Ho Lee had with his wife that day and evening, it obviously had an impact on Sylvia Lee. She phoned a friend, Pat Krikorian, whose husband worked at the lab, and related the call her husband had received. "Tell the people at the lab who should know," Sylvia Lee said. Pat Krikorian's husband reported the incident to lab counterintelligence the next morning.

The FBI agreed that lab counterintelligence should go talk to Lee, but not until the false flag agent contacted him by phone a second time. In the second phone call, Lee was no more eager to meet than the previous day. The agent said Lee could call back anytime and gave Lee a phone number. Covert phoned Terry Craig and told him to go talk to Lee.

Craig walked to Lee's office and struck up a casual conversation, waiting for Lee to mention the call. When he didn't, Craig told him that his wife had reported it. Craig looked for Lee's reaction.

"It was kind of like, no reaction," Craig said. "He said, 'Yeah, I was gonna come see you.' " Craig didn't believe him. Lee confirmed he'd gotten a phone call, but didn't mention that he'd been asked to meet with the caller, nor that the caller had inquired about an espionage case.

"I gave him every opportunity in the world," Craig said. He even prompted Lee, asking whether or not the caller had asked to get together.

"Oh, I forgot to tell you a couple of things," Lee replied. "He did want me to meet him." Lee told Craig that he had been a little suspicious.

Craig returned to his office one floor below. Within minutes, Lee appeared. Looking uncomfortable, Lee said he hadn't known that his wife had called Pat Krikorian, and he'd been surprised to see Craig. But Lee didn't add any more detail about the phone call, such as the callback number.

"He just was not level with me," Craig said. "He never told me the guy really pushed him [to meet], and he never said the guy spoke the wrong kind of Chinese."

In sum, "he really didn't do anything wrong," Craig said. "The question is, why would he lie by being silent?"

The FBI didn't know what to make of the situation. Wen Ho Lee had not reported an obvious approach by a foreign intelligence service, but his wife arguably had—apparently without his knowledge.

Whatever the conclusion, it was clear the false flag had failed.

The FBI didn't generate a printed translation of the phone conversation for more than a month. Levy, Covert, and their supervisors were apparently unaware of the one intriguing point in the entire exchange—Lee's apparent recognition of Chinese intelligence organization. Even when the translation was complete, nobody passed that information to the attorneys at OIPR who were reviewing the wiretap application. Nor were the attorneys informed that Lee failed to report the come-on. The new information might have impelled OIPR to forward the FBI's wiretap application to the Foreign Intelligence Surveillance Court, or so OIPR officials later claimed in congressional testimony.

The FBI missed a crucial opportunity to try to obtain a warrant to bug Lee's phone and home. If the warrant were granted, it would have been an easy matter to monitor of Lee's computer at the laboratory.

Levy now had very little to show for more than a year and a half of work. His propensity for documenting everything left him with a sizable written record of an investigation going nowhere. DOE counterintelligence chief Edward J. Curran, a former FBI spy catcher, was pushing the FBI to do something, anything. Washington FBI headquarters was increasingly displeased with the lack of progress, and Levy was on the receiving end of their reproach. Covert remarked to acquaintances that Levy appeared frayed.

Supervisors considered teaming up the two agents, but in the end, the case was handed to Covert.

———————

On December 2, Wen Ho Lee again left for Taiwan. He had notified laboratory officials of a family emergency; one of his sisters was ill. Lee also had a troubled nephew whom he would be escorting to Taiwan so the family could look after him.

Laboratory regulations required notification of any employee travel, even for personal reasons, to a sensitive country. Taiwan was a sensitive country, due to its earlier interest in nuclear-weapons research and its ongoing territorial dispute with China, a nuclear power.

Lee initially sought official sanction for the trip by saying that he had been invited to give a paper at the Chung Shan Institute in exchange for airfare. Los Alamos would not approve the travel officially, but would not keep Lee from visiting his family in an emergency. Lee departed in the company of his nephew.

Over the next three weeks, he would split his time between his family and business in Taipei. He delivered a luncheon speech at the Chung Shan Institute. According to later FBI investigation, he also performed more consulting work for AsiaTek Inc. in the realm of armor-antiarmor simulation.

In Albuquerque, meanwhile, a new supervisory agent, Will Lueckenhoff, arrived at the field office. He read Bruno's administrative inquiry and was appalled. For the first time, someone in the FBI questioned the AI's basic premise that the W88 design had been stolen by China, probably from Los Alamos, likely with the help of Wen Ho Lee. Lueckenhoff concluded the report was "a piece of junk." The field of suspects could easily number three hundred people.

– 16 –

Trulock and the True Believers

B_y *the autumn of 1998*, Notra Trulock was a frustrated man. For three years, the DOE's intelligence chief had been sounding his alert about the Chinese, but it seemed no one was paying attention. Over and over again, he had told his story, complete with slides and a red-bound briefing book. His message was that the Chinese had stolen W88 secrets in the 1980s, then designed and tested something almost identical in 1992. Security at the labs was a joke; the scientists were out of control. Chinese came and went, some for a week, some for a year. Americans were in China, virtually naked to clever solicitation techniques. No one seemed to care. There could be a spy in the labs right now, beavering away, undetected.

Trulock had been persistent. His evangelizing had spread beyond the Energy Department in 1995, to the White House, the CIA, and the Defense Department.

In April 1996, Trulock briefed Sandy Berger, then the deputy to National Security Advisor Anthony Lake. In the situation room of the White House, Trulock spent forty-five minutes using his charts to map his case. He warned of evidence of Chinese "successes" as recently as 1995 or 1996, when neutron-bomb secrets may have once again been lost from the weapons labs. Berger listened, and then approved Trulock's plans to inform Congress about the possibility of a spy. Berger "expressed his hope that the FBI would catch him and prosecute him," Trulock said.

Trulock became a traveling China-spy show. In all, he guessed he did sixty briefings. He told his story to Leon Fuerth, the national security advisor to Vice President Al Gore. In a spate of briefings in the summer of 1997, he talked

163

to FBI Director Louis Freeh, Attorney General Janet Reno, and Secretary of Defense William Cohen. He briefed at the National Security Agency and again at the White House's National Security Council. He met with the staffs of the two most relevant committees on Capitol Hill, the intelligence committees of the House and Senate, in June and July of 1996. Afterward, he felt the reaction was too subdued.

Trulock was persuasive. He had an air of credibility, speaking as if he were revealing secrets with every breath. His talks had a dramatic flair and visual impact. His W88 slide show was subtitled, "DOE Nuclear-Weapons Laboratory Contributions to Chinese Strategic Breakthroughs." "He was a very compelling briefer. He spent hours preparing for a briefing," said Ric Bloodsworth, a CIA officer who served as Trulock's counterintelligence chief at DOE in the mid-1990s. "It was his knowledge, his writing ability, his ability to cut to the heart of a problem."

"I'm not saying that Notra didn't have a point of view," Bloodsworth added. "And I'm not saying that didn't cause any problems."

A former senior DOE official said, "Like most intelligence analysts who are kind of tea-leaf readers, they often hypothesize worst-case events. And I took Notra's analysis not at face value."

"He was fine. He was intel," said Dan Bruno, the DOE investigator. "As far as I'm concerned, he was not an alarmist. He put them in the right church, maybe not the right pew."

Trulock claimed to have peppered his talks with caveats, but few in his audience heard them. According to Bob Vrooman, in 1998 word filtered back to the lab that Trulock was "briefing Kindred Spirit as if Wen Ho Lee was about to be arrested." Trulock berated Stephen Younger, the head of the Los Alamos nuclear-weapons program, for not taking the China threat more seriously. "The FBI is getting ready to slap handcuffs on a guy out there right now in X Division," he told Younger. Stories circulated that Trulock was claiming that China had deployed an exact copy of the W88 atop a missile.

John C. Browne, who became the Los Alamos director in November 1997, was briefed by Trulock and found him to be "a very strong, adamant individual."

"The way he put it, it was the W88 [that was lost] and the details could only have come from a weapons designer . . . 'This is one of your guys and you've got a big problem.' "

FBI agents referred to one of Trulock's "alarming" talks as the "nightmare presentation" and the "sky is falling" briefing. In tone and substance, the briefings shared the problems of the earlier administrative inquiry. Despite the dire claims, there was no consensus that the W88 had been "lost," and not a scrap of evidence that, if it had, Los Alamos was responsible. But the exaggerations had a very real effect. The AI and Trulock's briefing had prompted the FBI to investigate Wen Ho Lee for espionage—a death penalty offense.

Bobby Henson, the physicist who had worked with Trulock on the original intelligence assessment, remembered a 1996 conversation in the men's bathroom at Sandia National Laboratory in Albuquerque. Henson, like Trulock a man of strong opinions, was explaining his theory of how high-level interactions between the U.S. and Chinese labs involving some of Los Alamos's most prominent scientists could have resulted in the inadvertent compromise of weapons-design information. "Trulock's response was, 'I caught my sonofabitch, I don't want to hear what you have to say.' " Trulock later denied that he had made that statement.

Despite all his high-level access, Trulock still felt frustrated. There had been security initiatives, but on the ground at the labs, he thought, not much had changed. It didn't even cheer him up to know that he and Bloodsworth had played a role in creating Presidential Decision Directive 61. After Clinton signed it in February 1998, PDD-61 made counterintelligence for the DOE labs an independent organization that reported directly to the secretary of energy, with bigger budgets and a more professional staff.

It didn't matter, he felt, because the labs were still full of Chinese postdoc students, like the one Lee had hired. More experienced foreign scientists were hired as "assignees," and stayed on for a year or more. "For two years, the big flap in the office was Notra's concern there were too many foreign nationals from sensitive countries on campus in Los Alamos," said John Richter, the Los Alamos bomb designer who worked in Trulock's intelligence shop in Washington.

The list of "sensitive" countries has about two dozen names. They are countries that have weapons programs or might want one, such as India, Iran, Iraq, Israel, North Korea, Libya, Pakistan, Taiwan, China, and Russia.

DOE inspectors had gone to the labs and brought back "anecdote after anecdote" about scientists who had host responsibilities for foreign postdocs "but hadn't seen them for months," Trulock said.

He had a host of security horror stories. The rules for handling secret documents had been relaxed after the Cold War. The FBI once had agents stationed at the labs but had pulled them out in 1994 in frustration at the lab directors' lack of commitment to security. Los Alamos scientists had evaded the rules governing foreign visitors by meeting them off-campus. Trulock was familiar with the long history of studies that had frowned at poor security practices at Los Alamos and Livermore. A list later compiled by the President's Foreign Intelligence Advisory Board categorized 112 studies between 1980 and 1999 into topics ranging from missing classified documents to inadequate safeguards for nuclear material to unsupervised foreign visitors.

"The threat was a serious one. There was an explosion of visitors," Bloodsworth said. "You can see it happen in the statistics in the late eighties. The floodgates open. People are pouring into the laboratories. We needed a tighter knowledge of what was going on. Notra was concerned that the people in control at Energy were blowing him off." From the late 1980s to the mid-1990s, the number of foreign visitors had risen by 50 percent.

The General Accounting Office reported that a lab departmental newsletter containing classified information was mailed to eleven foreign visitors. In yet another incident, an undercover security assessment team went into an unclassified building and removed a complete computer system without anyone questioning their actions, even though they wore no security badges.

Between 1994 and 1996, there were 2,714 foreign visitors to Los Alamos. On ten occasions, according to the GAO, lab employees hosted visitors from sensitive countries without bothering to get approval in advance.

The list went on. Once foreign visitors arrived at Los Alamos or Livermore, it wasn't always clear what topics were cleared for discussion, the GAO reported. An Israeli scientist assigned to Los Alamos collaborated on research of high explosives used in nuclear weapons, while two Chinese scientists visited Livermore to discuss the manufacturing of special high-speed cameras used to record nuclear-weapons tests.

But, unlike Trulock, Vrooman thought the situation was well in hand. In 1997 Vrooman wrote an assessment of the threat posed to the lab by foreign intelligence that was met with derision at DOE headquarters. The assessment was "very shallow, very brief," according to Bloodsworth. "No problem here, and if we ever do have one, we'll get in touch." Parts of the assessment were so ludicrous, according to Trulock, that Bloodsworth read them aloud for entertainment.

In Trulock's view, lab management was clearly on Vrooman's side. In fact, Vrooman was given an award for his role in getting rid of the background checks on foreign visitors.

———————

The disputes between Trulock and the lab reflected a larger disagreement over the value of foreign interactions. Los Alamos maintained that to attract high-level employees, the lab must not deny them the stimulation and recognition gained from being members of the international science community. The GAO saw foreign scientists as "having the opportunity to identify and target" U.S. secrets, and warned of "relationships that foreign countries can use to obtain information."

Trulock very much wanted to tell his story to a larger congressional audience. Twice, he said, DOE officials had blocked his testimony. On one occasion, he said, he was told that his testimony would be used by the Republicans to attack Clinton's China policy, which included support for the comprehensive Test Ban Treaty.

The treaty, an effort to bring a worldwide halt to nuclear explosions, was an important goal of the Clinton administration. China, after a spate of tests to refine its design of new, smaller warheads, stopped testing in 1996. Some anti-Clinton conspiracy buffs in Congress whispered that the administration had willingly allowed China to steal the W88 so that the Asian country, having as sophisticated weapons as the United States, would agree to the treaty.

Trulock didn't go that far, but he accused the administration of using the labs, with all their secrets, as "bait" to engage not only the Chinese and the Russians, but Israel as well. (Some Los Alamos scientists claimed that the "pushiest" foreign visitors were not from Russia or China, but from France.)

———————

After years of disappointment, Trulock finally got a break, in the form of a congressional committee chaired by California Representative Christopher Cox.

The Cox Committee grew out of the bitter relationship between the Republican Party, which controlled both the House and Senate, and the Clinton White House. Republicans had relentlessly pursued allegations that money from the Chinese government had wound up, illegally, among campaign contributions to the Democratic National Committee during the 1996 elections. There was a clandestine plan by China to influence the U.S. elections, the Republicans said.

In May 1998, a dramatic new story emerged about Sino-U.S. dealings, fueling even more Republican rancor toward the Clinton administration.

The New York Times reported that two American aerospace companies that paid Beijing to launch their satellites may have violated export laws by helping China solve technical problems that had plagued its missiles.

A federal grand jury was investigating, but "the criminal inquiry was dealt a serious blow two months ago when President Clinton quietly approved the export to China of similar technology . . ." Justice Department officials had opposed Clinton's decision. The chairman of one of the companies, Loral Space & Communications, was the largest single contributor to the Democratic National Committee in 1997. One of the reporters on the story was veteran *Times* investigative journalist Jeff Gerth.

A month after the story appeared, House Speaker Newt Gingrich announced that Cox would head a select committee to look into the missile deal and other wrongdoing. Gingrich set the tone for what was to follow. "This has to do with the national security of the United States and the effort by a foreign government to penetrate our political system and the effort by some people to give the Chinese secrets in violation of American law," he said. "This is a profoundly deeper question than anything that has arisen in this administration."

On the same day, Gingrich compared the Clinton White House to the *Jerry Springer Show,* a reference to Clinton's affair with intern Monica Lewinsky. The tenor of the times was acrimony.

That same month, May 1998, Trulock was removed as director of intelligence at DOE. There was a new secretary of energy, former U.N. ambassador and New Mexico Congressman Bill Richardson, and he wanted his own man in the job. It was a double hit for Trulock. Presidential Decision Directive 61, which he had campaigned for, gave his counterintelligence responsibilities to FBI agent Ed Curran, who was detailed to the Department of Energy. Trulock was demoted to an advisor's position.

Representative Cox, a Harvard Law grad and a former legal counsel in the Reagan White House, set out a bipartisan course for his committee: five Republicans, four Democrats, a joint investigative staff. The House Select Committee on U.S. National Security and Military/Commercial Concerns with the People's Republic of China would operate largely behind closed doors, and have a report out by January 1. The size of its staff and budget was the envy of the Hill. It operated in secure, windowless quarters, with alarms and "burn bags" to dispose of classified documents.

Representative John Spratt, a South Carolina Democrat on the committee, found that Cox, as promised, kept partisan bickering out of the proceedings. But Spratt felt Cox had loaded the staff with people from the intelligence and national-security world who "had a certain attitude about China, its 'hegemonic' objectives in Asia." The committee was influenced behind the scenes by the "Blue Team," an informal group of Washington insiders from think tanks, academia, and government agencies who believed the Clinton administration was soft on China.

James Mulvenon, a China expert from the Rand Corporation, one of the country's oldest think tanks, was asked to talk to the committee about the number of U.S. firms secretly owned by the Chinese government. "I testified on Chinese front companies and immediately got into a fight with Cox," he said.

Mulvenon testified that there were perhaps two dozen such companies. "Cox turns around and says, 'The FBI tells me there are three thousand front companies.'"

Mulvenon had worked with the FBI's Los Angeles office on the front company issue, and he thought he recognized the source of the three-thousand figure. It was every company in the United States owned by Chinese citizens or corporations, regardless of size. When he told the committee that, he said, the response was "You can't prove that those companies aren't front companies."

On September 1, Trulock testified in closed session with the committee staff. He had come to talk about how China might use high-performance U.S. commercial computers—Clinton had eased export controls on high-end computers—to build advanced nuclear weapons. The computers would be especially helpful, he told the staffers, when combined with the design secrets China had stolen from Los Alamos and Livermore. "I was daydreaming and I sort of snapped my neck. What did that guy say? What?" remembers a staffer. "You could have heard a pin drop in that room."

At last, Trulock had found a welcoming audience. He was invited back to tell his story to the full committee on November 12. As committee members sat spellbound behind the closed doors of an Interior Committee hearing room, the political scientist told them about the W70—the neutron bomb believed given away by Tiger Trap's men in the late 1970s—and the W88.

The interesting part of the W70, he said, was the primary. It was different from the W88 primary and not quite as small. But still, it was small enough that the Chinese could mount it on a small "road mobile" missile that could be launched from a truck. A mobile missile would be harder for an adversary to find than a stationary missile, increasing its worth.

"When Notra Trulock presented [his chart], I got the message," recalled Representative Norm Dicks, the ranking Democrat on the committee. Another committee member remembered Dicks exclaiming, "This is incredible! I can't believe it!" Trulock described Dicks's reaction as "apoplectic." Dicks said, "Everybody in town knows how screwed up DOE is, but nobody knew it was this bad."

"I saw the look on their faces, I listened to the expression of emotion when we heard these things, and our hearts were in our mouths," Cox said. "The information on the W88 and W70 was so extensive that it permitted them successfully to test these weapons. Particularly with the W88, that is a remarkable thing." Despite Cox's description, the Chinese had not actually tested a copy of the W88 but had tested a device that shared some of its design features.

Spratt, a veteran of the House, saw immediately that Trulock had changed the course of the committee's investigation. "The Cox Committee had been cranked up expecting to find some significant lapse of security in the satellite launches," he said. "Instead, we went on into the fall with a ho-hum set of findings that weren't going to alarm anybody. And then Notra Trulock comes along with a story of nuclear espionage."

Trulock told the committee about the FBI's spy suspect at Los Alamos, a scientist the FBI agents called "Kindred Spirit."

Trulock's timing was perfect. The committee was set to expire on December 31. The staff hurried to write up Trulock's revelations and find a color photo of a nuclear mushroom cloud for the report. "All of a sudden we had this sensational story," Spratt said.

The committee's other senior Democrat, Rep. Dicks of Washington, hastened to the office of Energy Secretary Bill Richardson to warn him that the allegations were serious. Richardson had to act, Dicks told him.

Trulock would come back for one more hearing, on December 16, when he was once again the star witness. The hearings were a turning point in his life, although he wouldn't realize it for a few more months.

– 17 –

Exile from X Division

In early December, DOE counterintelligence chief Ed Curran found himself in the unenviable position of being questioned by the Cox Committee. The committee was demanding an explanation for the loss of multiple-warhead designs and the lack of progress in bringing the Kindred Spirit suspect to justice as the apparent thief of the W88 warhead.

It was only then that Curran learned that Lee, at that very moment, was out of the country. Curran was stunned. Their leading nuclear espionage suspect was less than a hundred miles from China. Who knew whether he really was in Taiwan at all? Could he have been spooked by the false flag and now be spilling secrets to the Chinese or even seeking asylum? He could easily slip into China, and no one would be the wiser. The committee was demanding answers. Curran didn't have any. He felt blindsided.

Curran was an old FCI hand, as one reporter called him, "an espionage troubleshooter." He had led a counterintelligence squad in New York City that tried tricks to "flip" Soviet agents and diplomats, even using call girls.

The ruddy, lanky father of four also helped manage the investigation of Harold J. Nicholson, a rising CIA star thought to be a Soviet spy. To catch him, agents slipped into CIA headquarters, where they bugged his office phone, installed a TV camera in the ceiling, and searched his car. Lately, Curran had been trying to do the job Trulock apparently couldn't—accomplish a huge overhaul of counterintelligence at DOE and its labs, which entailed quite a sales job to lab scientists. Now he was coming up to speed on another Trulock legacy—Wen Ho Lee.

A few days later, on December 15, Curran learned in a meeting at FBI headquarters that FBI Director Freeh had recommended removing Lee's access to classified weapons data. This was getting worse. Curran had thought Lee was still working in his regular job, on weapons codes and design data, at the FBI's insistence. And as Curran saw it, the Bureau had spooked Lee but its agents still were unprepared to interview the Lees and bring the investigation into the open.

He reported what was happening back to Energy Secretary Bill Richardson. Cox's committee was hot about the lack of progress on Kindred Spirit, and the FBI's case was going nowhere. The Department of Energy had to do something, and soon.

Richardson was a true Clintonite. He and the president were creatures of ambition and politics, deftly skirting the contours of public opinion and partisan minefields.

Richardson had been elected six times as the congressman of New Mexico's Third District, a Democratic stronghold in the northern portion of the state that included Santa Fe and Los Alamos. On the campaign trail, he shed his suit in favor of jeans and sportcoats. He assiduously cultivated reporters and was famous for yearly parties where the tequila flowed freely and Richardson casually dropped hints of his desire to become vice president, perhaps president. He and his perennial advisor and press secretary, Stu Nagurka, were reputed to sit down every week to map their strategies for the next week, the next year, and so on, all the way to the White House. In 1998, Richardson seemed to be closing in on his target: He was widely rumored to be on Gore's short list for a vice presidential running mate.

As a congressman, Richardson had trod a delicate line between Los Alamos's conservatism and support for nuclear-weapons research on one hand and Santa Fe's liberal disdain for weapons on the other. His political calculations led him to become a loud critic of a defense nuclear waste dump known as the Waste Isolation Pilot Plant. After a short tenure as U.S. ambassador to the United Nations, Richardson had the misfortune to be tapped as the Secretary of Energy, requiring a 180-degree reversal of his stand on WIPP. In New Mexico, Richardson had campaigned as the "Fighter for the North." Now he was fighting for WIPP, even if that meant going to court against many of his former constituents.

Richardson already could see where the Cox Committee was going. He had heard Trulock's briefing more than a month before, and had approved his testimony before the committee despite the misgivings of some of his staff.

Behind his desk on the ninth floor of the Forrestal Building, Richardson listened to Curran's conundrum. The Cox Committee clearly was out for blood, but the FBI investigation seemed to have stagnated. It was time to take action. If the FBI couldn't move the investigation, Curran suggested, the DOE could act on its own in the interest of self-preservation. Beyond the political considerations, the Energy Department had a legal and moral obligation to protect the classified data in its possession.

The false flag had blown any semblance of a covert investigation. Lee was spooked, and there was no longer reason to keep him in his job. At the least, Curran advised, the department could ask Lee, on his return from Taiwan, to undergo a polygraph examination under the pretense of the routine renewal of his security clearance or a post-travel debriefing.

Top Energy Department officials and the FBI later offered differing accounts of the motivations of Richardson and Curran for ordering Lee polygraphed. The FBI's version was starkly political: Richardson feared the Cox Committee's report and put pressure on the FBI to come up with an excuse to fire Lee posthaste.

Two drafts of an internal FBI memo supported this conclusion.

On December 18, a memo circulated among the Bureau's top brass, especially in the National Security Division, noting that DOE counterintelligence wanted to "neutralize their employee's access to classified information prior to the issuance of a final report by the Cox Committee." An earlier draft said DOE wanted to cut Lee's access before "the conclusion of the Cox Committee hearings this month."

Energy's counterintelligence officials decided they would send officers to LANL as soon as Lee returned from Taiwan and conduct what would be portrayed to Lee as a post-travel interview and give him a polygraph exam.

Supervisors in the FBI's National Security Division told DOE that its agents would not be ready to conduct their own "interrogation of the Lees on the W88 question" for a few weeks. They approved Curran's plan.

Albuquerque's new Special Agent in Charge, or SAC, David V. Kitchen, was ordered by FBI headquarters to prepare for an interrogation of the couple "aimed at resolving this case."

The China Unit's Craig Schmidt, who was supervising Kindred Spirit out of Washington, later testified in a deposition before staff of the Senate Judiciary Committee: "[T]he Cox Committee had been meeting for some time. They had focused very heavily on this investigation, and what they saw as being problems here concerning lack of security at the national laboratories. The Department of Energy was becoming more and more concerned about how they would appear, and how they were appearing, during the committee meetings. And it was becoming very urgent for them to look like they were doing something. Ergo, they decided that, 'On our own, we have to interrogate and interview Wen Ho Lee, and we have to jerk his clearance or his access, and we expect the FBI—we're begging the FBI, please resolve this investigation in the next 30 days or 60 days so we can fire this guy.' And at that point, I no longer had any control over the investigation, nor did Albuquerque or anybody else."

Curran later vehemently denied any political motivation for his decision to polygraph Lee. Counterintelligence officers who worked for him nonetheless got the impression that Curran and Richardson, at the least, were suddenly eager to fire Lee. Other DOE interviews suggest Richardson simply wanted to be decisive and proactive, or at least appear so. He had inherited this mess and wasn't about to become a victim of the Cox Committee and the political storm that was sure to follow.

In any event, on December 21, word came down from DOE headquarters to New Mexico that the Energy Secretary himself wanted "immediate action," to include Lee's removal from his job, regardless of the outcome of the interview and polygraph. Dick Schlimme, the DOE counterintelligence manager in Albuquerque, was on vacation when he got a phone call telling him to come into the office immediately.

Ken Schiffer likewise was unexpectedly pulled into the fray. By then Vrooman had retired, and Los Alamos had replaced him with Schiffer, a former FBI counterintelligence agent who spoke Mandarin and another Chinese dialect. He had years of experience in China cases. In his spare time, Schiffer was a rodeo champion; he roped steers for fun.

He had started work at the laboratory exactly one week before, on December 14. Terry Craig and Carol Covert had briefed him on Kindred Spirit. It was the first he'd heard of Wen Ho Lee. It wouldn't take long for him to conclude that Kindred Spirit agents were botching the investigation.

Schiffer already had committed to spending Monday, December 21 with his wife, getting settled in their new house in Los Alamos. He was supposed to make sure the movers got all of their boxes and possessions into the house. Instead, at 9 A.M. he was roped into a conference call with Curran's chief investigator and one of his deputies in the DOE Office of Counterintelligence. One of the DOE men said the Energy Secretary wanted Lee fired. They laid out for Schiffer the plan to use a post-travel debriefing as a pretext to interview and polygraph Lee.

On December 22, a contract polygrapher for the DOE, Wackenhut Security polygraph chief John P. Mata, huddled with Craig and Schiffer to plot their approach to Lee, who was expected back at the laboratory the next day.

December 23 was to become a frenetic and confusing day for all.

DOE's Schlimme left Albuquerque before 7 A.M. so he could meet the team being assembled in Los Alamos for the polygraph—Schiffer, Craig, Mata, and Wolfgang Vinskey, the polygraph operator from Wackenhut.

Schiffer, the FBI, and the DOE's polygraphers already had formulated the questions for the polygraph. Curran had instructed the polygraphers that their interview should be "cursory, non-alerting and non-confrontational."

If Lee refused the polygraph, his security clearance would be pulled on the spot and he would be sent home on investigative leave. If he failed it, Covert and another FBI counterintelligence agent, John Hudenko, would be waiting in the wings to interrogate him. It remained unclear what they would do if Lee passed the polygraph.

Lee arrived in his office shortly after 9 A.M. He was called to the lab's Internal Security Office, where he found Schiffer and Craig waiting with a third man. Schiffer and Craig asked him about his trip.

Lee clearly was pleased. He had managed to get his troubled nephew out of the United States and, in Taiwan, he had explored some promising work with AsiaTek. The company was thinking of creating commercial versions of one of his codes so that it could be marketed in the Pacific Rim. Lee didn't mention that the code to which he was apparently referring, MESA-2D, wasn't truly his. He had contributed to the code, but its primary developer was another laboratory scientist, and the code was export-restricted.

Schiffer introduced him to Mata, who gently asked Lee to take a polygraph examination. Lee reacted as though the request were a grievous insult. He had consented to a polygraph in 1984, he said, only because he was "a loyal American" and had wanted to clear his name. But after some discussion, Lee relented and agreed to be polygraphed.

The polygraph began at 10 A.M. in the Harold Agnew Conference Room. The polygrapher aimed a video camera at Lee and put a strap around Lee's chest to measure his respiratory rate, as well as a metal cuff around one of his fingers to monitor his skin conductivity and pulse rate. Then, in standard polygraph procedure, Vinskey laid out the questions that he planned to ask Lee.

He gave Lee definitions of espionage, disclosure of classified information, and unauthorized contacts with foreign nationals. The latter clearly embraced Lee's experience with senior Chinese weaponeers asking for a nuclear secret.

The FBI has a slang term for what happened next. It's called a hiccup. Lee began telling the polygraph things he had never admitted before. Lee revealed that Hu Side and Zheng Shaotang came to his hotel room on a muggy night in June 1988. He related Zheng's question about the two-point detonation system for the W88 primary, but said he hadn't answered. "I tell him I don't know and

I'm not interested" in discussing the question, Lee said. He hadn't given up any classified information, and Zheng hadn't pressed further. At first, Lee implied to Vinskey that he had reported the encounter on his trip report but later acknowledged that he hadn't, explaining that there didn't seem to be a place on the trip report for such information. Lee said he and Zheng exchanged Christmas cards for about three years afterward, then stopped.

Lee talked about his wife's work translating for the laboratory and the Lees' occasional entertainment of Chinese scientists at their home. Then he recounted the false-flag phone call from August.

He recalled being asked about the consequences of the Peter Lee case for Los Alamos Chinese. Lee said he then told the man that he was not interested in a meeting and ended the call. Lee recalled that Sylvia had said she would call a friend whose husband worked at the lab. Sylvia had said the call should be reported to lab security. Lee then misleadingly said *he* had reported the call. He still didn't mention that his caller had left a phone number for future contact.

Vinskey calibrated the machine by directing Lee to give incorrect answers to control questions so that Vinskey later could discern Lee's physiological responses when he was telling a lie.

Then Vinskey launched into the exam.

"Have you ever committed espionage against the United States?"

"No," Lee replied.

"Have you ever provided any classified weapons data to any unauthorized person?"

"No."

"Have you had any contact with anyone to commit espionage against the United States?"

"No."

"Have you ever had personal contact with anyone you know who has committed espionage against the United States?"

"No."

The preinterview and exam together lasted four hours. At 2:18 P.M., Vinskey stepped out and reported his conclusions to Mata, Schiffer, Craig, and Covert: NDS—no deception shown. Lee was telling the truth.

Schiffer walked into the conference room to talk to Lee. Why hadn't Lee brought up the 1988 meeting before? he asked. Lee launched into an elaborate explanation. He had suffered memory loss as a teenager when his appendix was removed, then again in 1987 after undergoing colon surgery. He said he had a lot of things on his mind.

At the time, Schiffer was unaware that Lee had embraced one of the Chinese scientists from the hotel room six years later, and Lee didn't mention the 1994 incident to him. But his explanation begged the question: How could he have forgotten meeting Hu in 1988 and having been locked in a hug with him in 1994?

Covert and Hudenko were not entirely surprised by the outcome of the polygraph. The Justice Department had not seen enough evidence for a FISA warrant, the false flag had failed, and now Lee had come up clean on a polygraph. Perhaps he was innocent after all. In fact, the Albuquerque FBI office increasingly suspected Lee had no connection to the supposed loss of the W88 and had begun to scrutinize the house of cards that was DOE's administrative inquiry.

Covert and Hudenko nonetheless missed a critical opportunity to rush in and explore Lee's admission. Here, under the pressure of a polygraph, he suddenly recalled being pressed for classified information by Chinese scientists more than a decade earlier. FBI counterintelligence agents are trained to suspect the worst: If a suspect acknowledges that he was approached by foreign operatives, an agent should assume that he gave something away. If the suspect acknowledges giving up only unclassified information, agents can be sure that he gave away secrets.

Lee's admission to the 1988 meeting could have been a stepping-off point for an interview: What else did the Chinese scientists say? Had there been other incidents in which he'd been asked for classified information? Where was Sylvia Lee when these high-ranking Chinese weapons scientists were in his hotel room? The agents arguably had the psychological edge to press for more but didn't. "It will bother me for years," said one official who was present.

Covert asked Vinskey for a copy of the polygraph charts. "Sure," Vinskey replied, "After the DOE releases it." The DOE's polygraph would be subject to rigorous quality assurance, Vinskey said. Mata and his supervisor would perform blind reviews of the polygraph charts and come up with their own interpretations as a check on Vinskey.

Presumably, everyone—the FBI, the DOE, and Los Alamos—might have been relieved by the result of the polygraph, which suggested that a laboratory employee had not stolen any secrets for a sophisticated U.S. nuclear warhead and given them away to China. But instead, DOE and Los Alamos were under orders to get Lee out of his job. The question was how to do that when he had a clean polygraph.

The FBI, DOE, and Los Alamos officials got together to decide what to do next. Covert said she would be ready to do a final interview with Lee in a couple of weeks. That left the laboratory and DOE people to decide how they were going to finesse pulling Lee out of X Division.

Eventually, Lee was told the DOE still had security concerns. He would be barred from his office in X Division for thirty days while those were resolved. Lee hung around the laboratory for a few hours, then went home.

Schiffer called Richard "Dick" Burick, the associate laboratory director for operations, and others for a meeting that ran into the evening. They decided to rescind Lee's access to his office inside the X Division Limited Exclusion Area or LEA. He would be transferred to similar but unclassified work in T Division's fluid dynamics group, known as T-3. That evening, the laboratory's computer-security officials were ordered to lock Lee out of the classified network, and X Division officials removed Lee's name from the computer that controlled the automated door locks to the LEA.

-18-

Panic

Lee left the polygraph in high anxiety. His security clearance, even his job was in peril. At 9:30 P.M., when most lab employees were gone and long after Lee typically went home to make dinner, he walked to the southwest corner of the Administration Building, where a door controlled by a badge reader gave access to a stairwell leading up to Lee's office on the second floor.

Lee pulled out his laboratory badge and, at 9:36, swiped it through the badge reader. It beeped a rejection. There was not the familiar click of the door lock disengaging, and the door did not open. Lee tried again, and again, his panic rising. He was locked out.

He absolutely had to get inside. If the laboratory searched his X Division office, he knew they would find plenty of reasons to fire him—hundreds of pages of classified documents should have been locked in his safe and weren't. Worst of all were the tapes he had made years ago, with so much painstaking effort. His office contained a vast and secret library of almost everything he had ever worked on, and more. Lee turned and swiped his card again; the door didn't budge.

He got into his Oldsmobile and drove home. Alberta was coming home for the holidays. Sylvia had picked her up at the airport and told her, "Your dad is being questioned for something." Alberta was worried: Her father never stayed at work this late. She fell asleep on the sofa, waiting for him, awakening when he came through the door.

"What's going on at work?" she asked. "Do you have a problem?"

"I don't know," he said.

"Do you still have a job?"

"I don't know."

Unable to sleep, Lee went back to the laboratory. It was 3:30 A.M. on December 24. He tried his card one more time. The reader just beeped—entry denied. Lee was not known for cursing, but he must have uttered a few choice words in those predawn hours.

On the morning of Christmas Eve, Lee was called to the office of Richard Krajcik, a primary designer and the deputy director of X Division. Dan Butler, the acting director of the Theoretical Division, was there. Krajcik informed Lee that he would be moved for thirty days to T Division, while the DOE looked into his 1988 contact with the Chinese and completed its clearance investigation. Butler told Lee that he had a project for him to work on and assured Lee that everything would be resolved as soon as possible.

Lee agreed. "If issues need to be resolved," he said, "I understand that."

Lab Director John Browne and most Los Alamos employees came back from their holidays on January 4. Ken Schiffer briefed Browne on the hectic events before Christmas. Browne instructed Schiffer to get a commitment from the DOE and the FBI to resolve the Lee case, one way or another, within thirty days. It wasn't fair for an investigation of a University of California employee to languish for years and disrupt his career, producing nothing except a clean polygraph. Schiffer made some phone calls and, within a few days, the FBI met Curran and his staff at DOE headquarters. Curran tried to get the Bureau to agree not to let the case drag on. The FBI committed to conducting an interview with Lee on January 17.

But while the laboratory was moving to protect Lee's reputation and career, Lee was moving to erase evidence of perhaps the most massive computer-security violation in Los Alamos history.

Lee was welcomed into the offices of T-3, the fluid dynamics group of the lab's T Division, located in a brick building a few dozen yards from his X Division office. There, Lee was teamed up with his old friend Bryan A. "Bucky" Kashiwa, with whom he had worked on and off since 1985. Kashiwa was the Japanese-American son of a hardware-store owner and a schoolteacher from a small town in upstate New York. He had married his childhood sweetheart, Linda, a girl he had known since kindergarten. Kashiwa was short and athletically built, with a long black ponytail streaked with a few gray hairs. Cheerful and easygoing, he loved playing country ditties on his guitar and favored a black cowboy hat. Every day, he drove an ancient Volkswagen to work at T-3.

Beneath his casual demeanor was a workaholic, an inventive scientist who couldn't switch his mind off. Years earlier, he had been a championship ski racer, and he had designed skis for Volant, a company he cofounded.

Kashiwa was a protégé of Frank Harlow, a pioneer in the field of fluid mechanics and computer simulation. It was Kashiwa who contributed the most to the research and papers that he and Lee had produced. In early January, T Division Director Dan Butler stopped Kashiwa in the hallway and laid out the situation: Lee was under investigation and would be working with Kashiwa in T-3 "for a while."

That night, Lee waited in his new office until he was sure he was alone with a computer and a telephone. He dialed up the lab's computer help desk and told the technician who answered that he seemed to be having trouble accessing his account on the X Division open network, also known as the Enchanted LAN. No one had told the help-desk technicians that Lee's account had been deactivated pending a security investigation. The technician helpfully reactivated the account, thinking someone else must have made a mistake. It would be almost a month before he learned the mistake was his.

At about 9:45 P.M., Lee typed in his password and regained access to his "kf1" directory, where he had accumulated the files of weapons codes, input decks, and data libraries that he had first begun downloading in 1988. He deleted three of the files. Eight days later he deleted more.

But his X Division office was still full of security violations, and Lee kept an eye out for any opportunity to get back inside.

On January 14, he got his chance—two, in fact. The first came at 2:45 A.M. The manner in which he gained access is unclear, but Lee made his way to his second-floor office. To his relief, it appeared just as he had left it. Once inside, he closed the door and booted up both the classified and unclassified computers. His classified account was still locked up. But it is reasonable to assume, based on his actions in the same time period, that he was eager to get rid of any evidence of mishandling classified computer files. Whatever he did, the job was incomplete: Over the next forty days, Lee made more than twenty-five attempts to get back in, the next one just hours later on that same day.

Around lunchtime on January 14, Lee waited outside the stairwell doorway for X Division, saw coworkers about to enter, and apparently slipped in behind them, tailgating his way into the Limited Exclusion Area. Another time, an unwitting security guard let him in.

On yet another occasion, a fellow X Division scientist escorted him to his office but declined to leave him alone there. Lee became angry and left. Another time, Lee called a friend, who came downstairs and let him in unescorted.

During one of his three returns to his office alone, Lee gathered more than a dozen 3M 6150 tapes that he had made in 1993, 1994, and 1997 and hauled them out of X Division.

On January 17, Lee welcomed FBI Special Agents Covert and Hudenko into his home. He excused himself to the kitchen and reappeared a few minutes later with a platter of cut fruit speared on toothpicks and a pot of his best tea, ordinarily saved for honored guests.

The agents responded amicably to Lee's hospitality. They began asking him questions about his 1988 hotel-room encounter with Hu Side and Zheng Shaotang. Lee said he didn't remember anything new about the conversation. He had told Hu and Zheng that he was not interested in talking about the question they asked; that was all.

The agents were solicitous. They wanted to help him—and perhaps get his help in finding whoever had stolen the W88. They asked him to go back to his very first meeting with the Chinese and recount every single contact. Lee said the first was in March of 1985 at a conference in Hilton Head, South Carolina, where a scientist named Li De Yuan had talked to Lee and invited him to a conference the next year in Beijing. At the 1986 conference, Lee told them, he had met a number of Chinese scientists—Li Wei Shen, who wanted help with a modeling problem, and at least three others—Li De Yuan, Li Wei Sew, and Wang Zhu Sheu—with whom Lee began corresponding with Christmas cards and letters. They were, in Lee's mind, just professional acquaintances of the kind the lab was encouraging at the time. He had reported all of them on his trip reports.

Lee tried to lend the impression of being cooperative. He flatly and repeatedly denied any role in the loss of any W88 information. In fact, the scientist said, he barely worked on anything classified.

The interview went on for four hours, but most of what Lee had to say merely reiterated what the agents had already heard. They noticed a Macintosh desktop in a work area off the living room. Later, when they asked Lee about it, he said it was lab-issued. "Sometimes I work at home," he explained. Covert and Hudenko thanked him for his cooperation and left.

The FBI had missed another opportunity. Each of Lee's admissions to a Chinese contact could have been probed further: What correspondence did you have with them besides Christmas cards? What are your perceptions of China? Instead, the interview lacked the tough questions from the heart of the case—for example: Why didn't you provide the phone number from the false flag to either lab counterintelligence or the FBI?

The FBI may have been squandering its chances, but Lee himself wasn't wasting time. Three days later, he spent twenty minutes on a T Division computer erasing forty-seven files from his unclassified directory. Each time he hit the delete button, however, he noticed that the files didn't disappear but simply became bracketed by parentheses.

On Thursday, January 21, he phoned the computer help desk and asked why the files he was deleting weren't "going away." The lab computer network had a safeguard against unintentional file deletions—hitting the DELETE button just queued them up for eventual erasure a week later. That way, if a scientist made a mistake, he or she could still retrieve the file.

But Lee wasn't making a mistake; he wanted the files gone. The technicians taught him over the phone how to override the deletion safeguard. A few minutes later, Lee made yet another attempt to enter X Division. His card still wouldn't work.

Later that day, FBI agents Hudenko and Michael Lowe brought to Lee a typed statement based on the January 17 interview, ready for his signature. What Hudenko and Lowe took back to the office that day would be the FBI's official record of Lee's account, as he saw it.

Covert and Hudenko had led Lee to believe the FBI's interest in him was coming to an end. They were trying to help clear his name. Lee was only too willing to cooperate in this regard. He carefully crossed out a number of the passages printed in the typed statement, amended it to his liking, and signed it. The FBI was almost ready to close the case.

Getting a signed, sworn statement was an unusual step in an investigation of alleged espionage. Such a statement is generally intended to lock in a suspect's story. By getting one from Lee, the agents were blocking Lee into a corner, making it almost impossible for him to alter or add to his story. And Lee's story kept changing—each time revealing more and more contacts with the Chinese—every time the FBI or anyone else questioned him. His version of the truth was fungible, varying with the time, the questioner, and the circumstances. The FBI's experience with Lee so far suggested that the more they poked at him, the more they would get. Instead, the statement locked the FBI into a story in flux.

But by then, the Albuquerque FBI had become convinced that Dan Bruno's administrative inquiry was hopelessly deficient, and perhaps dead wrong. "We couldn't understand how they came to the conclusion they came to, specifically about how Lee was the main suspect," said David V. Kitchen, the special agent in charge for New Mexico. Now Lee hadn't taken the bait in a false flag and had come up clean on a polygraph test. On January 22, Kitchen sent a memo to headquarters stating those conclusions, with Lee's sworn statement attached. "We worked the case for quite a while, and what did we have to show for it?" Kitchen asked.

But no one really worked the case until Covert. FBI Assistant Director for National Security Neil Gallagher later told the Bellows review team that the first two agents on Kindred Spirit—Lieberman and Levy—added up to "a third of an agent." But the fault lay most heavily on the supervisors who assigned them. The Albuquerque office frequently ranked the case as one of the lowest priorities in intelligence, itself a low priority. As a result, the Bellows team found, the case "proceeded at a pace that can only be described as languid, if not torpid." It "suffered from neglect, faulty judgment, bad personnel choices, inept investigation, and the inadequate supervision of that inept investigation."

Other counterintelligence investigators were critical in retrospect. "The FBI had uncovered nothing in three years, no evidence of wrongdoing, other than the admissions," a former counterintelligence agent said. "The admissions provided things to pursue. They didn't."

Lee, however, wasn't taking any chances. He continued his attempts to get back into X Division and to delete the weapons files from his unclassified directory. Over the next twenty days, he erased roughly 360 files that he had amassed since 1988. Every day the FBI increased his suspicion, Lee was covering his trail, and no one was watching.

One of those days in late January, Lee took a walk with his friend, Hsaio-Hua Hsu.

"Do you know anything about the W88?" Lee asked.

No, Hsu said. "It has a W on it, so it's a weapon."

Lee gave Hsu the impression that he knew nothing about the W88—a project on which he had worked.

Meanwhile, unwitting lab officials were agitating to get Lee back into X Division through the front door. The lab director had a commitment from the DOE to resolve the Lee case in thirty days, and time was up. T Division Director Dan Butler was needling senior lab managers, who in turn were needling the DOE's

Albuquerque office, who in turn were talking to Ed Curran at DOE headquarters: When could Lee go back to work?

Curran, for his part, kept nagging the FBI for something—anything—that would justify keeping Lee out of his old job. The Bureau had nothing. On February 2, after conferring with Secretary Richardson, Curran convened a conference call with DOE security officials, counterintelligence officials in Albuquerque and Los Alamos, and Dick Burick, the lab's associate director of operations. They came on the line one by one and, when all were assembled, Curran announced that, in the absence of any new information, he proposed to allow Lee to return to X Division. Schlimme in the Albuquerque Operations Office and Schiffer in Los Alamos said they had no new information and no objections. DOE Albuquerque agreed to formalize the decision in a letter to Burick that day.

A few hours after everyone hung up, Curran's phone rang, and an FBI official gave him jolting news: Something was wrong with the December 23 polygraph. The FBI had relied for weeks on the DOE's judgment that Lee was telling the truth. But DOE did not send the actual polygraph line tracings and videotape to FBI headquarters for review until the third week of January. FBI experts found that the test was inconclusive at best—and perhaps showed that Lee was being deceptive.

Curran reddened with surprise and anger. He told the FBI that he saw no other option but to interview and polygraph Lee again. But the Bureau was having none of it; its own polygrapher would test Lee this time.

Curran hung up, quickly dialed DOE Albuquerque and sought to rescind his order clearing Lee's return to X Division. He was too late; the letter had been faxed to Burick, who had drafted a letter to Lee saying the investigation was concluded and Lee could return to his old job. Burick had handed Lee the letter in person. Perhaps thinking his access was restored, Lee swiped his badge yet again at 4:52 P.M. but still could not gain admission to X Division.

Burick didn't learn of the last-minute snafu until the next morning and was annoyed. He had to go back to Lee and rescind the letter he'd just issued the previous afternoon.

That day, February 3, Lee made a total of six attempts to get into X Division, starting at 9:42 A.M. and running until 1:46, when he swiped his badge no fewer than four times. Ironically, Lee had come within hours of legitimately getting into the office to which he'd been denied access for so many weeks.

The different readings of the December 23 polygraph remain an open mystery. Questions were raised about why it took a month for the polygraph charts and videotape to reach the FBI for review, with DOE and the FBI each blaming the other for the delay.

The explanation for the polygraph's conflicting results could be as simple as flaws in the test itself and in its calibration. One of the control questions—"Are you the kind of person who would lie to cover up a mistake?"—may have been poorly worded to calibrate the machine to Lee's physiological responses. Lee's answer to that question sent the pin sailing off the graph paper, and most of his subsequent responses to espionage-related questions showed a significantly lesser reaction.

One espionage question—"Have you ever given classified weapons data to someone unauthorized to receive it?"—also generated an extreme response. But Vinskey penciled a notation of "SN" next to the spike representing Lee's response. "SN" generally denotes a "sniff," an involuntary and sudden change in breathing pattern on the part of the individual being tested, such as a sneeze. The spike therefore was ignored.

Therein lay the FBI's problem with the polygraph: He could have been lying on one of the espionage questions, but the entire test appeared to be invalid anyway because of Lee's response to a poor control question. DOE's polygraph manager took a closer look at the charts and sent them to the Department of Defense Polygraph Institute, which trains and certifies all non-FBI federal polygraphers. Both the DOE polygraph manager and the DOD experts agreed with the FBI analysis.

FBI headquarters notified its Albuquerque Field Office that it was sending one of its own polygraphers to New Mexico to retest Lee as soon as possible. Agents phoned Lee on February 8 and asked for a meeting later that day to discuss another interview and polygraph. Lee raced to a stairwell access to the X Division LEA and tried his card once more. He still was unable to gain access.

He met Covert and Hudenko later that afternoon and agreed to a second polygraph sometime within the next two days. No sooner were the agents gone than Lee appeared once again at the southwest door of the Administration Building, futilely swiping his badge through the reader. X Division remained locked to him.

At lunchtime the next day, February 9, Lee spent a half hour deleting more than ninety weapons-related files. The FBI showed up again at 1 P.M. The agents told him—disingenuously—that they needed his help solving a puzzle related to the W88, but first he had to be cleared with a polygraph. Lee agreed to take a polygraph the next day at the Los Alamos Inn. After the agents left, Lee decided to go see Schiffer, the lab counterintelligence chief. He asked why he should have to take an FBI polygraph. "I passed the other one," Lee said.

Schiffer advised Lee that it was in his interest to submit to the test. "Just settle this," Schiffer told him. "Help the FBI out and move on with your life."

At 9 P.M., Lee made yet another unsuccessful attempt to get back into his X Division office.

———————

Resigned, Lee reported to the Los Alamos Inn at 9 A.M. on February 10. He was shown into a room where the polygrapher, named Hobgood, was waiting. Agents had taken down the room's artwork and situated a table and a chair for Lee facing one of the blank walls. The room was uncomfortably warm, and Lee had the distinct impression that the FBI had turned up the thermostat. He took a seat and Hobgood hooked him up to the machine. The polygrapher cinched the finger cuff around his thumb to a painful tightness. Hobgood informed Lee that he was a suspect in an investigation into the loss of classified information on the W88 warhead—the first time the FBI had clearly told him. He was advised of his rights, just as he would be if he were being arrested. Lee found this upsetting.

Hobgood walked Lee through the questions he planned to ask, posed the control questions, then launched into the test proper. "Have you ever given [two sensitive nuclear-weapon] codes to any unauthorized person?"

"No," Lee replied.

Hobgood asked if he had ever obtained any W88 documents and got the same answer. He judged that Lee's responses were inconclusive.

The polygrapher and Lee talked about the questions, and Hobgood tried again, rephrasing them.

"Have you ever given any of those two codes to an unauthorized person?"

"No."

"Have you ever provided W88 information to any unauthorized person?"

"No."

Hobgood thought Lee's responses showed deception. He asked Lee whether he had anything further to say about his answers.

During his 1986 trip to Beijing, Lee said, a Chinese weapons scientist approached him for help with a simulation problem, and Lee had suggested a solution. He admitted the solution could be useful in nuclear-weapons simulation, but Lee apparently did not explain that his solution also could have applied equally to all kinds of unclassified simulations having nothing to do with nuclear weaponry. Hobgood merely recorded that Lee claimed not to have given up any classified information.

At one point, apparently at Hobgood's request, Lee drew diagrams of nuclear bomb designs to illustrate the information the Chinese scientists were soliciting. The drawing and the conversation were Secret Restricted Data, so both men technically were violating security rules by discussing them in an unsecure hotel room. It would later be argued that the circumstances of the test—the heat, the painful thumbcuff, the drawings, and being told he's a spy suspect—created enough anxiety in Lee to render the results of the test useless.

The two back-to-back tests and pre- and postpolygraph interviews took seven hours. Lee left the Los Alamos Inn at about 4 P.M. in a nerve-wracked state. He knew the test hadn't gone well.

He drove to the parking lot of the Administration Building and, once again, unsuccessfully tried to get inside X Division.

Lee next booted up his T Division computer and began deleting more files. Still overwrought by the FBI polygraph, he left his computer and made his way to the office of Dick Krajcik. According to Krajcik, Lee appeared upset and revealed that he had just failed an FBI polygraph. Lee also suggested that he might have inadvertently divulged classified information, perhaps in one of his scientific published papers, Krajcik later testified. Krajcik told Lee to report to Schiffer the next morning and repeat what he had just said. The moment Lee left, Krajcik picked up the phone and recounted the exchange to Schiffer. A worried Lee went back to his T Division office, sat down at the computer, and deleted more than three hundred files, a task that kept him at the keyboard until nine-thirty that night.

The next morning, Lee indeed did report to the counterintelligence chief. Schiffer waited, but Lee never said a word about his supposed revelation to Krajcik.

The Bureau's polygraph evidently had spooked Lee, but no agents were waiting to swarm into the hotel room and interrogate him on the basis of the polygraph results. No one said to him, why are you failing the polygraph? Nor did anyone apparently follow him when he left the hotel. An FBI expert on interview techniques who was familiar with the case said it was bewildering that agents were not poised to follow up on the polygraph. Another chance to coax a little more truth out of Wen Ho Lee was missed.

A few days later, Kashiwa talked to Lee about an idea for curing a longstanding problem with hydro codes, but it would be necessary to verify his solution by running it on several codes. One of the codes, Lee suggested, could be KFIX, an old Los Alamos code that he had modified for his own use years before. His only copy, however, was on a quarter-inch tape, a 3M 6150. To use it, the code would have to be uploaded off the tape, Lee said. Kashiwa hunted around and found an unused computer with a quarter-inch tape drive in the office of fellow T-3 scientist Mark Ulitsky. Lee carefully scrawled down the instructions for logging on so he could use the computer when Ulitsky was away from the office.

Soon, Lee was sliding his X Division tapes into the drive. He apparently intended to cleanse them of damning evidence but ran into a technical glitch. Once again, the help desk came to the rescue. Lee wanted to know a way to replace individual files on a tape while leaving others. Can't do it, a help-desk technician told him. You have to upload the entire contents of the tape to the computer hard-drive, then download the revised contents. So that's what Lee did.

He pulled dozens of weapons files and unclassified files off at least four tapes and stored them on the hard drive of the computer in Ulitsky's office. He then replaced the weapons files with more unclassified files and downloaded the new, wholly unclassified set back to the original tapes. It's not clear that he finished the job. But perhaps unknown to him, Lee's sanitization of the tapes worked at cross-purposes with his simultaneous efforts to get rid of weapons files on the unclassified network. The computer in Ulitsky's office automatically backed up its files to a central T Division server, so all of Lee's discarded weapons files that he so laboriously erased from his directory on the Green network were now resurrected elsewhere in the Green, on the T Division server.

Meanwhile, his FBI polygraph results sent shock waves through the Albuquerque FBI and headquarters. Perhaps they had a real spy, after all. Executives at Los Alamos also were stunned. Shortly afterward, Burick applied to the DOE for a revocation of Lee's Q clearance. It was granted February 23. From that day forward, it was virtually certain Wen Ho Lee's career in the weapons world was over. His blue badge, bearing the number 3 to indicate a Q clearance, was taken away.

On February 24, Lee took a last shot at sanitizing his X Division office. He phoned a colleague, Gary Pfeufer, and said he had lost his clearance. Lee described a box inside his office that he said was full of papers he needed. They were not classified, he assured Pfeufer.

Pfeufer found the box and worried about what might be inside. A cursory look showed none of the documents bore a classification stamp, but Pfeufer was leery. He asked a colleague for advice and decided to report the incident. He took the box to the lab's classification officers for review. It soon became clear that the documents Lee wanted—including a couple of viewgraphs—were classified Secret Restricted Data. Someone had removed the classification stamps.

– 19 –

"As Bad as the Rosenbergs"

The FBI was stuck in an awkward position. In January 1999, the Albuquerque Field Office had all but declared Wen Ho Lee innocent. Then in February, he flunked a lie detector test. Three years of investigation had left the Bureau holding a paper bag of loose suspicions but not a scrap of hard evidence that the gray-haired, fifty-nine-year-old family man was a spy.

At the same time, the classified version of the Cox Report was circulating in government circles and the unclassified version would be released soon. Chris Cox had issued a statement on December 30 that the committee had voted unanimously to approve its report. According to Cox, the panel had uncovered a sustained effort by China to acquire U.S. technology. In a story the next day, the *New York Times* patted itself on the back, noting that the committee had begun its inquiry as a result of stories in the *Times* about the Chinese satellite launches.

One of the authors of the *Times* story was Jeff Gerth, who had been the lead writer on the satellite story throughout 1998. Editors at the paper added this last story to several other articles the *Times* had published on the subject and mailed them off with a nomination for a Pulitzer Prize. The latest story served as the seal of approval for the earlier ones, and indeed the *Times* won the Pulitzer. The Pulitzer judges made special notice of Gerth's work.

The *Times* story also mentioned that Cox's panel had uncovered evidence that China had acquired nuclear-weapons-design technology from the U.S. weapons labs. The first detailed account of this story was published on page 3 of the *Wall Street Journal* a week later under the headline "China Got Secret Data on U.S. Warhead." In eight hundred words, the article accurately summed up the outlines of the investigation. The first sentence noted that the "top suspect is an American scientist working at a U.S. Department of Energy weapons laboratory."

On February 17, longtime national-security reporter Walter Pincus of the *Washington Post* wrote a story that made public the name of the investigation, Kindred Spirit, and the fact that the suspect was "an Asian-American scientist at Los Alamos who had contacts with the Chinese . . ."

Notra Trulock had hoped that the Cox Committee would be the vehicle to finally bring attention to his warnings about security at the labs. His testimony had riveted the committee. He was told that in the classified version of the committee's report, 90 percent of the nuclear-weapons section was footnoted to his testimony. But in early 1999, as the committee and Clinton Administration officials debated about how much of the still-secret report could be released to the public, Trulock began to get that sinking feeling again. He heard that the heart of the public report—his story of Chinese spies—was being cut out, supposedly for classification reasons.

He asked to see the unclassified version proposed by the administration. "What I was shown was a stack of blank sheets of paper." Trulock was convinced that the administration—"the White House or the DOE or the National Security Agency"—was trying to suppress his tales of theft. "Twice I had been asked to come to the Hill and testify about this. Twice I had been denied, and the third time it appeared that they . . . were going to be successful in bottling up the Cox commission report."

Trulock would find another way. If the Clintonites were going to silence his clarion call, he would shout the news with the biggest megaphone he could find. He chose one of the Beltway's most time-honored tactics—a leak to the *Post* or the *New York Times.*

Then, or perhaps at some earlier point, Trulock sent a message to Jim Risen at the *New York Times,* complimenting him on the paper's coverage of the Hughes and Loral satellite-launch controversy. Now he was ready to talk to Risen about Kindred Spirit, with the understanding that he would not be identified as the source of this information. Risen was receptive. He had a highly placed source on the line, offering intimate details of a top-secret nuclear spy case.

Risen had come to the *Times* in 1998, after covering the CIA in the Washington bureau of the *Los Angeles Times.* Both the *New York Times* and the *Washington Post* offered him their CIA beat. He chose the *Times* for its "visibility and impact—the same reason everybody else goes there." Trulock told Risen the story of Kindred Spirit. As always, he was a convincing briefer.

Zheng Shaotang, Chinese nuclear-weapons scientist and administrator who asked Lee about the W88 in a Beijing hotel room in 1988.

Photo taken during the 1994 visit of high-level Chinese weapons scientists to Los Alamos. It was during this conference that Wen Ho Lee was embraced by Hu Side. Prominent figures include: (front row, left) Yang Fujia, Chinese Academy of Science, president, Fudan University, director, Shanghai Institute of Nuclear Research; (third from left) Hu Side, deputy director, China Academy of Engineering Physics; (back row, second from left) Terry Hawkins, Los Alamos intelligence official; (third from left) Siegfried Hecker, lab director; (fourth from left) Danny Stillman, Los Alamos intelligence official, frequent traveler to China. (Los Alamos National Laboratory)

Lee's handwritten instructions for making his illicit tapes included instructions for operating the tape drive. (Court document)

Dan Bruno, the DOE investigator who suggested that the FBI investigate Lee.

Former DOE Intelligence Director Notra Trulock testified before the Senate Judiciary Subcommittee on Administrative Oversight and the Courts on Tuesday, October 3, 2000. At the hearing, Trulock disclosed that he had been a source for the *New York Times'* Jim Risen. (AP Photo/Dennis Cook)

At least eight W88 warheads form a ring around the final stage of the Trident II D-5 missile, shown here in a test launch at sea. (AP Photo/Lockheed Martin Corp.)

Longtime friend Cecilia Chang mounted a spirited defense of Wen Ho Lee. (AP Photo/Matt Bernhardt)

Bob Clark, Lee's friend, co-worker and supporter. (Dan Stober)

Former Los Alamos National Laboratory Counterintelligence Director Robert Vrooman, pictured testifying October 3, 2000, before the Senate Judiciary Subcommittee on Administrative Oversight and the Courts. Vrooman worried about Sylvia and Wen Ho Lee's "naïveté" in their dealings with Chinese scientists. Stephen Younger, LANL Associate Director for Nuclear Weapons (left), gave the overinflated "crown jewels" testimony that led to the initial denial of bail for Lee on December 13, 1999. (AP Photo/Dennis Cook)

Attorney General Janet Reno (right) appeared with FBI Director Louis Freeh (center) and Norman Bay, U.S. Attorney for the District of New Mexico, on Tuesday, September 26, 2000, to defend the Justice Department's handling of the Lee case before the Senate Select Intelligence and Judiciary Committees. (AP Photo/Dennis Cook)

George Stamboulidis, who in June 2000 replaced Assistant U.S. Attorney Bob Gorence as the lead prosecutor in the Wen Ho Lee case, gives a statement to reporters outside the U.S. courthouse in Albuquerque, N.M., September 13, 2000, after Lee pleaded guilty to a single count of mishandling nuclear secrets and was set free by an apologetic Judge Parker. (AP Photo/Jake Schoellkopf)

Energy Secretary Bill Richardson on May 25, 1999, called the Cox Committee's three-volume tome "a good solid report" and enumerated his steps to tighten security at the nation's nuclear weapons labs.

Wen Ho Lee's son, Chung Lee (left), daughter, Alberta Lee (center), and wife, Sylvia Lee, arrive at the U.S. courthouse in Albuquerque, N.M., Wednesday, December 29, 1999, for the last day of Lee's second bail hearing. (AP Photo/Jake Schoellkopf)

Don and Jean Marshall defended Lee, their neighbor of twenty-one years, from the day he was fired. The two weapons-code scientists volunteered to be his custodians and offered their house for bail to help secure his release from jail. (AP Photo/Sarah Martone)

U.S. District Judge James A. Parker took over the Lee case after the June 5 recusal of Chief Judge John E. Conway. Parker apologized to Lee for his jailing and lambasted the government's handling of the case. (AP Photo/*Albuquerque Journal*, Pat Vasquez-Cunningham)

John Richter, Los Alamos bomb designer whose testimony undercut the government's "crown jewels" argument. (Dan Stober)

Wen Ho Lee (center) walked free September 13, 2000, leaving federal court in Albuquerque with his attorneys Mark Holscher (right), Brian Sun (far right), and John Cline (left), and daughter and son, Alberta and Chung Lee. (AP Photo/LM Otero)

Wen Ho Lee topped the headlines on September 14, 2000, his first full day outside jail in nine months. (AP Photo/LM Otero)

In late November 2000, FBI agents sifted garbage in the snow-covered Los Alamos County landfill, looking for the tapes Lee had made. The FBI never unearthed Lee's tape library, although his attorneys are convinced it lies buried in the lab refuse. (AP Photo/Sarah Martone)

Cartoonist Tom Tomorrow offers a satirical reflection on the roles of *The New York Times* and the FBI in the Lee case.

Risen and Jeff Gerth, the main writer on the satellite stories, worked together on this one. Gerth had been at the *Times* for twenty-five years, almost all of that time in the Washington bureau. He was an investigative reporter who was not afraid of uncharted waters or complex subjects. He had shaken the Clinton Administration by breaking the Whitewater story and the tale of Hillary Clinton's wildly profitable commodities trading. He was widely respected but not without his critics. Some colleagues described him as practicing "a kind of connect-the-dots journalism in which individual facts are presented as patterns suggesting causation or culpability that may or may not be warranted."

By early March, Gerth and Risen were ready for publication. The date was set for Friday, March 5. FBI and DOE headquarters knew what was coming. They sent word to Covert. Time for interviews was running out. They had time for one, possibly two, final shots at Wen Ho Lee.

If Lee had taken note of the *Wall Street Journal* or *Washington Post* stories, he didn't let on to the FBI agents. For their part, the agents—having tried and failed to close out the case—now planned two interviews, the first on March 5, 1998.

Lee agreed to come in, apparently in hopes of finally convincing the agents of his innocence. When Lee walked into a conference room in the building that housed X Division, he was met by familiar faces around a long walnut conference table. Carol Covert and John Hudenko, the FBI agents who had been building a rapport with him, were there, along with their technical advisor, Dick Krajcik, who as X Division's deputy director was three levels of management senior to Lee and a primary designer well-schooled in the art of weapons design.

The FBI had placed a special clock radio in the room. Inside were hidden a tiny TV camera and a microphone. Lee's image and words would be carried live to a nearby room full of observers. Bob Vrooman was there as a lab consultant, along with his former assistant Terry Craig, lab counterintelligence chief Ken Schiffer, two or three more FBI agents, and an FBI technician to run the videotaping equipment.

The questioning went on all day. Covert, the lead agent, would occasionally slip out of the conference room to ask the hidden observers if they had any questions to suggest. Krajcik and the agents pushed Lee for answers, but the tone was not confrontational. At least one investigator thought there were missed opportunities to pursue Lee's answers further.

They quizzed him on his contacts with the Chinese, and he told them about some of the scientists he had met at the Chinese Los Alamos, the Institute of Applied Physics and Computational Mathematics in Beijing. He mentioned Zheng Shaotang, Pen Huiming, Li Wei Shen, and Wang Zixiu. "After I came back in '88, I did receive one or two mail from Wang," Lee told his questioners. "He asked me some questions about some numerical method." He wrote back to Wang, Lee said.

At one point, the FBI agents sought Lee's permission to search his offices in X Division and T Division. Craig, watching the television monitor, saw Lee agree, then left to help the FBI begin the searches. Until then, despite years of investigation, no one had searched Lee's office, computer, or home, nor had they listened to his phone calls or checked his e-mail. Then, simply by asking, they were into both his offices. In his X Division office, agents found improperly stored classified documents scattered around and decided to lock the door for a more thorough search later.

In his T Division office, they found a set of instructions, in Lee's handwriting, labeled "How to Move Files." In the middle of the document, Lee had written his classified computer password, a security violation, especially in an unsecured office.

At lunch, Lee went home to get a lab-owned Macintosh desktop he used for word processing and checking his e-mail. In his office, investigators took a Macintosh laptop that also belonged to the lab. Neither contained classified files.

The closest thing to a confrontation around the conference table that day came when the agents pressed Lee on why he had failed to report that the two Chinese weapons scientists, Zheng Shaotang and Hu Side, had asked him a classified question about the W88 in the Beijing hotel room in 1988. At the FBI's request, Vrooman had dug into the personal journals he had updated daily during his years at the lab. There, in black ink, was the entry for July 13, 1988, the day he debriefed Lee after his return from China. "Wen Ho Lee. Trip report not done yet. Gave talk at IAPCM, he was not probed for info on codes. He talked on hydrocodes for shaped-charge calculations."

A few lines down, Vrooman wrote, "Lots of good questions, but no inappropriate questions."

Covert showed Lee his trip report and a memo Vrooman had written for the FBI, based on his journal entry. Vrooman, watching on the monitor, thought Lee seemed flustered, that Covert had him on the defensive. Why, she asked, didn't he report the approach? Zheng, after all, had asked a question that went right to the heart of small U.S. primaries: "Does the W88 use a two-point primary?" Lee responded only that he had forgotten the encounter until 1998.

There was a tense moment between Lee and Krajcik as well. Lee said he didn't know anything about the Komodo, the primary for the W88; Krajcik insisted that of course Lee was familiar with it, he had worked on it. Krajcik thought Lee was being evasive, trying to deceive the agents. Vrooman again thought Lee was flustered, but the line of questioning went nowhere.

At another point in the questioning, Covert pressed Lee on what must have seemed to him an unfair point. In one of his published papers, Lee had included a number known to hydro-code writers as the "coefficient of artificial viscosity." It was an unclassified number, but wouldn't it be useful to the Chinese weapons program? As Lee later told his friend Bob Clark, the number was in the open literature, lots of people used it. Lee looked to Krajcik, who knew Lee and his work, to "tell them there's nothing special about that number," Lee told Clark. But Krajcik sided with the FBI. Lee was devastated. He denied wrongdoing, but the mild-mannered Lee didn't know how to debate with his high-powered opponents, "as if it wasn't his place to argue with management or the FBI," Clark said.

All that Lee knew was that his papers were unclassified and had been cleared for publication by the lab officials.

According to Vrooman, at the end of the day, Covert remained unconvinced of Lee's guilt. "I don't think he's the right guy," she said.

The FBI had asked the *Times* to delay running its story for several weeks so agents could continue to interview and investigate their chief suspect. The *Times* agreed to one day, possibly longer if FBI Director Louis Freeh made a personal request. Freeh never called. On Saturday morning, March 6, 1999, the *Times* printed the story that profoundly shook Washington and Los Alamos. "China Stole Nuclear Secrets from Los Alamos, U.S. Officials Say," the headline trumpeted. The lead paragraph summed up the story: "Working with nuclear secrets stolen from a U.S. government laboratory, China has made a leap in the development of nuclear weapons: the miniaturization of its bombs, according to administration officials."

The story, thirty-eight hundred words long, largely reflected Trulock's views, noting that "in personal terms, the handling of this case is very much the story of the Energy Department intelligence official who first raised questions about the Los Alamos case, Notra Trulock."

The story was researched in detail, but the tone was prosecutorial. The eighth paragraph stated, without attribution, that "some U.S. officials assert that the White House sought to minimize the espionage issue for policy reasons."

The next paragraph quoted a "U.S. official" as saying, "This conflicts with their China policy . . . It undercuts the administration's efforts to have a strategic partnership with the Chinese." Trulock would later say that he confirmed the accuracy of the quote to Risen, although the words came from someone else. This allegation of cover-up was Trulock's central thesis. It was his opinion, but in the *Times* it had the ring of fact.

The story quoted Gary Samore, the National Security Council official, as denying a cover-up, but then immediately undercut his denial with a sentence that began, "Yet a reconstruction by the *New York Times* reveals . . . delays, inaction and scepticism" in dealing with the situation. In making its case, the *Times* had not so subtly equated a poor investigation with a cover-up, in connect-the-dot fashion. "Now, nearly three years later, no arrests have been made," the article complained.

Readers could be forgiven for confusing allegation with fact. Scattered throughout the story were unqualified phrases such as "the espionage," "the nuclear theft," "the leak," "the crime," and "the Chinese spying."

Far down in the story, the reporters noted that the CIA considered Trulock's briefings to be a "worst-case scenario," and that the agency believed that in developing small warheads, the Chinese scientists had benefited from their own research and help from Russia.

Perhaps most inflammatory, the CIA's chief spy catcher, Paul Redmond, was quoted as saying, "This is going to be just as bad as the Rosenbergs" and "This was far more damaging to the national security than Aldrich Ames."

The *Times* quoted an anonymous source as saying there was a suspect, who "stuck out like a sore thumb." Lee was not named, but described as "a Los Alamos computer scientist who is Chinese-American." It was the echo of the misleading administrative inquiry, which had been bouncing around Washington for almost four years. By the time Gerth and Risen's story appeared, FBI agents had concluded that Lee had *not* stuck out from the other suspects. But the *Times* used the "sore thumb" description to virtually indict Lee.

Alberta Lee read the story in a library in Chapel Hill, North Carolina, where she held a software job. She knew by the details that the suspect was her father and that the story described her mother as well. They had traveled to a conference in China, they had been to Hong Kong, as the story said. Her mother had worked at the lab. "I can't tell you how mortifying it was," she said later. "They had all these incredibly horrible things—so many lies."

She looked up the Rosenberg case and was horrified to discover that they had been executed in the electric chair in New York's Sing Sing prison in 1953 for channeling Los Alamos atom-bomb secrets to the Soviet Union. She phoned her dad, told him about the story, and begged him to get a lawyer.

The *Times* article surprised the FBI—it wasn't expected until Monday. The *Times* had blown the FBI's case on the front page, wrecking any plan for a series of interviews. The article destroyed the investigation, but at the same time made it politically impossible to close the case.

Albuquerque FBI chief David Kitchen ordered Covert to turn her Sunday interview with Lee into an interrogation. He arranged for Covert to get a crash course in confrontational interview tactics and suggested that she bring up the Rosenbergs with Lee because of the *Times* reference. Covert had never done a confrontational interview, never taken the special course at Quantico. This would be the Bureau's final crack at Lee, and Covert was going to hammer him, armed only with a few tips that she had gotten from an expert over the telephone.

Lee agreed to go down the hill to Santa Fe to talk to Covert and Hudenko one last time. On the phone, they had said something about a package that had arrived from Washington. It was Sunday, the day after the *Times*'s story. Lee's friend physicist Bob Clark had stopped by Lee's house with his wife, Kathy, to see how he and Sylvia were holding up. Lee had confided in Clark about his increasingly difficult dealings with the FBI and the lab.

"He had very few people he went to talk to," said Kathy Clark. "So if our doorbell rang at ten minutes to nine, just after dark, we knew it would be Wen Ho." The couples had shared the ties of children, carpools, and science. At holiday time, the Clarks would open their door to find Alberta or Chung bringing a gift of Chinese roasted chicken, both food and breath steaming the night chill. Their father would wave from the car.

When Clark was laid off from the lab in the mid-1990s, Lee had testified on his behalf during an appeal. Yet, despite these years of friendship, this was the first time the Clarks had ever been in the Lees' home.

On this Sunday morning, Lee looked shaken. "He never really got afraid that something was going to happen to him until that Sunday morning after that *New York Times* story was published," Kathy Clark said. Lee asked Bob Clark to come with him to see the FBI agents, then awkwardly reconsidered. "Forget I asked you that," he said. "You don't want to get mixed up in this." Clark sized up the situation and told Lee he would drive him the forty miles to Santa Fe.

Lee didn't have a lawyer, though Clark had advised him to hire one. Time after time, Lee had told Clark, "I haven't done anything wrong. Why do I need a lawyer?"

Sylvia Lee ordinarily kept her emotions closeted, but now she was plainly scared.

Kathy Clark offered to keep Sylvia Lee company. No, Sylvia said. "I'll be all right."

The two men pulled on jackets. The wind was picking up and clouds were coming. Clark drove Lee's blue Honda Accord out of White Rock and onto the downhill highway. "Wen Ho knew something was going to happen. He didn't know what," Clark remembered. "He really did not want to go, but he knew he had to."

————————

They were to meet the two FBI agents in the wood-and-marble lobby of Santa Fe's Eldorado Hotel. The agents had implied that the package from FBI headquarters would almost certainly clear him and perhaps identify the real spy. Lee and Clark talked this over in the car. "It supposedly was all they needed to finish this investigation," Clark recalled. "I didn't believe any of it. I told him it smelled fishy. Why would they have to do this?"

The moment they walked into the Eldorado, the story changed. An apologetic Hudenko, who was there alone, said the agents had received "bad news" from FBI headquarters. "We didn't get what we expected out of Washington," Hudenko said. You lying sonofabitch, Clark thought, but he said nothing.

Hudenko said Lee must come immediately to the FBI Resident Agency three blocks away. The three men walked there together. The wind blew leaves around them.

Clark asked if he might come in, but Hudenko wouldn't let him into the office, and the guard wouldn't allow him to wait in the lobby. Lee wanted Clark with him during the questioning, but the agents refused. Clark should go get some lunch, they said.

It was Covert's show, and she was going for a confession, all or nothing. The *Times* story would surely drive Lee into the arms of a lawyer; this would be their last chance. But Covert told colleagues she was unsure the confrontational approach was such a good idea.

Schiffer, the lab counterintelligence head, who had been in the job for only a few months, thought it was clearly a bad idea and told anyone who would listen. He was an ex-FBI agent, a man of strong opinions. You don't do a confrontational interview unless you have something to confront the suspect *with*, he argued. There was no evidence of a crime by Lee, no self-contradictory tale to throw at him. There was no evidence that he gave away classified information, no photo, no electronic intercept, no defector.

The only thing they knew about the 1988 hotel meeting was what Lee himself had provided, and he maintained his innocence. The Bureau was moving from interview to interrogation with no foundation, Schiffer said. But the FBI was under pressure to solve the case.

The videotape was rolling.

"I, I, I don't to stay here very long. Okay, I, you know, I want to do as brief as possible. Just tell me what the package about very quickly and then I gotta go," Lee said to Covert. He had not yet eaten lunch, and it was well past noon.

Covert ignored his plea. She had a copy of the *New York Times* in her hand. "Have you seen the article in the newspaper?"

"I didn't, but my daughter told me everything."

Covert handed him the paper. He didn't read it, but he held it in his hands anxiously.

"It's uh, it's uh, very bad," Covert told him. "I think that there's some things in here that, that we have got to address based on that phone call I got from Washington a few minutes ago . . . it's boiling right down to your job, is what it's boiling down to."

Lee seemed surprised, but he did not flinch. "Can I, can I retire?"

Covert tried again to get him to read the article, then summarized it for him. Someone has committed espionage, she said, "and that points to you." Like the mathematician he was, Lee asked, "But do they have any proof, evidence?" He had already figured out Covert's obvious weak point.

The Bureau had decided to focus the interrogation on the hotel-room meeting. Besides a lack of leverage, there was a more subtle problem with this approach. The meeting had taken place in June 1988, but the walk-in document—the strongest hint that espionage had taken place—was dated earlier that year. If the W88 was lost, it was lost before Lee ever got to Beijing.

Covert turned accusatory: "I don't think that you can have a person in your hotel room for any period of time and not answer questions."

"No. I deny," Lee said. He told the Chinese scientists that "I don't know that question and I'm not interested in discuss that . . . I'm telling you the true. That's it." He sighed. It was the first of dozens of times that afternoon he would plead his innocence.

Covert tried again, summing up her case and the FBI theory of Chinese espionage as well: "You have an individual that's involved in the Chinese nuclear-weapons program. And they come to your hotel room, and they feel free and comfortable enough to ask you a major question about [the W88] . . . and then 1994, they come to [the] laboratory and they embrace you like an old friend. And people witness that and things are, are observed and you're telling us that you didn't say anything, you didn't talk to them and everything points to [something] different . . .

"I can understand, you know where, where these things could happen, I mean, you were treated very nicely in 1986 when you went to China. I mean they were good to you. They, they took care of your family. They took you to the Great Wall. They had dinners for you. Everything. And then in 1988 you go back and they do the same thing and, you know, you feel some sort of obligation to people to, to talk to them and answer their questions . . ."

Lee was adamant: "No, no, no. That's not true . . . you may think, when people, when the Chinese people do me a favor, and I will . . . tell them some secret, but that's not the case, okay? . . . I have a rule in my mind. If this thing is classified, if thing is nuclear, I'm, I'm not, I'm not suppose to say."

"Washington" was convinced Lee was lying, Covert told him. Tomorrow it would be on the TV. Everyone would know it was him. When that tactic didn't work ("You want me to swear to the God or whatever, okay? . . . I never tell them anything"), Covert attempted to unnerve him: "Do you know what's in the package that I got today and the phone call that I got from Washington? You failed your polygraphs."

That was half true. It was only on reexamination that the FBI and DOE experts changed the finding that Lee had been truthful.

Covert tried yelling: "You are, you are going to be an unemployed nuclear scientist. You are going to be [a] nuclear scientist without a clearance! Where is a nuclear scientist without a clearance gonna get a job?

"You got to tell us why you're failing these polygraphs."

Lee answered, "I can retire, to tell you the truth."

With every failure, Covert ratcheted up the threat: "A day, an hour, a week, and we come knocking on your door, we have to arrest you for espionage!"

Lee, though browbeaten, was steady. With a sigh, he told the agent, "You, you going to arrest me. I think you have to at least give me the evidence."

At times, Lee could barely get a word in:

> Covert: When somebody comes knocking on your door, Wen Ho . . .
> Lee: . . . No, no, no.
> Covert: . . . they're not going to give you anything other than your Advice of Rights and a pair of handcuffs! That's all you're going to get!
> Lee: But, but . . .
> Covert: And now, what are you going to tell your friends? And what are you going to tell your family? What are you going to tell your wife and your son? What's going to happen to your son in college?
> Lee: I know, I know . . .
> Covert: When he hears on the news. Instead of an article like that in the front page of the paper. It says "Wen Ho Lee arrested for espionage." What's that going to do?
> Lee: But, Carol, I'm telling you, I did not do anything like that.

There was a moment when Covert managed to coax an admission from her suspect that he had agreed to give a talk to scientists in Beijing as a favor, because they had treated his family well on their trip there in 1986. Perhaps sensing an opening, Covert shifted into a softer approach. If Lee had answered that hotel-room question in 1988 with a simple "Yes," (Yes, the W88 uses a two-point primary), it wouldn't be so bad. "Saying yes is no way near as bad as sitting down and say yes, and this is how they do it. And giving them a full-blown explanation . . . If you said yes to that question, it's not like that's a big deal."

It got her nowhere. "But, but I did not, I did not, say yes, I did not explain to them."

Then the interrogation gave way to threats again.

"What if they decide, okay. We're going to polygraph your wife. . . . And you're never going to have a clearance. And you're not going to have a job. And if you're arrested you're not going to have a retirement."

To this, Lee said, "Well, okay, I, let's stop here 'cause I'm very tired, okay," but Covert ignored him.

Eventually, Lee had had enough. "You want me repeat again? I, there's nothing I can tell you because I already told you everything, okay? And if they don't believe, it's too bad. If they want to put me in jail, fine."

Nothing had worked for Covert. Now she pulled out all the stops.

"Do you know who the Rosenbergs are? . . . The Rosenbergs are the only people that never cooperated with the federal government in an espionage case.

You know what happened to them? They electrocuted them, Wen Ho . . . They didn't care whether they professed their innocence all day long. They electrocuted them."

When she threatened that Lee would "rot in jail" like Aldrich Ames and John Walker, two famous spies of the last fifteen years, she was wasting her breath. Lee said he had never heard of them. Covert returned to the Rosenbergs. At least Lee knew who *they* were.

"Do you want to go down in history? Whether you're professing your innocence like the Rosenbergs to the day that they take you to the electric chair? . . ."

Lee gently reproached her.

"Carol . . ."

". . . Do you want to go down in history?"

"Carol . . ."

". . . with your kids knowing that you got . . ."

"Carol . . ."

". . . arrested for espionage?"

Covert, seemingly running out of threats, began to repeat herself. When she again bullied the scientist with the specter of unemployment, he told her, "I will open a Chinese restaurant here and you can give me welcome."

A minute later, Covert lost her patience. Lee cried out, "Oh, don't!" and then there was a loud snap in the room, as if Covert had slammed her hand on the table in frustration.

Eventually, Lee turned philosophical. "Okay, I, I, I told you before. I, I don't belong to any religion. I don't go to church. Well, I mean once in a while, but I don't believe in God, okay. However, I think there must be a something like a God, okay. Not, may not be a Christian God, but something like that, you know, super power, super creature . . . round the universe, and I believe he will make the final judgment for my case. And I depend on him. I don't depend on you or depend on John or depend on Washington, D.C., people. I don't depend on this, I depend on this God. I think he will make a final judgment."

Covert's response was: "You know what, the Rosenbergs professed their innocence. The Rosenbergs weren't concerned either. The Rosenbergs are dead."

Lee asked to leave, again and again.

"I'm sorry, I'm really tired. I have to go . . ."

"Let me, let me go, please . . ."

"Carol, let me go, okay? I [pause], I'm very tired."

Finally, it wound down, Covert all but giving up, and Lee talking about his religious beliefs and his joy in being alive after his 1987 surgery for colon cancer, how "the more important for me in my life is my children."

As he walked out the door, Lee thanked his tormentors. "Carol and John, I really appreciate your kindness and your efforts, try to help me out to clean up this stuff . . ." He bade them "good health," they wished him good luck.

"They want to put me in jail, whatever. I will, I will take it," he said. And then Lee was gone.

He found his friend waiting on a bench by the post office, and they drove home. As Clark drove again, a weary Lee told him the agents seemed most interested in a question a couple of Chinese scientists asked him in a hotel room. He said he was surprised that the Chinese would have asked such a question, "when they knew they shouldn't."

Lee was equally surprised at Covert and Hudenko. "They just wouldn't believe me. They just kept after me," he told Clark. "They kept harping on me that if you just admit you did this, everything would be okay, we will go easy on you.

"Should I have just said I did it? But I didn't do it."

Lee mentioned nothing about the Rosenbergs or execution. Clark got out at his home, and Lee drove away into flurries of snow.

– 20 –

Becoming the Enemy

*B*y *Monday morning, March 8,* the firing of Wen Ho Lee was little more than a matter of paperwork.

With marching orders from the highest echelon of the Department of Energy, everyone forgot about due process. Ordinarily, firing a lab scientist wasn't easy. In theory, the core staff of Los Alamos enjoyed the same job protection as a faculty member on a University of California campus. Dismissals took a recommendation from a case review board, notice to the employee, at least five days for the employee to respond, then a final decision and appeals. The more common prescription for a serious security violation was a thirty-day term of investigative leave, possibly followed by dismissal.

Wen Ho Lee received none of this. On the very morning Lee was being fired, Energy Secretary Bill Richardson was extolling his bold action to the *Washington Post* and *New York Times,* then going off the record to leak Lee's name.

Lee "stonewalled" the FBI, Richardson told reporters. According to the *Times,* Lee's "failure to fully cooperate" possibly left the FBI without a prosecutable case. The implication was, Lee didn't confess to espionage and this lack of "cooperation" led to his firing.

The reasons Richardson gave for the firing were "failure to properly notify Energy Department and laboratory officials about contacts with people from a sensitive country, specific instances of failing to properly safeguard classified material and apparently attempting to deceive lab officials about security matters."

The man tasked with the firing, acting Theoretical Division Director Dan Butler, had just assured Lee a few days earlier that his job was fairly secure: Even if the FBI came up with anything worthy of dismissal, Lee would have plenty of time to appeal. Or so Lee told friends. Lee even went so far as to say he'd been exonerated.

According to T Division sources, Butler wasn't keen on firing Lee, but he had no choice. He handed Lee a copy of the lab's formal termination statement and said his dismissal was effective immediately. Instead of his five-day notice, the lab issued him a check for five days' salary.

Lee handed over the temporary badge he'd been issued two weeks before. He signed a certification that he had returned all lab property. Security officers escorted him to his car. He was not allowed back into his office to collect his belongings.

People who saw Lee that day found him confused. He appeared disoriented. He went to the Clarks' house and showed them his termination paper.

"Does this really mean I'm fired?" he asked.

Bob and Kathy Clark read his firing notice and looked at him. They thought he was incredibly naïve. What could they say? His dismissal was spelled out in black and white. Lee stood in their doorway uncomprehending.

"I will carry my image of him that day to my grave," Kathy Clark said later.

Bright people worked at Los Alamos, and they loved to gossip. Rumor and innuendo traveled quickly and so did news of Lee's firing. The "official" word made the TV and radio by dinnertime, courtesy of Richardson and the DOE.

Don and Jean Marshall had just backed out of their driveway and were driving past Lee's house when three figures appeared out of the dark. They were reporters, and James Brooke of the *New York Times*'s Denver bureau did most of the talking.

The *Times* had broken the story, Brooke said, clearly proud. A number of people believed Lee was a spy, he said. Didn't the Marshalls know he was a spy?

"We told them we didn't know but we didn't believe it," Don said. Brooke left his card and a number at the Los Alamos Inn. The couple were headed back to work on Blue Mountain, the lab's massive supercomputer for weapons calculations. While they did some debugging work, they surfed the Web until they found the *Times*'s story. They got home close to midnight and Don headed straight for the telephone to dial Brooke's room.

"He's either a very, very good actor," the scientist told the *Times* reporter, "or he's not your man."

Lee had been a fabulous neighbor. Could their friend of more than twenty years, a colleague whose children had played with their own children, really be a Chinese spy?

Don and Jean turned their minds to every experience that they'd had with Wen Ho, Sylvia, and their children—the children especially. Don Marshall reasoned that adults can hide things, but children are guilelessly honest about their families. The Marshalls thought back to 1986 and 1988, when the Lees went to China, and recalled only that the family prepared for the trips like excited tourists who were eager to pack as much as they could into their itinerary.

"We asked ourselves, 'Can you remember anything? Can you remember any time he was gone for a suspiciously long time? Can you remember anything strange with the children?' " Jean Marshall said. Their talk ran hours into the night. "We couldn't think of a single thing."

Rumors of Lee's troubles had started earlier among Los Alamos's Chinese Americans. At least a few friends knew he had lost his Q clearance, and when the New York Times article appeared on Saturday, their speculation narrowed immediately to Lee. No one, however, knew for sure.

Now it was clear who the spy suspect was, and the majority of Lee's Asian friends judged it was in their best interests not to associate with him. Most of Los Alamos's Chinese Americans were Taiwanese. They were familiar with the aggressive tactics of Taiwanese intelligence agencies. In the McCarthy years, Kuomintang agents fed the FBI the names of Taiwanese in the United States who were KMT critics. They were painted as sympathizers to the communists on the mainland. Ever since, many Taiwanese Americans harbored a general distrust of intelligence and counterintelligence agencies, and worried that association with a publicly identified spy suspect might bring suspicion upon them.

And what if he really was a spy? All of them knew of the Lees' socializing with the visiting Chinese; several of them had done the exact same thing. What if, backed into a corner, he fingered *them* as being involved in spying? How would association with a spy suspect impact their Q clearances, the sine qua non of their careers in classified defense science? If nothing else, prudence dictated keeping their heads down and staying clear of Lee.

Jen-Chieh Peng had no Q clearance. He was a well-regarded physicist who performed unclassified research on the lab's particle accelerator. That evening, Peng phoned Lee's house and thought the phone connection sounded strange, as though it might be bugged. "Why don't we just go down to his house?" Peng said to his wife, Tze Huuy. At 8 P.M., the two slipped past the few remaining reporters. They rapped on the windows of the Lees' house, calling their names in Chinese.

"We saw a little light on inside the house," Jen-Chieh said.

In a moment, Wen Ho and Sylvia let them in. Reporters had been ringing the doorbell and rapping on the door all evening. For hours, the Lees had been hunkered down, hoping they would be left alone. But they were quite glad to see the Pengs.

"Many of your friends are concerned and want to talk to you," Jen-Chieh told Lee, "but they're worried. I have nothing to lose."

Jen-Chieh inquired whether Lee had hired a lawyer.

"I haven't done anything wrong," Lee replied. "Why should I get a lawyer?"

The next morning, the Marshalls knew what they had to do. Together they agreed to take a step that could throw their careers into jeopardy. They went into work early and reported to the lab Office of Internal Security. They told Terry Craig that they strongly disbelieved that Wen Ho Lee was a spy and offered themselves as character witnesses on his behalf.

Later, Don Marshall had a chance to talk to Wen Ho, who said he wasn't planning on hiring a lawyer. "I haven't done anything wrong," Lee said.

"He looked me right in the eye," Marshall said. "He looked like he thought, 'There's some mistake here.' I believe he really thought he had gone through the naturalization process and now was an American and would be cleared."

Lee had said much the same thing, in the same way, to Bucky Kashiwa a few weeks earlier.

Later that Tuesday, John Kammerdiener, a leading nuclear-weapons designer, walked into the offices of X Division Director Jon Weisheit.

"He didn't do it," Kammerdiener told Weisheit. "He did not give the Chinese the W88."

Kammerdiener had seen the 1995 intelligence data a year earlier, during a three-month stint working for Trulock. The W88 information in the walk-in papers looked exactly like the kind of data laid out in something known as an interface-control document or ICD. It defined which parts of a bomb were built by the Department of Defense and which by the Department of Energy. An ICD described the outside of the peanut, for example, so DOD could build a reentry vehicle around it.

Nuclear-weapons systems were assembled from parts made in more than a half-dozen states, at factories often hundreds of miles apart. As nuclear-weapons design labs, Los Alamos and Livermore were responsible for the "physics package" of a warhead—the primary and secondary that made up the actual nuclear explosive. Sandia was responsible for all the auxiliary systems—fuzing, timing sets for firing, technology to prevent an accidental or unauthorized detonation. Contractors for the Defense Department had everything else, beginning with the surrounding package, the reentry vehicle. An interface-control document laid out the size of the radiation case, the mass of the physics package, and its centers of gravity—but none of its internal components.

Unlike most people in X Division, Kammerdiener had worked with the Defense Department on ICDs. He knew that they were widely distributed to literally hundreds of addresses in Washington, D.C., northern Virginia, Colorado, and California, where defense contractors manufactured the reentry vehicles.

The measurements and other data in the 1995 intelligence looked to him as though they had come from a W88 ICD.

"The [1995] information was far too sparse to have described an actual device," Kammerdiener said later. "To define the W88 it's nice to know the outside, but you'd have to know a lot more about the inside. Your typical person in X Division, particularly a code developer like Wen Ho, doesn't have anything to do with ICD information."

Instead, Lee could walk down a hallway and into the main X Division vault, where extremely detailed weapons blueprints and testing data were stored. Most of the data had been scanned and made available online as well; Lee could log in to the online vault and see weapons designs down to every bolt on his screen, without ever leaving his office.

"He's got all this other stuff to choose from, a lot more detail on the insides," Kammerdiener explained. "If you're a spy, why just give them [the ICD], why not give them the whole pie? It's the information age, you could do it easily."

Weisheit heard Kammerdiener out. "As I recall, he said, 'Gee, I don't know anything about that,' " Kammerdiener said.

Weisheit was brand-new to the leadership of X Division, having just left an astrophysics post at Rice University a month before to take charge of Los Alamos's weapons designers. He knew that the FBI was pursuing a spy in his division. If he did anything with Kammerdiener's observation, it was not apparent.

Kammerdiener next went to Terry Hawkins, now director of the lab's Nonproliferation and International Security Division. Hawkins knew by then that Trulock's reading of the intelligence and his investigation were off course. A plan began to take shape: Los Alamos would take a fresh look at the 1995 intelligence.

A number of other weaponeers knew what Kammerdiener knew, but few said anything. Word didn't reach Los Alamos's executive management or DOE, and it was doubtful their opinions would have mattered. The laboratory was a secretive place where it paid to keep one's head down, particularly when Washington was involved. Besides, the FBI, the DOE, and factions of the lab's own management weren't looking for evidence of Lee's innocence—quite the opposite. They were tracking every lead suggesting he was a spy.

As one Los Alamos official put it, "There was a steamroller going at that point, and the mind-set was 'He's guilty and all we got to do is prove it.' "

Lee's guilt was accepted most unquestioningly in Washington. Reporters and congressmen were so caught up in the fever pitch of a spy hunt—a nuclear spy, no less—that no one stopped to examine the basis for the original suspicions. Instead, Washington slipped easily into one of the games at which it excelled—pinning blame wherever it might stick.

Even before Lee's firing, the New York Times reported over the weekend that "Clinton aides" conceded the administration had been slow to tighten security at the weapons labs. The nation's other major media scrambled to catch up with stories in the same vein.

The White House, the FBI, and the Energy Department mobilized defenses: Sandy Berger and Richardson became the point men and repeatedly cited Presidential Decision Directive 61's strengthening of DOE counterintelligence as evidence of the administration's "quick response." It was a weak argument from the start. Clinton signed PDD-61 almost a year and a half after Trulock had delivered the second, more dire briefing to Berger at the White House. DOE then took another year to get an implementation plan out to its laboratories.

Republicans in Congress quickly seized on the reported delays as welcome evidence that the Clinton administration had been remiss in protecting America's nuclear secrets. Such laxity dovetailed neatly with mounting Republican suspicion that Clinton had auctioned off the presidency for political contributions from the Communist Chinese.

Clinton's more jaded critics had come to view every aspect of his China policy of engagement as a bought political favor—sales of high-performance computers, leaking of rocket-launch technology, letting China off the hook for human-rights abuses and the sharing of weapons-of-mass-destruction technology with rogue nations. A few House Republicans already had begun using the word "treason."

Because many members of the House and Senate had not heard of the FBI investigation, Congress took up the *Times*'s charges of a White House cover-up. The president's men supposedly had kept the spy case under wraps to prevent Congress from derailing Clinton's China policy. It was Trulock's charge, repeated first in the *Times* and now in the halls of Congress.

Senator Don Nickles, a Republican of Oklahoma, was one of the first out of the gate: "They obviously received a lot of money from individuals who had some connections with the Chinese government. And evidently there was a lot of espionage ongoing, and that's very, very troubling . . . If they had that information and they were keeping that from Congress and they didn't do anything about it until this last weekend, that is grossly irresponsible and, needless to say, dangerous to our national security."

But Congress *had* been told. Trulock had briefed the staff of the Senate and House intelligence committees back in 1996, as the White House's Berger directed.

Even so, certain Senate and House members were blindsided. One of these was the leading champion of the nuclear-weapons labs, Republican Senator Pete V. Domenici of New Mexico.

The Albuquerque lawyer had accrued enormous power and influence over the labs and the DOE in the last two decades, most recently as chairman of the Senate Budget Committee and a key energy appropriations committee. In those positions, Domenici held the purse strings for the DOE and the labs, together the largest employer in his state.

Domenici's staff often slapped down DOE regulators when they annoyed lab executives or seemed to get in the way of job and mission expansions. DOE officials often joked that Domenici was the only real secretary of energy; the labs called him "Saint Pete."

For years, weapons-lab scientists and managers had filled Domenici's ear with complaints of micromanagement by DOE, of myriad regulations and endless waves of bureaucrats. Moreover, whenever Domenici wanted to communicate his desires to DOE, his staff ran into a tangled maze in which no one seemed to have ultimate responsibility. Domenici would rail about the lack of accountability at the DOE, neglecting to mention that he had shielded Los Alamos from accountability for years.

In 1998, word had leaked to Domenici's lead nuclear-weapons staffer, Alex Flint, that DOE counterintelligence had a hot case going at Los Alamos. Flint requested a briefing from Trulock, but Deputy Secretary Elizabeth Moler turned him down, indicating that the case was an FBI matter. As soon as she hung up the phone, according to Trulock, Moler stared ahead and said, "I can't believe I just said no to Pete Domenici."

On March 7, the day after the *Times*'s first Los Alamos spy story, Flint called Trulock and ordered him to Domenici's office immediately. Senate colleagues had been calling, asking, "Pete, what's going on? These labs are your baby." Domenici felt betrayed.

"Nobody told me," Domenici said, according to Trulock. "Nobody told me."

Within weeks, however, he and his staff dreamed up a solution. It was perfectly simple: Domenici's plan would take care of the mounting criticism in Congress over lax lab security and, at the same time, eliminate the bureaucracy that had bedeviled him. He would craft the most massive overhaul of the U.S. Department of Energy since its creation in 1977.

Meanwhile, a small army of reporters had blockaded the Lees in their home. The couple had their phone disconnected and didn't dare answer the door. Wen Ho decided that he should hire a lawyer after all. For once, Lee decided to take his daughter's advice.

Alberta Lee had put out feelers and, at the suggestion of a friend at Columbia Law School, she phoned Mark C. Holscher, a hotshot, white-collar criminal defense attorney in Los Angeles's oldest law firm, O'Melveny & Myers.

Holscher was thirty-seven, a California native who had gotten his law degree at Berkeley in the 1980s, when anti-Reagan sentiments ran high and conservatives like Holscher grew tough hides.

After a brief period in Justice Department headquarters, Holscher had been an aggressive young assistant U.S. attorney in the Central District of California. On the side, according to a friend, he was a "vicious" surfer.

Holscher pursued the high-profile mail-fraud and tax-evasion prosecution of "Hollywood Madam" Heidi Fleiss.

O'Melveny & Myers was perhaps best known as the law firm of senior partner and Democratic stalwart Warren Christopher. By 1999, it had grown to a small legal empire spanning three continents, with offices in Shanghai, Hong Kong, and Tokyo as well as London. The firm prided itself on its extensive client base on both sides of the Pacific, but the firm's partners looked on the Lee case with concern: What if he really was a spy? Holscher argued that defending Lee was the right thing to do and ultimately swayed the firm's executives.

Wen Ho and Sylvia Lee left shortly after he was fired to meet Holscher and spent nearly the next month living with family in the Los Angeles area.

————————

As FBI headquarters mounted a defense of its lackadaisical investigation of Lee, its agents in New Mexico persisted in trying to salvage something of their espionage case. They combed Lee's X and T division offices for any scrap of evidence that he had been a spy.

They were aided by a handful of weapons scientists, some drafted and some who volunteered to the lab Internal Security Office. One of the volunteers was a mustachioed physicist by the name of John Romero, who led a code-development group working on Big Mac, Los Alamos's premier code for modeling secondaries. Romero and Lee had worked together for more than a decade in the 1980s; Lee had written almost six hundred lines of code for Big Mac.

On March 23, as agents rifled through Lee's X Division office, Romero saw an old printout of one of Lee's computer directories. His eyes scanned down the listing of files, noting names very similar to virtually every major weapons design code Los Alamos had. He didn't think too much of it until he spotted a notation at the top of the directory listing: The directory was on the laboratory's unclassified network. "I couldn't believe it," he said later. "I just couldn't believe it."

Alarmed, Romero carried the printout from Lee's desk to the laboratory's computing center. Network managers immediately began tracing the files on the printout and discovered they'd been erased. But ghostly remnants of the files still existed on the system. The lab's Common File System had not yet overwritten the erased data, so computer experts could retrieve the files and read them.

What Wen Ho Lee had done now became astonishingly clear. He had created the largest unauthorized collection ever of nuclear-weapons simulation tools, nuclear data files, and input decks—long strings of words and numbers describing the shapes, sizes, and materials of nuclear weapons. And he had placed it on an open computer network with hundreds of Internet connections to the outside world.

————————

Romero's discovery was manna to the FBI. After all these years, they finally had evidence that Wen Ho Lee had committed such a massive security violation that the only explanation could be espionage. Agents quickly notified the U.S. Attorney's Office in Albuquerque. It took little discussion for U.S. Attorney John Kelly to assign the case to his most trusted prosecutor.

First Assistant U.S. Attorney Robert Gorence ran the office on a day-to-day basis and frequently took over the most challenging, high-profile cases. His favorites were rare death-penalty drug cases and complex white-collar crimes. He had been reared by a family of modest means on a Wisconsin farm, and discovered he not only had an affinity for the law but a talent for oratory, weaving complex facts into a dramatic tale for judges and juries.

Gorence, forty-one, was an intense man with startling blue eyes and short salt-and-pepper hair. He thought fast, spoke fast, and didn't have much time for people who couldn't keep up.

Gorence was in the process of separating from his wife, the daughter of Pete Domenici.

Gorence and the senator still got along, but the prosecutor was sensitive about the relationship. Gorence was ambitious and proud. He wanted no one to think that his successes were due to the senator's influence.

When word of Lee's downloads came from Los Alamos, Gorence and the FBI agreed they had to move fast. The FBI wanted an immediate search of Lee's house. In a flurry of phone calls with the FBI and Justice headquarters, Gorence and attorneys in Washington hammered out an application for a search warrant. Kindred Spirit, with all its flaws and embarrassments, was closed as an official FBI case. The Bureau opened a new case, code-named "Sea Change."

The FBI scrambled to assign a new case agent to Albuquerque to help out. He was Robert Messemer, a nineteen-year Bureau veteran who had spent most of his career working foreign counterintelligence cases, mostly in Los Angeles. Messemer specialized in Chinese cases and was proficient in Mandarin. He flew in from California, where fellow FCI agents knew him by the nickname "Stealth," for his crafty ways.

Messemer took charge of the growing team at Los Alamos, and he began working with Gorence and Special Agent Michael W. Lowe on assembling seventeen years of FBI experience with Wen Ho Lee into a compelling argument for a search of his home.

Meanwhile, the FBI was blaming the Justice Department for failing to have approved its FISA warrant applications. The Justice Department in turn was blaming the FBI for failing to have brought a strong enough case. Congress ripped into the White House almost daily for its supposed failure to brief members on the alleged espionage. And everybody was blaming the Department of Energy for poor security and general ineptitude.

Lee's downloads were more than anyone at Justice or the FBI could have hoped for. So far, the agents and Los Alamos's computer experts had found twenty-one weapons files on the unclassified network and the number was growing. Lee had no work-related reason to place them on the Green network, according to a leading weapons-code developer at Los Alamos, Charlie Neil. By the second weekend in April, Lee had returned from Los Angeles, and the FBI was ready to move on his house.

On the night of Friday, April 9, Gorence and FBI Special Agent Michael W. Lowe knocked on the door of a federal magistrate in Albuquerque and presented him with a nineteen-page application for a search warrant. The Bureau believed its agents could find evidence in Lee's house of Lee's "unlawful removal and retention of classified materials," lying to federal agents, and a low-level offense under the Espionage Act of 1918: "gathering, transmitting or losing defense information."

In two of its thirty-seven paragraphs, Lowe's affidavit argued that the magistrate should consider the Lees' ethnicity as a reason to search their home. The affidavit listed Wen Ho Lee's birthplace as Nantow, Taiwan, and noted that Sylvia Lee was born in Hunan Province, China. Lowe quoted an unnamed FBI expert as saying that "PRC intelligence operations virtually always target overseas ethnic Chinese with access to intelligence information sought by the PRC." Furthermore, Chinese intelligence agents routinely took advantage of visits by Chinese Americans to "establish and reinforce cultural and ethnic bonds with China . . ." It was the same ethnic argument the FBI had employed in its failed attempt to obtain a court-ordered wiretap on the Lees in 1997.

Lowe and Messemer then painted a picture of a man who had met with Chinese scientists, lied to coworkers and the FBI as far back as 1983, and now was spiriting away nuclear-weapons secrets that were "more valuable to a weapons designer than an actual bomb blueprint."

U.S. Magistrate Judge William W. Deaton had been a longtime federal public defender; he was not a judge to roll over for a weak search warrant. He signed his approval at 10:40 P.M. and ordered the affidavit sealed, a not-uncommon practice for a criminal investigation. Gorence and Lowe bade him goodnight. They went to notify the agents: The search was on for the next morning.

At 7 A.M. Saturday, fifteen agents met at the Santa Fe Resident Agency. Lowe handed out ten copies of the search warrant and affidavit for them to read. Then he briefed them on the search. They were looking for any form of computer equipment or material—laptops, desktops, floppy disks, tapes, anything—as well as printouts, correspondence, or financial records. Lowe kept his copy of the warrant in a maroon folder. He gathered the other copies back from the search team and shredded them.

At about eight-thirty, Lowe knocked on the Lees' door. The agent said he had a court-approved warrant for a search of the house and environs. The search team donned gloves and fanned through the house, each to their preassigned rooms, as well as the garage, front yard, and backyard garden.

Lee quickly dialed Holscher's number and soon had his lawyer on the phone. Holscher asked for the agent in charge and asked Lowe for a copy of the search warrant. Lowe arranged for a copy of the warrant itself to be faxed to Holscher, but the affidavit was under court seal and could not be released.

Holscher's confusion turned to frustration. The FBI was rifling through his client's house without alleging—in papers he was allowed to see—that Lee had committed a single criminal offense. The warrant said they could seize "all data," as well as any forms of communication. They could do this, as far as Holscher could discern, without revealing a single detail of their case.

As reporters gathered outside, agents swarmed throughout the house. They poked metal rods into Lee's yard and garden, and swept them both with a metal detector. They went through every drawer, every book on his shelves.

If they found a piece of paper with Chinese writing or a phone number on it, they took it. The result was the seizure of the *Selected Short Works of Guy de Maupassant* and a collection of plays by Tennessee Williams—books in which Lee had underlined English words and scrawled Chinese characters in the margins. But they were not secret spy messages; Lee was honing his English skills. Likewise, the agents took the Santa Fe–Los Alamos phone book, a directory for the Los Alamos Chinese Cultural Association, a list of phone numbers for a local Christian group, and loads of his children's belongings—Alberta's address book and diary, her and Chung's old school textbooks, a photo album filled primarily with shots of Milan, Italy. The agents also took a thick stack of computer printouts dating to 1977, letters that Lee had written to his old professors in the early 1970s, and even an old thesis of his from 1967.

Several of these came from a stack of more than twenty boxes in Lee's garage. It was there that agents came upon a potential gem—three letters from weapons scientists at China's Institute for Applied Physics and Computational Mathematics, asking Lee to send codes.

The agents also found a couple of computer-software manuals for Los Alamos weapons codes. The manuals were classified.

Lastly, they found a blue $8\frac{1}{2} \times 11$ notebook. Inside, Lee had handwritten, in typically meticulous detail, the exact steps for logging on to a T Division computer and creating tapes. His notes were carefully written in both Chinese and English, with a helpful diagram of the front of a computer tape drive.

On other pages, Lee had listed more than a dozen portable tapes and the exact file contents of each. The agents were stunned. Here in Lee's house, outside the lab, was a card catalogue to a private trove of U.S. weapons software and designs.

Elsewhere in the notebook, Lee had written descriptions of the FBI agents—Covert and Hudenko—and Los Alamos's Schiffer. They read as though Lee was considering how to manipulate the agents and the lab.

The FBI left Lee's house after four hours, hauling away almost a dozen boxes, including the hard drive and other components of his Macintosh. The vast majority of their take was completely useless. But the notebook, the letters, and the classified code manuals were prized finds, the kind of items that caught jurors' attention.

Lee's defense, meanwhile, had lost a crucial first round—the FBI had the elemental evidence of a criminal case and in return had shown nothing of its hand.

The FBI carried translations of Lee's notebook to Los Alamos and set computer experts to work on the largest computer-forensics investigation in Bureau history. Special teams of computer detectives flew in from the Bureau's National Infrastructure Protection Center in Washington.

It became clear that Lee had created at least fifteen tapes. The agents remembered finding six tapes in Lee's T Division office, all on first glance containing unclassified files. On closer examination, the FBI found the tapes indeed had contained weapons files but had been reconfigured. Lee had replaced those files with unclassified ones. Nine tapes had not been found—two believed to contain unclassified files, the other seven full of weapons files.

A full surveillance team was assembled and sent to White Rock. Lee had a library of weapons codes on portable tapes, and no one knew where they were. The FBI intended to watch him and his wife every minute from then on. The existence of the tapes was not made public. Quietly, so as not to alert foreign spy agencies to a loose prize, agents began a hunt on both sides of the Pacific for seven missing tapes of nuclear secrets.

Not long after the FBI search, Lee and Don Marshall had a neighborly chat over the stone wall between their houses. The FBI's surveillance team watched the two men talk among their roses. Marshall had been curious: Had Lee really put weapons codes on the Green network? Surely the newspapers had it wrong.

They did, Lee told him. He promised his friend that he hadn't put any classified files on the unclassified network.

————

It took only a few days for news of Lee's transgressions to leak in Washington. Far from blunting the criticism of the FBI and DOE, the news was like gas on a fire. Congress exploded in a tirade the likes of which few had ever seen.

In the House, Indiana Republican Dan Burton began a weekly series of harangues that linked Chinese campaign donations with "how the Clinton administration, either intentionally or through incompetence, has irreparably damaged and compromised the security of every man, woman, and child in the United States."

With the W88, "you can hit 10 cities with one missile launched from China, thereby endangering as many as 50 or 60 million Americans. And the neutron bomb data, that kind of information, would allow an enemy of the United States, Communist China, to launch a missile at the United States with a neutron bomb warhead, and when it explodes, kills everybody in the city but it does not destroy the infrastructure, the roads, the bridges or the buildings," Burton said, wildly exaggerating the effectiveness of the neutron bomb.

"Why would the Justice Department turn down this request for electronic technology to be put on this gentleman's phone when they thought and highly suspected and *even knew* that he was giving top secret nuclear technology to the Chinese communists that endangered every man, woman, and child in this country?" Burton continued.

Senate Majority Leader Trent Lott ordered the Republican chairmen of the China task force that Lott had formed in 1998 to now focus their energies on stolen nuclear secrets. Armed Services Committee Chairman John Warner took up the charge with fervor.

He and colleagues in both chambers repeatedly cited the view of CIA spy catcher Paul Redmond that the Wen Ho Lee case—even before the downloads were discovered—was "worse than the Rosenbergs" and "far more damaging to the national security than Aldrich Ames," invoking the nation's two most horrific spy cases of the century.

On April 12, Warner turned his rhetorical fire toward the PRC in opening his committee's third hearing on Chinese nuclear spying. "China is moving towards elevating its superpower status in the world, and it will be indeed America's and the West's natural enemy in the next millennium."

On a more measured note, Democrats on the committee sounded a caution about the intensifying witch-hunt atmosphere of Congress's inquiries into the China spy scandal.

"Obviously these are serious issues. They deserve a full investigation, full airing. In fact, there are nine committees in the Congress who are now looking into them," said Senator Jeff Bingaman, a conservative New Mexico Democrat and former state attorney general. "I think there's an appearance or a perception that we have got a piling-on going on here by the Congress. And just as . . . the administration motives and withholding information might be subject to question, I think actions of the Congress could also be subject to question if we don't watch it."

Instead of moderation, what Bingaman got was a scolding by Warner and colleagues.

"I resent the fact that as the committee and subcommittee with oversight responsibility that we were not informed," replied Republican Senator Bob Smith of New Hampshire. "And so if 'piling on' is reacting in a negative [way] to that and holding hearings, then I'm going to stand in line to pile. So I'm ready to go."

Smith had plenty of company.

"The information we're talking about took a half a century to develop in this nation; hundreds of billions of dollars of taxpayers' money," said Senator Frank Murkowski, Republican of Alaska, chairman of the Senate Energy and Natural Resources Committee. "We're not talking about, you know, helping Coca-Cola protect its secret formula. We're talking about protecting the most destructive and powerful information known to mankind."

Murkowski was "truly shocked" to learn "you can walk out of the most secret room in our laboratories with a zip drive disk such as this, full of the nuclear legacy codes, and nobody knows, with the possible exception of China's top spies. Not surprisingly, nobody appears to want to be held accountable for what may be the greatest loss of nuclear military secrets in our nation's history."

Republicans were fairly salivating at the chance to prove Clinton had sold nuclear secrets to the Chinese or at least turned a blind eye. "It was absolutely viewed as fair game for the elections, the question of how effectively he was protecting nuclear secrets," said one senior staffer in the Republican leadership.

No one, of course, publicly mentioned the hunt for ammunition to use against the Gore 2000 presidential campaign; in fact, several Republicans were quick to deny such a motivation. Instead, Congress was in the grip of a frenzy motivated by something almost as powerful as partisanship—the bottomless fear of an enemy stealing secrets of mass destruction and turning them against the United States.

"I am certainly not interested in pointing fingers in a partisan fashion or going off on some witch hunt," said Republican Senator Ben Nighthorse Campbell of Colorado. "But, holy smoke, we're talking about the potential loss of every major nuclear secret in the United States, I mean, not to say anything of the untold billions of tax money to do that research, but the potential of putting Americans in danger at some future point."

Congress and media outlets—not just the *Times,* but Fox News and others—were locked in a game of one-upsmanship, describing Lee's crime in ever more superlative-laden rhetoric.

-21-

Shock Waves

For five months, the Clinton administration and the Cox Committee warred over the public release of the committee's report. Each side strategically leaked portions of the findings to the networks and national newspapers—the committee staff dribbling out the most sensational details of Chinese thefts of warhead secrets, the White House and Energy Department revealing evidence of PRC espionage in the Reagan years, so as to blunt the report's impact.

If anyone could be said to have won this game, it was the Cox Committee and its supporters in Congress. The report was a bombshell. The unclassified version, at 872 pages, was literally full of bomb diagrams and photographs of missile launches and rising mushroom clouds.

On May 25, congressional aides wheeled stacks of the black-bound, three-volume set into the huge room they'd reserved in the Cannon Office Building. A hundred reporters waited to rip through the pages and extract any unpublished detail. One waiting journalist reported that the *New York Times*'s Jim Risen turned with obvious pride to his colleague Gerth and said, "Look at what we started."

The Cox Report was a slick production, unusual for congressional reports. Aides posted it on the Internet in a design reminiscent of a movie promotion. Web surfers were treated to a stark black background, the committee's name, and a glowing red button that bade them ENTER.

Inside the paper and Internet reports were ominous statements, in bold type often on a black or red field: "The People's Republic of China (PRC) has stolen design information on the United States' most advanced thermonuclear weapons."

Clinton campaign donations and the transfer of ballistic-missile technol-ogy to the PRC were almost an afterthought. The dominant theme of the report itself—and indeed of the next day's headlines in every major U.S. newspaper—was China's wholesale theft of nuclear secrets.

"The Select Committee judges that the PRC will exploit elements of the stolen U.S. design information for the development of the PRC's new genera-tion of strategic thermonuclear warheads . . . all of which will be able to strike the United States." Readers in Congress and the public were appalled, fright-ened—and angry.

The Cox Report was received in Congress with unbridled praise. Connecti-cut senator and future Democratic vice presidential candidate Joseph Lieber-man profusely thanked Cox and his colleagues "for an extraordinary act of public service and a very thorough, very comprehensive, very credible report." The enthusiasm with which he and fellow Democrats embraced the Cox Report was matched across the aisle. "The hair on the back of my neck stood up be-cause it's scary," said Majority Leader Trent Lott. "I haven't seen anything like it before in my 26 years in Congress."

Over the next week, Democrats and Republicans alike sent dozens of press releases to newspapers across the country citing China's threat to the security of the United States. The message often as not was this simple: China's spies were ubiquitous and unrelenting in their pursuit of weapons which China would use to threaten ordinary Americans.

———

In no time, a flood of fear and hatred washed over the Internet and talk radio. The notion of a Yellow Peril—that Chinese somehow could not be trusted—once again came simmering to the surface of the American consciousness.

It horrified Henry Tang, a New York investment banker and chairman of the Committee of 100, an organization of influential Chinese-American busi-ness executives. Driving on the freeways of Los Angeles on a business trip, Tang turned on his radio and heard Rush Limbaugh ranting about the Chinese. "It was like a gasoline fire," Tang said. Elsewhere, DJs playing pranks were making live phone calls to people with Asian last names, demanding to know if they were spies.

The Cox Report did not arrive in a vacuum.

Sino-U.S. tensions had escalated in the mid- and late 1990s, when the two nations joined in confrontation over Taiwan. In 1995 and 1996, China sought to intimidate the island and proponents of its independence with test missile launches and amphibious and airborne assault exercises that were billed as practice for the invasion of Taiwan. President Clinton responded by sending two U.S. carrier battle groups into the Taiwan Strait. But even before then, China issued what American hawks took as a clear nuclear threat against an American city.

Assistant Secretary of Defense Charles Freeman had gone to China in 1995 to warn PLA leaders against their planned military exercises.

A high-ranking PLA officer reminded Freeman that in the 1950s, the United States had threatened China with nuclear attack. "You're not going to make that kind of threat now, because if you hit us, we can hit back," he said. "And in the end you care a lot more about Los Angeles than you do about Taiwan."

Freeman himself didn't view the statement as much of a threat. He took it as affirmation of China's avowed policy of no first use of nuclear arms—if the United States threatened a nuclear strike to deter China from taking Taiwan, the Chinese would respond in kind. But to many in Washington, it became an article of faith that China had just threatened the annihilation of millions.

———————

The Cox Report invigorated notions of China as a dangerous new enemy. It inspired a new sinophobia. But the report also made sweeping assumptions, glossed over facts, and ignored much that might have added perspective. In style and content, it was Trulock's story.

It stated, "PRC penetration of our national weapons laboratories spans at least the past several decades and almost certainly continues today." The Cox Committee had no clear evidence that spies were currently busy stealing nuclear secrets. But that was arguably the smallest rhetorical leap in a report that quickly became famous for bold conclusions. In the Cox lexicon, possibilities became probabilities and qualified speculation became hard fact.

"They cherry-picked, and they disregarded the larger body of analysis," said one former CIA analyst. "It seemed fairly clear from both the process and the outcome that they went in with a set of conclusions already in hand and the cherry picking was to support that. The predetermined finding was: The Clinton administration is full of incompetents at best and willfully negligent on national security at worst, and all these things were sort of purchased with campaign contributions."

A wealth of intelligence suggested that Chinese weaponeers were quite capable on their own and had help from the Soviet Union. Soviet designers had told the Chinese as early as the 1950s that primaries should look like "a watermelon rind," the shape employed in many miniaturized U.S. designs. Yet the report stated, "Without the nuclear secrets stolen from the United States, it would have been virtually impossible for the PRC to fabricate and test successfully small nuclear warheads . . ." Such questionable assertions underscored the importance of having a nuclear-weapons expert on the Cox Committee staff. It had none.

Intelligence analysis is akin to assembling a puzzle without most of the pieces; it takes inference, deduction, and judgment of probabilities. The Cox Committee swept away those nuances. The facts behind the committee's assertions, members and staff said, were more often than not tucked away in the classified version of the report. In other words, if you didn't have a clearance and need to know, you couldn't challenge the committee's findings.

The Cox Report sounded an especially dark note about this new wave of modern Chinese nuclear arms to be targeted on the United States. But it failed to demonstrate that these new warheads and missiles represented a major increase in China's threat to American interests.

Unlike the United States and the Soviet Union, China had not built a nuclear arsenal to win a nuclear war but simply to deter a nuclear attack. Its missiles and warheads were designed for a retaliatory strike on cities in the United States but did not amount to a preemptive threat in the same way that the U.S. nuclear arsenal threatened China.

China's nuclear missile force was dominated by short- and intermediate-range weapons targeted on countries on China's periphery. In addition, roughly twenty long-range ICBMs were capable of striking American cities. Unlike the ICBMs of the United States—fast, highly accurate and ready to launch at a moment's notice—China's ICBMs were relics of the 1950s: large, obsolete, and inaccurate liquid-fueled missiles that took hours to prepare for launch. Their warheads were monstrous four-megaton nuclear explosives that were stored in pieces, unmated to the missile. Their launch sites were stationary silos. These factors helped protect the Chinese leadership against the risk of an unauthorized launch and were a reflection of a modest and inherently defensive nuclear doctrine.

By the 1970s, China's scientists were working toward a new generation of nuclear warheads and missiles that would be smaller, lighter, and more likely to survive a first strike by the United States or the Soviet Union. These new, more mobile missiles could be hidden, for example. The DF-31 and the longer range

DF-41 ICBMs would be carried on mobile road launchers that foreign satellites would have trouble detecting, tracking, and targeting. The JL-2 ICBM would be installed on a new class of nuclear ballistic-missile submarines that would have longer range. With smaller warheads, the DF-31 and JL-2 could be MIRVed to allow the delivery of more warheads for every missile. But China had not deployed any of these weapons, nor did intelligence in the 1990s suggest that the Chinese planned to build thousands of these modern thermonuclear weapons as the United States had.

The Cox Committee "judged" that some or all of these new weapons would incorporate stolen elements of U.S. nuclear weapons designs and be targeted on the United States. "The fact that these new nuclear weapons will be far more survivable than the PRC's current silo-based forces could signal a major shift in the PRC's current nuclear strategy and doctrine," the report said.

The Cox Report had recast the replacement of grossly obsolescent missiles and warheads as a greater threat to the United States, which wasn't necessarily true. China has targeted cities across the United States for decades, just as the United States has targeted China. China's new weapons, even if equipped with MIRVed warheads, would not substantially change this deterrent calculation: Both countries would continue to hold valuable assets of the other at risk. Even if China built hundreds of new warheads and missiles, it would remain well behind the United States in terms of nuclear might for years to come. A PRC nuclear attack on the United States or its forces abroad would be suicidal. The United States could counterattack with thousands of warheads.

For all of its frightening conclusions, the Cox Report turned out to be remarkably unappreciative of history and the nature of intelligence gathering at the time. The report's authors erred on numerous facets of Chinese political history and policy in ways that cast the People's Republic as a soon-to-be-superpower hungry for far-reaching dominance. The report failed to explain the context of Sino-U.S. relations going back to the late 1970s. It inaccurately portrayed China's gathering of intelligence as a one-sided pursuit.

For example, the report stated that "the China Academy of Engineering Physics has pursued a very close relationship with the U.S. national weapons laboratories, sending scientists as well as senior management to Los Alamos and Lawrence Livermore." Chinese weapons executives, the report said, used the visits to gather intelligence on U.S. weapons.

It was, in fact, the U.S. weapons laboratories—specifically Los Alamos's Harold Agnew and other senior managers—who first went to China and began cultivating relationships with the scientists of the CAEP. They went with funding and direction from the Central Intelligence Agency and with the blessings of several presidential administrations. From Carter forward, every administration used U.S. scientists and military officials as inducements for China to join the United States in a Cold War strategic alliance against the Soviet Union.

During the Carter and Reagan years, enhancing China's military power was in fact a key foreign-policy objective. As Rand China expert Jonathon D. Pollack observed: "A more militarily credible China would be better able to counter Soviet power, and it would require the Soviet Union to deploy additional assets in Asia . . . The United States therefore saw China as an asset rather than a threat to U.S. security interests."

Of course, China used those contacts to acquire every bit of technological and military insight possible. But the United States reciprocated. It took advantage of those visits to gather intelligence and later to reinforce Chinese understanding of U.S. scientific and military superiority as a form of deterrence. American scientists learned about the Chinese nuclear program, the drivers behind its modernization, and some of the thinking behind its strategic doctrine. Previous administrations had judged that intelligence to be in the national interest. The Cox Report mentioned none of this.

The Chinese assiduously cultivated trade and transfers of commercial technology with the United States, but the United States through four presidencies was an equally ardent suitor. President Ronald Reagan found it in the national interest to approve U.S. commercial satellite launches on Chinese rockets, a policy that ultimately led U.S. engineers to share informally their technical advice with the Chinese on making rockets more reliable. Likewise, the Reagan administration approved exports of computers, machine tools, and a host of other dual-use technologies to China—all part of the perceived U.S. security interest. Experts could debate whether the trade-offs in intelligence and national security were a net gain for the United States or not, but the Cox Report contained none of that debate.

Predictably, China disparaged the report as a pack of lies. Three days after its release, the PRC ambassador to the United States, Li Zhaoxing, went on national TV and sarcastically thanked Americans "for your extraordinary courage, for in the heat of the moment, when some sensational stories are running wild in downtown Washington, D.C., and when my motherland is being called every dirty name from pickpocket to enemy number one . . . you still have the courage and the boldness to invite me to be here, to be among you, without fearing that my presence might be endangering your security and welfare."

Li flatly denied that China had stolen "any nuclear weapon knowledge or information" and said it never would, preferring the path of self-reliance for its defense.

The Cox Report, he said, was "like most nightmares . . . not true." It was "but fabrications out of thin air, not worth the millions of taxpayer dollars, not serving any greater purposes of greater peace, stability and friendship," he said. "[T]he whole report is nothing more than a hodge-podge of distilled water, intentional ambiguities, misleading details, well-calculated conclusions."

Los Alamos's Dan Stillman happened to be in China that week and found a chilly reception from Hu Side.

"I wish I could testify before your U.S. Congress to tell them how much damage has been done," Side said, according to Stillman. "They have turned cooperation into conflict! I could tell them the truth, that we never found it necessary to steal any U.S. nuclear-weapon secrets."

Side went on to condemn the hubris of American scientists and politicians who seemed to believe the Chinese were incapable of matching U.S. weapons ingenuity. The Chinese were no nuclear thieves, and Wen Ho Lee was "a scapegoat."

China's scientists discovered watermelon-shaped primaries and two-point detonation systems in the 1970s, Side said, but they lacked sufficiently powerful and reliable computers to verify those designs by calculation. That power arrived with the Galaxy II, China's second generation of high-performance weapons computers. Side himself designed the device that China detonated on September 25, 1992, the device that three years later triggered Henson's alarm.

"You have overestimated the scientific and technical capability of the U.S. and seriously underestimated that of China," Side railed at the visiting American. "You have insulted us. You must have made these charges for political reasons and not on the basis of evidence of what we have done. We never learned anything from you . . . We did not need you!"

Stillman's own decade of observations inside the Chinese weapons program led him to agree. "I think they did it on their own," he said. "I don't think it was espionage."

China later released its own detailed rebuttal to the Cox Report, titled "Facts Speak Louder Than Words and Lies Will Collapse by Themselves."

But China's repeated denials were at least partly disingenuous. The walk-in documents alone were full of classified data on U.S. nuclear weapons, however rudimentary. Espionage had occurred. What remained uncertain was the magnitude and significance of the leaks. Yet the Cox Report, following Trulock's lead, did not reflect this uncertainty. Dozens of U.S. intelligence analysts, academics, and government consultants were, however, fully aware of this failing. Yet virtually none stepped forward publicly to critique the Cox Report out of fear for their careers, their influence, and their security clearances. In part, their reticence grew out of the inherent vagueness of U.S. intelligence on China and its nuclear-weapons plans.

"The stakes had been raised to something more than an academic argument," said one scholar of China's military modernization. "The claims were pretty serious. You don't want to speak out unless you've got a pretty strong factual basis. Because China is intrinsically vague, the facts simply are not available. People were hesitant to speak up because you knew the response would be an attack on your patriotism and your good judgment. You don't want to be on the wrong side of that when the music stops, particularly now that everything in Washington on China has gotten McCarthyesque."

"I've never seen anything like it," said a former intelligence analyst. "I can tell you the people who knew China were being very quiet, and they were intimidated into silence . . . I didn't appreciate the way they [the Cox Committee members and staff] used the intelligence. I'm not a fan of worst-case scenarios or conspiracy theories, and that's in large measure what's in the Cox Report."

Earlier in 1999, President Clinton had ordered an independent review of Chinese nuclear espionage by the government's intelligence agencies. Robert Walpole, the national intelligence officer for strategic and nuclear programs, assembled a panel of intelligence experts. That spring, they delivered their own assessment in more cautious, sober terms.

China indeed had obtained classified U.S. nuclear-weapons information by espionage, and that information probably accelerated its program to develop more advanced nuclear weapons, the panel said. But the Walpole panel drew a few important distinctions. Rather than suggest that China had acquired U.S. nuclear-weapons designs, as the Cox Report did, the panel said merely that China obtained information on a variety of weapons design "concepts and weaponization features, including those of the neutron bomb."

"We cannot determine the full extent of the information obtained. For example, we do not know whether any weapon design documentation or blueprints were acquired," the panel found. It added: "China's technical advances have been made on the basis of classified and unclassified information derived from espionage, contact with U.S. and other countries' scientists, conferences and publications, declassified U.S. weapons information and Chinese indigenous development. The relative contribution of each cannot be determined."

Nowhere in the unclassified or classified versions of the Cox Report did the name Wen Ho Lee appear. His case was barely discussed at all, and like so many of the report's more sensitive topics, was covered by the statement that "the Clinton Administration has determined that more cannot be publicly disclosed without affecting national security or ongoing criminal investigations." But Lee had become the face of every nefarious act alleged in the report; he was the prototypical Chinese spy, stealing the secrets with which the PRC might destroy American cities.

———————

Even so, the tide and tenor of media coverage began to shift. The *Los Angeles Times,* the *Washington Post,* and other newspapers began to report that classified information on the W88, and indeed other warheads, was available at hundreds, perhaps even thousands, of locations. At the same time, the administration and a few members of Congress, most notably Senators Fred Thompson and Joseph Lieberman, began unearthing the flaws in the original Kindred Spirit investigation.

Earlier in 1999, Clinton had tasked the little-known President's Foreign Intelligence Advisory Board with examining security failures at the national laboratories. To lead the panel, Clinton chose former senator Warren Rudman, a Republican trusted by both parties for his evenhandedness. For the panel's staff, Rudman drew on the CIA, the FBI, and the National Security Agency. In June, the Rudman panel issued the first official recognition that the analysis underlying Kindred Spirit was more equivocal than Congress had been led to believe.

The title of the Rudman Report—"Science at Its Best, Security at Its Worst"—prefaced a brutally honest critique of a quarter-century of tension between science and security at the nation's weapons laboratories. Rudman found that security had lost.

"Organizational disarray, managerial neglect and a culture of arrogance, both at the DOE headquarters and the labs themselves, conspired to create an espionage scandal waiting to happen," the Rudman panel wrote. "The Department of Energy is a dysfunctional bureaucracy that has proven it is incapable of reforming itself . . . Never before have the members of the special investigative panel witnessed a bureaucracy, a culture so thoroughly saturated with cynicism and disregard for authority."

At root, the panel said, DOE's security failings were not about poor counterintelligence by itself, but rather a bureaucracy that shunned accountability. "This report finds that the Department of Energy is badly broken, and it's long past time for half-measures and patchwork solutions. It's time to fundamentally restructure the management of the nuclear-weapons labs and establish a system that holds people accountable," Rudman said in presenting his report.

Senator Pete Domenici and colleagues were delighted with the salient conclusion of the Rudman Report—that the DOE required reorganization. Rudman advised the formation of a new, semiautonomous agency within DOE to handle all of its nuclear-weapons–related work, including the guarding of nuclear secrets. Members of Congress who for years found their influence over DOE diluted by its massive bureaucracy were primed to seize this opportunity.

"We would be negligent in our duties if we don't take advantage of the opportunity," said Republican Representative Mac Thornberry of Texas, a longtime critic of the DOE and its oversight of the Pantex nuclear-weapons assembly and disassembly plant near Amarillo. "If we don't protect our own nuclear deterrent against espionage . . . , the security of our nation and ideals will be threatened. We should act today when the path is clear and the time is right."

The proposed National Nuclear Security Administration nonetheless struck critics as a resurrection of an early Cold War relic, the Atomic Energy Commission, whose build-bombs-at-any-cost mind-set left a legacy of worker illnesses and a waste cleanup bill in excess of $10 billion.

A key finding of the PFIAB went relatively unremarked in the ensuing press coverage. The panel found that the wide availability of classified W88 information suggested that the Kindred Spirit investigation had wrongly targeted Wen Ho Lee. Rudman subtly chided Congress for leaping to conclusions.

"Possible damage has been minted as probable disaster. Workaday delay and bureaucratic confusion has been cast as diabolical conspiracies," the PFIAB wrote. "Enough is enough."

Congress by and large took little of this chastisement to heart. By midsummer 1999, all the feverish talk of Chinese spies had generated overwhelming pressure to do something—to come up with a legislative cure. Reorganizing DOE was coupled with a moratorium on foreign visits to the weapons labs and scientists' travel to sensitive countries. It seemed not to matter that there was little evidence that these exchanges had resulted in lost secrets. Members of Congress then engaged in a bidding war to require polygraph testing for larger and larger numbers of national lab scientists.

The headlines of Lee's firing sent waves of anxiety through Chinese-American communities across the country. Not only was China accused of a massive espionage campaign, but the suspect was ethnic Chinese as well, even if he had been born in Taiwan. They knew instantly, "in the belly and in the brain," as a business leader put it, that there would be a backlash against Chinese Americans and an attempt to revive a Cold War stance toward China.

E-mails circulated quickly. Lester Lee, president of a Silicon Valley high-tech company, wrote that the chill was immediate. "Even at my own company, where I am the boss, I detected a certain amount of distance from my non-Chinese employees when this subject was brought up in casual conversation."

In New York, Henry Tang was distressed. He was worried both about Lee and the threat to the growing economic ties between China and the United States. The community was calling for a reaction, but there was reason to hesitate. No one knew the facts of the case. What if Lee turned out to be a spy?

Tang decided to invite the secretary of energy to address the Committee of 100 at its annual meeting in New York. In his April 30 talk, Richardson acknowledged the anger of Asian Americans at Los Alamos and Livermore who felt "their loyalty and patriotism are being challenged." Afterward, Joel Wong, a Hong Kong–born scientist at Lawrence Livermore, handed him a two-page list of incidents at the lab, including allegations that managers had stopped promoting Asian Americans out of fear for their own careers. In one meeting, Wong said, there were titters of laughter at the speaker's Chinese last name.

At Los Alamos, there was exasperation that a DOE security trainer had joked during a class that the seven Chinese restaurants in town were obviously covers for Chinese spying.

"It showed that Asian Americans were still not accepted in their own country," Wong said.

Cecilia Chang, Wen Ho Lee's old friend from Albuquerque, had since sold her computer company and moved to the San Francisco Bay area. Even before the *Times* story, Alberta had told her that her dad was in some kind of trouble. Chang was in Hong Kong when Lee was fired. When she returned home and read through the emotion-laden e-mail waiting for her, she broke out in a cold sweat, shaking. "Then I knew that it had really got in my system. I thought, I can't turn away, I cannot. Never have I had that kind of experience."

She answered her messages, telling others that she knew the Lee family and that they were in need of money for their legal defense. In September, there was an organizing meeting of thirty or forty people at Ming's, an upscale Chinese restaurant in Palo Alto. Alberta was there, and Mark Holscher flew up from Los Angeles. Holscher talked about how the case came to him in the form of a young woman's shaky voice over the telephone, almost in tears, saying "My father is being harassed by the FBI."

He had agreed to meet with Lee, and quickly realized there was no turning back, he said. He was a Republican who defended white-collar and corporate defendants and had no previous interest in civil rights cases, but he was shocked at the way Lee was being treated. As he talked to the Chinese audience at Ming's, he was crying. "I am a German; I am not the kind of guy who can do this in front of people," he said, wiping the tears.

For Chang, "it was unbelievably moving." Afterward, she started a Web site—wenholee.org—that would become the central switchboard and organizing tool for Lee's supporters.

———————

Bob Vrooman had retired from Los Alamos and moved with his wife to Montana a year before Lee was fired. He was at home outside Bozeman when he heard on CNN about the *New York Times* story. Infuriated that the investigation had been blown and Lee would surely be publicly identified, he began yelling at the television.

He felt that Lee didn't have a chance, and decided, as he put it, to level the playing field. A week later, he was back in Los Alamos in a meeting with lab management on the fourth floor of the Administration Building, trying to put together a game plan to counter the negative publicity. He was defending the lab as much as Lee. Among some managers, Vrooman sensed shock and paralysis, a feeling that "this can't be happening to us."

Vrooman and Karl Braithwaite from the lab's Government Relations Office wanted to take a hard line, to go public with the message that the W88 was not lost from Los Alamos. Others urged a more conciliatory approach, because the lab did have some security problems. In the end, it was decided that the lab would take the high road and Vrooman would take the low road. Lab executives publicly would offer mea culpas in Congress and the press; Vrooman would take on the DOE and the FBI for incompetence.

On April 12, he was one of the briefers when the Senate Select Committee on Intelligence came to Los Alamos to hear firsthand about the W88 affair.

Meeting in a high-security, windowless room protected from electronic eavesdropping, the senators listened as Vrooman and others made their case. He told them he disagreed with Trulock's investigation and the *Times* story. Lee did not "stick out like a sore thumb," he said. Terry Hawkins, the lab division director over intelligence and a visitor to China, pointed out how the Chinese small-weapon design differed from the W88. The PRC warhead was, at the least, significantly larger. Vrooman's plan to defend the lab was under way.

Vrooman began preparing a personal press release, although he wasn't quite sure what he was going to do with it. Hawkins suggested he call it "The Ethnic Cleansing of a National Laboratory." Throughout the summer, Vrooman met with congressional committees, their staffs, and investigators from the DOE's inspector general. His message was consistent: Trulock and the FBI had done a poor investigation; security at the lab wasn't so bad; there was no evidence that Lee was a spy.

In August, Bill Richardson sent a letter to the lab demanding that Vrooman, his assistant Terry Craig, and former lab director Sig Hecker be disciplined for alleged shortcomings in the handling of the Lee case. Vrooman was cited for failing to remove Lee's access to secrets after the FBI signaled that its investigation no longer required him to remain in his job. Vrooman responded that the decision to leave Lee in place was made during a meeting with FBI and DOE representatives. A major factor, he said, was the FBI's desire not to alert Lee to the then-ongoing investigation. Vrooman thought Richardson was just posturing, looking tough for the press.

Vrooman's name was quickly leaked, which angered him more. He wrote another press release, had it cleared by the lab security office and the legal staff, then the public affairs staff, and got phone numbers for reporters Vernon Loeb of the *Washington Post* and William Broad at the *New York Times* from Jim Danneskiold in the public affairs office.

On August 16, the *Post* carried a story headlined "Ex-Official: Bomb Lab Case Lacks Evidence, Suspect's Ethnicity a 'Major Factor.' " It quoted Vrooman extensively: "I'm not going to go down in history as the guy who screwed up this case, because I wasn't. This case was screwed up because there was nothing there. It was built on thin air."

Vrooman told Loeb that documents with W88 information were widespread in contractor and government circles. One document was even distributed to the National Guard. But it was his comments on ethnicity that got most of the attention. Race played a role in singling out Lee, he said. The obscure code writer was a suspect in part because he had visited the Institute of Applied Physics and Computational Mathematics in Beijing, even though "caucasians at Los Alamos who went to the same institute and visited the same people" were not investigated. Vrooman was thinking specifically of Bob Clark. Lee and Clark were friends, worked together in X Division, and traveled to Beijing together in 1986. Lee was a spy suspect; Clark was not. Lee's supporters saw Vrooman's words as proof that their worst fears were true. He had established the foundation of a "racial profiling" claim.

In September, William Broad, a *Times* science and nuclear-weapons writer, wrote a long piece that had a profound effect on public opinion. Unlike his colleagues Gerth and Risen in their reporting of the original story, Broad talked to numerous people at Los Alamos, including physicists involved in the early analysis of the intelligence data from China, and Harold Agnew, the first Los Alamos official to visit the Chinese weapons scientists. In contrast to the Cox Committee's claim that it was "virtually impossible" for China to have made small warheads "without the nuclear secrets stolen from the United States," Broad reported that there was violent disagreement in the intelligence community about how much help the Chinese got—or needed—from espionage.

Broad cited one "top administration official" as saying, "Everyone has come to the same conclusion: We don't have a smoking gun."

———————

While the Cox Report was generating overheated rhetoric on the radio, a group of scientists at Los Alamos was going back to square one with the W88 case. As it became apparent in 1999 that there was no evidence that Lee had given away the warhead design, the group decided to reexamine the walk-in document that had helped launch the investigation four years earlier. Ken Schiffer, the counterintelligence director, was in charge.

"Schiffer did the good thing," said a scientist familiar with the team's work. "He said, 'What exactly are we looking at here?' " By then, more of the documents delivered by the Chinese defector had been translated into English, providing new insight.

The team concluded that the walk-in's document on nuclear weapons of interest was a cross between a report and a letter. It was apparently written as guidance for defense officials planning the future of China's missile force. "It was a high-level, lowquality paper, a here's-where-we're-going document."

It was filled with mistakes. Numbers and dimensions were not consistent from page to page. "It would get a C if it were a class paper," one scientist said. The dimensions in the document generally referred not to warheads, but to the cone-shaped reentry vehicles that carried them. The pages contained sketches of reentry vehicles for several warheads, with dimensions, weight, and information about the center of gravity. They were specifications intended for the manufacturers of the re-entry vehicles, not for Los Alamos scientists.

For the W88, there was slightly more information. The documents accurately listed two dimensions for the outside of the peanut-shaped warhead, information needed to fashion a reentry vehicle for the warhead. The document also accurately described the W88 as having an aspherical primary, and correctly concluded that the orientation of the warhead was "primary forward," i.e., that the primary was toward the small, pointed end of the reentry vehicle. But even these "secrets" were fairly basic.

Buried in the document—and apparently missed by the 1995 review—was similar information about the W87, the warhead for the silo-based MX missile. The Chinese knew that its primary was shaped differently from that of the W88, and that unlike the W88 it used insensitive high explosives, so it was less susceptible to accidental detonation.

Information about insensitive high explosives, however, could be gathered easily from the open literature. The Los Alamos researchers also discovered other data in the walk-in document that came from public sources. Dimensions related to the W62, the warhead for the Minuteman III missile, were wrong, a mistake that was traced to an inaccurate 1979 article in a publication by Jane's, the British publishing firm that chronicles weapons systems around the world.

The authors of the Chinese document compared the W88 and W87 and found the W88 more desirable—slightly smaller and more powerful. The Chinese analysts seemed to be saying that the W88 was the nuclear world's most advanced weapon. The document was warning Chinese defense officials, however, that China was not yet capable of building such a sophisticated weapon. "The author is saying that the W88 is as good as it gets. We're not there yet, and it will be a while before we get there," a U.S. scientist said.

The realization by the Los Alamos sleuths that the document had roughly as much information on the W87 as on the W88 changed the way they looked at the case. The sources from which the Chinese could have drawn this information were greatly expanded. The W87 was a Lawrence Livermore design. The MX missile and its reentry vehicle were made for the Air Force, built by a different set of prime contractors than those who built the Navy's W88. If there were a spy, the spy might be someone who had access to data about both weapons, perhaps from a company that worked on some detail of both systems, or an employee of a company consulting to the Pentagon.

———

Information on the W88 could have come from a wide variety of sources, the researchers concluded. The data seemed to come from reentry-vehicle manufacturers, or from "interface documents" that describe the outside of the warhead and how it should be bolted inside the reentry vehicles. As John Kammerdiener had predicted immediately after Lee was fired, one such document apparently had slipped into Chinese hands, the Los Alamos scientists concluded.

As they dissected the walk-in document, the scientists found what appeared to be a small error in one of the dimensions for the W88. But when they looked back through U.S. documents, they discovered it wasn't a mistake after all. For a certain period of time, before the W88 design had been finalized, it was the official number. The number was ultimately changed as the design moved forward.

That discovery suggested that some of the information acquired by China came from a specific document. But distribution of that document was in the hundreds, scattered to addresses throughout the Defense Department, the DOE, and contractors' offices.

"It's a systems compromise," said one scientist. "It could have come from dozens of companies, thousands of people, over fifteen, twenty years."

Investigators did discover one document that had all the relevant W88 information in one place, on a single page. It had been created by Lockheed Missiles & Space in Sunnyvale, California, the company that built the Trident missile and the reentry vehicle that enclosed the W88.

The team turned up nothing that pointed to Wen Ho Lee as a suspect. Working away in his office on mathematical codes, he had had no access to interface documents.

The Los Alamos "relook" at the walk-in document did not offer much hope that the FBI would ever find anyone who leaked documents to the Chinese. The situation contrasted starkly with most espionage cases. In the Aldrich Ames case, investigators had an idea of what was lost, then drew up a matrix of who had access to all the information. Slowly they narrowed in on Ames. But the W88 case was different, said a Los Alamos official, shaking his head. "Here, the matrix keeps getting bigger."

The team briefed its results to the FBI, where some agents had long harbored doubts that Lee had leaked W88 information. In September 1999, just months after the release of the Cox Report, Attorney General Janet Reno and FBI Director Louis Freeh announced a new investigation into the loss of the classified weapons data found in the walk-in documents. Kindred Spirit was finally dead. The new search faced tremendous odds. "You're looking at potentially a thousand points of compromise. So it becomes an undoable problem," a federal official said.

In 1996, Kindred Spirit had been opened with two ready-made suspects, Wen Ho Lee and Sylvia Lee. This time, the target was listed as "UNSUB," FBI-speak for "unknown subject." This was the case Kindred Spirit should have been, an investigation of the "potential" loss of the W88.

Notra Trulock's misleading briefings and FBI bungling had caused agents to spend four years investigating the wrong crime, as the Bellows review team later concluded. The man who wanted "one spy" had found none.

Although Lee still faced the threat of prosecution for his downloads of weapons files, the new investigation was a tacit admission that Wen Ho Lee was not the W88 spy.

– 22 –

Intent to Injure

U.S. Attorney John Kelly had been Bill Clinton's college roommate at Yale and had led his campaign in New Mexico. After his election, Clinton had appointed Kelly to be the top federal law enforcement officer in the state.

As a prosecutor, Kelly didn't make much of an impression on the lawyers who practiced in federal court; his administration was merely unremarkable. The powerhouse of the office was Gorence, and Gorence knew it. He loved tough, high-profile trials, and the Lee case was cracking up to be that and more.

In the late spring of 1999, Kelly and Gorence were rapidly losing their patience with Lee and his combative young defense attorney. For weeks, Holscher and Gorence had engaged in rhetorical warfare, neither willing to concede an inch of the field to the other. Gorence clearly had the upper hand in this clash, in no small measure because Lee was lying to his lawyer.

Holscher, eager to head off the case before it came to an indictment, went to the U.S. Attorney's Office in Albuquerque on June 21, 1999, with his client in tow. As Lee listened, Holscher told prosecutors that his client had never downloaded classified data to magnetic tapes. Holscher didn't know that his client had lied to him, but Gorence did. "We called them on that," said one of the prosecutors on the case.

Holscher talked to his client again and came back with a different story: If he put classified information on these tapes, he destroyed the tapes. Holscher could provide no evidence to back up the claim.

By late spring, Gorence and Kelly had had it. Sea Change investigators began preparing their case for indictment. They procured an unused lab office and interviewed scientists of X Division.

Gorence hurled himself into the arcana of bomb science. He read physics texts and headed to Los Alamos weekly to talk to weapons managers. He was a fast learner and quickly mastered the intricacies of weapons and weapons codes.

Los Alamos weapons executives confirmed what Gorence and his investigators already had heard from lower-level managers: Lee's tapes contained incredibly sensitive weapons data, and he had no legitimate reason to make them. Rank-and-file scientists gave insights into Lee's personality, suggesting that he had profound job insecurity. A few told the FBI that they had seen Lee inside X Division in January and February, after he was supposedly exiled from his old office.

FBI agents and psychological profilers started knocking on doors in Los Alamos and White Rock. At Bob Clark's house, an agent pulled a 3M 6150 tape from his pocket.

"Have you ever seen one of these?"

"Sure," Clark said.

"Did Wen Ho Lee ever give you one of these?"

"No, never," Clark replied. "Why?"

The agents wouldn't say.

Two agents of the FBI's Behavioral Sciences Unit paid a visit to Don and Jean Marshall. They began asking questions about the Lees' marriage. They were especially curious about Sylvia Lee.

Agents also assembled Sylvia's old supervisors in a room at the laboratory. They asked a number of personal questions about her and her past. They already knew of her cooperation with the FBI and her difficulties at work.

Gorence was careful to interview a number of Lee's friends and acquaintances to put them on the record. Before Lee even knew he was facing criminal charges, Gorence already would know the probable outlines of the defense and have locked in its witnesses' stories.

On June 9, FBI agents simultaneously visited every Lee relative in the United States, handing out grand jury subpoenas and performing searches. They found Alberta Lee at her Chapel Hill, North Carolina, office and served her a subpoena. Alberta phoned Chung in Cleveland, and minutes later agents appeared at his apartment door. The FBI returned with a search warrant for the clinic where Chung performed research on heart-valve mechanics. They checked his computer files and e-mail. The same day, the Bureau interviewed Lee's younger and older brothers Wen Ming in San Mateo, California, and Wen Tou, in an Arcadia, California, nursing home, as well as his younger sister, Angela Liang, in Arcadia. "It was straight out of *The Godfather*," Alberta told the

Los Angeles Times. "They orchestrated a hit on all my relatives across the country at exactly the same time."

Before long, Gorence was taking the same witnesses before a federal grand jury in Albuquerque. Every two weeks, FBI agents and Los Alamos weapons scientists waited their turn outside the grand jury chambers on the second floor of the Albuquerque Federal Courthouse. On June 18, almost all of Lee's relatives were questioned, one by one, in front of the grand jury. It was a small room. The jurors were seated in three rows before a raised platform for prosecutors and witnesses. Prosecutors probed the Lee clan for money problems or unexplained cash. They asked about the 1997 murder of Wen Tou's wife and son during a house robbery as well as Wen Ho's $16,000 loan to his older brother. Prosecutors asked whether Wen Ho liked to gamble.

"They were looking for motivation, money . . . for giving away secrets," Chung Lee later told a reporter. "They knew we often drove to California and usually stopped at Las Vegas. The reason was my mom likes the buffet and loves to shop. So my dad and I would go gamble. They wanted to see if my dad was losing a lot and needed money, so they asked what's the most he ever lost. I told them I once saw him lose $50 and he was really upset and stopped playing for a long time."

Los Alamos's computer experts had found evidence of multiple log-ins to Lee's unclassified network account from UCLA and from Lee's home. Alberta and Chung said they used their father's password—Chung to send e-mail to his girlfriend in San Diego when he was in White Rock and Alberta when she was at UCLA to join a multiplayer version of Dungeons and Dragons on the Internet. The lab's high-speed access was an advantage, she said.

Wen Ming Lee, known to his friends as Lucky Lee, was cheerful after his testimony. He said that he told the grand jurors "about God's love, about how there should be no weapons of mass destruction."

Prosecutors didn't ask Lee's colleagues much about their trips to China, but they did want to know what these potentially friendly witnesses thought about Lee's tapes.

"Why would he do this?" Gorence asked Clark in front of the grand jury, according to Clark.

"To look for another job," Clark testified.

———

While Gorence and his assistants grilled Lee's family before the grand jury, Lee himself was living in a fishbowl. On the day his home was searched, photographers thronged outside to capture stills or footage of Lee. Afterward, he rarely came out of the house, and one by one the photographers disappeared, except for the occasional freelancer.

The FBI, however, was a constant presence. Members of the FBI's Special Surveillance Groups, or SSG, were carefully trained in disguise and conceal-ment; for many jobs, they appeared as joggers, street repairmen, or bag ladies. In watching Lee, however, the SSG dispensed with any attempt at camouflage. Wherever Wen Ho and Sylvia went, the SSG was there in force, performing con-spicuous, bumper-to-bumper surveillance of the Lees' every move.

When Lee went fishing, as many as five government-issue sport utility vehi-cles trailed along. At Lee's fishing holes, his watchers piled out of their cars and stretched out on the banks of lakes and rivers while he dunked worms. Lee seemed to enjoy it. "It's good for me to take them fishing," he told friends. "It gets them out of their cars for a while." Sometimes, Lee even altered his itiner-ary for the convenience of his tailers.

The FBI, likewise, fell in behind Sylvia on her trips to the grocery store and even to the University of New Mexico–Los Alamos, where they surveilled her from the back of the Thai cooking class she was taking.

The Bureau nonetheless tried to enhance its watch on the Lees through sur-reptitious means. The FBI secured the approval of Los Alamos Police Chief Rich Melton to locate its command post in his driveway, one street over from the Lees' house. The Bureau's mobile command post bristled with antennae and appeared to residents of the neighborhood as though it were capable of electronically eavesdropping on conversations in all of their homes.

That summer, friends of Alberta began receiving notices from the phone company that their calling records had been subpoenaed by the FBI. Mean-while, back in White Rock, an unusual number of Lee's neighbors reported vis-its from the local telephone company. Repairmen arrived in US West vans and fiddled with the phone lines and boxes in the area. Several neighbors said their phones sounded different, full of new clicks and noises, and they became guarded about their conversations.

"It wasn't only Wen Ho who was under surveillance. We were all under sur-veillance," said Mary Norris, a family acquaintance who lived up the street. "When I had guests, the FBI would come by and get their license plate numbers, and they were followed home."

One night, a young member of the surveillance team made the mistake of parking her car outside the bedroom window of Norris's daughter. Norris grabbed a camera, raced out the side gate of her house, and started snapping photographs through the car window. She demanded some identification. Police Chief Melton arrived and eventually calmed Norris down. The surveillance team never parked in front of her house again.

The FBI did, however, seek to put an unblinking eye on the Lees' house. Agents asked the neighbors across the street whether the Bureau could install a camera in their bedroom window, pointed at the Lee home. They were turned down, and shortly thereafter some neighbors noticed a small camera affixed to the top of the streetlight nearest Lee's house. The FBI wasn't taking the risk of losing Lee the way it had lost Edward Lee Howard.

By late July, Gorence was just about ready to seek an indictment. He decided that he needed props. He drove inside Kirtland Air Force Base to the Sandia campus, to a special chilled vault where the government stored footage of U.S. atmospheric nuclear tests. Gorence sat and watched as fireballs rose from the Pacific and the Nevada desert like angry djinns, wreaking destruction for miles. It was an awe-inspiring sight, and Gorence planned to share it with the jurors sitting in judgment of Lee. They would witness the awful power of what Lee had put on his tapes. Gorence put in a request for some of the movies to be declassified for courtroom use.

Meanwhile, it became clear to the Energy and Justice departments that taking Lee to trial was likely to jeopardize the secrecy of a large amount of classified weapons information. The case against Lee was driven in large measure by the very sensitivity of the weapons software and designs he had put on his tapes. Somehow, prosecutors would have to convey that sensitivity to a jury without revealing the codes, input decks, or data files themselves.

By law, U.S. nuclear-weapons design information is "owned" by the U.S. Department of Energy. Earlier that spring, Richardson had hired General Eugene Habiger, formerly the head of the Strategic Air Command, as DOE's director of the Office of Security and Emergency Operations. Richardson called him his "security czar."

That summer, Habiger assembled a panel of scientists and classification experts to study the information on Lee's tapes, as well as Gorence's movies, with an eye to deciding what could and could not be publicly released. Their review took weeks.

In early August, Wen Ho Lee broke months of silence and made his first public explanation of his rationale for creating the tapes. He had his choice of any news organ in the country and chose CBS News's *60 Minutes* and Mike Wallace, venerated in his CBS Web site biography for his "no-holds-barred interviewing technique." But in Lee's case, *60 Minutes* reached an unusual agreement that had the potential to dilute the credibility of the interview. As Wallace acknowledged to viewers, during taping Holscher was allowed to veto—off-camera—any questions he didn't want his client to answer. These questions would then be edited out of the program.

Wallace introduced Lee as follows: "This man, Dr. Wen Ho Lee, is a nuclear scientist many, if not most Americans have come to believe stole America's most closely guarded nuclear secrets and passed them to the People's Republic of China. Even though he has never been charged with a crime, Dr. Lee was fired from his job in the top secret Division X at Los Alamos National Laboratory in New Mexico. He has been portrayed in newspapers across the country as a traitor, and now wherever he goes, he's trailed by government agents . . . Why are you talking to us, Dr. Lee?"

"It's a point I should try to tell the public," Lee replied. ". . . The truth is, I'm innocent. I have not done anything wrong with what they try to accuse me."

"Did you at any time pass any information, any U.S. nuclear secrets, to the People's Republic of China?" Wallace asked.

"No, I have never done that," Lee said, "and I have no intention of doing that at all, period."

Lee went on to say he had devoted "the best time of my life to this country, to make the country stronger . . . particularly in the nuclear-weapon area . . . so we can protect the American people. But suddenly, they told me I'm a traitor. I mean, I'm—I'm—just don't understand this—this whole, you know, things."

In the same segment, Bill Richardson said Lee had improperly transferred nuclear-weapons information from classified to unclassified computers, where it was accessible through the Internet. Lee responded that other scientists at Los Alamos did the same thing all the time.

"The reason I download the computer code from classified machine to—into unclassified machine is part of my job, to protect my code, to protect my file," Lee explained. "I do that routinely. I never give those, you know, information to any unauthorized person. Plus, I—when I download into unclassified machines . . . I have a three level of password. Three . . . It's—it's almost impossible for anybody to break in. You know, sometime I even had a hard time to break in myself. And so I think what he [Richardson] said was misleading."

But Lee's statements on *60 Minutes* were misleading as well. No other scientist at Los Alamos or the other weapons labs ever had been found to have downloaded all of the major codes for simulating nuclear detonations, as well as the input decks for more than twenty weapons. The FBI's best computer detectives found only two passwords barring access to the weapons files that Lee placed on the unclassified network—his network log-in password and the one he used to access the kf1 directory. That password was "WHLee."

Wallace asked, "Why do you think they focused on you, Dr. Lee?"

"My best explanation of this is they think I'm a—you know, Chinese people," Lee replied. "I was born in Taiwan. I think that's part of the reason. And the second reason, they want to find out some scapegoat. They think I'm the—perfect for them to—to blame me . . . I am the only one Oriental or Chinese people working on the top secret for the last eighteen years. There's no other people . . . Oh, I know the top secret of nuclear weapon very well, yes. I'm—I'm one of the very important people in our division."

Lee's *60 Minutes* interview reached millions of viewers. Holscher had scored major points in the court of public opinion, albeit at some risk—federal prosecutors now had a preview of his defense. Many of Lee's colleagues in Los Alamos were pleased for him. But they were taken aback at the same time— "one of the very important people in our division" and the only Chinese working on the top secrets of weapons? At least two other Chinese Americans outranked Lee in the weapons program, and Lee himself had at least two other Chinese-American acquaintances in X Division. He was hardly an important person in the division. How did his statements square with his professions of ignorance of the W88? Or for that matter, his claims to the FBI that he hardly worked on weapons?

It was becoming clear to Holscher that his bid to halt an indictment of Lee was not working. Several members of Congress already were calling his client "the spy of the century." Meanwhile, Kelly and Gorence seemed unreceptive to Holscher's claims in early August, right after the *60 Minutes* piece, that Lee had made his tapes to protect Los Alamos's files, by making backup copies.

In one of Kelly's latest letters, the prosecutor sounded a note of frustration: "In short, we want you to tell us why he made the tapes!"

Holscher needed help on the ground in New Mexico. His search led him to the Albuquerque firm of Freedman Boyd Daniels. Partner Charlie Daniels—a rakish and canny lawyer who raced cars and led a rock band, Lawyers, Guns and Money—was considered a dean of criminal defense in the state. But the lawyer who teamed up with Holscher was decidedly less flashy.

The house in Huntington, New York, where John D. Cline grew up never had a television; his mother was determined that her two sons be as well read as she was. His father was an airline pilot, trained as an engineer. Cline imagined becoming a university professor, but his disenchantment with college convinced him that teaching literature was not the right path. Almost as an afterthought, he decided to try law.

It turned out he was gifted at it. The lanky, mustachioed lawyer had his father's eye for technical detail and his mother's flair for writing. Both served him well at Williams & Connolly, a litigation powerhouse in Washington. There, Cline joined a team defending Iran-Contra figure Lt. Col. Oliver North. Cline helped tackle the classified portions of the evidence and became intimate with a little-known law called the Classified Information Procedures Act.

"John's just scary smart," said Tom Wilson, a defense attorney for Joseph Fernandez, a North partner in Iran-Contra.

Cline's first marriage hadn't worked out, but he followed his ex-wife to New Mexico to be closer to his son. On the side, he was a long-distance runner and a USTA-ranked tennis player. Cline was also a tournament chess player, consistently one of the highest ranked in New Mexico, and often sought out European and Russian opponents for Internet matches.

At Freedman Boyd, Cline dove into federal criminal defense, also tackling death-penalty cases in state courts. One of the other stars in the office was Nancy Hollander, who wrote textbooks on criminal defense and was an expert on Fourth Amendment protections against search and seizure. In March 1999, Cline and Hollander read about Wen Ho Lee in the pages of the *New York Times*. "There's a guy who needs a really good lawyer," someone had commented. Six months later, they joined the Lee defense team.

In October, DOE finished its study of the data on Lee's tapes and the risk of revealing the information in a trial. Habiger reported to Richardson and the Justice Department that the Energy Department had concerns, but had found "no show-stoppers."

"This train can leave the station," Habiger said.

Habiger himself reminded some people of the Manhattan Project's General Leslie Groves—less blustery but every bit as impatient with scientists and anyone else who failed to appreciate tight security. The fact was, the scientists of the Manhattan Project pioneered nuclear secrecy long before Groves and the Army took charge. They voluntarily withheld publication of the atom's promise for bombs of unbelievable destructive power. And they practiced compartmentalization—scientists who knew different secrets intentionally did not reveal them to one another. In 1940, three years before the Army set up a bomb lab in Los Alamos, the communications barrier kept physicists who were thinking about how to design an atomic bomb from knowing that another group of U.S. scientists had discovered a way to produce enough uranium-235 to actually build such a bomb. Without compartmentalization, the United States probably would have had the bomb years earlier and perhaps hastened the end of the European war.

———————

Not long after the bombing of Hiroshima and Nagasaki, with the world still in awe of the atom's destructive power, Congress sought to secure America's nuclear monopoly by drawing up the Atomic Energy Act of 1946. For the first time ever, an entire body of knowledge—much of it basic science and engineering—would be "born classified."

Scientists warned Congress that the line between basic science and real, practical weapons was blurry. They cited their self-enforced rules in an effort to dissuade Congress from restricting the flow of scientific ideas. But the stunning power of nuclear weapons had given rise to a new politics of secrecy and even paranoia. Some congressmen feared that the Espionage Act of 1918, despite penalties as severe as execution, was not sweeping enough to cover every possible compromise of nuclear secrets. As a result, lawmakers insisted on punishing not just disclosures of nuclear secrets but even the mishandling of them with penalties up to and including life imprisonment. The Atomic Energy Act would be the nation's only set of laws allowing the government to lock up a defendant convicted in a nuclear-secrecy case indefinitely without any proof of espionage.

Aides from the White House and the Defense Department who worked on the Act perceived its potential to clash with the tradition of open scientific exchange. But Congress was being driven by more primal motivations, as two of the Act's drafters would later write:

> The information section of the Act reveals the atavistic depths that have been stirred by the release of atomic energy. The response to this greatest of all triumphs of scientific method and creative intelligence has

been in some respects closely akin to the practice of magic among the most primitive of tribes. Having in their possession a fearful image of the god of war, which makes them stronger than all their enemies, the tribe is obsessed with the fear that the image may be stolen or duplicated and their exclusive claim to the deity's favor lost. So a temple is built, ringed about by walls, and guarded by untiring sentinels. Those whose function it is to attend the deity are carefully chosen and subjected to purification rites; they are forbidden ever to look upon the whole image or to speak of what they have seen. They are guarded with unceasing vigilance, and at the slightest sign of defection condign punishment is visited upon them.

In 1999, when Gorence went looking for the law that fit the FBI's assessment of Lee's crime, the Atomic Energy Act—a throwback to the early Cold War—seemed to "fit like a glove," according to prosecutors.

Gorence had encountered the Act earlier when hundreds of peace protestors marched on Los Alamos, and the lab and DOE wanted to arrest them. Gorence shot the idea down. But in the Lee case, the law seemed particularly apt.

Gorence argued to Justice headquarters that the Lee case was more egregious than a simple mishandling of classified information. Lee had no work-related purpose for creating the tapes. He had meticulously assembled what one senior lab executive had described to Gorence as "the crown jewels of the U.S. nuclear-weapons program." Gorence felt that Lee's meetings with top Chinese weapons officials would help meet the required proof under the Atomic Energy Act that Lee acted "with intent to injure the United States or . . . to secure an advantage to any foreign nation."

Lee obviously knew what he had done was illegal; why else had he been so desperate to get back into X Division? Why had he erased hundreds of files, lied to the laboratory, and lied to the FBI?

But at root, Gorence's case was simpler: the "injury" was denying the United States its exclusive use of its nuclear secrets, no matter whether Lee gave his tapes to the Chinese or Taiwanese or, as Clark suggested, he was trying to get a new job. Jurors, Gorence believed, would easily be convinced of Lee's guilt.

Gorence laid out his logic in a prosecution memo that he and John Kelly hand-carried to Washington in early November. Attorney General Janet Reno was hesitant. She summoned Los Alamos Director John Browne and one of Gorence's lead witnesses, Associate Laboratory Director for Nuclear Weapons

Stephen Younger, to assure her that Lee's tapes posed a dire threat to national security.

Right before Thanksgiving, Reno called a meeting of prosecutors from New Mexico and Justice headquarters. Everyone in Reno's conference room that day was in agreement to seek a full fifty-nine–count indictment, dominated by thirty-nine charges under the Atomic Energy Act. The prosecutors were so confident that they unanimously decided the indictment would charge Lee for copying bomb secrets with intent to injure the United States *and* to aid a foreign country. The remaining twenty counts, brought under a low-level statute of the Espionage Act, would charge Lee with illegal gathering or retention of defense information.

One step remained. Reno needed clearance to put the weapons information on Lee's tapes potentially at risk in a trial. She called a meeting of the leaders of the nation's top intelligence and law enforcement agencies for December 4. They gathered in the White House Situation Room. It was a Who's Who of national security in the Clinton administration: In attendance were National Security Advisor Sandy Berger, FBI Director Freeh, Energy Secretary Richardson, CIA Director George Tenet, Deputy Defense Secretary John Hamre, U.S. Attorney Kelly, Robert Walpole of that spring's CIA review of the W88 case, and assorted aides.

Walpole, the national intelligence officer for strategic and nuclear issues, opened the meeting with a summary of the information that the FBI said was on the tapes. Its potential value to a foreign country, he said, depended heavily on the receiving country. Beyond the codes and input decks, any nation would require plutonium and uranium, sophisticated machining capability, and strong engineering skill to turn the contents of Lee's tapes into deliverable bombs and warheads. But losing the data, he concluded, would pose a serious threat to national security. Everyone agreed the government should act to keep Lee's tapes out of foreign hands.

In the end, it was Reno's decision. She ended the meeting by assuring the room that her prosecutors would drop the case if Lee's defense somehow persuaded a judge that the contents of his tapes would have to be introduced in open court.

Kelly carried home the news: Gorence could take his indictment to the grand jury. *U.S.* vs. *Wen Ho Lee* was a go.

– 23 –

The Crown Jewels

*O*n *the morning of December 10, 1999,* Holscher faxed an offer to the U.S. Attorney's Office: Wen Ho Lee would take a polygraph test, administered by a mutually agreed-upon operator, on the narrow questions of whether he had destroyed the tapes he had made and whether he had ever given their contents to an unauthorized person.

He was too late. The federal grand jury, gathered in a second-floor room of the U.S. District Court in Albuquerque, had voted out the indictment of Lee.

The FBI and the U.S. Attorney's Office had press releases ready to go. The largest computer investigation in FBI history revealed that Wen Ho Lee had "removed from the Los Alamos National Laboratory" a mountain of nuclear-weapons design and "construction" files. Right from the start, the government was laying out a case theory that was inflated and not provable. It was a hint of the miscalculations to come.

John Cline was in Los Angeles for a legal conference. He carried a speech that he was to deliver that afternoon. But for the morning, Cline figured he would drop in on Holscher. A phone call interrupted the visit.

"Your client will be arrested at noon," Gorence said to Holscher.

Holscher and Cline were staggered. A week before, they had asked Gorence to issue a summons for Lee, ordering him to appear at the courthouse at a certain time to be arraigned and presumably released on bail. This was the traditional practice in the District of New Mexico for nonviolent, white-collar criminal cases. Gorence had quickly rejected the idea. The defense then asked whether Gorence would notify them of an impending indictment so Lee could turn himself in and be arrested privately, without the humiliation and damaging publicity of Lee pictured in handcuffs. Gorence had said he'd think about it.

On the phone now, Gorence told the two lawyers that FBI agents were en route to White Rock and would knock on Lee's door momentarily.

Kelly was about to hold a press conference on his nuclear spy case. The government was determined to portray Lee and his downloads as a dire peril to the nation, and that caught his defense flat-footed. Cline quickly dialed the Lee home.

"Wen Ho, the FBI's coming to arrest you in about fifteen minutes," he said.

Cline then rattled off his standard advice for clients about to be arrested publicly: Don't take anything with you. No clothes, toothbrush, or books. They'll just take them away and supply their own. Most of all, don't talk to the government. And no covering up, say, with a blanket to hide from photographers. "It makes you look guilty," Cline warned.

A few minutes later, Special Agents Mike Lowe and Dave Oldham knocked on the Lees' door. Lowe knew Lee, having gotten a signed statement from him in January and having headed the team that had searched his house in April. The agents read Lee's rights to him but were nonetheless soft-spoken and courteous. Lee pulled a beige windbreaker over his plain white shirt. He was then handcuffed and led to their waiting car.

Lee had known for a while that he could be arrested. But as he was handcuffed and taken to court, the enormity of the moment settled in. He forgot Cline's advice and began chatting nervously in the agents' car. They gently reminded him that perhaps he shouldn't say anything.

Meanwhile, prosecutors and the FBI were flooding newsrooms with press releases and copies of the indictment as the FBI drove Lee the hour and a half to Albuquerque. A newspaper photographer, Albuquerque Journal photo chief Paul Bearce, arrived just in time to shoot a picture of Lowe leading a handcuffed Lee into the courthouse.

Lee was taken before U.S. Magistrate Judge Don Svet. His attorney Nancy Hollander was there. Prosecutors notified Svet that they were seeking detention—they wanted Lee jailed until his trial—triggering a provision that allowed Lee to be held for up to seventy-two hours until a full detention hearing could take place. The magistrate set the detention hearing for 11 A.M. Monday. Wen Ho Lee was going to spend not just his first night in a jail but an entire weekend.

The U.S. Marshals Service took custody of Lee and drove him fifty-five miles north to the Santa Fe County Detention Center. He was driven into a walled enclosure topped with barbed wire and escorted into a cinder-block hallway, a booking area of stark white walls and gray floors. Guards towered over Lee and asked him to empty his pockets. They rolled his fingers in ink and got prints. He was given a huge reddish coverall that had to be rolled up several times at the cuffs to fit him. Lastly, he put on a pair of jail-issue flip-flops and was given a thin, vinyl-covered mattress pad to drag back to a cell. The cell itself had a blue metal door, with sliding metal plates on the outside so that jailers could deliver food and look in on him.

He had no family visits, no books, no music, just the echoed shouts of fellow inmates. He was three weeks from age sixty.

———————

Cline and Holscher scrambled to prepare. Alberta Lee caught a quick flight home. Lee's friends and neighbors phoned each other and agreed to make a strong showing at the federal courthouse come Monday. Cline hunted for character witnesses, someone to show Lee's roots in Los Alamos, anything to make him seem unlikely to flee. Next-door neighbor Jean Marshall was ideal. She looked as though she had stepped out of the American heartland—tall, dressed often as not in floral dresses, neat, practical, and smart. She went to church regularly, spoke and smiled in a way that exuded trustworthiness. She was a Q-cleared scientist in X Division; she had the government's own imprimatur of trust. Moreover, she seemed to Cline as though she had strong faith in Lee.

Privately, Marshall was virtually certain that Lee had lied to her and Don, even to his own family. One night Alberta came next door to visit and said her father had pledged to her that he had never downloaded weapons codes to tapes. By then, Don and Jean had seen the indictment. The government couldn't be *that* wrong. "We sat her down and had a little talk with her," Jean said.

Regardless, the Marshalls felt in their gut that Lee was innocent of any criminal intent, and they were determined to defend him at almost any cost.

Cline coached Jean Marshall briefly on the phone: Think of anything that shows your neighbor would stay put to face the charges. The hearing shouldn't take long, he told her. Lee wasn't charged with a violent crime, and the officer from Pre-Trial Services—an arm of the court—had recommended Lee be released on $100,000 bail. They'd be in and out in a little over an hour.

———————

On Monday morning, the federal marshals drove Lee to Albuquerque and placed him in a holding cell in the basement of the courthouse. His lawyers carried a suit and tie to him. Lee was escorted to Svet's courtroom, its gallery packed to its limit. Lee looked up to see reporters studying him intently, but he also saw lots of familiar faces—Cecilia Chang, Sylvia, the Marshalls, the Kashiwas, the Clarks, other neighbors and coworkers. They were a hopeful lot. A friend told Jean Marshall: "You know, your little two-year-old grandson is more of a risk to our community than Wen Ho Lee is. He bites."

Lee sat down with Holscher and Cline. Holscher had a cold and sat pale and coughing. Across the aisle was the federal government: U.S. Attorney Kelly, his first assistant and lead prosecutor Gorence, and Assistant U.S. Attorneys Paula Burnett and Laura Fashing.

Svet called on Lee to stand and give his name and other details. Lee couldn't remember his full Social Security number. Yes, he had read the indictment. He didn't understand Svet's next question until prompted by Cline.

"I plead not guilty," Lee said.

The government came out swinging. Gorence intended to show Lee was a flight risk—pointedly noting to Svet that Lee faced a potential life sentence in prison—but more important, he argued, Lee posed a danger to the community. Gorence called his first witness.

Stephen M. Younger had straight salt-and-pepper hair and gray-blue eyes behind steel-framed glasses. Almost fifteen years before, Younger had made a principled stand against Edward Teller. Younger had led a team of scientists at Lawrence Livermore who were designing part of Teller's dream machine—a space-based laser known as Excalibur that Teller had advertised to President Ronald Reagan as a sure-bet defense for shooting down Soviet nuclear missiles. Inside Excalibur was an H-bomb surrounded by laser rods. In event of a Soviet attack, the bomb would detonate and pour energy into the rods, firing hundreds of intense laser beams at Soviet missiles or warheads. But Teller's sales job masked the persistent fact that no one at Livermore knew whether Excalibur would ever work. After years of Teller's driving his team to meet the elusive goal that he'd promised, Younger became an outspoken critic of Excalibur and later resigned. Some speculated, however, that the real reason for Younger's departure was that he was passed up for a higher post. Regardless, Teller despised him, and Younger reciprocated.

As Younger had climbed the management ladder at Los Alamos, colleagues wondered whether the headiness of senior management had not carried him closer to the hyperbole and arrogance of his nemesis.

He developed an air of chilly disdain, a kind of steely stillness in his manner that could be off-putting. Lab insiders resented his constant reminders that he controlled 80 percent of the budget for the lab that designed 85 percent of the

most advanced nuclear arsenal on Earth. The mission of the lab—meaning primarily the divisions he headed—was to erase any doubt about the capability of
the United States to "project overwhelming force" across the globe. It had a
Strangelovian ring.

"I am responsible for the nuclear-weapons program at Los Alamos. That's
approximately a $900 million program. It's the dominant program at Los
Alamos. And I also have oversight for the five core nuclear-weapons divisions at
the laboratory, which is approximately 3,500 people," Younger told the courtroom by way of introduction.

Gorence then led Younger through an hour-plus tutorial on nuclear
weapons and weapons codes. His testimony was masterful, crushing for the defense. Neither Cline nor Holscher knew much about nuclear weapons. Gorence
and Younger turned the court into a classroom—Bombs 101—and the defense
lawyers found themselves in the uneasy role of students.

Younger laid out the basic workings of nuclear weapons—the primary of
high explosives and plutonium produces nuclear energy to compress the secondary, which provides most of the yield. Weapons codes had been the principal design tools ever since the first bombs. The weapons codes were annotated;
code writers inserted their reasons, in plain English, for solving the equations in
a particular way or for setting a mathematical constant because of a certain nuclear test.

"You put a number of what are called comments in to remind yourself how
the equations are being solved," Younger said. "The source code can be hundreds of thousands of lines long so it's the equivalent of a very thick book . . .
You can read it so it represents, in essence, a graduate course in nuclear
weapons design."

"Could you characterize their complexity?" Gorence asked.

Younger went on: "They have been among the most complex computer
simulation tools ever developed on the planet. They have person-centuries of
effort devoted to them. They are hundreds of thousands of lines long. They are
very carefully designed, very well protected. And they have inside them the results of, well, a thousand nuclear tests that the United States has done over the
past 50 years . . . It's not that all of the results are included in the code, it's the
experience derived from the test that is in the codes."

Every nation designs nuclear weapons the same way—with numerical simulations—"but I think I can say with some confidence that American simulation codes are the best in the world, bar none," Younger testified.

America lavished billions of dollars and the best tools on its weapons scientists. They were put to work in a many-faceted competition—Los Alamos versus

Livermore, the Air Force versus the Navy versus the Army, everyone against the Russians, democracy versus communism, scientists challenging themselves. Predictably perhaps, U.S. nuclear weapons rapidly evolved into complex, high-performance killing machines, the Jaguars of mass death—with more than six thousand parts and exotica like gold, plutonium, and lithium deuteride.

The physics at work inside an exploding thermonuclear device is extraordinarily rich, counterintuitive, and fast—no other devices on the planet are comparable. Skilled physicists starting at square one logically would assume they needed an incredible volume of very precise equations and data to simulate such a thing.

At first, American weaponeers thought the same. They blew up hundreds of bombs and built extraordinary instruments to mine the data—insights of physics that they added to the codes. The codes swelled in size, became more detailed, more accurate.

But as explosions rocked Nevada and scientists learned more, they figured out shortcuts, too. It seemed that certain pieces of bomb physics were not critical; they didn't really affect the overall accuracy of the simulation. Scientists could replace some complicated calculations with fairly simple equations and numbers, saving significant amounts of computer power and time.

"And that, indeed, is one of the biggest secrets within the codes," Younger said.

No other nation could afford to spend billions of dollars on a thousand nuclear tests.

For decades, U.S. weapons codes ran on the world's fastest computers. In fact, Younger said, H-bombs were a dominant force in creating and propelling the U.S. supercomputer industry. Congress and the Energy Department and its predecessors made sure Livermore and Los Alamos had the most powerful machines available.

Yet the supercomputers used in the 1970s to design all of the highly sophisticated nuclear weapons now in the U.S. arsenal were no more powerful than a modern laptop. A nation of moderate computational power could use U.S. codes to design fairly complex weapons.

If a foreign nation acquired Lee's tapes, the task would be easier: The tapes contained the critical data files that the codes draw upon when running, as well as many numerical depictions of nuclear-weapons designs. These are called input decks, and they are the starting points for a nuclear-weapons simulation. To the untrained eye, they appear as ranks of letters and numbers. Yet they describe the shapes, dimensions, and materials of the component being modeled—the exact radius of the plutonium and high explosives in a primary, for example. Common programs called "utilities" can translate those numbers into a two-dimensional picture of a bomb.

Lee's tapes contained some two dozen input decks. "They represent a spectrum of nuclear explosive designs [from] relatively simple designs to very sophisticated designs," Younger testified. "I might say that some of these designs were successfully tested." The fact that one was the W88 was classified information and went unmentioned.

The data files on Lee's tapes were mostly unclassified. Known as the Sesame Tables, they contain numbers showing, for example, the speed of radiation through bomb materials and the behavior of those materials at various temperatures and pressures. They are unclassified for elements of low atomic weights—the plastics, high explosives, and light metals in the bomb—as well as some heavier elements. But the numbers are classified for the qualities of plutonium and uranium at extremely high temperatures and pressures, when they are crushed to liquid and gas.

"These conditions are really only found in nuclear weapons. Those properties are secret," Younger said.

What time and money did America invest in the data? Gorence asked.

Fifty years of calculations and lab experiments, Younger said. Nuclear tests supplied the rest, and it didn't come cheaply. Scientists and engineers created new technologies for capturing high-precision measurements hundreds of feet underground and close to the hostile environment of a nuclear explosion. Nothing down the hole survived for another test.

Younger placed the price tag for the data at "hundreds of billions of dollars."

Its quality was unparalleled, in Younger's opinion. No other country had the money and technology to acquire it in the heyday of nuclear testing. Most of the world stopped nuclear testing in the early- to mid-1990s. The United States began its moratorium in September 1992, France and China persisted until 1996. China's blast that September was thought to be the world's last until India and Pakistan detonated weapons in the spring of 1998. The testing moratorium had closed the window of opportunity for acquiring the data.

"I don't think it's possible, no matter how smart you are or how much technology you have, . . . to reproduce tools of this sophistication without nuclear testing," Younger said. "So in a sense they are priceless, they can't be duplicated."

Could the weapons codes, data libraries, and input decks be used for something other than designing thermonuclear weapons, Gorence asked—perhaps some commercial application?

"The input decks, no, because they describe specific nuclear explosive designs. It is possible to use the computer codes for other things but, certainly, in a sense of using a Ferrari to haul cement, yes, you could do that. But it's not the vehicle of choice," Younger said.

Gorence walked Younger through four of the most important codes on the tapes, identified only by letters. Younger identified Codes A and D as design software for secondaries, Codes B and I were used to design primaries.

If a scientist wanted to work on the codes, Younger said, he might pull down a piece at a time. Working on code modules in such a way was faster than moving around inside the entire code. In every case, Younger said, Lee downloaded and copied the entire codes for his tapes. The implication was clear: It was unlikely that Lee made the tapes to make his work easier or to take his work home.

Together, the four codes "represent the complete nuclear weapons design capability of Los Alamos at that time," Younger said. "There may have been small codes that weren't included in there, but they were the big ones. And they would enable the possessor to install the complete nuclear weapons design capability at a remote location without a great deal of effort."

For a group or nation without its own weapons program—a beginner in the world of nuclear weapons—Lee's tapes amounted to the "immediate capability to design a credible nuclear explosive, perhaps without nuclear testing, I can say without testing."

A developing nuclear nation—India, Pakistan, perhaps China—could use Lee's tapes to "greatly advance" its arsenal with smaller, vastly more sophisticated weapons. Such a nation could, for example, go from clunky, single-warhead missiles to MIRVed missiles carrying several small, efficient warheads—more overall explosive yield over a larger area, perhaps targeted on several cities.

An advanced nuclear nation—only the former Soviet Union fit this category—could in Younger's opinion learn a few extra tricks of the trade but, more important, could glean vulnerabilities of U.S. nuclear weapons. The Russians, for example, might devise a missile defense to home in on the weakest, most sensitive part of American warheads and be especially proficient at destroying them before they reached their targets.

Until those statements, Younger's testimony had been straightforward and factually difficult to attack. But it was not quite gospel to assert that a foreign nation, a terrorist group, anyone could take U.S. weapons codes and design a weapon with them. The codes Lee copied were finicky beasts. Even a fledgling Los Alamos bomb physicist would need at least a year to run them successfully, typically several years to get useful results—and that's with extensive, classified apprenticeship to senior designers or code developers.

And that point was precisely where Gorence was headed. He aimed to leapfrog the judge past the lack of any espionage evidence to the conclusion that the fifty-nine-year-old scientist was a dangerous man who had taken the secrets to America's most lethal weapons.

Wen Ho Lee could be the mentor. In fact, part of Lee's job, Younger said, was to help designers make the codes run.

"It is possible to run them in an incorrect fashion so that you will get the wrong answer," Younger said. "Even if you had the manual for the code, it's helpful to have someone who understands how to set the parameters, how to describe the geometry, the practical details associated with using any complex skill. It's sort of the difference between giving someone a toolbox and saying, 'Now I want you to make a chair,' or giving someone a toolbox and a carpenter to help them."

By implication, Wen Ho Lee would coach a U.S. adversary past the sizable technical challenges of using the codes to design nuclear weapons. He carried the know-how in his head, Younger said. Gorence had skillfully turned a weakness of the government's case—the cranky resistance of the codes to an uninformed user—into an advantage and at the same time painted the diminutive Lee as a walking danger to national security.

The courtroom gallery sat stunned. It occurred to several scientists that they, too, met the implied definition of a danger to the community. The defense had suffered a staggering blow. Gorence led Younger in for the *coup de grâce*.

"Let me ask you my last question, Dr. Younger," he said. "If you were to assume that Dr. Lee had control and access to seven missing tapes containing the information that you just described in this courtroom, do you have an opinion as to whether or not Dr. Lee, assuming he had that control and could get them to an unauthorized possessor, would he pose a risk to U.S. national security?"

Younger's reply would become notorious.

"These codes and their associated databases, and the input file, combined with someone that knew how to use them, could, in my opinion, in the wrong hands, change the global strategic balance," he said. "They enable the possessor to design the only objects that could result in the military defeat of America's conventional forces. The only threat, for example, to our carrier battle groups. They represent the gravest possible security risk to the United States, what the president and most other presidents have described as the supreme national interest of the United States, the supreme national interest."

Within hours, the news broadcasts of every major U.S. television network would carry some version of Younger's statements. They would appear in some form on the front page of almost every major newspaper the next morning.

Younger's testimony was, however, a massive exaggeration. Scientists sat upright in the gallery. "That's a lie," one whispered. "That's an outright lie."

First, Younger's testimony suggested the codes and input decks in the hands of another nation would vitiate the United States' overwhelming nuclear power overnight. But having a weapons code and building a weapon were altogether different things. Younger implicitly suggested that anyone who had the codes also could engineer, machine, and assemble some of the most complicated devices on Earth. Learning those skills took decades, too. He also glossed over profound problems with U.S. weapons codes—their tendency to crash and deliver bad answers, to predict bombs would work that wouldn't. His testimony assumed that Wen Ho Lee, whose skills were run-of-the-mill at best, could convey the intuitive expertise of generations of U.S. weapons designers.

On a lesser scale, Younger depicted the Lee tapes as "the gravest possible security risk." Yet not one byte of Lee's downloads was classified Top Secret. Lastly, Clinton had described the maintenance of the nuclear arsenal as *a* supreme national interest—not *the* supreme national interest of the United States.

Lee's defense team knew none of this.

What they did know was that the government had circumstantial evidence at best of Lee's intent to share his tapes or his classified knowledge with a foreign power. Holscher hammered at that point. It was almost all he had to work with.

"Your Honor," he objected, "we are now beyond the allegations of the indictment. There is no allegation of any unauthorized possession. There is no allegation of any transfer here."

Svet was having none of it. He overruled the objection.

Satisfied he had portrayed a world in danger, Gorence turned to the FBI and Lee himself.

Special Agent Robert Messemer took the stand and sketched out his credentials—a sixteen-year veteran at foreign counterintelligence, proficient in Mandarin. It soon was obvious that Messemer was a prosecutor's dream: He answered in carefully chosen phrases, and addressed his testimony directly to the judge, often turning to make eye contact.

Together, Gorence and Messemer tried to put Kindred Spirit, with all its flaws and baggage, to eternal rest. Sea Change and the indictment of Lee were a clear break with the bumbling of the past, having "no connection whatsoever with the original W88 investigation," Messemer testified.

It was a disingenuous statement, made within Messemer's first three minutes on the witness stand. Sure, the FBI had put a different name on the investigation and had opened a new file. But Sea Change inherited a lot of evidence from Kindred Spirit and the earlier Tiger Trap—Lee's lies about calling Min in 1982, his admission to sending export-controlled information to Taiwan, Hu Side's expressions of gratitude for help with codes in 1994, Lee's failure to report his contact with Hu—not to mention at least nineteen FBI interviews, four polygraphs, and a no-holds-barred interrogation. All of these were pieces of evidence that federal prosecutors intended to use against Lee in court. Sea Change was clearly "connected" to the earlier, flawed case.

In the courtroom, the investigation was depicted as exhaustive: more than sixty agents, more than a thousand interviews, the Bureau's largest and most thorough detective work on computers. Scientists, agents, and technicians had examined more than a million files—a total of four terabytes of data, or nearly 40 percent of the entire collection of the Library of Congress at the time.

Messemer held up a 3M 6150 magnetic tape—the government's Exhibit 2. Lee had created at least fifteen of these, packed to the brim with both classified and unclassified data. Lee's classified downloads tallied 806 megabytes—if printed out, 403,000 pages of nuclear secrets. Stacked up, they would reach 134 feet high—about a quarter of the height of the Washington Monument.

Massive as that sounded, all those supposed secrets would fit on one and a quarter compact discs. Los Alamos's Common File System at the time stored more than a hundred terabytes, over a hundred thousand times as much information.

Ferreting out Lee's few hundred classified files in the lab's network was painstaking, "a veritable needle-in-a-haystack operation," Messemer said. Some files had been overwritten and the exact record lost forever. But the FBI was able to re-create everything that had been stored in Lee's kf1 unclassified directory.

"We came very, very close, within literally days, of having lost that material," Messemer said.

Messemer gave a brief biography of Lee—his birthplace, his education, his family, his work at Los Alamos, the security violations that justified his firing. He then laid out a compelling case that Lee was secretive and deceptive. He described the way Lee "declassified" the weapons codes and other files and shifted them to the open, Green network. The agent then told the story of Lee getting password access to Kuok-Mee Ling's computer in T-15, in the unlocked trailer.

According to Messemer, Lee lied to Ling in order to use his computer. Lee had claimed to Ling that he needed to put his résumé on tape.

Next came the notebook. Found April 10 in the FBI search of Lee's house, it was a gold mine, a linchpin of Gorence's case. Holscher stood and noted that the search was illegal, in the defense's eyes, but he knew he couldn't keep the notebook out of this hearing.

In a mix of Mandarin, English, and diagrams, Lee had described Ling's tape drive, the 3M 6150 tapes, exactly how to use them, and exactly what was on each tape. The government's Exhibit 3 was a series of color photocopies of several pages, in which the FBI had blotted out the names of the files and translated the Chinese writing.

The notebook was a powerful piece of evidence. Nothing else more strongly suggested that Lee had a non-work-related purpose in making the tapes. Its presence in his home fed the inference that Lee physically had taken the tapes somewhere.

For the FBI, the notebook supplied a nearly exact match with what Los Alamos computer experts found in the lab's computer network. It also was a heads-up for agents and lab scientists to look more closely at the six tapes found in Lee's T Division office.

On closer examination, it was obvious that some of the tapes once had contained weapons files but had been reconstructed with unclassified files. Computer forensics showed that those original weapons files had suddenly appeared on an unclassified server for T Division's Fluid Dynamics Group, known as T-3. They traced back to a workstation in the office of a scientist whom Messemer did not name. The scientist said Lee gained access to the workstation by claiming he had to pull a code off a tape for use in some calculations with another scientist. The notebook effectively led to the tapes, to the files, and ultimately to evidence of another Wen Ho lie.

"From a counterintelligence perspective Dr. Lee's actions are secretive, appear to be clandestine," Agent Messemer said.

Kashiwa sat transfixed in the courtroom. Hearing the story, he recognized himself and Ulitsky. Lee had lied to him. But he'd also listened to Younger mischaracterize the weapons codes so grossly as to amount to a lie. On one hand, a colleague of fifteen years, and on the other, the government to which he had entrusted his career. "I didn't know who to believe anymore," he said later.

A lot of Lee's friends felt exactly the same way. The amiable man they trusted looked more and more like a figure of shadows and gray. And the government they worked for was no different.

Lastly, Messemer testified that all the while the FBI was pursuing the W88 investigation, Lee was busily destroying his collection of files on the network. After the FBI's January 17 interview at his home—when agents concluded that he was an unlikely suspect in the theft of the W88—Lee began what Messemer termed "massive file deletions" on his unclassified network directory. His deletions totaled more than 360 files and ran sporadically through late February, with peaks every time the FBI talked to him. One of the largest file-deletion sessions was within two hours of his February 10 polygraph, when Lee was told he was under investigation and appeared to be lying.

The FBI had searched far and wide for the tapes, which Gorence repeatedly called "America's nuclear secrets." The Bureau transmitted leads to agents all over the country and to its legal attachés in Europe and the Pacific Rim.

"Your Honor, we have undertaken an extraordinary investigation to locate and return these tapes to the proper authorities," Messemer said. "We have been unable to locate them." In the agent's opinion, Lee and his "unfettered access to these seven missing classified tapes represents a clear danger to the United States' national security."

———————

The prosecution's case was devastating. Gorence had painted a compelling portrait of a would-be spy—a man who lied to friends and meticulously, covertly assembled a digital library of bomb secrets supposedly capable of changing the global balance of power.

Holscher repeatedly counterattacked with his strongest point.

"There is no allegation in the indictment that a single one of the files that you described on direct exam has ever been seen by any unauthorized person; isn't that true?"

"The indictment does not discuss that," Younger replied.

"There is no evidence that Dr. Lee has ever attempted to transfer these files to unauthorized persons, is there?"

"Not those files."

"Let me make sure we are very clear," Holscher pressed. "I am referring to every file in the indictment. There is no evidence that Dr. Lee has ever attempted to transfer any one of the files listed in the indictment; is that correct?"

"I believe that's correct, to the knowledge that I have," Younger conceded. "However, I do not believe that I know everything about this investigation."

But Messemer did. And even he admitted there was no evidence that Lee had given nuclear secrets to any foreign country or to anyone for that matter.

Younger conceded that Lee had worked on some of the codes. Further, almost all of the codes shared certain bits and pieces. Code writing was an incestuous craft; developers such as Lee borrowed algorithms, lines, even entire modules when writing a new code. So it was not necessarily unusual for Lee to want access to multiple codes, even if his immediate work pertained to just one or two codes.

Younger further admitted that Lee had not downloaded any of the codes' user manuals. Some manuals instruct users on setting the parameters in the input deck for a successful code run. Others help a user decipher the mass of numbers that come out in the end. But Younger denied that the manuals were "critical," as Holscher argued.

"They are a very important part of using them but, on the other hand, you could reconstruct that user manual with enough time, given the source code."

"You would also agree that the source code and the input data files are not complete by any means without the user's manual?" Holscher asked.

"Oh, they absolutely are complete without the user's manual, yes. It just takes a little longer to figure out what they mean."

Holscher was in potentially dangerous territory. Part of the justification for firing Lee was the discovery in his office of his supervisor's classified code manual, printed without classification markings.

Hadn't other X Division scientists downloaded classified codes, Holscher asked Younger. Rumors of routine computer-security violations had abounded before Lee's arrest.

"We did computer forensics which looked at millions of file transfers and millions of files. We have no reason to believe that this has ever happened before in the history of the program. We have searched extensively," Younger said. "As a matter of fact, we have never seen anything even comparable to it."

Younger admitted, however, that he did know of a scientist who had downloaded classified information to an unclassified computer. In March 1998, a weapons engineer had moved a classified document known as the Green Book to his unclassified office desktop.

The Green Book was the blueprint for Stockpile Stewardship, the federal program of maintaining and refurbishing U.S. nuclear weapons. The document was more or less a schedule for research into existing weapons and their components, as well as design and production of new weapons parts. The engineer had indicated that moving the file onto his unclassified machine, "contaminating" its hard drive with classified data, was inadvertent, but the incident had triggered a major flap and there had been pressure on senior Los Alamos managers to make an example of the engineer, perhaps fire him.

"I am aware that classified files have been put onto an unclassified machine due to an error made on the part of the operator or on the part of the person," Younger said.

But an abundance of anecdotal evidence also suggested that some Los Alamos scientists took classified information home so they could work on it. In some cases, scientists had carted away classified documents in their belongings when they retired. But those situations were fairly rare, and at this early stage, Holscher didn't know enough to rely on them. He drew instead on the Rudman Report and its scathing critique of lab security. The report cited a "deeply rooted culture of low regard for and, at times, hostility to security issues." Younger disagreed with that statement. But he had to concede some of the report's key findings—that Los Alamos's classified system was linked with the unclassified system and further had many connections to cleared researchers outside of the laboratory.

The fact was, Los Alamos's computer security in the early 1990s was indefensible. The lab prided itself as one of the birthplaces of the digital age, yet had failed to secure itself against insider threats and, to a degree, hackers on the outside.

Younger offered the only real defense the lab could offer: The system operated on a "sacred" trust, and Wen Ho Lee had violated that trust.

"We trusted our people that they would not move secret data that shouldn't be, just as we trusted people that they would not carry secret documents out of the gate," he said. "Every federal agency that deals with secret information trusts their people to some extent, and we did too."

———————

Gorence quickly repaired what little damage the defense had done to his case. Holscher had suggested that Lee made the tapes as backups after losing massive amounts of his work files in an early 1990s computer crash. Younger countered that there was no reason to do this. The lab's Common File System was quite stable, and besides, each of the code-development groups in X Division kept formal copies of their most precious codes in secure places.

Even if Lee had lost files, Gorence asked, "would there ever be a legitimate work-related purpose to downpartition and download onto tape the major source codes and data files to operate them?"

"There is never, never a reason to downpartition a nuclear weapon source code to an unclassified place, ever, never," Younger replied. "I believe that everybody in the nuclear-weapons program understands that as a mortal sin, a mortal sin."

Holscher tried to show that the government did not have a single document or witness providing evidence that Lee intended his downloads to "injure the United States" or "secure an advantage to any foreign nation."

Svet stopped him, however: Save it for another judge, another time. When Holscher persisted, he was scolded.

"I said I'm not changing my ruling," the judge said sternly.

Ordinarily, lawyers are supposed to limit their second round of questioning— the redirect—to issues raised by the other side in its cross-examination. But Gorence saved a gem for his redirect of Messemer.

Lee had asked a T Division scientist, apparently Ling, to market his skills overseas as a consultant, Messemer said. "In fact, he sent letters expressing interest in employment overseas to seven separate institutes."

Lee had written letters to the National University of Singapore and Nanyang Technological University in the same city, the Swiss Defense Technology Procurement Agency, Germany's Messerschmitt-Bolkow-Blohm, the Hong Kong Institute of Science and Technology, and National Chung Cheng University and National Cheng Kung University, both in Taiwan. The FBI search team had found those letters on Lee's computer at home.

Twice in 1998, Messemer continued, Lee had visited and worked at Chung Shan Institute of Science and Technology in Taiwan. At Chung Shan, a Taiwanese government military lab, Lee had acted as a consultant, giving lectures and interacting with the faculty, for six weeks in the spring, then for several days in the fall, according to Messemer. For the first trip, Chung Shan had paid Lee a fee of $5,000. At the same time, Lee toured AsiaTek, a Taiwanese company with links to Chung Shan, and met its chief executive officer. The two men discussed whether Lee might act as a consultant to Pacific Rim countries. The company's chief interest was in Lee's expertise with armor/anti-armor codes. Those codes were close cousins to parts of the U.S. nuclear-weapons codes. They were unclassified, Messemer said, but export restricted—they were not to be transferred to a sensitive country such as Taiwan.

"Given family members abroad, the ability to speak another language, travel abroad and, in fact, the contemplation of employment prospects abroad," Gorence asked, "does that modify in any way your response to Mr. Holscher about whether or not Dr. Lee has ties to other communities besides this one in New Mexico?"

"I think it's clear from our investigation that Dr. Lee has close ties outside of the New Mexico area, including foreign ties, more specifically, in Singapore and in Taiwan. And, moreover, he has excellent prospective employment opportunities in the event that he should try to pursue that."

"Would that be particularly true if he was in possession of seven missing tapes?"

"Even more so."

————————

Weaponeers have been portrayed by social scientists as a closed and ritualistic society, a "nuclear priesthood," for their secrecy and elaborate codes of conduct for indoctrination and for research into the tools of massive destruction. Younger's statements were startling for their frank confirmation: Here was a senior man of the cloth condemning an initiate for committing a "mortal sin" that broke the "sacred trust" with "the supreme national interest."

Public exile of a weapons scientist is rare, but defense of an outcast is rarer still.

Don and Jean Marshall felt duty-bound to their neighbor and friend. Testifying for Lee, effectively in opposition to the government and the head of the weapons program, an executive at least three levels above them in the lab hierarchy, was a tremendous risk.

"I was so unprepared for Younger to be there," Jean Marshall said. "I realized I would be in hot water at work, so I had to be careful. It was obvious which side the laboratory was on. Here he's sitting right there in front of me and he's my boss."

She walked to the stand in a dark turquoise knit dress, on her way casually dropping a note on the defense table. Kashiwa had slipped it to her as she rose from the gallery; he had been restlessly jotting down the inaccuracies of the prosecution testimony. But it was too late. She was the only witness left. Cline asked what kind of neighbor Lee was.

"I have loved living next door to Wen Ho," she said. "He likes to work out in his yard and he's outside lots and he never fails to stop what he's doing and come over and chat any time we step outside. So I talk with him often. And he almost always talks for a brief time, makes a real witty quip and then takes off and it always brightens my day."

In the spring, Marshall found Lee clambering in the branches of the large apple tree in front of his house, pruning the limbs. "What trees do you want me to prune over at your place?" Lee asked her.

"He really meant it. He would have come over and done it," she told Svet.

Marshall recounted meeting Lee as their houses were being built, Lee introducing himself as "Wen Ho, like Santa Claus—Ho, ho, ho!" He'd taken them inside his freshly framed house and, pointing to the photograph tacked on the mantel, introduced each member of his family.

"To the best of my knowledge, he lived the life that he was dreaming about in front of his hearth that day," she testified.

It was clear Lee's family was behind him, Marshall said, and she pointed out Sylvia Lee and Alberta in the back of the courtroom. Sylvia stuck by Wen Ho when he had cancer and now stood by him in his condemnation as a spy. Alberta Lee had caught a flight home Friday when she was warned of the arrest.

"Beautiful, tall young woman with long dark hair," Marshall described her, so Svet could pick her out. "If I wanted to guess what kind of a dad Wen Ho has been to Alberta, I think she says it all by the way she came home . . . She has been her dad's staunch defender, I think except for you lawyers. She has done research every night on the Internet trying to come up with any information. She has . . ."

Cline cut her off: "In the interest of brevity, would you say that she is standing by him 100 percent?"

"I think that's an understatement," Marshall said. "They had a very close relationship. He was very active in his children's lives, in their education. He expected a great deal from them but he stuck around to make sure it happened. He was there for, nearly every night for working with homework. He made sure they had piano lessons, and he arranged Chinese lessons in town so that they would have that heritage . . . [If] he would lean his head out the door and say something, those kids would just go skittering off home. So they obviously respected him. And they have grown into two wonderful young people that I think any of us would be proud to call son or daughter."

Cline drew her toward the answers likely to show Lee was a man of good character and wasn't going to run. Did he try to dodge the surveillance; did he show signs of preparing to flee?

"To the contrary, I think no one could have demonstrated any more strongly or effectively than Wen Ho has with his conduct over the last nine months that he is not a flight risk," Marshall said. "He has cooperated with the federal agents, with the tracking team in every way that I can imagine. He's stayed calm, he's stayed stable."

In fact, Lee in the last month had winterized his house, trimmed his bushes, cleaned away the autumn leaves, and climbed the apple tree for the topmost apples. He put new, red-painted gates on his backyard fence and replaced some of the pumice blocks on the wall between his house and the Marshalls'.

"It seems to me Wen Ho has done this year exactly what he does every year, which is prepare his house for spring just like he expects to be here in the spring," Marshall said. As instructed by Cline, she turned to make eye contact with Svet. The magistrate looked distracted, staring off through the window far above Marshall's head.

"I don't believe there is any possibility [Lee would flee], and the reason is that I believe his most pressing concern right now is for the future of his children," she said. "I believe that he shows every indication of staying and fighting the charges and clearing his name so his children's future can be what it ought to be."

It was strong testimony, clearly heartfelt. Gorence aimed to knock it in the dirt.

Had Marshall ever heard of anyone at work in X Division downloading "America's nuclear secrets"? No, she said, and she probably wouldn't have heard anyway. And what did she think about Younger's testimony?

Marshall was horrified. Younger looked right at her.

"Did you disagree in any way with his characterizations of the significance of the information alleged in the indictment?" Gorence pressed.

"Well, I, I think Dr. Younger at one point made the comment that these codes read like a novel and I guess I would say that we really should have him writing all of our codes, because the ones that I've worked on do not read that easily at all," she said. "And 134 feet tall to read through? . . . Usually people in the division are given about a year to come up on a code with all the expertise around. So it seems a little bit optimistic that these codes would be usable immediately by people."

That's it, she figured, a career down the drain. Later that evening, a distraught Marshall told a restaurant waitress, "You better be nice to me because I just committed suicide today." The waitress brought her a thick wedge of chocolate cake, unasked. Marshall brightened. "I may have died, but I'm going to heaven happy."

Gorence had laid out a compelling case in the last four hours, and he knew it. His argument for Svet to deny Lee's freedom took less than two minutes.

The federal government had asked repeatedly, but Lee never would explain what happened to the tapes, he said. The tapes, combined with Dr. Lee's knowledge, could change the balance of world power.

"I cannot contemplate a more serious risk to U.S. national security than to have a person like Dr. Lee walking around with access to that type of information, information that Dr. Younger has said could lead to the military defeat of our conventional forces," Gorence argued. Ordinarily, judges sit on detention hearings about armed bank robbers and their danger to the community, "but quite frankly, Your Honor, the 'community' in this case is 270 million persons that face a degree of peril by virtue of what he did and the information that remains unaccounted for, if he's walking around."

The defense seemed doomed along with 270 million other Americans. Cline took his shot nonetheless.

From March 1999, almost every major U.S. newspaper had played up the allegation that Lee was a spy, a death-penalty offense. "If Dr. Lee was going to flee or if he was going to do something with these supposedly missing tapes, he would have done it then. That was the time, you know, the game is up and he's caught. But he didn't," Cline said. Instead, Lee surrendered his passport and even altered his daily movements to accommodate his FBI tailers. His defense had told the government that the tapes had been destroyed. After a massive investigation—a thousand witness interviews, a million files examined, almost four years of scrutiny—the FBI hadn't a shred of evidence to the contrary.

"There is no evidence whatsoever in this case that he has the tapes. There is no evidence that he has ever disclosed the tapes, attempted to disclose the tapes to anyone. There is no evidence in this record that he has ever disclosed any classified information to any unauthorized person," Cline said. "That's not clear and convincing evidence; that's an absence of evidence.

"He has stood his ground. He's made repeated representations to the government about why he's innocent. He's prepared to fight these charges. He's going to be here for trial, he's going to prove his innocence. There is no chance . . . that he's going to flee."

Svet already had made up his mind.

"I don't need to address the matter of flight risk because I'm going to order the detention of Dr. Lee based on what I have heard here, indeed, the concession that certain classified materials were in the possession of Dr. Lee outside of his requirements of employment," he said. "I am convinced that I'm right because of the testimony of Dr. Younger, who essentially gives us this equation. The knowledge of the defendant, plus the missing tapes, the source code, are a clear and present danger to the national security of the United States. So I will order him held."

A deputy U.S. Marshal led Lee away. He was hauled back to the Santa Fe jail until his lawyers could appeal.

-24-

"It's Conceivable That This Is Possible"

When a guard slid Wen Ho Lee's first meal through the metal slot in his jail door, Lee didn't reach for it immediately. "Aren't you going to eat?" the guard sitting outside his cell asked. Lee replied politely, "You haven't been served yet."

In the ensuing months, Lee seldom ate his full ration of jail food. Nearly every meal centered on meat, which he didn't eat. He shared some of his meals with fellow inmates—as he walked past, they shouted, "What have you got for me today, Wen Ho?" And he began to lose weight.

Lee's cell was in Block A100, the administrative control wing of the Santa Fe County Detention Center, an area normally reserved for the jail's trouble-makers, the mentally infirm, and others thought at risk of harming themselves or being hurt in the general population. The cell was small, measuring 8×10 feet, with a metal-frame double bunk bed of vinyl-covered mattresses and a stainless steel sink/drinking fountain/toilet combination by the door, facing the rear. A single 18-inch window in the rear wall gave out onto flat pastureland, with mountains in the near distance.

The location of the cell made it easier to watch Lee than if he had been housed with the regular population. Guards placed a chair not far from his door and noted his activities at least a couple of times an hour. A blue-painted fluorescent light overhead illuminated the cell, even at night. It interfered with his sleep, but far more aggravating were the echoing shouts and shrieks of his fellow inmates in administrative control. Lee's request for earplugs was denied, and his family was not allowed to bring him a pair.

The first bail hearing left the Lee family in shock, especially Alberta. She was unprepared for the sight of her father in jail. "I was shown into a yellow room with very bright lights and a glass partition. My dad came in in a red jumpsuit, with handcuffs attached to a metal belt and shackles on the ankles. He looked like an animal being led around. He sat down and tried to reassure me that everything would be all right. But I just kept crying. He said, 'It's going to be OK.' But I felt hopeless."

Every weekday, Lee was permitted one hour of solitary exercise. His jailers walked him to an enclosed exercise yard, and as time went on, they gave him a soccer ball that he kicked around the yard while shackled. Later, Lee demonstrated for friends the way he got around, with a short shuffle constrained by the chains.

Unlike most other prisoners, Lee was permitted no radio, TV, books, or newspapers. His only knowledge of the outside world came through his lawyers and weekly visits from his family. They spoke to him through a thick glass partition and only in English. The Mandarin that was his family's household language was prohibited to accommodate the FBI. An agent sat in on every visit and took notes on their conversations.

Attorney General Janet Reno and Energy Secretary Bill Richardson had personally approved each of these conditions, known as "special administrative measures," or SAMs, with the express purpose of silencing Lee. He was to have no means of communication, in order to bar him from signaling potential accomplices about the location of the tapes or the use of their contents. SAMs typically were reserved for extraordinary cases of espionage and terrorism. Wen Ho Lee was accused of neither.

The government, however, desperately wanted to recover the tapes. Wen Ho Lee's library was inimical to national security, advisors to Reno and Richardson had said.

Some administration officials admitted the hefty offenses in the indictment and the SAMs were intended to coerce Lee into confessing his reasons for making the tapes and revealing what he did with them.

"We pushed for solitary confinement to make life as difficult as possible, because if he were sent home, there would not be a lot of incentive for him to come clean," one senior official told the *Washington Post*.

For Lee's sixtieth birthday, even a cake was out of the question. In Chinese society, a man who turns sixty is accorded greater respect and seniority, and his relatives gather to honor him. Cecilia Chang was saddened at the thought of Lee in jail, seeing no one. She knew of a wealthy Chinese American in the Bay Area, a man she'd never met, and phoned him.

"I need a place for a party," she said. "I know I'm asking for the impossible, but this is an impossible case."

On December 21, some eight hundred miles from Santa Fe, two hundred Asian Americans feted Lee in Foster City's Crowne Plaza Hotel, south of San Francisco. A number of TV and newspaper reporters showed up. Lee's supporters lit the candles on two pink-and-white-iced cakes, then turned to the cameras to sing "Happy Birthday" to Lee. They raised $20,000 that night for Lee's defense fund.

Several of them likened their advocacy of Lee's rights to the struggle to win an apology for the internment of 120,000 Japanese Americans in World War II.

"Like the Japanese-American community learned, alone we have no strength," Chang said. "Together we have power. The government had poor security at the labs. Instead of finding out what was wrong, they blamed someone—Dr. Lee. A computer-security coverup."

Alberta Lee had hopped a plane to San Francisco after appearing on ABC-TV's *Good Morning America* in New York. In the past, she told her father's supporters, the Lees enjoyed Christmas quietly, with a meal of roast chicken, a family game of bridge—she was her father's partner—and a line of silver candles glowing in paper-bag *farolitas* along the driveway.

"I feel that the leaks in the beginning in March, maligning my father and my mother, were extremely detrimental to the investigation, and that is why he is in jail today," she said. "And that is why I won't be able to spend Christmas with him."

A jail guard in Santa Fe caught the news about the party and went to Lee's cell.

"I don't think you're going to get a cake here, so I brought you a small piece of cookie," the guard said.

Lee took the proffered tidbit. "I really appreciate it from my heart," he said.

———

Six days later, on December 27, U.S. marshals drove Lee back to the federal courthouse in Albuquerque. His defense team was upbeat. They were appealing

Svet's denial of bail, and the judge hearing the appeal had a reputation as a fair and open-minded jurist.

The case had been assigned to Chief Judge John Edwards Conway. But on this day in December 1999, Conway happened to be far away from Albuquerque, vacationing with his wife in Australia and New Zealand. His stand-in was the district's next-most-senior judge, James A. Parker, known to the local bar as "Gentleman Jim." Lawyers had come to terms with Parker's inquisitive and deliberative style. It often seemed as though the judge stretched his rulings so as to accommodate both sides of a dispute as much as possible; they called him a "split-the-baby" judge.

Like Conway, he was a Reagan appointee and generally conservative. But Lee's defense was thankful to have him on the bench for this hearing. Federal law set a high bar for taking away the freedom of a nonviolent defendant, and if any judge would hold the government's feet to the fire, it was Parker.

The courtroom was packed. Lee's friends and supporters filled the right side of the gallery and spilled over into the left, where they joined several prosecution witnesses and a throng of reporters. In attendance were representatives of the wire services—the Associated Press and Reuters—as well as the *Washington Post,* the *Los Angeles Times,* ABC News, and Fox News. The *New York Times* sent James Sterngold from its Los Angeles bureau. Just before the hearing opened, a half-dozen people filed in, led by Alberta Lee and a publicist for one of her father's defense lawyers, and took seats in the front row behind the defense table.

Marshals brought Lee in through a door by the judge's bench wearing a charcoal business suit. He glanced up, spotted Alberta and his friends, and brightened. He sat down with Holscher, Cline, and Hollander. Nearly twice as many lawyers flanked the prosecution table across from them. U.S. Attorney Kelly rose and introduced them: Gorence, Supervisory U.S. Assistant Attorney Paula Burnett, Assistant U.S. Attorney Laura Fashing, and Michael Liebman, a leading espionage prosecutor with the Internal Security Section of Justice headquarters.

If anyone in the courtroom doubted that Wen Ho Lee had downpartitioned classified information to an unclassified network, the prosecution quickly eliminated that uncertainty. Under questioning from Burnett, a Los Alamos computer expert gave the courtroom a step-by-step description of Lee's precise actions in gathering together the weapons files, marking them unclassified, shifting them to the lab's Green network, and ultimately downloading them to tapes. Cheryl Wampler, the deputy leader of the lab group in charge of scientific computing and data storage, brought detailed diagrams depicting every computer Lee used and a series of spreadsheets tracing his every keystroke down to the creation of the tapes.

Lee's storage of weapons files on the unclassified network ended up crippling scientific computing at Los Alamos for three weeks, Wampler testified. As soon as the FBI had gathered evidence of Lee's transfer of weapons files to the unclassified network, lab computer personnel realized they had to take down the entire Common File System to "decontaminate" it. Los Alamos shut down almost the entire lab computing network on April 2, 1999, and it took almost three weeks to make absolutely certain all of the classified files had been removed.

Likewise, when agents learned from the notebook at Lee's house that he had made tapes, they realized that Ling's computer in T Division also was contaminated, as well as other computers above it in the network hierarchy. Ling was not Q-cleared; ten other people had access to his machine, and his computer was connected to the Internet. "It was imminently available to not-very-sophisticated hackers from the Internet, for example, or whatever actions [Ling] might have chosen to take with the files," Wampler testified.

Prosecutors next began chipping away at Lee's defense that he was backing up his files. Wampler testified that the CFS was "a phenomenally robust and reliable system." Lee had told friends that he lost almost an entire year's work on the CFS once. Wampler testified, however, that she had checked the CFS records and found no "massive loss of data" to users during the early 1990s, when Lee was making the tapes.

But Lee had begun his downpartitioning in 1988, and in the late 1980s the CFS did experience a large-scale loss of data. Just one of thousands of data-storage disks became corrupted, and dozens of users temporarily lost files. Lab computer staff pulled the disk full of corrupted classified data and took it to California, where experts were able to retrieve almost all of the information and return it to Los Alamos scientists.

Lab scientists were expected to maintain backup copies of their work. But it was wholly unnecessary to make backups on the unclassified network or portable tapes, Wampler said. The standard practice was to save file backups to a different disk or tape on the secure side of the CFS.

"It's difficult for me to put into words the comparable risk involved in moving data into the open environment . . . and onto portable tapes," Wampler said. "That is a far, far, far riskier handling of this material than anything you could do by handling the material properly . . . in the classified environment."

Yet Lee hadn't done much to hide his stash of files in the 1990s, Wampler conceded under cross-examination. He hadn't significantly changed the names of the files, so that Romero instantly recognized them five or more years later, during the March 1999 search of his office.

"Wouldn't it make more sense," Cline asked, "for someone who was trying to conceal what he was doing to disguise the contents of the files he was putting on the Green system?"

Wampler eventually acknowledged: "It would make sense, yeah."

Nor had Lee compressed or encrypted the files, or done anything to prevent a computer administrator or colleague from stumbling upon their contents.

"Is it fair to say that, as you sit here today, you have no evidence that any hacker ever accessed any of the files . . . as they sat on the Green partition?" Cline asked Wampler.

"That is correct," Wampler said. "I don't have evidence of that today."

Lee's defense attorneys theorized that their client was being made a scapegoat for the Los Alamos National Laboratory's failure to protect classified information, and Cline went on to use Wampler, the government's own expert on Los Alamos's networks, to depict the lab's poor state of computer security. Wampler admitted that the laboratory did not monitor the specific movement of classified information to the unclassified network.

In the early 1990s, scientists could move supposedly unclassified files from the classified network to the unclassified network through a computer known as Machine C, nicknamed "the washing machine." It was not even necessary to be physically seated at Machine C; any cleared scientist could remotely log onto that machine from his own computer and mark files as unclassified so that they could be moved. Nothing in the laboratory's network verified that the files marked as unclassified and transferred were, in fact, unclassified.

"By the action of logging in and using the machine, they are certifying that the action they are taking is involving unclassified material," Wampler testified. "They accepted responsibility for their action." In short, Los Alamos relied on an honor system.

But the laboratory did have a security program, the Network Anomaly Detection and Intrusion Reporting system, or NADIR, that generated profiles of scientists' typical computer usage and flagged unusual activity. NADIR flagged Lee in 1993 for moving volumes of files from the classified system to the unclassified.

Earlier the laboratory had installed a new computer for running scientific calculations, and a large number of scientists were moving volumes of files in preparation for the change. In 1993, NADIR flagged an average of 180 computer users every week for altering their computer use. The woman who watched NADIR's reports decided that Lee's downpartitioning appeared to be part of a mass migration of computer files in anticipation of the new computer.

She had been wrong, however, Wampler said. By the time Lee started moving his files, the transition to the new computer was complete. Nor had the woman ever picked up the phone and called Lee to verify her theory of what he was doing. Even the lab's minimal security measures had been, in effect, defeated by its own staff.

Likewise, although Lee made numerous phone inquiries to the lab's computer help desk in 1998 and 1999, the technicians with whom he spoke were never informed that he was under investigation for potential espionage. They logged his inquiries but never raised an alarm.

Further, Los Alamos for much of the 1990s kept records of remote log-ins from outside of the laboratory, but not detailed records of the files that were accessed. Hence, it was impossible to say whether anyone had tapped into Lee's weapons files as they sat on the Green network.

Los Alamos's shoddy computer security, surprising for an institution that believed it was on the cutting edge of the digital age, was a serious problem for the prosecution. It handed Lee's team a strong argument that Lee was being crucified for the lab's security failings. As one prosecutor said, "LANL [Los Alamos National Laboratory] security was awful, and we just had to work around it."

Yet, Lee also paid a high price for the lab's lax computer security. If anyone had delved deeper into Lee's file transfers that NADIR flagged in 1993, he or she could have halted those transfers. Lee might have been disciplined, perhaps even fired. But it was unlikely that his case would have become so politically charged, or that he would have found himself under criminal indictment.

X Division Director Richard Krajcik picked up where Younger had left off in the earlier detention hearing. "When I first realized what was downloaded by Dr. Lee, I realized that I was looking at a chilling collection of codes and files," he testified. "They contained devices across a range of weapons, from weapons that were relatively easy to manufacture, let's say, to weapons that were very sophisticated and would be very difficult to manufacture . . . [I]n terms of designing something new or checking something old, it was all there."

Despite the fact that he was a runner and occasional rock climber, Krajcik presented a stooped and gaunt, almost sepulchral, figure in the courtroom. He was a gray man who appeared to wear heavily the responsibilities of an entire career designing nuclear weapons. A couple of spectators jokingly compared him to *The Simpsons'* cadaverous nuclear-power-plant owner, Mr. Burns.

Krajcik had climbed the ranks of Los Alamos's weapons program for almost a quarter century, and he was respected by colleagues for the understanding of weapons design that he brought to management of the division. Under questioning by Gorence, Krajcik waxed almost poetic about witnessing nuclear tests at the Nevada Test Site. "In particular, when the ground rolls—and we are talking about the Earth moving—you really understand the incredible power of the devices you are designing," he said. "And it's really an inspiring experience . . . It really amplifies the sacred trust that has been given to the people in the nuclear weapons arena."

Lee's actions, he testified, were inconceivable. "[T]o make such a library and put it in an unclassified environment would be an egregious offense of enormous magnitude," Krajcik said. He characterized the files as "the crown jewels" of the nuclear-weapons program. Krajcik could think of no job-related reason for Lee to put such files on an unclassified system and on tapes.

It was, he claimed, "highly unusual" for a code developer such as Lee to perform work on any of the weapons codes in their entirety. Instead, Lee and other code specialists worked almost exclusively on pieces of the code known as modules. What frightened Krajcik was not merely the presence on the tapes of entire weapons codes, but the files for data on radiation opacities and neutron cross sections that were outside of Lee's area of specialty, plus his collection of a large number of weapons input decks.

"Would there be any reason, any work-related reason, to have some of these very specific, successfully tested designs as represented in these input decks?" Gorence asked.

Krajcik replied that there would be reason to have some of the files in order to test a code writer's algorithms. "What was surprising to me was that there was a collection of these files . . . ," he said. "It meant to me that basically what you were collecting was an entire capability to evaluate nuclear weapons."

He could not imagine Lee destroying the tapes. Lee had taken extraordinary care in assembling a full library in unmarked, portable, and easily copied form. "You can do anything you want with it," Krajcik testified. "I see no reason why someone would be compelled to destroy that information."

At one point, Gorence depicted the weapons files as having been "stolen by Dr. Lee," drawing a quick objection from Lee's defense. Gorence gave a tight grin. "Okay," he said. "Let me strike that word, and I will say 'downpartitioned onto an open system and downloaded onto portable, walk-around tapes.' "

Judge Parker cut to the chase, asking, "[D]o you have a personal opinion as to whether he has already disclosed all of this to unauthorized people?"

"From my perspective, if you have information in an unclassified system for so many years, on a system that is not designed to protect that information," Krajcik said, "I think it's reasonable to expect that this information, in one way or another, has been compromised."

"If Dr. Lee has already passed on to unauthorized persons the Secret Restricted Data . . . what dangers, if any, are now presented by Dr. Lee being allowed to live at home?" Parker asked.

If a foreign nation had the codes and the input decks, said Krajcik, "the next thing you would want to do would be to talk to somebody knowledgeable of the codes." If Lee were free to talk to a possessor of the codes, he said, he could reveal the secrets to their operation and elaborate on their capabilities. "And if you had access to the person who actually wrote the code, then you've basically got it all."

As Krajcik testified, Gorence drew the weapons designer into more and more superlative descriptions of the files' sensitivity. His testimony for the prosecution ended with the assertion that foreign powers could use them to build U.S.-style nuclear weapons and "significantly increase the risk to 270 million Americans."

Cline stared at his legal pad. With every mention of the phrase "crown jewels," the prosecution looked more and more vulnerable to a rare but effective legal maneuver. Defendants charged in national-security cases could sometimes escape prosecution merely by threatening to blurt out the nation's secrets in open court. It was a strategy known as graymail, and it worked for the guilty as well as the innocent.

Cline wondered: Could he push the government into playing up the value of the tapes' contents so highly that it could not tolerate even the slightest exposure of the same information at trial?

It had worked for Joseph Fernandez. In the late 1980s, Cline worked on the defense of Oliver North in the Iran-contra scandal. Special Prosecutor Lawrence Walsh had brought an indictment against Fernandez, the former CIA station chief in Costa Rica who had helped North funnel arms to the Nicaraguan contras, on charges of lying to federal investigators and to Congress about the contra supply campaign.

Fernandez's defense was not unlike Lee's. He had to show that he had no criminal intent to deceive anyone. Fernandez claimed that his superiors in the

CIA right up through the National Security Council and the White House and, ultimately, President Ronald Reagan knew and approved of his actions, or at least should have known.

Fernandez's defense pressed the government to disclose classified documents that proved his claims, and a federal judge agreed he needed them to mount an effective defense. Yet the Bush administration remained adamant in its refusal to declassify the documents Fernandez sought, and on November 24, 1989, Walsh was forced to dismiss the indictment.

Cline carried his pad to the podium in preparation for a delicate cross-examination, which would be somewhat at cross-purposes with itself. On one hand, he was trying to prod Krajcik into playing up the highly secret and valuable nature of Lee's downloads. Because Cline himself did not have a Q clearance, he also needed to learn as much as possible about the codes in open court from Krajcik. At the same time, he hoped to persuade Judge Parker that the downloads did not necessarily constitute a dire security breach.

Cline got his brief tutorial in the use of weapons codes to design thermonuclear warheads. But he found himself barred from exploring issues of the codes' sensitivity. Krajcik declined, for example, to answer Cline's questions about the degree to which the physics and mathematics in the codes were published in open literature. Cline pressed further: "In the hands of what country, organization or person could the files change the global strategic balance?"

"I don't think I can go there," Krajcik said.

Classification of various aspects of the weapons world frustrated Lee's defense at every turn. But Cline was determined to turn the tables. In time, he would use the government's fear of exposure as a cudgel on the prosecution.

Judge Parker himself turned to the witness.

"Let me ask you to put yourself in Dr. Lee's shoes for the moment," Parker began. "If you were asking to be returned to your home until your trial took place, tell me how you might be able to communicate about this highly sensitive information, if all computers, cell phones, two-way radios and any other wire or wireless communication devices were removed from your home to the satisfaction of the FBI; your telephone was left intact; however, a wiretap was placed on the phone so that all communications by phone were monitored.

"You personally were required to wear an electronic monitoring anklet that would alert monitoring personnel that you had gone a certain distance from your home . . . plus 24-hour FBI surveillance; that you would be permitted to leave your home only in the company of your lawyers for the purpose of preparing your defense for the trial and to attend pre-trial court hearings; that you would be allowed to leave your home only in the company of Jean Marshall as a third-party custodian, also accompanied by an FBI agent, for essential personal matters such as going to doctors' appointments; that your mail would be screened; that the only other person who could live with you at your home would be your wife; and that the only other persons who could visit you in your home would be your children or grandchildren, if you have any—I am particularly partial to grandchildren—and that would occur only with the third-party custodian present; and that before you were allowed to go to your home, your house and environs and your vehicles would be thoroughly searched by the Federal Bureau of Investigation.

"Now, if you were allowed to go to your home under those restrictions, tell me in what ways you could somehow communicate with unauthorized persons about supersecret information."

Krajcik looked queasy. Gorence saw where the judge was headed, and he didn't like it. Parker seemed to be contemplating an array of restrictions only imposed in the most extreme cases involving terrorist suspects and mob bosses who had the capability of ordering murders. In some ways, Parker's notional conditions of release even went beyond those situations.

Gorence objected: "Quite frankly, Your Honor, Dr. Krajcik just said he is a scientist and not a cop."

Parker let Krajcik off the hook and agreed he would get his answer shortly from the FBI.

First, Gorence called two more weapons managers to underscore the extreme value of Lee's downloads. John Romero, the scientist who had volunteered to help the FBI, also could think of no work-related reason to move weapons files to an unclassified network. "You can't do that. I mean, people have, by accident, moved classified data into the open. But believe me, it is by accident. And the first thing we all know is you have to report it," Romero testified.

Had anyone, to his knowledge, accidentally moved 806 megabytes of weapons codes and other files? Gorence asked.

"Absolutely not," Romero said. "It's unimaginable. I could not believe it. I still cannot. I have trouble believing it. It's just—all the codes, all the data, all the input files, all the libraries—the whole thing is there, the whole ball of wax. Everything."

Next, Sandia National Laboratories President Paul Robinson took the stand and regaled the court with his qualifications. Besides eighteen years in the weapons program at Los Alamos and ten at Sandia, he chaired an advisory panel to the Strategic Command in Omaha on weapons policy. Robinson liked to be referred to as "Ambassador" because he had served three years as a U.S. negotiator on nuclear testing treaties in Geneva. Robinson's rhetorical skills and quick thinking were renowned.

"I think the risk to U.S. national security is truly a devastating one," Robinson testified. With most of the world no longer conducting nuclear tests, a lot of the tapes' contents were now unattainable.

He drew a vivid picture of the consequences of Lee's tapes falling into foreign hands. "These tapes could truly change the world's strategic balance. The previous worst case [in which] I am aware of classified information being stolen also happened at Los Alamos—Klaus Fuchs taking a design that, if detonated, could demonstrably kill 100,000 people in a city . . . These would allow the design of weapons that would kill several million people, if a single weapon were detonated in a city."

Gorence prompted him to assess the risk of releasing Lee, given the FBI's fruitless search for the tapes worldwide.

"I have got to say that this court, I believe, faces a you-bet-your-country decision," Robinson said. "I would take, if it were in my power, every action I could take to make sure this information . . . does not get transferred to another nation or other powers."

If Lee's tapes were never found, he suggested, the United States would be forced to recalculate its strategic posture and retain higher numbers of nuclear arms as a deterrent. As did every witness, Robinson conceded to Lee's defense that he had no knowledge of any foreign power acquiring the contents of the tapes.

His testimony clearly aggravated Parker. The judge appeared annoyed that the weapons-lab director sought to rest the fate of the nation on his shoulders.

"In your opinion," the judge asked Robinson, "was the Federal Bureau of Investigation and the Department of Justice taking a you-bet-your-country risk during the period from March 1999 to December 1999 by not taking Dr. Lee into custody, when they learned clearly in March what he had done?"

Robinson dithered, but finally answered. "Perhaps there is only one thing that is more important to me than the national security, and that is the rights of individuals."

To cap off his case, Gorence called on the FBI. Supervisory Special Agent Messemer was ruddy and tall, standing 6 feet 3. He had a long face, thinning black hair, and a thoughtful gaze he now cast on the packed courtroom.

"From a counterintelligence perspective, I would characterize Dr. Lee's activities as appalling, nefarious and deliberate," Messemer testified.

The FBI and the Justice Department intentionally held off arresting Lee in the spring of 1999 for fear of announcing to the rest of the world the loss of America's nuclear secrets, explained Messemer. The FBI had kept the existence of Lee's portable tapes secret for months in hopes of finding them before a foreign intelligence service did.

By placing Lee under tight surveillance, the Bureau hoped it would catch some clue as to the whereabouts of the tapes. Meanwhile, agents conducted a global investigation to find them, retracing Lee's steps since the early 1990s. Messemer made the unlikely claim that agents searched almost every safe-deposit box and storage locker in New Mexico.

It was finally decided that prosecution might be the only way to recover the tapes. Yet even indicting and arresting Lee in December came at "enormous cost," Messemer testified. The world now knew with certainty that Lee had created the tapes and they were missing.

Now it was no longer feasible merely to keep Lee under surveillance. "Let me underscore that now that the public knows about the existence of these tapes, there are going to be all kinds of people who are equally as interested as we are in obtaining these tapes," Messemer said. "[T]here are those people who are going to approach Dr. Lee, or perhaps one of his family members, in an effort to elicit their, shall I say, assistance in locating these tapes."

The many dialects of Chinese could make those communications harder for the FBI to thwart, Messemer said. "It's quite easy for him to have a conversation which may seem innocuous initially, but really has a hidden meaning." Messemer said he didn't mean to disparage the Chinese or their language, but the dialects could hide certain unique cultural meanings "that are not necessarily discernible to an outsider."

Monitoring Lee's phone would require a team of Chinese-speaking agents fluent in three dialects working around the clock, Messemer continued, in addition to translators working on tapes of his conversation. Even then, they might not recognize the import of coded language.

"[I]t could be something like, 'How is the weather today?' " Messemer testified. "It could be as simple as, 'Say Uncle Wen says hello.' " Such a message could signal someone to do something with the tapes, he explained. "Even messages appearing to be nothing but goodwill . . . will have to be taken with a grain of salt."

Parker suggested the FBI could track down the recipients of any odd-sounding messages and see whether they were up to anything nefarious.

"Well, what about conversations with his wife?" Gorence asked the judge.

"Well, what about it?" Parker replied briskly. "Is your assumption that Mrs. Lee is conspiring with Dr. Lee to commit offenses against the United States?"

Sylvia Lee hadn't been charged, Gorence said, but she or the Lees' children could be used to send messages to accomplices or foreign spies.

Holscher objected. "Your Honor, this scenario that is being strung here of spies, and the inference that Dr. Lee will commit a death-penalty offense while under the most heightened security ever in the United States, is just a ludicrous premise."

In just a few minutes, the FBI had suggested that Lee's household language was uniquely suited to conveying coded signals to foreign spies, and that his wife and children would be conduits for his nefarious plans. Chinese Americans in the courtroom gallery and Lee's colleagues from Los Alamos recoiled at such testimony. Some tittered. Most were simply awestruck by its fantastic nature.

This was only the beginning. In closed testimony the next morning, prosecutors laid out reasons to keep Lee locked up that were at least as surreal.

As if depicting Lee and his tapes as the fulcrum of world power weren't enough, now millennial terrorists and foreign commandos entered the scene. That very morning, according to Messemer, FBI Director Freeh and Assistant Director for National Security Neil Gallagher had complained that the Bureau was so inundated with terrorism investigations that it could not spare enough agents and electronic surveillance equipment to watch Lee's house. Keeping an eye on a sixty-year-old scientist who by court order would not be allowed to leave home would take as many as a hundred agents and professional watchers, the government claimed.

"You would have to have around-the-clock surveillance of his house and everybody coming and going," Gorence told Parker.

"Beyond that, we'd have to understand fully every single utterance that Dr. Lee made to a particular person," Messemer added. "For example, what if he were to say to someone, his brother in California, 'The fish are not biting today.' "

"Don't go so real," Gorence said dramatically.

Messemer pressed ahead. "I will tell you that Dr. Lee has a sixteen-year history of deceiving the FBI . . . then later recanted those deceptions and had made admissions to us when faced with incontrovertible evidence."

He and prosecutors now offered a new motive for Lee to give the tapes to a foreign power. "Today, there's an additional factor for him," Messemer said. "To want to take revenge against the United States for removing his liberty, this is a strong motivating factor for persons who commit espionage."

Lee may conclude that he would spend the rest of his life in a federal prison, Kelly said, and ask a foreign country to spirit him away. The FBI's unarmed watchers could not fight off such an "exfiltration" team.

"It could be something as simple as 'I've decided it's time to go' in some code fashion, and then we would be dealing with a situation in which an individual not in custody is going to be snatched and taken out of the country," Kelly said. "These surveillance people are not there in Ninja suits with assault weapons to prevent a foreign intelligence service from doing something like that."

Holscher tried to get a word in, but Parker cut him short. The judge had crafted an extraordinary set of rules to address all of the government's concerns, but now prosecutors were throwing flying, foreign spy commandos into the mix. He seriously seemed to be thinking over this new threat.

Holscher had heard enough. Every minute, it seemed, the government was inventing new obstacles to letting his client out of jail.

"These scenarios are extremely far-fetched," he interjected. "My concern is every time a condition is put in place, [an] extremely bright FBI agent who has a clear goal in mind comes up with a new scenario. We now have an airlift from a foreign country dropping down at his house to take him . . . [T]his has become kind of a free-for-all."

Messemer was unstoppable. Foreign spies might try almost anything—for example, smuggling a micro–e-mail device into Lee's house so he could send messages about the codes. "It's conceivable that this is possible," he told the judge.

Without a clearance, Cline had to wait outside for the closed hearing to end. "How'd it go?" he asked Holscher.

The younger attorney rolled his eyes. "You wouldn't believe it if I told you."

Back in the courtroom, Holscher went after Messemer. By mid-October, he noted, news of the tapes had leaked into the media. Messemer had to concede that since October the FBI had not noted any foreign intelligence services hunting for tapes in New Mexico.

Messemer had portrayed Lee's contacts with Chinese weapons scientists in pernicious terms, making much of his failure to report the letters found in his garage in which the IAPCM scientists asked for copies of codes. But under Holscher's questioning, the agent reluctantly admitted that the requested codes were unclassified and indeed the U.S. Department of Energy in 1989–90 was encouraging Los Alamos scientists to share their unclassified codes in a spirit of Sino-U.S. scientific cooperation.

Last, Parker heard from the FBI's Scott Larson, leader of the Bureau's computer-crimes squad. Given the number of times Wen Ho and his children logged into his account from outside the laboratory, it was likely that someone else had captured his password as it traveled the Internet or went through Los Alamos's network.

The FBI had no evidence that anyone then accessed Lee's kf1 directory, where the files were stored. But hostile intelligence services used skilled hackers who probably could breach the lab's network security, copy the files, and completely erase any trace they had been there. No one would have been the wiser, including the FBI.

The Marshalls were the only defense witnesses. Jean Marshall said she was willing to be Lee's custodian. She wouldn't hesitate to report any unauthorized people in Lee's home or any suspicions that he was communicating classified information or attempting to flee. Parker reminded her that if she failed in her duties, she could be held in contempt of court. He pried for details of the roads in and out of White Rock, the travel time to the Los Alamos airport (ten minutes) and the kinds of planes that fly out of Los Alamos.

Don Marshall took the stand, and the judge tried to put him in the shoes of a fugitive spy. "If you had contact with foreign operatives who had committed to assist you in leaving the United States . . . in the quickest manner possible, what would you arrange with them to do?" Marshall set his imagination free. The more he talked, the more Lee's friends chuckled.

"Well, probably the easiest thing would be to ask that they bring a helicopter just right down in the neighborhood," he said. Someone did just that ten years ago, landed in an open field near their house. "I mean you could just run a block and you are on the plane and out you go . . . You know, if you want to get more and more James Bondish kind of stuff, you could hypothesize all sorts of things."

He suddenly realized the judge was talking about the escape of his next door neighbor and reddened. It was a welcome moment of levity. A number of reporters already were quietly whispering that Lee was headed back to jail.

Parker retired to his chambers for a half-hour, then delivered his ruling.

"With a great deal of concern about the conditions under which Dr. Lee is being held in custody, I find on the basis of the record before me that the government has shown by clear and convincing evidence at this time that there is no combination of conditions of release that would reasonably assure the safety of any other person and the community or the nation," he said.

Lee posed a danger because of the missing tapes and his failure to explain when and how they were destroyed, Parker said, as well as his potential for signaling to foreign agents about their location and contents.

He urged lawyers on both sides to continue negotiating a polygraph test so Lee could certify that he hadn't divulged the tapes' contents to anyone unauthorized. If so, his release could be reconsidered in a new light.

"As I mentioned earlier, I have great concerns about the extreme restrictions imposed on Dr. Lee while he is being held in custody, and I ask the government attorneys to explore ways to loosen them, while preserving the security of sensitive information."

With that, Lee went back to jail. His daughter cried quietly as marshals led him out the rear of the courtroom.

– 25 –

Swords of Armageddon

After the New Year, John Kelly resigned as U.S. attorney to run for Congress. He shaped his image as a conservative Democrat, tried to organize a Republicans for Kelly Committee, and promoted himself as a tough, no-nonsense prosecutor. His uncompromising stance on the Wen Ho Lee case might give him a political boost; voters would see him as the man who locked up China's nuclear spy.

After Gorence assumed command of the office as acting U.S. Attorney, he and Lee's defense team made an attempt at negotiation on a polygraph test. But Gorence was winning and not inclined toward a compromise likely to result in Lee's freedom. Even if Lee passed a polygraph, the government would gain nothing—no tapes, no proof they were destroyed, and no recovery of the information on them. The polygraph that Hollander and Cline proposed—administered by a neutral, mutually agreed-upon examiner—would consist of just a few questions: Had Lee ever disclosed classified information to any unauthorized person? Had he, in fact, destroyed the tapes? And, had he made or retained any copies? Gorence quickly shot down the idea.

He fired back a counteroffer: The FBI would submit at least thirteen questions to Lee to answer, focused on exactly when, where, and how the tapes were destroyed and whether their contents had been copied or transmitted to any unauthorized person. Then, Gorence proposed, the FBI would attempt to confirm Lee's answers through investigation, return with another round of questions, and only then subject his answers to a polygraph, administered by the FBI.

Lee's lawyers knew the talks were going nowhere. The judge had specifically asked for a polygraph to determine whether Lee truly had destroyed the tapes. If he had, Parker had said he would reconsider Lee's release from jail. Instead, it seemed the FBI wanted a full-blown interrogation—even as Lee remained under threat of trial on fifty-nine criminal charges. No sane defense lawyer would agree to such a thing, and Gorence had to know it. It wasn't a negotiation, they felt; it was the government trying to strong-arm their client.

Cline and Hollander wrote back, declining Gorence's offer of an FBI interview.

"When Dr. Lee attempted to cooperate with the FBI in 1999, the agents lied to him about his previous polygraphs—telling him he had failed the December 23, 1998 polygraph when they knew he had passed—[and] used his close relationship with his children to coerce him, and even used repeated references to the Rosenbergs to threaten him with execution," they wrote. "In light of these tactics, it should come as no surprise that Dr. Lee does not trust the FBI to deal with him fairly and honestly."

Lee's best chance at going home before trial was lost in the sparring match between attorneys, each side unable to see any point in continuing.

Both sides, meanwhile, were preparing for a rehash of their battle over detention before the Tenth U.S. Circuit Court of Appeals in Denver. The Tenth had rarely considered a national-security case. Lee's defense attorneys knew it was a long shot: The appeals court could reverse Parker's ruling only if it believed his findings were "clearly erroneous" or an "abuse of discretion." Still, Lee's attorneys were so outraged by what had transpired in front of Parker that they had to give it a try.

In their appeal brief, they argued that the government had bullied Parker. Prosecutors and the FBI had worn down the judge's resistance with a relentless barrage of alarmist possibilities, however thinly supported by evidence, that Lee would commit espionage. At the same time, the government had failed to prove that the seven "missing" tapes actually existed, or that Lee had access to them and intended to give them to a foreign power—i.e., that facing life imprisonment, he now would commit a death-penalty offense. In tandem, the government and Parker were keeping Lee jailed largely because he remained silent on the exact circumstances of the tapes' destruction, a violation of his Fifth Amendment rights.

Gorence fended off their challenge easily. He paraded out the evidence of

Lee's lies, the unanimous condemnation of his actions by nuclear-weapons managers, and the extreme threat posed by the tapes to U.S. national security. His brief was replete with such characterizations as "deviously," "surreptitiously," "perniciously," and "unimaginable." Many countries yearned for the kind of power encoded in Lee's tapes. And his deceptions—coupled with the threat of life imprisonment—suggested he would give the secrets to them.

Gorence further drew on Lee's ethnicity and overseas ties to argue that he had a propensity to flee. "Lee was born abroad, speaks a foreign language, has siblings who live abroad, applied for foreign employment in 1992 and 1993 and recently taught and lectured abroad," prosecution attorneys argued. "[H]is background indicates an ability and willingness to live abroad, which makes him more of a flight risk than someone without such international contacts." The argument was not rare for a case involving a defendant with foreign ties, but Lee's ethnicity had once again come into subtle play; it had contributed to his targeting as a suspect in Kindred Spirit, indirectly led to his indictment in Sea Change, and now became part of the rationale for his jailing.

The Tenth Circuit's ruling in February read like a prosecution brief. "The 'potentially catastrophic' risk to the safety of the community, indeed the nation, presented by Lee's ability to communicate information about the location of the missing tapes or their contents if he is released pending trial is unprecedented," a three-judge panel ruled.

The defense was facing a grim reality. As Gorence pointed out on the day of the appellate court ruling, five federal judges had now concluded that Lee's freedom posed an unacceptably high risk to national security.

When Chief Judge John Conway returned from vacation, he took charge of the case eagerly. He gathered both sides into the courtroom and let them know that he planned to move this case along expeditiously.

Conway was a sixteen-year veteran of the federal bench. He had grown up in southern New Mexico, received his law degree at Washburn University Law School in Topeka, Kansas, and returned to Alamagordo, the town close by the site of Trinity, the world's first nuclear test. For years, Conway practiced general law with a focus on defending insurance companies. He served as a Republican state senator, and he brought to the federal courthouse a measure of the same garrulous manner and charm for which he was known in the legislature. His spacious office on the top floor of the courthouse was filled with mementos:

photographs from his Air Force days in the late 1950s as a pilot on B-47 Strato-jets carrying nuclear weapons, his judicial commission from President Ronald Reagan, and a couple of joke gifts that poked fun at Bill Clinton.

Conway was intrigued by spy books, and he had lobbied for a seat on the Foreign Intelligence Surveillance Court, the supersecret panel often afforded the first glimpse of spy investigations. "God, I'd love to be on that," Conway said later. "It would be exciting."

As chief judge of New Mexico's federal bench, Conway had befriended Louis Freeh when the FBI director was on an inspection tour in New Mexico. They talked and "we became good friends," the judge said. He also was friends with acting U.S. Attorney Bob Gorence, not uncommon in a legal community as small as New Mexico's.

In court, Conway often sat deadly still and stared into the distance, snapping rapid-fire rulings to objections as if to belie any perception that he was inattentive. He was regarded as a no-nonsense, pro-business, and pro-prosecution judge, and he was proud of it.

Conway told the lawyers in early January that he had issued orders to the General Services Administration to renovate two mediation rooms on the third floor of the courthouse into a secure facility, where Lee and his defense could review classified documents. The room would be equipped with special high-security locks, video monitoring, and an alarm system; GSA expected the work to be finished in late March. Defense attorneys suggested they would need several months after the completion of the secure facility to work with Lee in preparing their case.

Fine, Conway said. He set Lee's trial to begin November 6. The trial was expected to last anywhere from six weeks to three months, and Conway wanted to get the proceeding well underway before the holidays.

The judge already had contemplated the enormous public interest in the case and laid out his plan to commandeer a second courtroom for trial spectators. The trial courtroom would be equipped with closed-circuit cameras, wired to monitors in the second courtroom. For many spectators, the trial of Wen Ho Lee would unfold on a TV screen.

While Holscher and Hollander prepared an attack on the FBI's search of the Lee home, Cline was preoccupied by the information on the tapes. On one hand, Lee's scientist friends had for weeks been telling him, quietly, that the weapons codes were nowhere near as valuable as the government claimed. They were unreliable, they gave wrong answers, and they crashed so often that Lee's friends could scarcely understand their utility to the Chinese or anyone else. On the other hand, Cline had Steve Younger talking about the global strategic balance.

How could people in the same profession disagree so sharply on such an apparently simple matter? What really was on those tapes? Until Cline got a Q clearance, no one could actually show him.

He threw himself into the task of learning every detail he could about nuclear weapons and the federal government's case against Wen Ho Lee. Cline directed his executive assistant Barbara Bond to order *Swords of Armageddon*, the multivolume CD-ROM by civilian nuclear-weapons chronicler Chuck Hansen.

Hansen's pursuit of the minutest details of nuclear-weapons designs, nuclear tests, and warhead systems had been dogged, even fanatical. Over the years, he had learned to wield the federal Freedom of Information Act expertly. By matching up separate, redacted documents on similar subjects, Hansen was able to discern censored information and beat government classifiers at their own game. His *Swords* was the most exhaustive nongovernmental resource on the internal details of U.S. nuclear bombs and warheads.

Meanwhile, Bond and paralegal Ann Delpha were given their own obsessive research tasks on the Internet. They were to venture out on the Web and bring back to Cline any technical information they could find on nuclear weapons, weapons codes, and their physics. They also scoured the Web for scraps of information about computer security at Los Alamos National Laboratory. Nearly every day, Bond deposited two thick stacks of printouts on a chair in Cline's office.

In bed at night, Cline sat awake next to his wife, racing through Richard Rhodes's *The Making of the Atomic Bomb* and *Dark Sun,* as well as Bond's Web gleanings, and propping his laptop on his knees to study Hansen's *Swords.* He became immersed in the arcane world of nuclear weaponry and found he had little trouble understanding it. Cline's father, a retired airline pilot, was an engineer by training, and his son evidently had inherited his technical bent.

During the day, Cline planted himself inside the U.S. Attorney's Office, where clerks brought him boxes of documents on the Lee case. Cline pored over the FBI's interview memos (known as 302s), affidavits, and reports, dictating the entire time into a small tape recorder. He was not permitted to take any notes back to his office, and he had to leave the tapes with one of the prosecution clerks, who saved them for the day Bond would be cleared to transcribe them.

As Cline contemplated a graymail defense, he knew that he had one major obstacle to overcome. In the late 1970s, the U.S. Justice Department moved to curb the proliferation of graymail by drafting the Classified Information Procedures Act.

CIPA, as it was known, forced defendants to divulge early in a criminal prosecution exactly which pieces of classified information they proposed to use at trial. That way, prosecutors could weigh up front the potential cost to national security—measured in lost secrets—of going forward with a prosecution.

Defense attorneys hated CIPA. Ordinarily, criminal prosecutors must show their evidence to a defendant before trial, but the defense is under a lesser obligation. CIPA changed that: Now defense attorneys had to reveal a significant measure of the evidence they planned to use at trial.

Legal challenges to CIPA had been filed in a handful of cases, primarily in northern Virginia, where most national-security prosecutions originated. None had been successful, but most of these had been hasty, pro forma efforts. Cline didn't have much hope that he could knock CIPA down, but he felt it was imperative to take advantage of the Lee case as a venue for a more thoughtful, rigorous attack.

CIPA was inherently unconstitutional, Cline argued, because by preemptively revealing a blueprint of defense strategy to the prosecution, the law infringed on Lee's rights to a fair trial and to remain silent.

In effect, months before trial, prosecutors would see virtually every argument that Lee's lawyers planned to make in his defense, as well as have a sense of the content of Lee's own testimony if he took the stand. Armed with that knowledge, prosecutors could tailor their witnesses' testimony to defeat Lee's defense. No other criminal procedure gave the government such an advantage at the outset.

But a constitutional attack had failed in the Iran-Contra case, and Conway now drew upon those rulings to reject Cline's challenge. CIPA didn't require Lee to divulge up front whether he would testify, the judge noted, or what he would testify about. Nor, Conway reasoned, did CIPA impose a one-sided disadvantage for the defense. Prosecutors also must disclose their use of classified information in the trial, as well as any evidence they plan to use for rebutting classified information introduced by the defense. Besides, CIPA was nothing special; ordinary rules of criminal procedure required the defense to disclose before trial its plans to use an alibi, a claim of insanity, scientific tests, or expert testimony.

"The overall balance of discovery is not tipped against Lee," Conway found. He ruled that CIPA was a "carefully balanced framework" for preserving the government's interest in its secrets, and violated none of Lee's constitutional rights.

Lee's defense now had argued aspects of his case in front of six federal judges and had been shot down every time. Cline's larger graymail strategy was still alive, however.

———————

For years, advocates for Chinese Americans had been a fractious bunch, with several groups competing for status as the community's lead voice in legal and political realms. They had disparate strategies for the assertion of Chinese-American civil rights and political power. Those differences faded in light of the Lee case. His prosecution and jailing coalesced Chinese Americans into a unified front on his behalf and their own.

By early 2000, the small displays of support for Wen Ho Lee that Cecilia Chang and friends had organized in the San Francisco Bay Area had reverberated outward to engage Asian Americans elsewhere in the country. Lee's plight came to be seen not merely as a Chinese-American issue, but as a profound challenge to the rights of all Asian Americans. Rallies sprang up in Los Angeles, New York, Chicago, and on the campus of every university with a significant ethnic Chinese student population.

But a quiet force also was at work among Americans generally. Lee's case forged common cause among civil libertarians, advocates of racial diversity, and the nation's scientific community.

Since the late 1960s, Asian Americans had come to constitute a greater and greater proportion of the students seeking U.S. technical degrees in every major scientific field—physics, chemistry, mathematics, and computer science. While Asian Americans made up a minority of the larger body politic, in the realm of science and technology they had become critical players in the New Economy. The nation needed them in an unprecedented way, especially the national laboratories with their heavy emphasis on the hard sciences.

Suddenly, Asian Americans were shunning U.S. defense science. Fear of racial profiling and spy accusations, coupled with the imposition of widespread polygraph tests and bans on international contact, had poisoned the workplace atmosphere at Los Alamos, in particular. In a normal year, the laboratory could expect at least a handful of the brightest Chinese students in American universities to accept its prestigious postdoctoral fellowships. Now no Chinese students were applying.

"I looked further down the list, and there weren't any Chinese names down there either," lab director John C. Browne told a conference of Chinese-American engineers in late February. "The students are being told, 'Don't come to Los Alamos. It's not a good time to be there.' "

Asian students made up the largest portion of U.S. doctoral candidates in the hard sciences, and the best of them wanted nothing to do with Los Alamos. Older weaponeers were leaving, and the lab desperately needed new blood to assume responsibility for its majority share of America's nuclear deterrent. The fallout of the Lee case was becoming a national-security risk in its own right.

Alarm over the Asian boycott resonated not only in the labs and the Energy Department, but in the nation's leading scientific societies as well. Already, scientists there had deep misgivings about the testimony that the federal government had used to keep Lee jailed.

Nuclear-weapons veterans were jolted by Younger's equating the Lee tapes with a change in the "global strategic balance." They and leaders of the scientific societies began talking about how such a hyperbolic claim was being used to deprive an American citizen of liberty.

American scientific societies prided themselves on their role as bulwarks against attacks on the free exchange of ideas worldwide. For decades, they had written letters to repressive regimes in the Middle East, Asia, the Soviet Union, and elsewhere to protest the jailing of scientists who were political dissidents. Now, it seemed, their own government was betraying basic notions of civil rights that they had stressed in their letters abroad, and worse, scientists themselves were complicit in doing so.

In late February, American Physical Society president James S. Langer wrote the same kind of protest letter that the APS had addressed to foreign governments. This time, it went to U.S. Attorney General Janet Reno.

"[W]e make no judgment about Lee's guilt or innocence. That will be decided in a court of law," Langer wrote. "However, we are deeply disturbed by the inhumane treatment that he has received in his pretrial incarceration. The extraordinarily harsh conditions under which he is detained suggest to the outside world that he is presumed guilty, and is being punished, before his trial has even begun."

The American Physical Society also viewed itself as a guardian of U.S. scientific strength. The Lee prosecution was dissuading the most qualified foreign-born scientists from careers in the weapons labs, Langer noted. "We are deeply concerned therefore, that our scientific capabilities and national security are being compromised by our government's actions in the case of Wen Ho Lee."

Likewise, human rights advocates within the American Association for the

Advancement of Science protested Lee's treatment to Reno. "Our concern stems from the possibility that Dr. Lee is being maltreated and may have been the target of special scrutiny because of his ethnic background," wrote Irving A. Lerch, chairman of the AAAS Committee on Scientific Freedom and Responsibility. Lee's solitary confinement, shackling, and lack of contact with the outside world were "harsh in the extreme," "exceedingly cruel," and could be construed as "intimidation," Lerch wrote. "Court records and prosecution documents give the distinct impression that many measures were imposed simply because he has Chinese associates and speaks Chinese. AAAS believes very strongly that place of birth or ethnic background should never be used to impugn the loyalty of scientists."

Lerch didn't mention Younger and other government witnesses by name, but he advised Reno to consult other, perhaps retired, experts on Lee's supposed threat to national security. "Otherwise, we worry that serious damage could be done to the U.S. scientific enterprise and to this nation's . . . security if the government is perceived by scientists as treating Dr. Lee unfairly and relying on unfounded claims regarding threats to national security," Lerch wrote.

The scientists only received bureaucratic replies.

Ever since the first hearing in Lee's case, defense attorneys had been intrigued by a contradiction. Weapons executives and federal prosecutors kept describing the files Lee had collected in the most extreme terms—"potentially catastrophic to the nation's security . . . the crown jewels . . . the gravest possible risk to the security of the United States." To Cline, the description seemed fitting only for Top Secret Restricted Data. In describing the contents of Lee's tapes, prosecution witnesses almost echoed the definition of TSRD in federal regulations as information that, if disclosed, "could reasonably be expected to cause exceptionally grave damage to the national security."

Yet not a single byte of Wen Ho Lee's tapes was classified as Top Secret Restricted Data. The indictment showed that some was unclassified and some was Confidential and Secret RD.

To add to the confusion, the spreadsheets prepared by Los Alamos's computer experts didn't show CRD or SRD classifications for the files—instead, each one was listed as something called PARD, which Wampler had said stood for Protect As Restricted Data. Cline was intrigued. He and Bond dug up DOE manuals on information security and found that PARD wasn't a classification at all. It was a handling designation for large volumes of information that have never been reviewed for classification but might contain small amounts of classified information.

PARD was devised by the Atomic Energy Commission in the 1950s, the early days of weapons computing. As bomb designers ran calculations every day, they churned out prodigious stacks of punch cards and paper printouts. No safes were large enough to hold all this material; it filled filing cabinets, then boxes, and finally spilled into hallways, becoming a fire hazard. The PARD designation allowed them to leave these masses of data out on their desks or other low-security places.

"PARD was a way to circumvent some laws we thought were too restrictive, to get some work done," said Bob Clark. "At the same time, it was well known that PARD was not a security classification. Therefore, you didn't stamp 'PARD' on something that was really secret. If it was Secret RD, it was stamped and treated as such."

Inevitably, despite its name, scientists came to view and treat PARD differently from Restricted Data. "It's in-between stuff," said one Los Alamos physicist. If a scientist carried home a printout of a code run, he got a verbal dressing down or a written reprimand. He didn't go to jail.

In time, however, advances in data storage made PARD obsolete. No longer were there reams of printouts everywhere; PARD disappeared back into the computers, where it filled hard drives and network storage disks. But when DOE officials tried to discontinue its use in the 1990s, Los Alamos and Lawrence Livermore executives resisted: PARD was part of the culture, a slightly more relaxed way of doing business.

So how did Lee's files go from PARD to classified in the indictment? The DOE had reviewed the files for classification upon discovering that Lee had made his tapes. To the defense, it looked as though the government had pulled a fast one. Now Cline had a strategy for deflating the government's overblown descriptions of the information Lee had collected. Gorence had to persuade jurors that Lee intended to injure the United States or help a foreign country, and he was relying on the extreme sensitivity of the information to lead them to that conclusion. But PARD meant no one had reviewed the files for classification before Lee made the tapes. Lee easily could have been in the habit, as many Los Alamos scientists were, of treating PARD in a more casual fashion than he treated classified Restricted Data—a significant erosion of Gorence's argument that Lee acted with criminal intent.

The computer still treated the files as if they were classified, even if not all the scientists did. But Los Alamos computers used a hierarchy of numbers to rank the classification level of files in the system, and Cline found that PARD was automatically given a numerical ranking below that for Restricted Data—as though it weren't necessarily classified at all.

PARD took federal prosecutors by surprise. They discovered its implication for their case almost by accident while interviewing Los Alamos weapons scientists, one of whom was John Kammerdiener.

In January 2000, he was called to a lab room full of prosecutors, FBI agents, and lab scientists who were assisting in the case. Kammerdiener believed he had been identified as a potentially indignant witness for the defense. "I hadn't much more than gotten through introducing myself and they said, 'Aren't you incensed that Wen Ho took this top-secret information from the Mossler [a safe brand] and put it on the unclassified?' I said, 'Wait a minute. As I understand it, he didn't do that. The information he downloaded was PARD information.' And they said, 'What is that?' That was the first time they had heard about it. They said that can't possibly be."

Romero was in the room and confirmed that indeed everything on the tapes was PARD.

The federal government had indicted Lee on life-penalty charges and portrayed him as a thief of the nation's nuclear crown jewels. Yet prosecutors didn't understand a potentially major flaw in their argument.

Meanwhile, Cline began inserting his PARD argument into almost every legal brief. In the public, the news became contorted into a conclusion that none of Lee's files was classified at all, and the government suddenly had turned them into state secrets when it wanted to send him to prison. The reality was more complex. Like all weapons information, PARD was "born classified." It was presumed a state secret until DOE ruled otherwise. Cline nonetheless had found the first weakness in the prosecution's case.

Meanwhile, the jail diet was taking its toll on Lee. Since his bout with cancer in the late 1980s, he had strictly adhered to a diet of fish, chicken, fruit, and vegetables. Sticking with this regime in jail, Lee was getting thinner week by week. It surely didn't help that Lee, at one point, suspected the government might even be trying to poison him. He had shared food with another inmate, who promptly became ill, and the incident made Lee wary of his meals afterward.

To keep himself busy, Lee pored through the case documents that piled up on the cell's empty second bed. He also began writing a mathematics textbook. He was allowed to purchase small personal items from the jail canteen, and friends said he confronted a dilemma between buying pencils and paper or purchasing small cans of tuna fish to supplement his meager diet. Usually, his hunger won out.

In mid-April, Lee got a much-needed break from solitary confinement in Santa Fe. Workers put the final touches on the secure room inside the Albuquerque Federal Courthouse, providing a place where Lee could escape his cell for hours to work on his defense. Cline, in almost daily meetings with Lee, was becoming the case expert on nuclear weapons. On weekdays, Lee left the Santa Fe jail early in the morning with the federal marshals, spent almost a full day in the secure room, and returned to his cell in the late afternoon.

Nancy Hollander and other defense team members were scandalized that their client appeared to be starving. They brought fruit and aluminum-wrapped home cooking to the secure room inside the courthouse. Lee would serve the food and tea to the defense team as well as visitors, including those from the government. Marshals brought Lee in wearing shackles and handcuffs but agreed to remove the handcuffs inside the secure room while he ate and consulted with his lawyers.

Meanwhile, in preparation for the trial, the U.S. Department of Energy had to restore Lee's Q clearance. It was necessary for Lee to be able to view classified documents to participate in his defense. The man who threatened the global strategic balance could look at U.S. nuclear secrets again. DOE also was required to give Lee a Los Alamos laboratory badge, allowing him to enter a separate secure facility that had been established on the Hill so that Lee, his attorneys—who also were given clearances—and potential witnesses could review the files on the tapes. Oddly enough, this secure room was located at Technical Area 52; Lee was revisiting the place where he'd started at Los Alamos, albeit this time in chains.

In early May, as Lee tutored Cline on nuclear-weapons codes, tragedy struck Los Alamos. On May 4, well-meaning managers at Bandelier National Monument sent a crew equipped with hand torches to light a fire on the rounded summit of Cerro Grande.

Named for a turn-of-the-century anthropologist, Bandelier was rich in prehistoric Indian sites and artifacts. But heavy grazing in the late nineteenth century opened the way for trees to encroach on Bandelier's original grasslands, increasing the risk of dangerous wildfires and the erosion of its archeological treasures. On Cerro Grande, the park service intended to burn off potential fuel for more intense fires, as well as bring back the mountain's grasses.

But the Los Alamos area had been bone-dry for weeks, and Bandelier's fire managers neglected to provide for sufficient backup fire crews. Early on the morning of May 5, winds began to fan the fire out of control and by May 7, the flames were racing toward Los Alamos.

The federal government brought in a small army of firefighters, helicopters, and slurry-dropping tanker planes. They put up a heroic battle, but on May 10 embers leapt Los Alamos Canyon into the forested hillsides above the townsite.

Los Alamosans grabbed what possessions they could and beat an orderly retreat to find refuge off the Hill. They watched on TV as the blaze consumed house after house. In the end, more than two hundred homes and apartments were destroyed.

Blazes also cropped up inside the lab boundary and ran down its canyons. More than two-thirds of the laboratory's 43 square miles was blackened or singed. Many employees who worked in trailers came back weeks later to discover their offices gone or their computers melted, their experiments destroyed.

Many New Mexicans feared that the clouds of smoke billowing northward and eastward were full of the radioactive legacy of a half-century of nuclear-weapons research. Tests later showed minuscule amounts of manmade radioactivity in the smoke, but those facts collided with decades of distrust.

The Cerro Grande fire nonetheless battered the spirits of many Los Alamosans. Lee's case and the condemnation of the laboratory by Congress and the media had already made the year one of the darkest in laboratory history. Polygraph tests and a moratorium on foreign travel created an image of a scientific institution isolated from the rest of the world and unable to keep or recruit staff. The Cerro Grande fire deepened those discontents and plunged laboratory morale to a new low.

A number of American weaponeers had watched helplessly as federal prosecutors used the "crown jewels" testimony of Younger, Krajcik, and Robinson to keep Lee locked up. That spring, scientists flooded each other's phone lines with calls and e-mails, decrying what they saw as an injustice borne out of partisan politics and the self-interest of weapons managers.

For years, nuclear-weapons executives had coaxed billions of dollars out of Congress and the White House for pricey new supercomputers and experimental facilities. These machines—Blue Mountain, the National Ignition Facility,

Blue Pacific, the Dual-Axis Radiographic Hydrotest Facility, and others—would be the vanguard of a reinvigorated nuclear-weapons program in which actual explosive testing was replaced by computer simulation. In a crude sense, a deal had been struck: The weapons budget would remain healthy and in return the labs would forgo nuclear testing, the most hallowed and unifying event of weapons science and culture. The labs reserved the ability to resume testing if needed, and the politicians were reliant on the labs' advice to decide when that might be.

The linchpin of this deal was a technical gamble: The United States would bet its nuclear deterrent on weapons-design codes. Virtual testing, in full 3D, would replace the real thing. No one was certain how to model all of the complex physics inside a detonating nuclear weapon in three dimensions, with enough resolution to be certain the bombs would continue to work thirty, forty, one hundred years down the road.

Congress and the White House were staking the nation's nuclear deterrent on the redevelopment of the legacy codes, such as those on Lee's tapes, into more capable, more detailed 3D codes. They poured billions of dollars into new experimental machines and supercomputers that lab executives argued were critical to this new effort, known as stockpile stewardship. Weapons executives such as Younger and Robinson were expected to sustain this flow of funding and projects to keep their laboratories vital without nuclear testing. They hardly could be expected to take the witness stand and say the weapons codes were less than the crown jewels.

Several rank-and-file weaponeers thought the prosecutors had been oversold on the value of Lee's tapes. The price, they feared, was not just the freedom of a fellow weapons scientist, but the reputation of the labs and arguably even of American science as exemplars of truth and the free exchange of ideas.

Ed Gerjuoy, a former chair of the American Physical Society's Committee on International Freedom, followed the Lee case from his teaching post at the University of Pittsburgh and was appalled: "There were aspects that resembled the kinds of things that I saw done when I was working for physicists in the Soviet Union." Gerjuoy got in touch with Cline, who sent him the transcripts of the bail hearings. "It confirmed my worst fears," he said.

Cline needed help "rounding up witnesses in the physics community to counter what these other witnesses said." Gerjuoy, as both a lawyer and a physicist who had studied at Berkeley under Robert Oppenheimer, was in an ideal position to help find volunteers.

Gerjuoy heard that Walter Goad, a retired Los Alamos scientist whose experience with nuclear weapons began in the early 1950s, had written a letter to the *Albuquerque Journal* equating Lee's bail hearings with the anti-Communist paranoia of the McCarthy era.

Goad had worked on "Mike," the world's first thermonuclear device, and the weapons that followed in the 1950s heyday of innovation in U.S. weapons design. In the 1960s, Goad was drawn to molecular biology and went on to become a pioneer of bioinformatics, the application of computer technology to biology and especially genetics. He successfully lobbied the National Institutes of Health for the creation of an enormous computer database to track the genetic code of humans and other organisms. GenBank was the first U.S. storehouse for data on the human genome, and Goad was its first director. Goad was a Renaissance man of sorts, a mountaineer, sailor, poet, gardener, and environmentalist. He was among the few lab physicists who not only could use computers but could build them—his office was an electronics junkyard, typically with smoke rising from a hot soldering iron.

In early 2000, Goad was outraged at Younger's testimony and the use federal prosecutors had made of it to imprison Wen Ho Lee. When Gerjuoy contacted him, it took little to persuade Goad to weigh in on the side of Lee's defense. He submitted a sworn declaration to Cline. In it, Goad derided Younger's and Robinson's characterizations of the national-security threat posed by Lee's code library as "apocalyptic."

"My experience and expertise tells me that these assertions are exaggerations, grossly misleading in their import," he wrote. "[T]he scientific knowledge and computational expertise required for nuclear weapons design is now widely dispersed. Therefore, any nation with a substantial scientific establishment is capable of designing nuclear weapons on its own. Only a group already deeply engaged in the design of nuclear weapons could profit from the Lee tapes (if they still exist). At most, the U.S. codes and data could augment, not revolutionize, their efforts. Furthermore, changes in the world strategic balance require not just scientific expertise and information, but the commitment of extensive technical and industrial resources to the practical development, production, and deployment of weapons and weapons carriers."

Younger's "crown jewels" and Robinson's "betting the country" testimony amounted, in Goad's opinion, to "unbridled exaggeration."

"The result is not a measured judgment of risk," he said, "but incitement of apprehension, even paranoia, that can override fairness and justice. Unhappily, our history has seen other examples in which exaggerations of danger have overridden the traditional American values of fairness and justice—most memorably to people of my generation, in the era of Senator Joseph McCarthy. These currents of fear are always deeply troubling and damaging, and in this case are doing specific and incalculable damage to the very military-scientific establishment that is ostensibly being protected."

In time, more retired weaponeers would join Goad in contesting the government's witnesses. They were challenging the assumptions at the very heart of the Lee prosecution and shifting the playing field. Prosecutors had thought they would have a monopoly on nuclear expertise and could argue the extreme sensitivity of Lee's tape library without being contested. Now, experts who were equal or superior to government witnesses were stepping forward with contradicting testimony.

Such a "battle of the experts" is common in civil cases. But it often is a death knell for a criminal prosecution, where reasonable doubt is enough to win acquittal.

That spring, President Clinton named a new U.S. attorney for New Mexico. He was Norman Bay, the son of a leader of Albuquerque's Chinese-American community. Bay was a serious-minded and workaholic bachelor, well regarded for his thoroughness and knowledge of the law. But his selection immediately prompted cynical criticism of the Clinton administration; Lee's defenders saw the appointment as putting a Chinese-American face on the prosecution to neutralize Lee's claims of racial profiling.

The real upheaval in the U.S. Attorney's Office was still to come, however. Soon after Bay took charge, someone complained about Gorence's earlier dalliance with an office intern as well as his involvement with another staff attorney. The allegations were not new, and no one could point to any proof that Gorence's personal life had impaired his judgment in the conduct of the Lee case. But the Justice Department chose not to take any chances with such a high-profile and increasingly embattled case. Gorence was removed as the lead prosecutor—although he remained on the prosecution team—and Justice arranged for a replacement.

The new lead prosecutor was George Stamboulidis, a federal prosecutor from Long Island who was known for aggressive prosecution of organized crime figures such as reputed Genovese crime boss Vincent (The Chin) Gigante.

Stamboulidis had a taste for double-breasted suits and colorful ties and walked with a rolling swagger. He was selected for the New Mexico case after an interview with Janet Reno, who had put out the word that Justice was in need of a prosecutor to parachute into a high-profile case. He was a talented lawyer and had handled complex cases, had even dealt with CIPA issues, but he was new to nuclear weapons. He was diving into a case full of scientific and legal ambiguities.

One of his first actions after arriving at the U.S. Attorney's Office in downtown Albuquerque was to reduce the public relations damage done by Lee's onerous jail conditions. He convinced the warden of the Santa Fe jail to allow Lee to get his daily hour of exercise without being hobbled by shackles. It was a change from Gorence, who would later say that his own failure to improve Lee's conditions was the "single greatest mistake" he made in handling the case.

It had taken Gorence months to learn the ins and outs of nuclear weapons, computer systems at Los Alamos, and the subtleties of counterespionage. He knew his opponents, and he knew the case inside out. But in May he was relegated to the back bench, and by mid-July, after warring with Stamboulidis on strategy, he was gone from the prosecution team.

"I'm not just gonna hang around and be the guy's briefcase carrier," Gorence grumbled to friends.

———————

On June 5, Judge Conway surprised observers of the Lee case by suddenly withdrawing as the trial judge. The old lawyer had seemed to relish the prospect of presiding over Lee's trial. Now he claimed the trial was shaping up as an arduous task and cited longstanding promises to his wife to go on senior status, a kind of semiretirement that allows senior federal judges to take a diminished caseload. It was rumored around the courthouse that Conway's physician had recently informed the judge that he had Parkinson's disease.

But Conway had another possible reason for stepping down. In the previous week, a woman connected to the defense team had reported to Lee's attorneys that Conway had made an inappropriate advance to her earlier that month in his chambers.

Lee's defense attorneys were troubled by the allegation but immediately realized what they had to do. If they did not raise the allegation with the judge and he remained in charge of the case, it was possible that no harm would come to Lee, perhaps even conceivable that the judge would soften his rulings to favor the defense. But it was likelier that the judge could turn vindictive, out of either a sense of rejection or a fear of having his indiscretion exposed.

Ultimately, the matter wasn't up for debate: No prudent defense attorney could take such a chance with his client's freedom. Lee's attorneys wrote Conway, requesting that he recuse himself based on "an unwanted sexual advance." If he resisted, the defense knew it was in for a painful recusal hearing in which the woman would be testifying against a sitting chief judge.

"I was so taken aback by that letter," Conway said later. "I couldn't believe it." But the next Monday, he issued an order formally recusing himself from the Lee case and vacating the hearings and trial date that he had scheduled.

Months later, Conway initially declined to discuss the allegation and the role it played in his recusal. But then he began to explain.

"If you're a judge, whenever you have an allegation like that, it doesn't matter whether there's any truth to it whatsoever . . ." His voiced trailed off. "Well, I'm just not going to talk about it."

———————

The departures of Gorence and Conway from the cast of the Lee case rewrote the story line in a way that dramatically favored the defense. The prosecution was now in the hands of a newcomer and the case itself returned to Judge Jim Parker, who was deeply troubled by the conditions of Lee's incarceration.

"I don't believe in a God," Lee told his attorneys. "But something's going on."

– 26 –

The Momentum Shifts

Cecilia Chang picked up a megaphone and informed the crowd of mostly middle-aged Chinese Americans that it was time for a protest chant. Awkwardly, the Silicon Valley professionals and elected officials attempted, "You say he's a spy, we say that's a lie!" The cheer drew smiles, but the mere fact that this reserved group of Asian Americans would participate in a street rally in downtown San Jose was proof of Lee's broad support.

"It's not just what he did," Chang told the crowd. "It's what he looks like. He looks like us." Some of Lee's supporters wore signs on their backs that read, "I am Asian-American. Arrest me too."

The movement had long since outgrown its hesitant beginnings when a leader of the influential Organization of Chinese Americans turned down requests to get involved, saying, "But what if he's guilty?"

Supporters coordinated protests on June 8, 2000, a "National Day of Outrage for Wen Ho Lee" to mark his sixth month in jail. They held a rally outside the federal courthouse in Albuquerque and other events in Detroit, Los Angeles, Salt Lake City, and San Francisco. There had been two or three dozen events before June, most in cities with universities and large Chinese-American populations. Many of them were panel discussions on civil liberties, reflecting the academic orientation of Lee's supporters.

Chang's Web site—wenholee.org—had its own office, staffed by volunteers who updated the news hour by hour. Chang had learned by experience that to be a voice for Lee in the news media, one had to be where the story was. Six months earlier, she had attended one of Lee's bail hearings in New Mexico. She watched the reporters looking for interviews during a recess. None of them approached her, because none of them knew who she was.

By the next hearing, she had a banner that read JUSTICE FOR ALL—WEN HO LEE DEFENSE FUND. She gathered all of Lee's friends and supporters to stand behind the banner on the courthouse plaza. The cameras flocked her way. The next day, her picture was in the *New York Times*.

"If you have a banner and are an organization, the media will talk to you," she said. "You have to be there, not expect them to hunt for you and find you." Her son called it "Wen Ho Lee theater."

While Chang was working on the outside, others had an inside political track. Charlie Sie, a former Xerox executive and cochair of the Committee of 100, the organization of prominent Chinese-American businesspeople, was invited to a gathering of Asian-American leaders at the White House. He talked to the president about the case of the jailed Los Alamos scientist. Clinton, turning on the charm, said he thought that Lee was getting a bad deal. "That Clinton's a smart guy," Sie said later. "He told me one thing" about those who were using Lee for political gain. "When you spit in the wind, it might come back at you."

Lee's Asian-American supporters had multiple reasons for speaking out or donating money to his defense fund. Some thought him innocent, while others spoke up for due process of law, regardless of whether he was innocent or guilty. All were concerned about discrimination against Chinese Americans. Many were protecting the reputation of China as well. It was ironic that Lee was from Taiwan, but the majority of his supporters traced their roots to the mainland. One donor, upon reading a newspaper story suggesting that Lee might be a spy for Taiwan, not China, declared, "If he's a spy for Taiwan, I'm not giving any more money."

"In the early stage, the Taiwanese organizations did not show their hand at all," Sie said. "They were not interested in this case."

An intellectual force in support of Lee was Ling-chi Wang, director of Asian-American studies at the University of California at Berkeley. A longtime community leader and civil rights activist, he laughed often and spoke bluntly. He organized an effort to have Asian-American scientists boycott jobs at the weapons labs, a move that prompted frightened lab administrators and DOE officials to fly to the West Coast, where they begged him to call it off.

Wang could talk for hours about the history of the Chinese in America. White Americans did not understand Asian-American alarm at the Lee case, he said, because they did not comprehend that Lee's troubles, far from an isolated occurrence, were part of an unbroken pattern going back to the arrival of Asians in America in the early nineteenth century.

Chinese laborers working in the goldfields of California at mid-century were forbidden citizenship but required to pay a special tax. The state legislature was busily enacting laws such as "An Act to Protect Free White Labor Against Competition with Chinese Coolie Labor." In Washington, D.C., in 1877, a congressional immigration committee reported that Chinese "can never assimilate with us; that they are a perpetual, unchanging, and unchangeable alien element that can never become homogenous; that their civilization is demoralizing and degrading to our people; that they degrade and dishonor labor; that they can never become citizens . . ."

In 1882, Congress passed the Chinese Exclusion Act, banning Chinese laborers from the country and denying citizenship to those already here. It was a legal status shared by lepers and "morons." Never before or since has Congress barred the entry of an entire ethnic group. The act wasn't repealed until 1943, when China was fighting with the United States against Japan. Even then, the immigration quotas were set far below those of European immigrants. Those last vestiges of the Exclusion Act were not removed until 1965, under President Lyndon Johnson.

The expression "not a Chinaman's chance" grew out of the Chinese experience in nineteenth-century California, where their odds were grim, from the courtroom to the railroad construction crews.

When Lee was fired and publicly branded a spy in 1999, Wang said, "He didn't stand a Chinaman's chance."

During World War II, 110,000 Japanese Americans were forcibly relocated and interned. Newspaper editorials alleged that Japanese-American farmers would otherwise plant their tomato fields to point toward U.S. airbases, to guide Japanese bombers toward their target.

In the summer of 1999, a Chinese-American researcher walked into Terry Hawkins's office at Los Alamos and put an editorial cartoon on his desk. "This is what the Chinese Americans at Los Alamos are concerned about," he said. Hawkins looked. "The cartoon was showing Chinese Americans as buck-toothed rodents running out of Los Alamos. Frankly, I haven't seen this kind of thing since 1944 or 1946."

These events and more shaped the world view of Asian Americans and became the prism through which they viewed the Cox Report and the Wen Ho Lee case.

Lee's supporters were delighted in June 2000 when Cline, Hollander, and Holscher filed a motion claiming that Lee was the victim of "selective prosecution," singled out because of his race. Politically, the timing was right. There was already much public discussion of "racial profiling," in which police stopped African-American motorists for minor traffic offenses in order to search their cars for drugs. The police based their actions on a "profile" of the average drug dealer that concluded black drivers were more likely to be carrying drugs than whites.

Claims of selective prosecution were usually difficult for defense attorneys to prove. This was not the same as proving that a specific law was discriminatory. In selective prosecution cases, the law itself was fair, but its enforcement was directed at a specific group. It would be poetic justice if Lee's defense team succeeded in having his case thrown out on a selective prosecution claim; the legal history of selective prosecution grew out of mistreatment of Chinese workers.

In San Francisco in the 1880s, restrictions on Chinese workers drove them to specialize in certain businesses, notably laundries. White laundry owners who didn't want the competition convinced the city to pass a fire safety ordinance allowing laundries only in brick buildings. The law, while nondiscriminatory on its face, was only enforced against Chinese. White owners continued to operate in wooden buildings without interference from police.

One of the arrested laundry workers was Yick Wo, whose case made its way to the U.S. Supreme Court in 1886. The Constitution did not speak directly to such a case, but the justices ruled that the situation was intrinsically unfair, a violation of the constitutional right to equal protection under the law. The remedy was to free Yick Wo and the others, even if they had violated the brick-building law.

It would be a stunning victory for the defense team if it could convince a judge to throw out the heavyweight national-security charges against its client on a selective prosecution claim. But it would be an uphill battle, no less because the evidence would have to come from the prosecution itself. The lawyers asked Parker to order the government to turn over certain materials, including a videotape of the security briefer who had joked about the number of Chinese restaurants in Los Alamos. More important, they wanted the government to produce records of other security cases in which the violators—presumably white—were treated much more leniently than Lee.

The defense provided a list of such cases in its paperwork, drawn from newspaper accounts. First on the list was John Deutch, the former CIA director who was in the news for keeping a collection of highly classified documents on his unsecured home computer. Like Lee, Deutch erased a number of classified files when investigators let him know their suspicions. But unlike Lee, Deutch's home computer contained documents classified at the Code Name and Top Secret levels. These documents concerned covert intelligence operations and named undercover operatives, arguably a more immediate threat to lives and national security than Lee's files. Worse, the machine was used to access the Internet through America Online. Somebody in the family had been surfing pornography sites with the computer.

Deutch was everything Lee was not—white, powerful, and well connected. The CIA was slow to investigate his security violations, and he had not been charged with any crime.

———

With John Conway's departure, the case was turned over to Jim Parker, the same district court judge who had presided over Lee's second bail hearing. Parker's expressions of concern about the harsh conditions of Lee's confinement gave hope to the defense team. They had not heard the same sympathetic remarks from Conway.

Parker did not disappoint. In his first hearing, on June 13, the lanky, understated judge from Texas asked about Lee's jail conditions. Cline and Hollander told him that their client was being driven by the U.S. marshals from Santa Fe to the defense's secure room in the Albuquerque courthouse four or five days a week, so he was getting out of his solitary cell often.

His family was now allowed to visit him in jail for an hour a week, with a Mandarin-speaking FBI agent in the room to make sure he didn't provide any secret messages or nuclear secrets to his wife and children. He was allowed two phone calls a week to his family, in English only, monitored by an FBI agent. "In fact, if they start to speak in Chinese, they pull the call," Hollander told the judge.

Parker asked that the defense and prosecution get together with a retired judge to mediate an acceptable set of conditions for Lee's release on bail. More remarkably—and this struck a note of fear in the prosecution—Parker suggested both sides also enter mediation to see if a plea bargain were possible for Lee. In those few remarks, he seemed to have downgraded *U.S. vs. Lee* from the worst case since the Rosenbergs to something far more routine.

———

Just as Parker was coming on board, beleaguered Los Alamos was hit with yet another security controversy. Two computer hard drives, each about the size of a pack of cards and loaded with nuclear-weapons design data, were discovered to be missing during the fire in May. Worse, lab workers had failed to report the missing hard drives immediately, hoping instead they could find them quickly and avoid another public relations nightmare or a criminal investigation.

The hard drives were for laptops used by Los Alamos scientists who served on DOE's elite Nuclear Emergency Search Team, a group of specially trained, beeper-wearing experts who were on call for nuclear emergencies. NEST team members were prepared to respond on short notice to the threat of a lost, stolen, or homemade terrorist nuclear weapon, in the United States or abroad. The high-tech snoops regularly practiced searching in crowded cities, disguised as telephone repair crews, secretaries, or delivery people. They cruised the streets in pizza vans or postal trucks, scanning for telltale signs of radiation.

If they ever came face-to-face with a real terrorist weapon, NEST team members would type the available information into classified software on the drives. The programs were designed to spit out suggestions on how to disarm the weapon. The hard drives were a master reference work on nuclear weapons, a trove of atomic advice for as wide an array of potential bombs as NEST members might encounter.

With the forest fire approaching the lab in May, a worker had gone to the high-security vault in X Division to retrieve the drives and found them missing. When they weren't returned after the fire, the search began. In June, the FBI was called in, and the lost disks became front-page news across the country. Cartoonists ridiculed lab security. Republicans went after the Clinton administration. Senator Frank Murkowski of Alaska, after admitting he didn't know how serious the security breach was, then said, "However, this could be one of the most significant losses of nuclear weapons information in recent times." Murkowski and colleagues had said the same thing a year earlier about the Lee case.

Lab workers theorized that someone simply forgot to put the hard drives back in the proper vault and then was too frightened to step forward. In the political atmosphere, a security violation could quickly be elevated to a crime.

As an energized FBI moved into X Division to find the hard drives and a suspect, tensions grew between the investigators and the Ph.D. physicists, who accused the FBI of Gestapo tactics—polygraph tests and confrontational late-night interviews. After a physicist greeted an agent in an X Division hallway with a Nazi salute, several dozen bomb scientists were given a week off with pay to go home and cool off. When the hard drives were eventually found stashed behind an X Division copying machine, David Letterman's jokes on late-night television grew worse. The scientists hired lawyers and stonewalled the FBI. Agents were irate that someone was lying to them, but their own hard-nosed tactics were to blame. Months later, they gave up. X Division was happy to see them go.

The missing hard drives had an immediate political effect. Bill Richardson had for some time been angling for the vice presidential slot on the Democratic ticket with Al Gore. He already had opposition from some Asian-American groups as a result of his handling of the Lee case, and then the hard drives went missing. Republican Senator Richard Shelby of Alabama, presiding over a meeting of the Intelligence Committee, told Richardson he ought to resign: "You've lost all credibility."

The heaviest blow came from Democratic Senator Robert Byrd of West Virginia, a senior statesman of Richardson's own party. "You've shown a contempt of Congress that borders on a supreme arrogance of this institution," Byrd said. "I think it's a rather sad story, because you've had a bright and brilliant career. But you would never, you would never again receive the support of the Senate of the United States for any office to which you might be appointed. It's gone. You've squandered your treasure, and I'm sorry."

Later, Richardson would observe, "That Los Alamos incident, the hard drives, cost me being in serious consideration for the ticket."

The hard drives had no direct connection to Lee's case, but prosecutors feared the incident would feed into the defense strategy of depicting the lab as a place of notoriously sloppy security, where only one person, a sixty-year-old Chinese American, was prosecuted. Indeed, Holscher was quick to claim that the data on the missing drives was much more sensitive than the information on the tapes, "a world of difference from the computer codes that Wen Ho Lee had."

Lee's lawyers looked for other tools to attack the government and found one in the Privacy Act of 1974. Early on, the Lee family's civil lawyer, Brian Sun, filed a lawsuit in federal court in Washington, charging that the FBI, the Justice Department, and the Department of Energy had violated the Privacy Act of 1974 by leaking Lee's name and other personal information to the press. Sun, who had represented Democratic fund-raiser Johnny Chung during the campaign contribution controversy, aimed his suit at future leaks as well as past. Sun judged that the threat of depositions would give officials pause before talking to reporters. The suit may have had a psychological effect on public opinion as well. Lee appeared to be fighting back, not only declaring his innocence, but accusing the government of misconduct.

As the case moved into court, Holscher and Cline split the defense's media dealings—Holscher taking the *New York Times,* the *Washington Post,* and his hometown paper, the *L.A. Times,* and Cline taking other news outlets, especially in New Mexico. Their skill at cultivating reporters had been matched early on by Gorence and the FBI, but Stamboulidis avoided media contact when he took over, in effect ceding the tug-of-war for public opinion to the defense.

Lee's case, which had been moving slowly through the first half of the year, picked up speed now. There were continuous filings, frequent court hearings. Unresolved issues were everywhere. The government alleged that Lee made the tapes with the intent to aid a foreign country. The defense demanded to know—which country? Stamboulidis didn't want to say. He argued that he didn't have to name a country, it could be any country. Perhaps Lee himself hadn't decided what country to help, he just had the intent to help someone, somewhere. Finally, at a hearing on June 26, Stamboulidis was cornered and had to come up with a list of countries he wouldn't rule out. China or its rival Taiwan, he said, or perhaps Germany, Hungary, Australia, or France. "We're in the process of refining our legal theories," he told the judge. Stamboulidis later added Singapore, Switzerland, and Hong Kong.

There were chortles from the spectators' rows where the defendant's friends and family sat. On the other side of the aisle, reporters scribbled madly. Had the government's case come to this? After months of implying that he was a spy for China, the government now was suggesting he might be a spy for Australia, one of the most antinuclear countries in the world?

Lee had written letters inquiring about work in the countries Stamboulidis had listed, with the exception of China. Stamboulidis was suggesting that Lee might have made the tapes to take with him to his next job. If it were an overseas university or company Lee had in mind, that could constitute intent to injure America by depriving the country of the sole use of the computer codes.

Stamboulidis had just enunciated a novel motive for espionage. Instead of money or ideology or fear, Wen Ho Lee had become a kind of immigrant striver with an international portfolio—a job seeker rather than a spy.

By the next hearing, Parker's suggestion of mediation had become a court order. He provided a list of semiretired judges as candidates. The two sides privately agreed on Judge Edward Leavy of the Ninth Circuit Court of Appeals, which is based in San Francisco, and began a series of secret negotiations.

In the courtroom, Parker was ruling for the defense, rulings that Conway probably would not have made. Parker ordered the government to turn over computer-security audits, which the defense team would use to show Lee wasn't the only Los Alamos scientist to break the rules. Parker himself agreed to take a look at classified documents describing Sylvia Lee's cooperation with the FBI, the CIA, and Los Alamos, as well as FBI memos written by agents who had concluded Lee was not the W88 spy. If the documents were helpful to the defense, he would turn them over.

Cline doggedly moved ahead with his graymail defense, claiming he might have to show the jury a bomb blueprint, as well as every line of code in every file from every tape in the indictment, to refute the "crown jewels" claim. He knew that if he won that battle, the war was over. The government would drop the case rather than disclose the codes. In a conversation with U.S. Attorney Norman Bay in June, Cline made his intent clear: "My guy's not going to take a plea to a charge in the indictment, and if you don't like that, I'm going to take you on a long, slow, death march under CIPA."

Cline was also targeting the obvious weak link in the case against Lee—the requirement that the government prove intent. His client's belief, the lawyer said during a hearing, was that the tapes were either flawed or already in the public domain, and thus no harm could come from storing them on tapes or in the unclassified section of the computer file system. If Lee believed the tapes were harmless—whether they were or not—then he could not have intended to harm the country by creating them.

To prove his point, Lee would have to point out the flaws in the tapes to the jury or show the court which parts of the codes had been published elsewhere. That brought Cline back to his graymail attempt.

The PARD issue fit the same mold. The defense could argue that since the government had assigned the codes a low security priority, Lee had no reason to believe he was harming the country by putting them on tapes.

Stamboulidis, of course, disagreed with all of that.

Yet in closed hearings, Cline's hard-won knowledge of nuclear weapons left Stamboulidis at a disadvantage. With Cline and his client both cleared for security, Lee became his lawyer's personal tutor on weapons and codes. Cline then wielded his newfound knowledge to give the judge a short course on nuclear weaponry. "I would like to take two minutes and tell the court a little bit about these codes and how they work," he said during a closed hearing in July. His classified lecture took up seventeen pages in the transcript of the hearing. Stamboulidis had raced to learn nuclear weapons and codes but was still behind. As Cline lectured on the shortcomings of the "crown jewels," Stamboulidis could scarcely do more than listen.

As time went on, the court hearings developed a familiar routine. Parker held court in the Rio Grande Courtroom, an elegant third-floor room in the brand-new courthouse. The bailiffs in their sports jackets would open the double doors to let in the spectators. There were a half-dozen rows for the public, on either side of the center aisle. On the right, toward the back, friends and lab employees gathered. Bob and Kathy Clark were usually there, as were Sandia National Laboratories engineer Bill Sullivan and his wife, Nance Crow. Lee's next-door neighbors Jean and Don Marshall were always there, as well as Los Alamos lawyer and activist Phyllis Hedges.

Employees of various federal agencies kept to themselves in the front row, left side, now and then handing a folded note to someone to pass to the prosecution table. Some wouldn't identify themselves; others admitted to working for the Justice Department, the FBI, or the Department of Energy. When a tall man walked in on a hot New Mexico summer day wearing a suit and a black trench coat, nobody had to guess—he'd just gotten off a plane from Washington.

The press corps usually took the middle rows, a handful of reporters on a slow day, twenty or thirty for a key hearing. Family members usually came in just before the proceedings began and took seats in the right front row, as close as possible to the defendant. Chung Lee came when he could break free from Case Western Reserve medical school in Cleveland, Ohio. Sylvia Lee, uncomfortable in a crowd, was almost never there.

Alberta Lee, on the other hand, was a fixture. Articulate, emotional, and attractive, she had become an accomplished advocate for her father, especially after an appearance at Harvard. "If I can talk to Harvard Law School, I can talk anywhere," she said afterward. Alberta Lee didn't organize rallies; she didn't do legal research. Instead, she traveled the country talking about herself and her father in a heartfelt way that moved people. She became the human figure in the story, the alter ego of her dad, who was silent behind bars. The news media needed her to bring life to their stories, and she was willing. She often came to court in the company of a Southern California publicist, Stacy Cohen, who had volunteered to be her de facto media manager. Together, they sought favorable stories from national magazines such as *Esquire* and *Vanity Fair*, offering access to the family as an enticement for journalists.

Attorneys, assistants, prosecutors, FBI agents, and federal security officials—the latter present to make sure neither lawyers nor witnesses uttered a classified word—took their places at two heavily polished dark tables in the courtroom. A marshal would bring in Wen Ho Lee, always wearing his same gray suit. He was noticeably thin at early hearings, when he was losing weight in jail, but appeared healthier as the months passed.

During breaks, Lee would steal a glance at the audience. Prosecutors and security officials, apparently believing their own spy stories, watched Lee for signs of surreptitious communication. One morning a prosecutor whispered to two FBI agents to watch Lee's eyes. Perhaps he was making contact with some-one. Who?

At one hearing, Lee flashed a hand signal to Chung in the gallery. First one finger, then two, then five, to reassure his family that his weight was back up to 125 pounds, nearly normal.

- 27 -

Freedom

In July, John Cline's immersion in the government case files paid off in gold.

He had studied every document the U.S. Attorney's Office turned over to him. He read the FBI reports, or 302s, of every FBI witness interview he could get hold of. He practically memorized the grand jury testimony used to indict his client. And as he read, then reread, the FBI interviews and grand jury testimony of Kuok-Mee Ling, the T Division scientist whose computer Lee had borrowed to make the tapes, Cline realized something was wrong.

At Lee's bail hearings, Messemer had testified that Lee asked to borrow Ling's computer "in order to download a résumé." This apparent deception seemed so indicative of ill intent that the judge specifically mentioned it in his order denying Lee bail. But as Cline reviewed Ling's grand jury testimony, one of the questions jumped off the page.

Q. Did he tell you—Did Mr. Lee tell you what information he wanted to download onto this tape that you're referring to?
A. No. Just that he wanted to download some files.

There was no mention of a résumé. The notes of one interview that Messemer himself had conducted stated that Lee "didn't discuss what was going to be placed on the tapes." Here was the new evidence Cline needed to request a new bail hearing. It looked like outright misrepresentation. But Cline needed to attack the other mainstay of the government's case and Parker's bail ruling, the overheated testimony about the significance of the tapes and their position as the "crown jewels" of the country's nuclear-weapons program. That testimony had carried tremendous weight because of the prestigious positions held by the witnesses, Stephen Younger, Paul Robinson, and Richard Krajcik. Yet for all the education and nuclear-weapons experience of the three men, their testimony was mere opinion, not fact. What the defense needed was its own opinion from an even more influential name. Through a connection in Holscher's office, the defense hit the jackpot—Harold Agnew, a veteran of the Manhattan Project, a nuclear-weapons advisor to five presidents and the first visitor to China from Los Alamos. It was Agnew who first dreamed up the half-megaton warhead that would become the W88. The former lab director was retired now, silver haired, comfortably rotund, and doing part-time consulting.

In May 1999, Agnew had written a letter to the editor of the *Wall Street Journal* questioning the furor over the Lee case and the exalted status of the codes. "No nation would ever stockpile any device based on another nation's computer codes," Agnew had written. He was happy to provide a declaration for the defense.

In late July, Cline filed his renewed motion for bail. It hit heavily on Messemer's "résumé" testimony. Cline included the excerpts he'd found from the grand jury transcript and FBI documents to make his case that the prosecution had presented false evidence.

The motion then attacked another key element of the bail decision, the theory that Lee, the small sixty-year-old man who quietly fished and gardened in his spare time, could be a secret spy for China who might be whisked away from his home by armed foreign agents in helicopters. The government itself seemed to have all but abandoned that notion with Stamboulidis's announcement that Lee might have made the tapes to find a new job.

Cline wrote: "The prosecution now claims that he intended to provide the tapes to aid Australia (a firmly non-nuclear nation), Singapore (which has no known nuclear capabilities), France (an ally), Germany (an ally), Hong Kong (then controlled by Great Britain, another ally), or Switzerland (non-nuclear and neutral), in addition to one or the other of two historically antagonistic nations, Taiwan and the PRC."

"Dr. Lee, the alleged job seeker, cuts a far less threatening figure than Dr. Lee, the alleged spy," the lawyer wrote.

Agnew's declaration was devastating. The missing codes, he wrote, "would be of little or no value to the People's Republic of China." If China obtained the codes, "it would have little or no effect whatsoever on today's nuclear balance." China had its own nuclear codes, which had been benchmarked against its own nuclear tests. Cline also had a similar declaration from Walter Goad.

Judge Parker scheduled a bail hearing for August 16. It would be Lee's best shot at getting out of jail since his arrest in December.

Cline had always felt that the most powerful weapon in his legal arsenal was the threat to use classified information in open court. Now his guerrilla graymail struggle in closed-door hearings paid off.

In early August, Parker handed him a crucial victory by ruling that a wide variety of classified information was relevant to Lee's defense. Cline couldn't have hoped for much more. He was one step away from using secret data from live nuclear tests in Nevada, bomb blueprints, operating manuals, input decks, and the codes themselves in court. Cline's strategy had pushed the government closer to its quitting point.

But there was more. The judge said he would hand over to the defense files that reflected well on the Lees as informants for the FBI and CIA during the 1980s. These documents were sure to undercut the prosecution if it persisted in describing Wen Ho and Sylvia's friendships with Chinese scientists as nefarious.

Wen Ho Lee walked to his usual chair in the courtroom for his new bail hearing on August 16, 2000. After eight months in the Santa Fe jail, he was getting his best shot at freedom. He had every reason to be optimistic. The judge seemed to be on his side. The gallery was full of Lee's friends and family members who had come to put up their homes as collateral if he was released on bail.

The first witness was the physicist John Richter, who had been recruited for the defense by Ed Gerjuoy. Five years before, Richter and his colleagues Bobby Henson and Larry Booth had read blue-border intelligence in the intel vault in Washington and announced that China had tested something resembling the W88. Richter was retired now, but still imposing in an amiable, self-confident way. He knew bombs inside and out, and it was almost impossible to stop him from offering his opinions. Today the dean of primaries at Los Alamos was a witness for the defense.

Richter was paying penance for his inadvertent role in provoking the investigation that put Lee in solitary confinement. When he had joined the other scientists in 1995 to guess the extent to which espionage had helped China solve the puzzle of smaller warheads, Richter didn't know that their judgments would lead to an FBI investigation, especially one as misguided as Kindred Spirit.

Richter had another reason for coming to Lee's aid. In the hard-drives episode, he thought the FBI had acted like "thugs" toward the scientists of X-4, the lab's primary design group that Richter had once led. The agents' behavior angered Richter; they seemed like the secret police of an increasingly undemocratic government, and now they were going after Lee.

On the witness stand, Richter was "results-oriented," as one prosecutor put it, a man on a mission. No matter what question Stamboulidis asked, or how he phrased it, Richter managed an answer that downplayed the importance of Lee's tapes. The message to Judge Parker was clear: There was no reason not to release Lee on bail. Lee could defect to China tomorrow, taking with him the codes he copied, and it would not harm U.S. national security, Richter said. "I don't think it would have any deleterious effect at all. I think that keeping him locked up the way he is is much more injurious to the reputation of the United States. And that is one reason I am here."

Lee may have helped write the codes, Richter said, but he knew little about weapons design. If another country had the tapes, Lee's personal help "wouldn't make much difference." At any rate, 99 percent of the material in the codes was unclassified, Richter told the judge, maybe 99.9 percent.

In fact, Richter said, Lee's codes would be about as useful to the Chinese as widely available unclassified codes such as Dyna 2-D. "We have a myriad of unclassified codes that are within a gnat's eyelash of the real ones, and I'm sure they [Chinese weapons scientists] have worked through those fairly well. And there is very little more they could get out of anything that has been described today."

Richter scoffed at testimony from the earlier bail hearings that the tapes represented a complete nuclear weapons design capability. Other nations might be curious about the codes, he said, but they would never attempt to use them to design their own weapons. They would use their own codes instead. Moreover, the W88 itself was so tricky to build that no country could make it work without nuclear testing—and China had given up testing in 1996.

At any rate, the tapes, even the graphics, didn't contain all the necessary details. The W88 had a key engineering item, unique to its submarine mission, that was not in the codes. Like other warheads, the W88 carried a bottle containing two isotopes of hydrogen—deuterium, and radioactive tritium—that would be injected into the hollow center of the plutonium primary just before detonation. This "boosting" was critical to creating a primary explosion powerful enough to ignite the fusion secondary.

But eventually, the tritium would decay into helium, ruining the effectiveness of the gas. In other missiles, the tritium bottles were simply changed frequently. In a submarine, the bottle was out of reach, impossible to switch often enough. The solution was a system named Terrazzo, which filtered the built-up helium from the bottle. Terrazzo, Richter said during a closed hearing, was not reflected anywhere in the physics codes or the input decks. Even if the Chinese had Lee's codes, they didn't have the W88.

In Richter's world view, the W88, America's most advanced warhead, would be of little use to anyone. A technologically unsophisticated country like Iraq couldn't build it and didn't need such "fancy stuff" to intimidate its neighbors. "A grumpy old bomb will go 'boom,' and kill you just as dead as a fancy one . . ." he said.

China didn't need the expensive, difficult W88, either. "The main thing is, they already have weapons that work. Why would they want to build other ones that they don't know about?"

U.S. weapons scientists, he implied, were motivated to design extreme weapons specifically because they were difficult. He called it "this self-challenging thing which many of us get involved with."

He put no stock in the earlier testimony by Younger, the Los Alamos weapons chief; Robinson, the president of Sandia; and Krajcik, the veteran Los Alamos physicist. They had called the codes the crown jewels of the weapons program, so important that their loss could change the balance of nuclear terror. Their testimony, like his own, was only opinion, not fact, Richter testified.

Richter had an explanation for their testimony: "I would probably have said the same things if I were in their position. If they returned to their labs after having said that their work there was less than the most important in the world, then they'd most likely be lynched.

"There would be a furor about it, believe me . . . if you have employees working and they don't think what they are doing is the most important thing in the world, they are no good."

In his folksy way, Richter minimized even the drawing of the interior of the W88 that was included on one of Lee's tapes. "The big question is, 'How would that be translated into the materials that make up a nuclear bomb?' And there is a huge gulf between what you can shine on a wall in your opaque projector and what you build with real materials like plutonium and explosives and uranium and so forth."

Under cross examination by Stamboulidis, Richter freely admitted that he had told a friend that if he were a juror he would vote to acquit Lee, even before seeing the evidence. Richter testified that his intelligence work in Washington taught him that the capital was a sieve of leaks but no one was ever prosecuted. "The proper punishment for leaking classified information was you get your clearance pulled and you get fired. Well, that happened to Dr. Lee sometime back, and I think that is enough. That's why I would vote to acquit."

At the December bail hearings, Parker had been convinced to keep Lee in jail by what appeared to be a consensus of scientific expert opinion that Lee was a danger to the country. Now the judge was being told, by equally or more prominent scientists, that it simply wasn't true. Armageddon retreated; there was a far different tone in the courtroom. Richter even offered the judge an alternative explanation for Lee's actions. "Never attribute to malice what can be adequately explained by stupidity," he said. "There has been a great effort to find a connection, an espionage connection, and that hasn't been found. And so what is left? Stupidity is the best I can come up with." A murmur of agreement rose from a handful of weaponeers in the gallery.

"Finally, somebody has said what tons of us have been wanting to say for eight months," said Bill Sullivan who, with his wife Nance Crow, was among Lee's staunchest advocates.

To the delight of many weapons scientists, Richter was debunking a myth used both to jail Lee and artificially prop up political support for Stockpile Stewardship, a $4.8-billion-a-year program. Many felt the testimony of Younger, Krajcik, and Robinson smacked of political boosterism for the program rather than reflecting the quirky nature of the codes themselves.

In truth, Richter said, the weapons codes are often faulty: Real nuclear bombs often behave very differently from the software's predictions. "Nuclear devices are kind of funny and tricky that way," said Richter. The true expertise of a designer lies in the intuitive knowledge of where to tweak the codes and the weapons design to make them work, he said. Those are real nuclear secrets.

After the lunch break, Holscher demonstrated Lee's support in the community. In dramatic contrast to the technical testimony of the morning, Holsher asked the judge's permission to bring up to the bench seventeen of Lee's family and friends who had pledged their homes as collateral for his bail. All of them—including people like Sullivan and Crow, who had never met Lee—stood and reiterated their understanding that any violation of the release conditions would cost them their life savings. The judge thanked them all.

In the courtroom the next morning, the atmosphere was electric. Messemer was called by the defense to face up to his errant "résumé" testimony from eight months earlier. As quickly as he could, he admitted the obvious, that he had

provided "incorrect" testimony. He had made an "honest mistake" in character-
izing some of Lee's actions as deceptive, and he apologized to Parker.

But Holscher wouldn't let him off that easy. Animated and angry, he hammered away at the agent. Hadn't he read Ling's grand jury testimony before the
bail hearing? Didn't he review the 302s, in which Ling never uttered the word
"résumé" in connection with Lee and his tapes? Wasn't it true that Messemer
knew at the December hearing that the defense did not yet have copies of the
transcript and reports, and thus had no way of knowing that his testimony was
false? Wasn't he the government's most important witness?

"Do you agree, Agent Messemer, that you testified under oath on December 13th, 1999, quote, 'Dr. Lee represented to the T-15 employee that he wished
to download a résumé'?"

"Yes," Messemer said.

"And that testimony was false?"

"Mr. Holscher, at no time did I intentionally provide false testimony. I
made a simple inadvertent error."

"That wasn't my question," Holscher prodded. "That testimony was false?"

"My testimony was incorrect."

Messemer, who had made it a point in December to turn in the witness box
and address the judge directly, wasn't looking at the judge now. He had no explanation for his mistake except that Ling had once remarked in passing that a
tape might be useful for keeping a résumé.

In rapid-fire questioning, Holscher showed that Messemer had no room
for excuses. The agent had interviewed Ling, written up the 302, and had spoken with Ling again three or four times in person and two or three times on the
phone before the December bail hearings. He also helped Ling prepare for his
grand jury testimony. Messemer should have known Ling's words inside out.
No one mentioned that Gorence, as the lead prosecutor, also had a responsibility to review Ling's words and guard against false or inaccurate testimony by his
lead witness.

The agent then confessed to other discrepancies. He earlier testified that
Lee had sent letters overseas seeking employment. The assumption was that
Lee might steal the codes to take with him to a new job. But Messemer admitted that while agents found the letters in Lee's house, there was no evidence
that he had actually mailed them, despite an international investigation. (Ironically, it turned out later that there *was* some evidence that Lee had mailed the
letters.)

Messemer had claimed that Lee had failed to disclose meetings with several
Chinese weapons scientists when he traveled, with laboratory approval, to the

Beijing conference in 1986. But Holscher produced a copy of the trip report that Lee filed upon his return, which clearly listed his contacts with the scientists.

Messemer had also testified that Lee failed to disclose his correspondence with Chinese scientists, beyond acknowledging that he had received a Christmas card. But again Messemer retreated. He agreed with Holscher that Lee had indeed disclosed his correspondence. Specifically, Lee had told FBI agents during the March 5, 1999, interview that he had discussed math problems in an exchange of letters with the Chinese.

Messemer's credibility was in shreds.

The next morning, he was back on the stand. Holscher shifted his approach, using the prosecution's lead witness to paint a rosy portrait of the defendant who sat nearby. Messemer readily admitted that in numerous interviews, Lee's coworkers in X Division portrayed him as apolitical, uninterested in foreign affairs.

"Oblivious?" Holscher asked.

"That is the theme that has emerged," Messemer said.

Holscher asked whether Lee had a myopic, tunnel-vision view of work, showing interest only in writing his own computer codes.

"He did have a rather limited focus," Messemer conceded.

Despite years of investigation, there was no evidence Lee had ever passed classified information. Messemer acknowledged that Lee willingly talked with FBI agents on twenty occasions, breaking off the relationship only after agents threatened him with the death penalty by invoking the Rosenbergs. The FBI agent also agreed that Lee seldom went into a special high-security area known as the weapons vault, where full-scale models of nuclear weapons were stored. A spy presumably would find the vault a useful place to visit.

The half-day bail hearing had stretched out to three days. The courtroom regulars scored it a clear victory for the defense. But the lawyers were quick to point out that, even if Parker granted bail, the government could appeal. The appeal could take weeks or months to resolve, during which time Lee would remain in his cell. Could the prosecutors, having advanced such extreme scenarios about the consequences to the country, now let him go on bail without an appeal?

And how would it look when Lee went home and nothing happened—no helicopters, no commandos, no secret messages? Cline predicted to associates that once Lee got bail, the case would be, for all practical purposes, at an end. Overnight, Lee would go from being the fictional spy of the century to just another Los Alamos retiree tending his garden, albeit a retiree with around-the-clock FBI surveillance. Lee could stay home while the lawyers finished off what was left of the case.

Six days later, Parker announced his ruling. Classification questions were holding up his long memo of legal points, but he didn't want to wait any longer to reveal his intentions. Lee would be going home. Gentleman Jim Parker was polite in his language. His order explained that the "totality of relevant information" that he had read and heard from December to the recent bail hearings "no longer has the requisite clarity and persuasive character" needed to keep the defendant behind bars.

Lee's lawyers phoned the detention center in Santa Fe and asked jailers to get word to him about the ruling, but they guessed he would hear it on the radio first. Alberta was overjoyed with the news that her father would be getting out of his orange jumpsuit and coming home to his own bed and his home cooking. Brian Sun, the family's civil lawyer, was more reserved. "We just do not know" about an appeal, he said.

———————

Parker convened a hearing the next week to hammer out the details of the house arrest. Lee would go home Friday, August 30, the judge said. Bail of a million dollars would be secured by the homes of Wen Ho and Sylvia, their neighbors the Marshalls, and Lee's younger brother and sister-in-law, Lucky and Patty Lee.

The conditions of his "house incarceration" were extreme. They seemed to validate the government's assumption that Lee, his wife, and their two grown children were spies, even though no one had been charged with espionage and the government was now alleging that Lee's crime was related to a job search. The conditions called for Lee to be monitored by a radio transmitter attached to his ankle. His telephone—cordless not allowed—would be electronically blocked from receiving calls except for a handful of court-appointed numbers. Only Lee and his wife would be allowed to live in their three-bedroom house, not Alberta or Chung. No one else could enter, except the Marshalls, who had agreed to act as Lee's court-appointed custodians, and Lee's children. Alberta and Chung could visit only with an FBI agent sitting in the room. In his usual back-row seat in the courtroom, Lee's friend Bob Clark was steaming. "To suggest that the entire family would engage in espionage is absurd," he complained.

No matter how restrictive the conditions, Stamboulidis continued to say that they were insufficient. Desperate to keep Lee in jail, he even expressed his anxiety that Wen Ho and Sylvia would be able to talk to each other alone. With the hearing teetering toward the surreal, Stamboulidis suggested that Lee might give his wife a secret coded message, which she would pass along to a foreign agent in the grocery store—while trailed closely by FBI agents—that would direct the agent to the missing tapes. Parker questioned why, after all Lee had been through, would he now involve his wife in an espionage scheme "that might subject her to the death penalty."

At one point in the hearing, Parker agreed to amend his bail order to allow firefighters to enter the house if it went up in flames. There was, mercifully, a moment of comic relief. Stamboulidis asked the judge to allow FBI agents to inspect all deliveries to the house, such as "a clown" or "flowers or whatever."

"Flowers?" the patient judge asked incredulously, provoking laughter in the courtroom.

———

Friday, August 30, came with an air of celebration. In White Rock, Lee's neighbors prepared to line Barcelona Street with waving American flags to greet him as he passed into house arrest. The Marshalls were throwing a party in his honor, though he wouldn't be allowed to travel any further than his backyard. Supporters had hung signs on mailboxes and trees proclaiming WELCOME HOME, DR. LEE and FBI GO HOME.

The FBI had conducted an exhaustive search of Lee's home, cars, and garden the day before, finding nothing of interest.

In Albuquerque, Stamboulidis had requested an emergency hearing to urge Parker to delay Lee's release until an appeal could be filed with the Tenth Circuit Court of Appeals in Denver.

That morning, Parker gathered the lawyers together in his courtroom, and federal marshals drove Lee down from Santa Fe. As noon approached, a smiling Parker was prepared to reject Stamboulidis's request. In his hands, the judge held a seventeen-page memorandum that he was ready to read aloud before sending Lee home on bail. Suddenly, the judge's assistant walked to the bench and handed Parker a fax. His face dropped. It was a one-line order from the Tenth U.S. Circuit Court of Appeals. "Release of appellee Wen Ho Lee is stayed pending further order from this court," was all it said.

The stay was a surprise to both Parker and the defense attorneys. "It is not clear to me that this is any longer under this court's jurisdiction," Parker said softly.

Cline and Hollander were outraged. They had specifically asked the appeals court and Stamboulidis to inform them if the appeals court was going to consider issuing a stay, so the judges could hear Lee's side of the issue. That was the federal rule. Stamboulidis denied that he was party to any deception. The request for the stay came from Justice Department headquarters in Washington, he said.

Hollander phoned Patrick Fisher, the clerk of the court in Denver, seeking an explanation. Someone from Justice Department headquarters had called to say that a request for a stay would be forthcoming. Two of the appeals court justices, Deanell Tacha and David Ebel, had acted on their own instead of waiting to hear from Justice officials in Washington. Hollander faxed off a motion of her own, asking for a reconsideration of the stay, but it did no good.

Holscher, Hollander, and Cline had been snookered. The marshals drove Lee back to jail.

———

Parker didn't get to read his memo aloud, but it went far beyond recognizing Lee as a proper candidate for bail. It was a withering critique of the merits of the case.

New evidence, he wrote, "tends to show that the information Dr. Lee took is less valuable than the government had led the court to believe it was and is less sensitive than previously described to the court." In other words, he had been misled.

The judge described a case in which the government's evidence had failed to live up to claims made by federal prosecutors and their witnesses. The defense attorneys had produced "evidence that FBI agent Robert Messemer testified falsely or inaccurately" the previous December. The memorandum implicitly raised serious doubts about the government's ability to win a conviction. Parker methodically moved through the government's evidence and concluded that it lent itself to a less sinister interpretation of Lee's actions than prosecutors had claimed.

In December, Holscher and Cline, then strangers to the world of nuclear weapons and not yet armed with grand jury transcripts and witness reports, had had no way to counter the testimony about "crown jewels," the "balance of power," and nefarious behavior that Gorence used to paint "an extremely dark picture of Dr. Lee and his actions."

"The totality of the information of which I now have knowledge presents a tableau different from that described by the government last December," Parker wrote. In another passage, he went straight to the crucial issue of intent. "The government has never presented direct evidence" of such intent, he said. Even the circumstantial evidence presented by witnesses had been "tempered" since December.

Parker cited the declarations from Agnew and Goad that much of the information on the tapes was already in the public domain—in newspapers, magazines, and on the Internet. Some of the codes existed in unclassified versions, Parker noted. Holscher and Cline's efforts to match the prosecution expert-for-expert had paid dividends.

There had been new testimony, "all of which tends to show that the information Dr. Lee took is less valuable than the government had led the court to believe it was."

Federal prosecutors faced a high threshold of proving beyond a reasonable doubt that Lee intended to harm the United States or help a foreign nation. The supposedly extreme sensitivity of the contents of Lee's tapes was a linchpin in the proof of his intent. Now the sensitivity of the tape's contents—and therefore Lee's intent—had slipped into a haze of ambiguity, and any such ambiguity could be fatal for the government's chances of getting a conviction.

As one government official said, "We wouldn't have [sought the indictment] if we thought it would come down to a battle of experts . . . it always hinged on the value of the information."

Parker's memorandum could have been written by Cline. The judge cited a declaration that Vrooman faxed from Montana, swearing as the former head of counterintelligence at Los Alamos that he believed that Lee "did not intend to harm the United States, is not a danger to United States' security, and will not turn the tapes over to a foreign power."

Page after page, Parker went on, sometimes reading into the evidence a meaning opposite from what the government had argued. Lee's calls to the computer help desk for advice on deleting files? "This suggests that Dr. Lee's actions may not have been as surreptitious, clandestine, and secretive as the government originally indicated."

The memorandum was understated, but Parker had taken an ax to the government's case. The "job prospect" motive hardly seemed to merit life-penalty charges. "Enhancing one's résumé is less sinister than the treacherous motive the government, at least by implication, ascribed to Dr. Lee at the end of last year," Parker dryly noted.

Between the lines was the unmistakable message that the easygoing judge was very angry at having been misled by the prosecutors and their witnesses from the FBI and Los Alamos. The prosecutor undoubtedly had counted on using the same witnesses at trial. The judge's memo raised the question: How much of a case did Stamboulidis have left?

After missing freedom by mere minutes, Lee was driven back to Santa Fe, where he put on his orange jail clothes again and went back into his cell. The lawyers went back to their offices. The flags were put away in White Rock. A hearing in Denver on the bail appeal was set for Monday, September 11.

———————

In Washington, Justice Department officials read Parker's memo and winced. No one wanted to see this happen in such a high-profile case. The presiding judge didn't seem to like anything about the case—not the evidence, the heavy-weight witnesses, or the lead FBI agent.

Bad news was everywhere, and worse loomed ahead. Cline had won the first round of CIPA hearings and another crucial one was approaching. With the judge on Cline's side, it was a good bet that the graymail defense was going to succeed, forcing the government to free the defendant with no conditions at all. He could go straight to China if he wanted, and it was obvious he wouldn't spend a minute telling the FBI what he had done with the tapes. It was a bleak picture. It was time to cut a deal.

On September 5, the first day after the long Labor Day weekend, Attorney General Janet Reno gathered her advisors on the case in a windowless confer-ence room on the top floor of the Justice Department. FBI Director Louis Freeh, who had argued for an aggressive prosecution the year before, was now supporting a plea bargain. "What I care about more than punishing this guy," Freeh declared, "is finding out where those tapes are."

He also wanted to head off courtroom disclosure of internal memos criti-cal of Messemer. The prosecutors in New Mexico were ready to deal as well.

The mistakes of the case were piling up. The heavy-handed decisions at the onset, first the gamble of indicting Lee on charges that required proof of ill in-tent and then the orders to keep him in solitary confinement, had sent the case down the wrong track from the beginning. The exaggerations required to sup-port such a case had given the defense an easy target to shoot down. The hy-perbole became the focus of the case rather than Lee's tapes, putting the prosecution on the defense.

Judge Leavy was already talking to both sides about mediation, as Parker had ordered. Mediation in a criminal case is unusual, but now the framework would prove handy. Plea negotiations went forward beneath the radar of public attention. For the Justice Department, any deal would have to require Lee to tell the truth about what he did with the tapes. The explanation had to be physically verifiable by FBI agents in the field; the Bureau had no trust in Lee's word.

For his part, Lee wanted to get out of jail, of course, and never go back. He had not confessed behind bars, as the government thought he might. That notion was apparently wishful thinking from the beginning; the FBI's behavioral profile of Lee had not supported the theory, according to an official who read it.

Lee's lawyers wanted a guarantee he wouldn't be further prosecuted. If possible, they wanted him to plead guilty to a charge that was not among the fifty-nine counts listed in the draconian indictment they loathed so much.

The extraordinary news of a deal was announced on Sunday, September 10. The arrangement called for Lee to plead guilty to one felony count on Monday morning and go home immediately afterward with no strings attached other than a requirement that he fully answer the questions of the FBI for a year.

Alberta and Chung Lee released a statement. "We are just simply thrilled that he's coming home," they said. Their father "never had any intent to harm a country that he loves."

The crowd at the Albuquerque federal courthouse on Monday morning was full of familiar faces. The same friends, family, supporters, and reporters who had been there ten days ago expecting Lee's release were back again. In White Rock, the flags were again readied. But before the hearing began, Cline telephoned Stamboulidis. There's something you should know, Cline said; we don't want you to be surprised. There are not just seven missing tapes. There could be fourteen, or twenty. Wen Ho made copies, but he's not sure how many.

The prosecution was caught flat-footed. Despite the largest computer investigation in its history, the FBI had missed the copies completely. Once again, the agents' prime source of information was Lee himself. His story, as he would later tell it, was that he began making copies around 1995, soon after the computer in his X Division office was equipped with a tape drive. The tapes, according to Lee, were not exact copies of the weapons codes that he had put on his tapes in 1993 and 1994. He had only copied the unclassified material, he claimed. And like the other tapes, the copies had been destroyed.

Stamboulidis didn't say much in response. But forty-five minutes later he called Cline back and said, "We need to delay this."

The crowd in the courtroom could only guess at the reason for the delay. For three hours, spirits slowly sagged as lawyers came and went from closed-door meetings. The plea-bargain agreement would have to be adjusted to account for the additional tapes.

Late in the afternoon, a disappointed Parker returned to the courtroom to "regretfully" announce that the hearing on Lee's plea and his release would be postponed until Wednesday. At the end of the day, as the prisoner was being led back to jail, a spectator cried out, "Hang in there, Dr. Lee," and the usually reserved audience burst into sustained applause.

The joke circulating in the courtroom was that the biggest danger Lee faced now was food poisoning from the aging potato salad waiting for him at his homecoming in White Rock.

Judge Leavy, the mediator, flew in from Portland, Oregon, the next day to meet with the lawyers. Late that night, the plea bargain was revived.

———————

At 7:50 A.M. the next morning, Holscher strode up the courthouse steps with a broad smile. "It's a good morning, a very good morning," he said.

But the 9 A.M. hearing was postponed until 10, and then another hour, as lawyers went over the final wording of the deal. In the courtroom, Lee was relaxed. He wore his usual gray suit with a blue tie. This time, the security officials didn't object when he waved to friends in the audience. Sylvia Lee sat in the front row with her two children.

Finally, at 11:02, Parker took the bench in his black robes. "I understand the parties have finally agreed," he announced.

The courtroom was alive with anticipation. Courthouse clerks and secretaries curious to see the end of a celebrated case took seats in the jury box. Lawyers and FBI agents with a connection to the case, including Messemer, showed up to witness the the assent.

The 5-foot-3-inch Lee stood between his much taller lawyers, Holscher and Cline, in the center of the room. He raised his right hand awkwardly and swore to tell the truth. He looked up at Parker behind the high bench and spoke in court for the first time since his arraignment nine months earlier. He told the judge his name was Wen Ho Lee—spelled "Wenho Lee"—he was sixty years old, with a Ph.D. in mechanical engineering from Texas A&M.

He answered a string of questions from the judge confirming that he understood his plea-bargain agreement. He was pleading guilty to Count 57. Reading from a sheet of paper, he admitted that "on a date certain in 1994, I used an unsecured computer in T-Division to download a document or writing related to the national defense." His sentence was 277 days, the time he had already served.

Lee agreed to submit to ten days of questioning by the FBI and remain available for additional questions for a year. If he lied, he could be prosecuted for perjury. Parker seemed pained to have to advise Lee that as a convicted felon he would not be allowed to vote. "You will be giving up your right to cast a ballot that would express your opinion of what was done to you." Parker's language hinted at his anger. Lee said he understood.

Lee leaned forward into the microphone and entered his plea: "Guilty."

As required by the plea agreement, Cline immediately handed Stamboulidis a sworn statement from Lee, explaining what he had done with the tapes. The Justice Department had been waiting for that piece of paper for eighteen months. Parker called a break. Stamboulidis, who was headed for the bathroom, took Lee's statement with him. There he read Lee's claim that he threw the tapes—for which the FBI had searched worldwide—into a trash dumpster in X Division. The prosecutor came back down the hall with Lee's folded declaration jutting from his suit pocket and a smile on his face. If Lee was telling the truth, it meant the crown jewels never got any farther away from the lab than the local dump.

When the formalities of the plea were over, Parker shifted slightly and spoke.

"Dr. Lee, you have pled guilty to a serious crime. It's a felony offense. For that you deserve to be punished. In my opinion, you have been punished harshly, both by the severe conditions of pretrial confinement and by the fact that you have lost valuable rights as a citizen."

Beginning with that statement, the conservative Republican jurist embarked on a heartfelt soliloquy about democracy, politics, justice, and his own personal feelings.

At Lee's early bail hearing, Parker said, he had been convinced by the extreme arguments of former U.S. Attorney John Kelly and his assistant, Bob Gorence, "that releasing you, even under the most stringent of conditions, would be a danger to the safety of this nation." Parker was particularly bothered by Kelly's resignation to run for Congress shortly afterward. When Parker had asked prosecutors to improve jail conditions, they had ignored his requests. Until the plea bargain, the "Executive Branch" still fought bail as an "unacceptable extreme danger."

"What I believe remains unanswered is the question: What was the government's motive in insisting on your being jailed pretrial under extraordinarily onerous conditions of confinement until today, when the Executive Branch agrees that you may be set free essentially unrestricted? This makes no sense to me. Why were you charged with the many Atomic Energy Act counts for which the penalty is life imprisonment, all of which the Executive Branch has now moved to dismiss and which I just dismissed?"

Parker noted pointedly that the decision to use the Atomic Energy Act charges was made by Attorney General Janet Reno.

Something extraordinary was happening in the courtroom.

"Dr. Lee, you're a citizen of the United States and so am I, but there is a difference between us. You had to study the Constitution of the United States to become a citizen. Most of us are citizens by reason of the simple serendipitous fact of our birth here."

Parker offered a brief civics lesson on the branches of the federal government, with this moral: "The Executive Branch has enormous power, the abuse of which can be devastating to our citizens.

"I believe you were terribly wronged by being held in custody pretrial in the Santa Fe County Detention Center under demeaning, unnecessarily punitive conditions. I am truly sorry that I was led by our Executive Branch of government to order your detention last December."

The courtroom, crowded though it was, was deathly quiet. The judge's apology was spellbinding.

"I am sad that I was induced in December to order your detention, since by the terms of the plea agreement that frees you today without conditions, it becomes clear that the Executive Branch now concedes, or should concede, that it was not necessary to confine you last December or at any time before your trial."

There were teary eyes across the courtroom. Bill Sullivan was crying in the back row.

"It is only the top decision makers in the Executive Branch, especially the Department of Justice and the Department of Energy and locally, during December [a reference to Kelly], who have caused embarrassment by the way this case began and was handled. They did not embarrass me alone. They have embarrassed our entire nation and each of us who is a citizen of it.

"I might say that I am also sad and troubled because I do not know the real reasons why the Executive Branch has done all of this. We will not learn why because the plea agreement shields the Executive Branch from disclosing a lot of information that it was under order to produce that might have supplied the answer.

"Although, as I indicated, I have no authority to speak on behalf of the Executive Branch, the President, the Vice President, the Attorney General, or the Secretary of the Department of Energy, as a member of the Third Branch of the United States Government, the Judiciary, the United States Courts, I sincerely apologize to you, Dr. Lee, for the unfair manner you were held in custody by the Executive Branch.

"Court will be in recess."

"I've never seen anything like it," said Cline, who was not known for displays of emotion. "It was like a movie. I was shaking when I walked out." Lee met with his family in a tearful, joyous private reunion in a conference room before marching outside, flanked by his family and lawyers, to stand before the television cameras.

In the blinding New Mexico sun, he thanked his supporters and said he was looking forward to being home with his family. Then he smiled. "Next few days, I'm going fishing."

EPILOGUE

George Stamboulidis soldiered out to talk with the reporters outside the courthouse. He did his best with what little he had. He defended the plea agreement, saying it would prevent nuclear secrets from being revealed in open court—an admission that Cline's graymail defense had won the war. At any rate, the prosecutor said, the case was always about national security first, and secondarily a criminal trial. Seen that way, it was more important to the country to have Lee finally say under oath what he had done with all the missing 3M 6150 tapes than it was to send him to prison. Even if a jury had returned guilty verdicts, Lee "might go to prison for a very long time, but we might never learn what happened to those tapes."

Similar sentiments were echoed in Washington by Attorney General Reno and FBI Director Freeh. Parker's apology was the only one Lee would get.

Lee arrived home in late afternoon to a warm welcome. The flags and signs at last served their purpose. The party at the Marshalls' house was alive with smiles. Lee thanked his neighbors for their support, saying, "They made me very strong when I was in jail." As the night wore on, Lee stood in a corner discussing computer codes with his friend Bob Clark. It was as if Lee had just left the room for a moment and then come back to resume his conversation.

Sylvia had rearranged the furniture to her liking in Wen Ho's absence, guided by the principles of Feng Shui, the Chinese tradition of design that seeks harmony by observing the flow of energy through the home. Awful as it was to have her husband in jail, for a few months she had been out from under his thumb. But within hours of his return, he had moved the furniture back. A family friend joked that life had been easier for Sylvia with Wen Ho in jail. In his first real conversation with his daughter, who had campaigned so hard for his release, he asked Alberta what she was going to do with her life. Just like old times, she thought.

Parker's speech created a nationwide stir. When asked about it the next day, President Clinton said, "The whole thing was quite troubling to me."

"I think it's very difficult to reconcile the two positions," he said, "that one day he's a terrible risk to the national security, and the next day they're making a plea agreement for an offense far more modest than what had been alleged." Most of Lee's supporters didn't give the president much credit for his sympathy. They wondered why, if Clinton was so troubled, he didn't talk to his own attorney general about the case much sooner.

As he was leaving office a few months later, Clinton issued a pardon for John Deutch's security transgressions. Lee, however, did not get a pardon, despite a petition drive by Cecilia Chang and others.

In the weeks after Lee's release, there was a series of congressional hearings in Washington. "Dr. Lee is no hero," Reno testified. "He is not an absent-minded professor. He is a felon. He committed a very serious, calculated crime, and he pled guilty to it." Senator Arlen Specter, Republican and ardent foe of Reno, chastised her one minute for being too tough on Lee, the next minute for being too lenient, with no apparent sense of irony.

At another hearing, Bob Vrooman and Notra Trulock appeared together. The highlight of Trulock's testimony was his disclosure that he was told by *New York Times* reporter James Risen that the anonymous source who gave Wen Ho Lee's name to the *Times* on March 8, 1999, the day Lee was fired, was Secretary of Energy Bill Richardson. Risen, who was in the committee room, left quickly.

The Lee family quickly announced that deals had been struck for a book and a TV miniseries on ABC, easing the Lees' financial worries. Alberta was soon scouting scene locations around Los Alamos with the producer.

Notra Trulock also began writing a book, which he called *Kindred Spirit*. When he circulated a portion of it after leaving the Energy Department, the FBI came to his house and took the hard drive from his computer, claiming that the manuscript he sent out contained classified information. Whether or not it did, it definitely contained a lot of criticism of the FBI, which Trulock believed was the real motive for the raid.

Trulock fell in with Judicial Watch, a conservative organization that repeatedly sued the Clinton administration. In 2001, he found himself out of a job and bankrupt. "If I'm such a mastermind," he groused, "how come I'm unemployed and broke?" On Trulock's behalf, Judicial Watch sued Lee, Vrooman, Bill Richardson, and DOE official Charles Washington for slander. Los Alamos picked up Vrooman's legal fees, accepting his argument that his statements were accurate. His criticism of Trulock was part of his official and unofficial campaign to defend the lab.

Danny Stillman wrote a book about his overseas adventures called *Inside China's Nuclear Weapons Program.* When he submitted it for classification review, the government said it couldn't be published, being full of classified information and potential to upset China. Stillman argued that it was the Chinese who willingly gave him the information in the first place, and filed a lawsuit.

The *New York Times,* battered for its accusatory, worst-since-the-Rosenbergs coverage, ran a long note from the editors that strived to apologize without admitting guilt, a sort of journalistic nolo contendere. The paper promised to take another look at the case. When that follow-up story ran four months later, it hardly addressed the *Times's* own role.

Judge Parker made the news again. In October, he scolded federal prosecutors for seeking a five-year sentence for a convicted New Mexico perjurer, pointing out that the prosecutors' boss, President Clinton, had asked leniency for his own false testimony in the Paula Jones case. Parker instead imposed a fifteen-month sentence.

In November, Walter Goad died of a stroke. He was seventy-five. Wen Ho Lee came to the memorial service and offered his thanks and condolences to Goad's family.

Back in White Rock, friends asked Lee how he could stand jail so long and resist the government's pressure to confess to something. But only rarely would he talk about his incarceration—it was behind him and no more needed to be said. As for the government, he would retell a story that is supposedly about Beethoven and Goethe. The composer and the poet were walking beside a street and encountered a group of noblemen. Goethe stepped into the street to accommodate them, but the composer plowed ahead. When Goethe asked how he dared be so impertinent, he replied, "Why should I step aside? I am Beethoven, and they are but noblemen."

So Lee would tell his listeners, "Why should I yield to them?"

No one wanted to say it publicly, but the defense team was well aware that its client's incarceration had its strategic advantages. Every day he spent in solitary was a black mark against the government, in the eyes of the public and the judge.

Lee's debriefings were held in the fall and winter, in a cramped secure room at Sandia National Laboratories in Albuquerque. The camera was on him the entire time as he went through his required sixty hours of sworn testimony. Stamboulidis was there, along with other Justice Department lawyers and FBI agents. More investigators were in another room, watching on television and sending additional questions to Lee's inquisitors via a laptop. Outside stood a Winnebago command center, possibly sending a live feed to Washington.

Lee wore his habitual blue jeans and was always accompanied by Cline. One of the FBI agents translated questions into Mandarin when Lee appeared to have trouble understanding them in English.

The FBI and the Justice Department clashed over what to pursue during the limited time available. Prosecutors were after the fate of the tapes. The FBI probed for details of Lee's involvement overseas, particularly in Taiwan, apparently still trying to prove he was a spy. The agents held up photos. Do you know this person? And this person?

At lunchtime, everyone—Lee, Cline, FBI, prosecutors—headed to a nearby McDonald's for burgers. Diners recognized Lee from TV and newspapers. They introduced themselves, shook his hand, and wished him well. The FBI agents, sitting nearby, bristled at the notion of Lee the celebrity.

The code writer provided new details. Lee told of more dinners with Taiwanese and Chinese weapons scientists at his home. He at first denied, then admitted to, viewing design data on his office computer for the three latest U.S. warheads—the W87 Peacekeeper, the W80 Tomahawk, and the W88.

Lee offered two explanations for his famous tapes. He claimed to have made the classified tapes as backups in case of computer failure, as he told 60 Minutes a year earlier. The unclassified tapes, Lee said, contained codes that he planned to use to launch a consulting career when he retired from the lab. The question of how many tapes he made in all will probably never be answered. Lee told the FBI he didn't remember. Lee took a polygraph test. The results were kept secret, but it appeared that Lee did not pass with flying colors. One person familiar with the case said the outcome "was as inconclusive as all the others."

In late November 2000, while the questioning continued, the FBI dug up a section of the Los Alamos landfill in search of the tapes. If Lee had thrown them in the X Division trash dumpster, as he said, they should have been buried in the area of the dump reserved for the lab's garbage. The agents zeroed in on a specific section that was filled around January 1999, when Lee said he had tossed out the tapes.

Los Alamos employees were tickled by the image of the agents in their biosuits crawling around in the stench of the refuse. The agents uncovered a handful of tapes, which they quickly shipped off to Washington for analysis. A DOE official, summoned by the FBI, found the smelly tapes to contain nothing but unclassified files unrelated to weapons work. They weren't Lee's, however. The tapes that had created a national furor were never found.

Lee had lied about the tapes to his family, his co-workers, his lawyer, and prosecutors. The FBI agents had always insisted on verifiable proof that the tapes had been destroyed, but they never got it.

The plea-bargain agreement stipulated that Lee could be charged with perjury if he lied, but there was no way to disprove his story about the trash dumpster, and no appetite for another public fight. The mystery of the tapes, and Lee, remained intact. The entire episode of Lee's debriefings and the unsuccessful search for the tapes ended on a frustrating note of ambiguity. With Lee, it always ended that way.

For Lee's sixty-first birthday in December, Cecilia Chang organized a large party in a hotel banquet room near San Francisco, as she had the year before. But she ran into conflict with the Southern California nexus into whose orbit the Lees had fallen: Holscher, the criminal lawyer; Brian Sun, the family lawyer; Stacy Cohen, the publicist; and the TV and book people. Holscher had some concern about Lee making public statements while the FBI still had an interest in him. But from the perspective of some Bay Area supporters, it seemed as though Lee's new handlers didn't want any part of an event they couldn't control. The e-mails among Lee's supporters were filled with the controversy. Was this really about the FBI, or was Wen Ho saving himself for the publicity tour for his book? Had Wen Ho and Alberta gone Hollywood?

San Francisco attorney Edward Liu joined in the electronic discourse from a slightly different angle. Isn't it about time, he wrote, that Lee told us what he did with the tapes? That idea, however, went nowhere.

Chang did not give up on the birthday party. She had started wenholee.org, helped get the defense fund off the ground, organized rallies, learned how to deal with the press. She had butted heads with the middle-aged Chinese businessmen who ran the prestigious Committee of 100, who thought she was stubborn. She *was* stubborn, but she got things done. Berkeley's Ling-chi Wang thought the criticism of her was largely sexist. On December 21, five hundred people showed up for the dinner party. For some, publicly supporting Lee was easier now that he no longer was under the cloud of federal prosecution.

The entire Southern California contingent was there, too, and Holscher charmed the audience with a short talk about the work of the defense team. But it was Lee who seemed most eloquent. Speaking haltingly, very much with a Chinese accent after almost forty years in America, he told the story of the guard who brought him a cookie in his cell on his sixtieth birthday.

"I come from Taiwan. Like many people, I get a job. I work hard like so many people." He followed the American dream of house and family. But his experience showed that was not enough. "You cannot just work hard and do the best you can. I think you need to do some project related to politics."

"My lesson," he said, "you must respect yourself before others can respect you." The crowd offered a standing ovation, then sang "Happy Birthday" in Chinese and English.

Back at Los Alamos, a scientist asked John Richter asked him why he "did it," why he brought his considerable reputation to bear on Lee's behalf. "People in this country should have a speedy trial," Richter replied. "Eight months is enough, and somebody had to do something about it." Later, he told a reporter, "If I had any influence in getting him out, I figured that's a payback."

As Lee quietly endured in jail—listening to classical music and writing a math textbook—a number of key players became casualties of the government's investigation. As former FBI China analyst Paul Moore put it, Lee's evasiveness and security breaches made him into the tar baby of counterintelligence. Suspicions of Lee didn't just add to one another; they *multiplied* upon one another, each new revelation making the odds of an innocent explanation vanishingly small. After a point, no one engaged in the case could let go.

"Once you get attached to him, you can't get unattached because you would have to suspend disbelief. If you're in counterintelligence, you just can't do that," Moore said. "You would be remiss or just incompetent to stop looking at him, because every time you look at him, he looks worse."

In the end, however, many of Lee's pursuers ended up as tarred as he was.

A year after Lee's release, the declassified portions of the Bellows Report took broad swipes at almost every investigator who touched the case. Bruno's administrative inquiry in particular was brutally dissected, though Bruno himself remained DOE's chief investigator.

Gorence and Conway had relinquished their posts as the state's top federal prosecutor and chief federal jurist. In 2001, Gorence was in private practice in Albuquerque, taking cases against the U.S. attorney's office. Conway presided over a diminished caseload, as a senior judge in semiretirement.

Two years after his committee's report made national headlines, Rep. Chris Cox was considered by the new Bush administration for appointment to the federal bench but did not get the nod. The Cox Report, however discredited, was reincarnated as a Republican fund-raising tool. Brent Bahler, the committee's press spokesman, abbreviated the report into a campaign mailer for the Republican National Committee. Bill Clinton and Al Gore shared its bright crimson cover with a communist star and a mushroom cloud.

Having lost his shot at becoming Al Gore's running mate, former U.N. ambassador and Energy Secretary Bill Richardson in 2001 was spreading word of his more modest ambition to be New Mexico's next governor. In the meantime, he straddled the political fences, as a board member for the Natural Resources Defense Council and as a consultant with Kissinger Associates.

In 2000, Steve Younger authored a paper, "Nuclear Weapons in the 21st Century," advocating the development of new, low-yield nuclear weapons for the United States. He argued they were necessary in part because of foreign espionage. In the spring of 2001, he was promoted to a lab job that took away his command of budgets and scientists. Soon after, Younger left Los Alamos for a Pentagon post.

The *Times*'s Risen and Gerth had reported that the story of Chinese nuclear espionage was the story of Notra Trulock III. That turned out to be truer than most knew. One man, hewing to his own ambitions and theories, had triggered an investigation of Wen Ho Lee for the potential death-penalty offense of espionage, sent Congress into a furor, and indirectly contributed to the heightening of Sino-U.S. tensions.

Trulock did manage to tighten security at the U.S. weapons labs and for a time prevent scientists from hobnobbing with the Russians and Chinese. Yet his hyping of the theft of the W88 not only failed to produce his "one good espionage case," it also misdirected the FBI from the real case—the compromise of fairly rudimentary secrets about the W88—and delayed that investigation by four years. Instead of propelling Trulock and the Energy Department to higher regard in the U.S. intelligence community, Kindred Spirit damaged the reputations of both. As of September 2001, the W88 spy, if one existed, had not been found.

Later, Trulock claimed the scientists of the Kindred Spirit Advisory Group and the FBI had sold him out to cover their own failings.

The FBI was tarred as well. The Bureau might have acted as a check on Trulock's excesses but did not. The FBI received clues at every level that its investigation was awry. Vrooman told Lieberman that the predicate was wrong; Lieberman passed those misgivings to his superiors in Albuquerque and Washington. One of them, Craig Schmidt, also received Dan Bruno's unedited administrative inquiry, which recommended a broader selection of institutions and people for investigation. Bruno's partner, Magers, had written a memo to headquarters advising the same. In September 1997, the CIA briefed Freeh himself on its assessment that the Chinese hadn't necessarily stolen the W88. The FBI director jotted notes on the discrepancy with what DOE was telling the Bureau, but he never made sure word reached Kindred Spirit's agents in the field. From Freeh down to the street, the FBI at every level had reason to question and perhaps halt Kindred Spirit.

The FBI and the Justice Department also seemed to miss one of the critical lessons of Kindred Spirit—that a case comprised of inflated claims is likely to collapse at some point. By December 1999, the Bellows review team, commissioned by Attorney General Janet Reno and staffed with prosecutors and FBI agents, already had discovered Trulock's overselling of Chinese espionage and the resulting misdirection of the FBI. In turn, Reno and the Justice Department might have taken extra care not to oversell the allegations of Sea Change. Yet that is precisely what Gorence and the Justice Department did from their first court appearances onward in December of that year.

In the spring of 2001, Freeh stepped down as director, amid criticism of the Bureau's handling of the Lee case, the Timothy McVeigh prosecution, and other problem cases. Congress and the White House called for a new accountability at the FBI and repair of its tarnished image.

"If a hostile intelligence service had launched a covert operation against the United States, it could not have been more successful in discrediting the criminal justice system, exploiting suspicions of racial profiling, demoralizing the career services of the Energy and Justice departments and the FBI, and diverting investigative attention from other suspects," observed John Martin, former chief of the Justice Department's Internal Security Section for twenty-six years.

"This case is a collusion of ineptness and political opportunism," said Bob Vrooman. "The only competent ones are Wen Ho Lee's attorneys."

As of 2001, Lee himself was retired, tending his garden and fishing. By September, a year after his sentencing by Parker, he was officially beyond the reach of the FBI's questions and collecting the proceeds of his miniseries and his ghost-written book, also released on audio CD and tape.

"He's beat the system," said Moore. "He knows it and everyone else knows it too." That, at least, was the counterintelligence view.

In spite of one of the largest investigations in FBI history, Lee remains an enigmatic figure.

"Ultimately," the *Times* observed in February 2001, "the case of Wen Ho Lee was a spy story in which the most tantalizing mystery was whether the central character ever was a spy." Ironically, it was the *Times*'s uncritical embrace of Trulock's story that hamstrung the FBI's chances to answer that question with more interviews. Instead, he got a lawyer and stopped talking to the FBI.

As former FBI Albuquerque chief David Kitchen said, in a comment as revealing of the FBI as of Lee, "It seemed like the more times you hit him upside the head, the more truth comes out."

Taken in sum, Lee's actions leave a sense of ambiguity. No single, overarching theory explains everything he did, perhaps because Lee's own motives were not necessarily coherent or well thought-out. In the end, his story fails to perfectly fit any pattern and remains stubbornly, idiosyncratically human.

Lee's own explanation for his actions—that he simply was backing up "his" computer files on tape—falls short of convincing. It is undercut by a number of critical facts. The tapes he created were most comprehensive in their collection of nuclear-weapons design codes, not—as one would expect in Lee's backup scenario—in his own specialty of hydrodynamics. And most of the codes weren't his.

Second, with just a few keystrokes, Lee easily could have made backup files on the secure side of the network. Los Alamos maintained a bank of tape drives specifically for the purpose of archiving files. Making backup copies there was the common practice among Lee's colleagues. If Lee distrusted that arrangement, he could have done what at least one coworker did—get permission to create a set of backup disks and store them within a laboratory safe.

Last, Lee claimed to friends that he began making backup tapes because he lost a year's worth of work in the late 1980s. But he began moving weapons files from the secure network into the open in April 1988. That's a full eight months before a disk crash on Los Alamos's Common File System resulted in temporarily lost data for a large number of X Division scientists. The January 1989 event was the most significant CFS crash in the late 1980s or early 1990s. If Lee lost data then, it was well after he began putting together his collection of weapons codes.

In any event, given Lee's history of dishonesty—his lies to the FBI, to friends, and to his own family—it is difficult to trust his version of his motives.

An alternative theory suggests Lee saw his tapes as an investment in semiretirement, the nest egg for a second career in academia or private consulting. Lee identified himself in the 1980s as a consultant to Taiwan, moonlighted with a hydrodynamics firm in the mid-1990s, and courted a Taiwanese consulting outfit in 1998. He spoke to friends about doing consulting work together after their retirement from Los Alamos. When Bob Clark asked whether Lee had in fact moved weapons codes to the lab's unclassified network, Lee replied that, no, he merely had copied MESA-2D—an unclassified but export-controlled code—to a tape for the purposes of consulting work down the road. "He said he would go to a university, get some grad students, and publish a lot," Clark said.

But if Lee wanted to be a consultant, many unclassified hydro codes were his for the asking. In fact, a number of the weapons codes and data files on Lee's tapes existed in unclassified form. He could have used these as he desired. Not only did he know of these codes, he busily tried to replace the weapons codes on his tapes with them in February 1999. Plenty of hydro experts turn to consulting using unclassified codes, and Lee easily could have done the same. Lastly, Lee the consultant wouldn't need input decks for H-bombs.

Another school of thought holds that Lee was a spy for China. Yet another claims he was a spy for Taiwan. Lee's actions—his longstanding relationships with scientists of both countries and his willingness, at least in Taiwan's case, to violate export controls—lend support to both theories.

In the Chinese case, Lee fit the FBI's model in myriad ways. He tried to be helpful to China's weapons scientists, coaching them on simulation problems that can be applied to weapons research but also to a wide variety of unclassified scientific simulations. He revealed his 1988 hotel-room encounter only under duress a decade later, and it was precisely the kind of encounter that FBI experience suggests poses the greatest risk for the loss of U.S. scientific secrets. Finally, the imbalance between Lee's inflated impressions of his own talent and his actual capabilities made him supremely vulnerable to one of the most common Chinese intelligence approaches—the obsequious but skillful appeal to ego.

Yet Lee's actions also clashed significantly with the FBI model. The very nature and size of Lee's downloads were, according to Moore, wholly inconsistent with the kind of information sought by China. Strange as it seems, Lee's tapes were too large a target for China's incrementalist method of gathering information. Even if Lee were directed by Chinese intelligence to steal America's weapons codes, it made no sense for him to leave the weapons files sitting scattered on four unclassified network directories, in some cases for as long as eleven years. An intelligence officer would have ordered him to sweep his trail clean well before his file erasures of 1999. Last, Lee had access to the physical and online vaults where Los Alamos stored nuclear-test data and actual bomb blueprints, arguably a more valuable target for Chinese intelligence. Yet no evidence suggests he copied any of these.

Taiwan was at least as plausible a suitor for Lee's knowledge. It was common for Taiwanese intelligence to seek recruits inside the Republic of China's air force, where Lee served a year. Early in Lee's career in the United States, he made contact with Taiwan's unofficial embassy and began sharing technical information, soon followed by what clearly appeared to be a formal tasking relationship with a Taiwanese intelligence officer.

Lee did not obtain approval before giving export-controlled documents to Taiwan and, again, only acknowledged the relationship under the duress of an FBI polygraph. And he openly offered his assistance to a Livermore scientist whom he thought in trouble for sharing technology with Taiwan. In the late 1990s, he literally spent weeks on the campus of Chung Shan Institute of Science and Technology—a longtime research partner of Taiwan's air force—and sought hydrodynamics work with a closely associated consulting firm. Both Chung Shan and at least one principal of the firm had been engaged in Taiwan's drive to research nuclear weapons in the 1970s and 1980s. While at Chung Shan, Lee dialed into Los Alamos's unclassified network, reached into his cache of weapons files, and pulled out an unclassified—but export-controlled—code.

But the evidence for Lee, spy for Taiwan, is just as contradictory as the evidence for Lee, Chinese spy. Lee just as easily could have snatched up a copy of one of the classified weapons codes and given it to his colleagues at Chung Shan, but there is no evidence that he did so. Moreover, while Taiwanese intelligence has a distinct element of ethnic appeal, its spy recruitment methods are traditional; like the United States, Taiwan pays handsomely for stolen secrets. And no evidence has been found that Lee suddenly came into large and unexplained sums of cash or other assets.

The last contingent of spy theorists holds that Lee was a novelty in the annals of espionage—not a spy, exactly, but a freelance purveyor of secrets. In this theory, Lee was both player and pawn, shopping his talents as a code developer to any prospective buyer, and yet naively vulnerable to manipulation by China, Taiwan, or, for that matter, any other country.

In the opinion of one China counterintelligence expert familiar with the case, Lee imagined himself as an international wheeler-dealer in codes. "He was flattered by anyone who would listen to him, and both countries are very good at this," he said. "I think Lee convinces himself that what he's doing does not damage the United States. It doesn't enter his mind. That makes it easy for him. Where does his loyalty lie? Nowhere."

Proponents of the theory argue that Lee was preparing to commit espionage or something very close to it. His collecting of the codes on tapes was akin to a bank robber "gassing up the car" for the getaway, says Moore, now the director of analysis at the Centre for Counterintelligence and Security Studies in Alexandria, Virginia.

"When you step back and look at all the things he would do if he wanted to commit espionage, he would have had to go through many of the same steps," Moore said. "He moved the information to an insecure place, made it portable, and then it disappeared. The record seems to be very clear: He's a liar and a thief. Is he a spy? I don't know."

If he was, the question then is, for whom? "You end up working by process of elimination," Moore said. "He's not working for the Russians, he's not working for the Taiwanese, and he's not working for China. You end up with the conclusion that he's working for Wen Ho Lee. It's not about helping China, it's about helping Lee."

This is roughly the scenario that federal prosecutors fell back on in the June 26, 2000, court hearing in front of Judge Parker, in which Stamboulidis suggested that Lee was a free agent, looking for work in any number of countries and drawing on the tapes to bolster his own abilities. This was a viable argument, however weakly presented: Lee very well could have seen the codes as a storehouse of ready-made algorithms, honed by hundreds of scientists on the basis of billions of dollars in experiments and nuclear tests. Those algorithms were a gold mine. Their efficiency and accuracy would have been a boon to a range of academic, commercial, and military endeavors. They were capable of narrowing the supercomputing gap between the United States and other nations. The theory fits Lee's collection of bomb files, as well.

But carrying that argument a step further to say Lee intended to commit espionage requires a stretch. The FBI scrutinized Lee for more than five years. Agents conducted more than 1,000 interviews. They studied Lee's mail, his phone calls, even his garbage, not to mention a quantity of data files equal to a fourth of the Library of Congress. They spent hours interviewing him, including ten full days of sworn debriefings. They cobbled together a case of suspicious circumstances. But they never found evidence of espionage.

Spies typically leave a trail of clues and suspicions among the people who know them best. Lee's longest and closest associates find any notion that he was a spy inconceivable. Even as he lied to them, they consistently hewed to the conviction that Lee was, at root, genuine, as well as faithful to his adopted country and wholly invested in his life in the United States.

Perhaps the more plausible explanation for Lee's assembling so comprehensive a library of U.S. nuclear-weapons design tools goes back to his formative years on Taiwan. His essential character was forged in a time of war, poverty, and hunger, culminating in the violent loss of both his parents. It is reasonable to assume these circumstances had a lasting effect on Lee, leaving him with a powerful sense of insecurity, a fear that at any moment the trappings of his success might be taken away.

What Lee acquired in the United States—his education, his family, his position and assets—he obtained solely on his own. He was a striver, making up for his poor language skills and mediocre talents with hard work. But Lee's professional aspirations collided with his own skill level and the antagonism of at least one supervisor. He was fired from his first job, driven out of his second, and worked under recurrent threat of layoff at Los Alamos.

Ultimately, the most reasonable explanation for Lee's collection lies in the gap between his scientific skills and his craving for job stability and professional recognition. It is possible however that his original downpartitioning was done simply to facilitate his habit of working at home.

The timing of Lee's first file transfers to the open network in 1988 coincides most neatly with his wife's problems at work. That spring, Sylvia Lee led personnel staff at the laboratory to believe that her husband was helping with her computing work, sometimes at home. The easiest way for Wen Ho Lee to work on his wife's files from home would have been to place them on the open network, where they were easily accessible by dial-up connection. Years later, Lee told FBI agents that he, too, sometimes logged onto the Los Alamos network and did work at home.

Lee's growing collection on the open network sat there for years. Only in 1993, when he was told that he was at risk of being laid off, did Lee begin making his tapes. A number of Lee's closest acquaintances are virtually certain that he initially created the tapes in case he was forced out of the laboratory and put at risk of losing access to two decades' work.

"What he did was just to help himself," said Los Alamos physicist Jen-Chieh Peng, who has known Lee since 1978. "He felt pretty insecure about his job, it was pretty clear. It was just his body language . . . he was uncomfortable. I'm guessing the reason he downloaded all those programs was because he wanted to be able to have something to go back to in any new jobs that he might find. Because in any of his new responsibilities, if he can already have the solutions based on that huge code, then he will feel more secure in his new job."

It is not at all uncommon in the software industry or in basic, unclassified research for departing scientists to take their work, as well as the work of others. Lee himself suggested to friends that he wanted to be ready for such a departure.

The former founder and president of the Los Alamos Chinese Cultural Association, Hsiao-Hua Hsu, said Lee told friends that "he'd been working on these things for twenty years, and he just wanted a copy."

Lee may well have seen the tapes as a crutch, a replacement for the expertise of colleagues on whom he relied for collaboration and scientific papers. In science, the coin of recognition and legitimacy is publication. By the secret nature of their work, weaponeers are constrained from recognition by the larger scientific community. They must find satisfaction behind the fence, where the measure of prestige is innovation and insight into the understanding of weapons physics. But according to coworkers, Lee's own insights were generally derivative and incremental. He was forced to depend on more imaginative collaborators for help in producing papers of note. If he had to leave the lab, Lee would be left more to his own devices. The weapons codes would have helped fill the void. He would appear more talented to a potential employer.

Federal prosecutors used the completeness of Lee's collection—all of Los Alamos's most important design software, files of data derived from nuclear tests, and detailed bomb descriptions—as powerful evidence of his nefarious intent. Combined with the absence of an innocent, work-related reason for creating the tapes, this comprehensiveness was the heart of their case. Yet this comprehensiveness just as easily demonstrates Lee's well-known proclivity for hoarding. Colleagues and friends describe him as an unusually thorough pack-rat. A man who owns 700 vinyl LPs of classical music, alphabetized by composer, does not collect things in an incomplete way.

The FBI saw the same phenomenon in his garage and office—huge stores of papers and documents dating back to the 1960s. The habit of near-obsessive collecting is not uncommon among code developers. Theirs is a profession of accretion. New codes are often as not created from old ones, and code writers never know when they might need a scrap of code for a future project. Lee was no different. As one officemate noted, "He kept absolutely everything."

Likewise, a Los Alamos physicist who collaborated with Lee said he took meticulous notes on everything, down to an inane level of detail. Even when the computer spewed garbage results, Lee filed away a copy.

Peng was certain that Lee's motivation for his ties to Chinese scientists and the making of the tapes wasn't espionage at all. Peng believed the two activities had a common link in Lee's insecurity.

"I have no doubt in my mind that he did not copy it for the purpose of copying it for other people," Peng said. "It's not surprising that he feels his job is in constant jeopardy, that he feels he needs to protect himself well. And it's that same mentality that makes him one of the most active people in these gatherings with the Chinese people, because he feels it will make him more important, that it will improve his job security at the lab."

Whether Lee was preparing to share bomb secrets or just collecting tools for his uncertain future, by making his tapes, he committed an egregious security offense. No other weaponeer in the country was known to have placed so many of the nation's basic tools of weapons design at such great risk. Even in the case of Klaus Fuchs, the Russians assembled two competing teams of scientists to figure out whether the nuclear secrets from Fuchs actually constituted a working atom bomb. If a foreign country obtained Lee's files from the unclassified Los Alamos network where they sat for years, it would have been readily apparent that the input decks described tested and operational warheads.

His downloads, said former Los Alamos nuclear-weapons chief John Hopkins, were "something that would horrify anyone in the weapons program. What Wen Ho did, no one else did. His explanation of backing up tapes is like a bank examiner finding $400,000 in his home and his telling the bank, 'I was protecting you against bank robbery.' You just don't take home $400,000."

Lee broke the fundamental trust that underlies the weapons world and, in the end, his betrayal of that trust—witting or not—seriously eroded America's confidence in the weapons labs and the ability of his colleagues to protect secrets. Los Alamos's shoddy computer security and the overreaction in Congress certainly contributed to that erosion and the resulting punishment of Lee's colleagues with polygraph tests and barriers to international exchange. But Lee deserves a share of the blame for the state of the weapons labs today.

"He created an enormous vulnerability for this country," said former lab director Sig Hecker. "It was deliberate, it was systematic—he did it over and over again—and it was egregious. He betrayed everyone at this laboratory. He was given a trust, and he betrayed this trust."

Even so, Hecker said, "The way he was hung in public and the way he was jailed was really un-American."

———

Regardless of Lee's motives, the Wen Ho Lee affair was an ugly chapter in U.S. history. It was a time when democratic ideals were forgotten in the name of national security, when ideology and ambition overpowered objectivity, and when partisan warfare trumped statesmanship.

At the turn of the twenty-first century, the United States was the world's last remaining superpower. Foreign policy analysts wrote of the "American century" and our "unipolar moment." But in the Lee affair, the nation revealed a dark side, compromising its moral authority to decry human rights abuses in China and elsewhere. The Lee case held a mirror up to a powerful nation, and the reflection showed fear, hatred, and a willingness to abandon its principles.

In the summer of 1999, as political pressure mounted on Lee's prosecutors, China had its own "spy" case. While visiting relatives in China, Pennsylvania-based researcher Song Yongyi and his wife, Helen Yao, were arrested by the Ministry of State Security because of a book Song had written about the Cultural Revolution. He was charged with sending state secrets abroad. The state secrets, according to Song's attorney Jerome Cohen, consisted of the contents of wall posters and newspapers from thirty-three years earlier.

Song and Yao were held in solitary confinement. Ministry of State Security officials told them that if they confessed, they could win leniency and perhaps their freedom. Security officers watched the couple in their cells twenty-four hours a day and steadfastly resisted their release into house arrest at the home of Song's brother in Beijing.

The pattern of the Song case was typical. Chinese authorities routinely jailed academics on espionage accusations and used their detention to coerce confessions.

"This is the essence of the Chinese criminal process," said Cohen, a New York University law professor who has defended more than a half-dozen academics charged with spying in China. "They tell people, 'You hold the key in your own hand.' If you confess, you can get out . . . The Chinese Communists say, 'Leniency for those who confess, severity for those who resist.' "

Ironically, the hysteria surrounding the Lee case drove the U.S. government into these same kind of strong-arm tactics—practices that its own State Department had long condemned in China. Ever since the 1989 Tiananmen Square incident, the single unifying factor among critics of America's China policy has been the PRC's willingness to arrest, detain, and even execute its own citizens with only the thinnest semblance of due process. In the Lee case, the United States betrayed its seminal ideals of justice.

Nonetheless, the best nuclear-weapons software and designs in the world are a far cry from the stuff of wall posters and old newspapers. The fact that Lee was able to put them on portable tapes is a testament to historically poor computer security at Los Alamos.

The Rudman panel and most of Congress carried their critiques too far, however. They properly decried the micromanagement of the laboratories by DOE and the lack of accountability. Yet they missed the critical connection between these problems and scientists' apparent resentment of security.

The overwhelming majority of weaponeers take secrecy seriously. They know perhaps better than anyone the enormous destructive power of the weapons they devise. It is illogical to assume that scientists who have devoted their careers to providing the U.S. government with such weapons will then divulge their secrets to a potential adversary. The Rudman Report is dead-on in its assessment that the denizens of the weapons labs have "a culture of arrogance." But part of this arrogance stems from dealing with those at the DOE and in Congress who believe that everything about a weapon is secret. Nuclear weapons are a blend of basic physics, practical testing experience, and prodigious feats of engineering and manufacturing.

Yet by virtue of the Atomic Energy Act, every aspect of weapons design is "born classified." The DOE and its predecessors traditionally have been reticent about declassifying weapons information. Keeping "secrets" locked up always is the safer bet, at least politically. As a result, enormous quantities of basic physics and engineering remain classified because they have some application to nuclear weapons, however remote. Many weapons scientists believe that 90 percent or more of classified Restricted Data should not be secret at all. This overclassification breeds complacency and resentment of security rules. It also frustrates public scrutiny of new weapons research and its justification.

This inherent tension between weapons science and government secrecy dates back to the Manhattan Project. The Lee case was merely the latest manifestation. The potential compromise of the W88 and the debate over the sensitivity of the contents of Lee's tapes might have compelled a reassessment of what is truly "secret" about nuclear weapons. Such an assessment, in fact, was performed. In the mid-1990s, a panel of veteran weaponeers recommended declassifying significant volumes of information and guarding some secrets more closely. Its study, sometimes called the "higher fences" initiative, was shelved.

But weapons science and secrecy are not mutually exclusive. The tension can be managed, but only to the degree that scientists can perceive a justifiable rationale for the protection of certain information. For security to work, scientists must be able to trust the Energy Department and Congress to make informed and judicious decisions on secrecy and security. Rather than undertake that challenge, Congress and the Energy Department left the roots of the laboratory's security problems in place.

Instead, Congress took the easier, less responsible path. It banned foreign travel, ordered sweeping polygraph tests, and instituted other punitive measures—all geared toward making lawmakers look decisive and strong in protecting national security. In the end, however, these overheated actions and the inordinate response by the Energy and Justice departments threatened the scientific vitality of the weapons laboratories. By extension, they undermined the critical base of talent and good technical judgment that the United States requires to maintain its nuclear arsenal without testing.

The pursuit of Wen Ho Lee at almost any cost—to civil rights, freedom, and scientific vitality—exacted a high price in long-term national security. It could take years, even decades to fully gauge the cost to U.S. defense science. But the episode clearly added to mounting Sino-U.S. tensions. The Cox Report and other voices in the American body politic cast China as a powerful and implacable enemy—sentiments which, left unchecked, could become a self-fulfilling prophecy.

On a more profound level, the Lee affair suggested Americans had lost sight of the true national interest. Nuclear weapons are the nation's ultimate defense, a supposed tool of last resort for safeguarding democracy. But H-bombs are never *the* supreme national interest, as Steve Younger claimed. Presumably, the national interest lies in the guarantees of freedom that the nation so cavalierly discarded in the futile search for a spy.

NOTES

PROLOGUE: "THEY ELECTROCUTED THEM, WEN HO"

Details of the "Rosenberg" interrogation were derived primarily from the transcript and interviews with Bob Clark, Alberta Lee, and others.

1. NANTOU TO LOS ALAMOS

The story of Lee's early life came from profiles in the *Washington Post,* the *Albuquerque Tribune,* Lee's fellow students at Texas A&M, coworkers and supervisors at the Idaho National Engineering Laboratory (now the Idaho National Environmental and Engineering Laboratory) and at Argonne. A few confirmatory details were taken from a biographical sketch that ran in the *New York Times* on March 10, 1999, and a two-part series published in February 2001, five months after his guilty plea and release from jail.

2. THE HILL

Historical details on Los Alamos and the Manhattan Project were derived from Richard Rhodes's *The Making of the Atomic Bomb,* Robert Serber's *Los Alamos Primer,* Jo Ann Shroyer's *Secret Mesa: Inside Los Alamos National Laboratory,* a public history published by the laboratory, as well as interviews with members of the Los Alamos Historical Society, local architectural historian and outdoorsman extraordinaire Craig Martin and White Rock architect Elwood Cardon.

3. A NEAT AND DELICATE PACKAGE

Much of the information in this chapter came from scientists who requested that their names not be included for obvious reasons.

There is a world of information about nuclear weapons in the public domain. On the Internet, the Web sites of the Federation of American Scientists (www.fas.org) and the Natural Resources Defense Council (www.nrdc.org) contain reliable information.

For a detailed technical history of nuclear weapons, there's nothing quite like *The Swords of Armageddon,* the self-published CD-ROM of private archivist Chuck Hansen of Sunnyvale, California. For more than twenty years, Hansen has gathered declassified weapons documents. He probably knows more than anyone else about what weapons data the government itself has made public. His Web site is www.uscoldwar.com

Teller's joy at the success of the Olive shot comes from "Roundtable Discussion [parts of title redacted] the Olive Event," *Research Monthly,* Lawrence Livermore National Laboratory, November–December 1990.

For an interesting history of how competition between Los Alamos and Lawrence Livermore led to highly optimized weapons like the W88, see the MIT dissertation (617-253-5668) of Sybil Francis, "Warhead Politics: Livermore and the Competitive System of Nuclear Weapon Design."

Some information about MIRVs came from Daniel Buchonnet, "A Brief History of Minuteman and Multiple Reentry Vehicles," Lawrence Livermore National Laboratory, 1976.

On the development of the shapes and configurations that make the W88, see "Shrinking the H-bomb / Miniaturization Key to Warheads," Dan Stober, *San Jose Mercury News,* April 8, 1999.

4. THE CHINA CONNECTION

Biographical information on Chen Ning Yang came in large measure from the Nobel Foundation. The experiences of Agnew, Keyworth, and Browne in China were derived from interviews with those three men, supplemented by information from former DOE and LANL intelligence officials. The brief section on radiochemistry and other forms of technical surveillance of foreign nuclear tests comes from interviews with scientists and intelligence officials who gathered and analyzed the data. Chuck Hansen's CD-ROM version of *The Swords of Armageddon* supplied details of the Mk 12A.

5. TIGER TRAP

Many details of the Tiger Trap case came from interviews in California, New Mexico, and Washington, D.C. FBI Agent Bob Messemer testified about Tiger Trap during a closed bail hearing for Lee on December 29, 1999.

The case was first publicly disclosed in 1990, but the story did not create a stir except inside government circles. See "Chinese Neutron Bomb May Have Local Origin," Dan Stober, *San Jose Mercury News,* November 21, 1990.

When Lee was polygraphed in 1998, he told the polygraph operator about his 1988 phone call to Tiger Trap. The polygraph operator's report is a part of the court file.

Attorney General Janet Reno discussed the phone call in closed testimony to the Senate Judiciary Committee on June 8, 1999.

Quotes from a secret government report offering Lee's explanation for the call are from the *New York Times,* February 4, 2001.

There is a brief reference to a connection between Gwo-Bao Min and a "foreign agent" in the appendix of "Science at Its Best, Security at Its Worst," the report of the President's Foreign Intelligence Advisory Board, June 1999.

Accounts of Lee's phone call can also be found in "Report on the Investigation of Espionage Allegations Against Dr. Wen Ho Lee," issued by Senator Arlen Specter on March 8, 2000. It was written by the senator's indefatigable investigator, Dobie McArthur.

6. THE NARROW NECK OF THE HOURGLASS

CIA funding of certain Los Alamos scientists' trips to China comes from a February 2001 interview with a former CIA officer. Observations on the Lees' domestic life come from interviews with family friends and the Lees' lab supervisors, as does the depiction of Sylvia Lee's difficulties in her lab job. Account of Sylvia's involvement in the visit of Madame Su Wei comes from an interview with Jean Andrews Stark. Her continuing involvement with visiting Chinese scientists, as well as the FBI and the CIA, come from interviews with a former CIA officer, a former FBI officer, FBI testimony in 2000, and Lee family acquaintances and coworkers. Accounts of Lee's initial acquaintance with Li De Yuan and the Lees' trips to China in 1986 and 1988 were derived from FBI testimony, Bob and Kathy Clark, Don and Jean Marshall, coworkers of Sylvia Lee, and former lab intelligence officers. FBI concerns about lab interactions with the Chinese were described by former FBI officials.

Numerous not-for-attribution interviews contributed to this chapter.

The note that ends, "His name is Dr. Zheng Shaotang. Please check if they are unclassified and send to them. Thanks a lot, Sylvia Lee," is quoted in the Justice Department's failed application for a wiretap on Lee's phone.

"I will be very happy if we can learn something in computational hydrodynamics . . ." is from "The Making of a Suspect: The Case of Wen Ho Lee," *New York Times,* February 3, 2001.

On the Lees' dealings with the FBI and the CIA, see "Lee's Wife Worked for CIA / Link May Undercut Nuclear-Secrets Case," Dan Stober, *San Jose Mercury News,* July 23, 2000.

References to Lee's travels and papers come from records of the Los Alamos National Laboratory.

Li Wei Shen asking Lee for help with a code problem is mentioned in the FBI application for a search warrant for Lee's home, dated April 9, 1999.

7. ALARM BELLS

The description of Sylvia Lee's continuing problems at work and her conflict with the late Rich Davidson (who died climbing one of the Annapurna peaks in the mid-1990s) comes from interviews with a number of her coworkers and supervisors.

8. ASKINT MEETS *GUANXI*

The account of Stillman's initial encounters with the Chinese and subsequent visits by Stillman, Hawkins, and others comes from former Los Alamos and DOE intelligence and weapons officials. We are especially indebted to John C. and Adele Hopkins and Hawkins and Stillman. For the historical tidbits about China's weapons program, see *China Builds the Bomb,* by Prof. John Wilson Lewis and Xue Litai (Stanford, 1988). The account of the interplay between Congress and the Bush administration in the wake of the Tiananmen Square incident is drawn primarily from James Mann's exceedingly informative *About Face.*

9. THE COLLECTOR

Lee's movement of files from 1988 to 1992 is outlined in a court document known as 404(b), which listed the evidence the government expected to use at the trial.

Lee's downloading of files is described keystroke-by-keystroke in court exhibits and testimony.

The descriptions of the Hug come largely from eyewitnesses.

10. KINDRED SPIRITS

The description of NN-30 comes from a number of the people who worked there. The comment about needing "one good espionage case" comes from a Trulock deputy, Charles Washington. The account of Henson's discovery comes in part from Henson himself and from others who have seen the intelligence upon which he and Booth based their initial report and which was reviewed by members of the Henderson panel. Confirmation and additional details were gleaned from several *Washington Post* stories by Walter Pincus and Vernon Loeb, who deserve kudos for excellent reporting throughout the Lee case. Additional details and chronological assistance is owed to the May 2000 report of the Attorney General's Review Team, headed by Assistant U.S. Attorney Randy I. Bellows. The report, released in segments starting in the summer of 2001, is hereinafter referred to as the Bellows Report.

11. A SHALLOW POOL

Knowledge of the administrative inquiry comes from numerous people who were involved as well as the Bellows Report.

There is also a substantial written record. See, for example, "Department of Energy, FBI, and Department of Justice Handling of the Espionage Investigation into the Compromise of Design Information on the W88 Warhead, Statement by Senate Governmental Affairs Committee Chairman Fred Thompson (R-TN) and Senate Governmental Affairs Committee Ranking Minority Member Joseph Lieberman (D-CT), August 5, 1999."

Information about the list of seventy names comes from the list itself.

12. MASS-MARKET ESPIONAGE

The accounts of the Larry Chin and Peter Lee cases come from Paul Moore, now director of analysis at the Centre for Counterintelligence and Security Studies in Alexandria, Virginia, plus congressional testimony by the DOJ's John Dion, Michael Liebman, Tom Cook, and the few newspaper stories that ran at the time, primarily in the *Los Angeles Times*.

13. THE OUT-OF-TOWNER

Interviews with a former FBI agent, a former CIA officer, and David Wise's *The Spy Who Got Away* form most of the basis for the observations on the FBI's Albuquerque Field Office and the Edward Lee Howard case. The account of the Pruvosts' suspicions comes from a former FBI agent, a former Los Alamos intelligence officer, and acquaintances of the Pruvosts, who declined to be interviewed, saying, "We learned one thing through all this and that's not to talk to reporters and not to talk to the FBI."

Vrooman's take on the flaws of the DOE administrative inquiry comes from him, supplemented by interviews with others cleared to see the AI. The account of the FBI briefing to lab director Sig Hecker comes from interviews with several participants. The exchange between Lieberman and Craig about access to Lee's computer comes from interviews, correspondence from Energy Secretary Bill Richardson to lab director John Browne in the late summer of 1999, and the Thompson-Lieberman Report. Further details of FBI Agent David Lieberman's investigative actions come from the Bellows Report.

The "dead donkey" reference to FBI agent David Lieberman is from the Bellows Report, as quoted in "FBI Errors in Lee Case Detailed," Dan Eggen, the *Washington Post*, August 27, 2001.

14. THE FISA

The description of Genong Li is drawn from laboratory records, interviews, and the Thompson-Lieberman Report.

Portions of the FISA application were quoted by Senator Arlen Specter in a June 8, 1999, closed session of the Senate Judiciary Committee.

The number of FISA applications is drawn from "U.S. Attorney General's 1997 Annual Report on FISA Requests."

Lee's credit card charges in Hong Kong are mentioned in Janet Reno's testimony to the Senate Judiciary Committee, June 8, 1999.

A description of the FISA application is included in the Thompson-Lieberman Report. Further details were drawn from the Bellows Report.

Louis Freeh's briefing by the CIA is taken from a story by the Associated Press, August 31, 2001, by John Solomon.

15. FLYING THE FALSE FLAG

The account of the investigation in the summer and fall of 1998 comes from interviews with two former intelligence officials, a former FBI agent, FBI testimony, congressional sources, Bob Vrooman, Terry Craig, and former DOE counterintelligence chief Ed Curran.

The description of FBI agent Levy as a "reject" is from the Bellows Report, as quoted in "FBI Errors in Lee Case Detailed," Dan Eggen, the *Washington Post*, August 27, 2001.

Information about Lee's activities in Taiwan comes in part from the *Washington Post*, "Lee Was Paid Consultant to Taiwan Businessman," Walter Pincus, December 23, 2000.

16. TRULOCK AND THE TRUE BELIEVERS

The descriptions of Trulock's briefings as "nightmare," "alarming," and "sky is falling" come from the Bellows Report.

Descriptions of Trulock's testimony to the Cox Committee come from people present at the hearings and Trulock himself.

Rep. Norm Dicks's advice to Bill Richardson is from the *Washington Post,* "Blunders Undermined the Lee Case," by Walter Pincus and David A. Vise, September 24, 2000.

17. EXILE FROM X DIVISION

Curran's responses to the hearing of the Cox Committee and his meetings with the FBI come primarily from interviews with him, as well as his correspondence with the FBI, his responses to interrogatories posed by the Senate Judiciary Committee, and committee depositions taken of other counterintelligence officials at the FBI, DOE, and LANL.

The biographical sketch of Energy Secretary Bill Richardson is derived from interviews with Energy Department staff and news reporters who have covered him.

Lee's account of his trip to Taiwan comes from FBI testimony at Lee's bail hearings in December 2000 as well as interviews with LANL officials. The account of his December 23, 1998, polygraph comes from the polygraph report itself, FBI testimony, interviews with Curran, and various LANL and former FBI officials.

"It will bother me for years," is from the *New York Times,* "The Making of a Suspect: The Case of Wen Ho Lee," February 3, 2001.

18. PANIC

The account of Lee's actions after being polygraphed comes largely from an FBI chronology released during congressional hearings in October 2000, as well as a prosecution 404b filing in the spring of that year. The exchange with Alberta Lee was reported in Ed Klein's "The Hunting of Wen Ho Lee," published in the December 2000 edition of *Vanity Fair.*

Details of the actions of the laboratory management in early 1999 come from lab director John C. Browne, Bryan "Bucky" Kashiwa, and other LANL officials.

Lee's actions upon gaining entry to his X Division office come from the FBI chronology and prosecution filing noted above, as well as Lee's statements to the FBI and Justice Department at the time of his plea agreement and in the months thereafter.

The account of Lee's January 17, 1999, interview by Agents Covert and Hudenko at the Lee home was pieced together from FBI testimony in December 1999 and interviews with a former FBI agent, lab officials, and acquaintances of Lee. Other facts about FBI actions in the winter of 1998–99 were supplied by the Bellows Report.

Additional details on Lee's continuing attempts to get back into his X Division office and his file erasures come from the same two documents cited above, as well as the testimony of FBI Special Agent Robert Messemer in the first and second bail hearings and the December 27, 1999, testimony of Cheryl Wampler, deputy group leader of LANL's former CIC-7 (the production computing group).

The reexamination of the December 23 polygraph is derived from interviews with congressional staff, a former FBI agent, Ed Curran, and reviews of both Curran's correspondence with the FBI and his reply to interrogatories by the Senate Judiciary Committee.

The account of the February 10 polygraph comes from Messemer's closed testimony on December 29, 1999 (coupled with questions by Lee attorney Mark Holscher), the June 1999 congressional testimony of Attorney General Janet Reno, as well as interviews with Lee acquaintances and lab officials. Those recollections differ on the location of the hotel where the polygraph was administered. Messemer says it was in Albuquerque; others say Los Alamos.

Lee's request of colleague Gary Pfeufer and Pfeufer's response were recounted by Messemer at the December 28, 2000, bail hearing and in the prosecution 404b filing.

The "third of an agent" quote is from the Bellows Report, as quoted in "FBI Errors in Lee Case Detailed," Dan Eggen, the *Washington Post,* August 27, 2001.

19. "AS BAD AS THE ROSENBERGS"

The dialogue of the March 7 interrogation of Lee is from the FBI transcript.

The description of the March 5, 1999, FBI interview of Lee comes from witnesses.

Trulock's dealings with the *New York Times* were described by Trulock in an interview.

Risen choice of the *Times* for its "visibility and impact" is from "A Reporter Under Fire," Lucinda Fleeson, *American Journalism Review,* November 2000.

The description of Gerth as practicing "a kind of connect-the-dots journalism" is from "Eye of the Storm," Ted Gup, *Columbia Journalism Review,* May 2001.

Alberta Lee: "these incredibly horrible things—so many lies" is from "Crash Landing," Robert Schimdt, *Brill's Content,* November 1999.

"I did receive one or two mail from Wang" is from the transcript of Lee's interview by the FBI, as quoted in court during a mail hearing on August 17, 2000.

20. BECOMING THE ENEMY

The section on Lee's firing and Richardson's leaking of his name come from Notra Trulock, laboratory officials, reporters who knew of the leak, Lee coworkers, and Bob and Kathy Clark.

Observations on the initial reaction of the Chinese-American community to Lee's firing come from interviews with members of that community.

Romero's reactions to finding a directory listing of weapons files on Lee's unclassified account comes from his testimony at the second bail hearing in December 1999, as well as Cheryl Wampler's testimony.

The profile of Bob Gorence was drawn from interviews with him, as well as with members and observers of the local bar.

Details of the search-warrant application and the search itself come from the warrant, affidavit, prosecution, and defense briefs on the issue of suppression of seized evidence and testimony at the suppression hearing itself in June 2000. The reaction in Congress comes from the *Congressional Record,* hearing transcripts, and current and former congressional aides.

21. SHOCK WAVES

The account of Gerth and Risen watching the arrival of the Cox Report comes from "Crash Landing," in *Brill's Content,* November 1999.

The ahistoric nature of the Cox Report was first the subject of a commentary by Rand's Jonathon Pollack, followed by a more thoroughgoing critique by Professors

Michael May, W. H. K. Panofsky, Marco di Capua, and Lewis R. Franklin at Stanford and Alastair Iain Johnston at Harvard.

The phrase, "in the belly and in the brain" was spoken by Henry Tang.

"A thousand points of compromise" comes from "The Making of a Suspect: The Case of Wen Ho Lee," in the *New York Times,* February 4, 2001.

22. INTENT TO INJURE

The account of the early Sea Change investigation and shift toward prosecution comes from correspondence exchanged between Holscher and the U.S. Attorney's Office, interviews with Holscher, Clark, the Marshalls, and a former FBI agent, and news accounts in the *Los Angeles Times,* the *New York Times,* and *Newsweek.*

The history of the Atomic Energy Act was drawn from the first volume of Arvin Quist's excellent *Security Classification of Information.*

The description of Gorence's argument for prosecution, Reno's decision to prosecute, and the meeting in the situation room comes primarily from a September 24, 2000, piece in the *Washington Post* by Pincus and David A. Vise.

Lee's denials that he put classified codes on tapes comes from the testimony of U.S. Attorney Norman Bay and FBI Director Louis Freeh at a joint hearing of the Senate Select Intelligence and Judiciary committees, September 26, 2000.

Lucky Lee's testimony about God's love is drawn from an interview with Bob Clark.

23. THE CROWN JEWELS

The conditions of Lee's jailing comes from testimony during the second bail hearing, interviews with family friends, and a jail official.

The biographical sketch of Younger is drawn from interviews with him, his colleagues in lab management, and employees under him, as well as William Broad's *Teller's War* and Jo Ann Shroyer's *Secret Mesa.*

Details added on to Younger's testimony regarding the makeup and value of the weapons codes comes from interviews with code developers and weapons designers.

Clinton's actual statement, made in September 1997, was as follows: "I consider the maintenance of a safe and reliable nuclear stockpile to be a supreme national interest of the United States."

24. "IT'S CONCEIVABLE THAT THIS IS POSSIBLE"

Conditions of Lee's jailing and his health come from the sources cited above for chapter 23, as well as Ed Klein's *Vanity Fair* piece and interviews with his attorneys and court statements they made in the winter and spring of 2000. The story of the birthday cookie comes from Lee himself, while celebrating his sixty-first birthday as a free man.

Details of the Fernandez case and Cline's graymail strategy come from the report of Iran-Contra Independent Counsel Lawrence Walsh, defense attorneys on the cases Walsh brought, and Cline's CIPA arguments, both in filings and hearing transcripts. Alberta Lee's visit to her father in jail is taken from Ed Klein's *Vanity Fair* article. The remainder of the chapter is derived from hearings transcripts.

25. *SWORDS OF ARMAGEDDON*

Kelly's desire to derive political benefit from the Wen Ho Lee case is an inference based on the following: Kelly was preparing his congressional campaign for months before the Lee case was ready for indictment. He had every indication that incumbent representative Heather Wilson would try to paint him as soft on crime, which she did. The Lee case was the most politically charged investigation during Kelly's seven-year tenure as U.S. attorney. Yet rather than avoid the appearance of political taint by leaving the case with his eminently skilled first assistant, Bob Gorence, Kelly MC'd a press conference to announce Lee's indictment and arrest, then insisted on making the final legal argument for keeping Lee jailed in late December.

The biography of Judge Conway was derived from interviews with him and members of the local bar. The defense allegation of a sexual advance came from an anonymous interview in April 2001 and was confirmed by the judge in a June 2001 interview.

The PARD is described in the *Albuquerque Journal*, "Lee Data Constraints Unclear," by Ian Hoffman, April 10, 2000.

26. THE MOMENTUM SHIFTS

"Long, slow, death march . . ." is from Norman Bay's congressional testimony on September 26, 2000.

27. FREEDOM

"There was bad news everywhere . . ." is in part from "Statement by FBI Director Louis J. Freeh Concerning Wen Ho Lee Case," September 13, 2000, and "Statement for the Record of Attorney General Janet Reno and FBI Director Louis J. Freeh," September 26, 2000, before the Senate Select Committee on Intelligence and the Senate Judiciary Committee, Washington, D.C. Details of Reno's decision to approve a plea bargain are from the *Washington Post*, "Blunders Undermined the Lee Case," by Walter Pincus and David A. Vise, September 24, 2000.

EPILOGUE

The description of Lee's debriefings comes from people familiar with the case.

"He said he was a paid consultant" is from "Lee Was Paid Consultant to Taiwan Businessman," Walter Pincus, *Washington Post*, December 23, 2000.

The account of Freeh's briefing by the CIA was drawn from an Associated Press piece by John Solomon, published August 31, 2001.

Kitchen's comment and the "most tantalizing mystery" came from the *Times*'s two-part series, published in February 2001.

INDEX